Christmas 1995

A little more info on two of
your favorites
~ Carter

WILL ROGERS & WILEY POST

WILL ROGERS & WILEY POST:

DEATH AT BARROW

Bryan B. Sterling & Frances N. Sterling

M. Evans and Company, Inc.
New York

M. Evans and Company, Inc.
216 East 49th Street
New York, New York 10017

Library of Congress Cataloging-in-Publication Data

Sterling, Bryan B.
    Will Rogers & Wiley Post : death at Barrow / Bryan B. Sterling and
Frances N. Sterling.
        p.   cm.
    Includes bibliographical references and index.
    ISBN 0-87131-725-7 : $24.95
    1. Rogers, Will, 1879–1935—Death and burial.   2. Post, Wiley,
1898–1935—Death and burial.   3. Humorists, American—20th
century—Biography.   4. Air pilots—United States—Biography.
I. Sterling, Frances N.   II. Title.   III. Title: Will Rogers and Wiley
Post.
PN2287.R74S74   1993
792.7′028′092—dc20
[B]   93-2411
                                                                      CIP

Design by Charles A. de Kay
Typeset by AeroType, Inc.
Manufactured in the United States of America

9   8   7   6   5   4   3   2   1

CONTENTS

CONTENTS

"Aviation, like the sea,
is not inherently dangerous;
but it is less forgiving
of carelessness or neglect."
—Anonymous

The End

It is just past seven o'clock on the summer evening of August 15, 1935. The place: The Top of the World, the treeless northern tundra of Alaska's Arctic Slope. The only sound offending the stillness is the steady drone of an airplane engine. A pontoon-equipped plane has been lazily ranging over hundreds of square miles for almost two hours. The tiny plane, an odd assemblage of ill-matched components painted red with silver trim, carries two men.

      The weather above is perfect, blue sky and radiant sunshine; but below the plane, from horizon to horizon, lies an impenetrable white carpet of clouds and fog. The picture of this aircraft cruising so leisurely below a faultless sky is deceptively serene; for in minutes the plane will be smashed, the pilot and his passenger killed . . .

CHAPTER ONE

THE PILOT

That Post is just full of determination. I would hate to tell him he could not do anything.
—Will Rogers, *Weekly Article*, July 26, 1931.

Few heroes, even genuine, national heroes, manage to retain a hold on the public's memory for as long as fifty years. There are not many people about these days who can tell with certainty, just what it was that this man, Wiley Post, did. And yet, he was one of the true American heroes of his time.

In 1986, when Americans Richard Rutan and Jeana Yeager flew non-stop around the world in their spindly aircraft *Voyager*, they were justly hailed. Great pilots of the past—famous names like Charles Lindbergh and Amelia Earhart—were recalled, yet no American television network even alluded to Wiley Post, the first man to fly around the earth alone.

Like Rutan and Yeager, Post had his picture on magazine covers, and his name had been front page news. He had been idolized and honored. He had received ticker-tape parades, a White House reception, keys to various cities, and stage and movie offers. Yet despite all that, what is remembered by those still familiar with his name is the fact that he died in a plane crash with Will Rogers.

It is lamentable that a trail-blazer like Wiley Post should be remembered primarily because of his companion in death. But history is not known to be fair, even though it is never a participant in an event, merely the eyewitness. It is not "history's" offense that man is callous. When in November 1979 the United States postal department showed a long overdue flicker of appreciation for Wiley Post's accomplishments by issuing two postage stamps in his honor, they were twenty-five-cent air mail stamps, which are rarely needed or used.

But Wiley Post's short, productive life should be remembered prominently: he was born Wiley Hardeman Post, on November 22, 1898, on his father's quarter-section near Grand Saline in Van Zandt County, Texas, some sixty-five miles east of Dallas. He received the unusual middle name in honor of a farmer near Denison, Texas, for whom Wiley's father had worked during the summer as a sharecropper. Wiley was the fourth of what would eventually be seven children, born to William Francis and Mae Quinlan Post.

After farming in various areas of northern Texas, the family moved in 1907 to southwestern Oklahoma, settling on a small farm near Marlow, an area known as the Palmer Community. Here Wiley received his junior education. Here, too, he attended the Palmer Baptist Church and its Sunday school. There were other moves in the coming years, other small towns and other dismal farms. Finally, the family sank permanent roots near the little town of Maysville, Oklahoma, some forty miles south of Oklahoma City. Wiley became increasingly restless on the land. Although the boy came from several generations of southwestern pioneers who made their way in agriculture, farming never much interested him.

Nor did school. When one of Wiley's rural teachers seriously suggested that Wiley had better improve his work in grammar, the boy replied that he was not much interested in that study—he wanted to be an aviator.

His mother recalled that even when he was a "small, barefoot, freckle-faced youngster," he had an inordinate desire to tinker with things. He read adventure stories avidly and showed a preference for mechanical toys. By the time he reached the age of eleven, there was only one thing Wiley pursued with interest: mechanical devices. He even gained the local reputation as a kid who could fix almost anything. "In the days when flying was only something to read about with raised eyebrows, the boy whittled out models of airplanes. He was always tinkering with something," reported *The Oklahoma City Times*.

Wiley was fourteen before he saw his first real airplane at the County Fair at Lawton, Oklahoma. It was a Curtiss Pusher piloted by Art Smith, one of the early "barnstormers." Wiley decided at that moment—so he would recall later—that he would become a pilot. His mind was filled with dreams of airplanes and heroic flights; he even envisioned one day "The Wiley Post Institute for Aeronautical Research." At this Fair, Wiley also saw his first automobile. Persuasive, as he could be if the occasion called for it, he managed to get a ride in it.

By mid-1916, a seventeen-year-old, stocky Wiley was fully grown; he was handsome, with a broad, freckled face with expressive eyes and a shock of unruly hair. Finding life on the primitive farm finally unacceptable, he left home. He soon discovered the harsh economic reality that even the simplest necessities of life had to be paid for. Somewhat cowed but wiser, he returned home and struck a deal with his father. He would work a ten-acre cotton field for part of its profits. Wiley stayed home just long enough to harvest one crop. Once he had the money in hand, he was off to Kansas City, Missouri, where he enrolled at the Sweeney Auto and Aviation School. He caused some behind-the-back derision, when he announced—somewhat grandiosely, it was thought—that he would fly around the world some day.

The Kansas City course cost $85 and young Wiley Post had to get part-time work after school hours to pay for his living expenses; the ten-acre cotton patch had not produced enough to allow that.

Strangely, the youth who had been so indifferent to grade school now proved he could easily digest a book on subjects close to his heart. But as mechanics could not be learned wholly from books, Wiley took a "post-graduate" course in garage machine shops in the oil fields of Oklahoma.

America entered World War I in April 1917. Wiley was eager to enroll in flight training; for hours, every day, he would hang around the military airfield at Fort Sill near Lawton. The closest he could come, however, was a job at the airfield with the Chickasha and Lawton Construction Company.

When his older brothers joined the army, Wiley enrolled in the Students Army Training Corps at Norman, Oklahoma. He also studied radio in Section B of the Radio School.

At war's end, Wiley went looking for a job, determined never to return to the farm. He was hired on as a "roughneck" in the Walters oil field, one of the most promising in southern Oklahoma, where wood derricks and rotary drilling equipment were just coming into use. The men worked twelve-hour tours, from noon to midnight and from midnight to noon, "rassling iron" and "firing pots." Wiley's boss was W. L. Klingman, who remembered the raw farm youth well. Accidents happened almost daily and Klingman's first instruction to his new worker was, "Be careful!"

"Wiley just looked at me sorter funny, and said he knew how to take care of himself. It wasn't long before I realized he could. He was always a careful fellow and never talked much. He never got drunk and raised Cain like some of the boys in the field. After about a year and a half, Wiley drifted with the 'oil gang' to other fields. He went through Graham, Healdton, and the other fields of Carter and Stephens county. He was always a roughneck in those days; it was a job carrying little responsibility, but a lot of hard work," Klingman recalled.

Little is generally known of Wiley Post during the next couple of years. No one bothered to ask, and Wiley certainly was not going to talk about it. The world simply accepted Wiley Post for his heroic accomplishments and never asked questions.

The facts are that Wiley Post, No. 3009, was convicted in the District Court of Grady County, Oklahoma, on April 28, 1921, for the crime of Conjoint Robbery. Brandishing a gun, diminutive Wiley had tried to hold up four men on a quiet country road. They promptly overpowered him, and he was arrested and tried. The sentence: a term of ten years in the State Reformatory, at Granite, Oklahoma.

Wiley, the free spirit, could not adapt to life in the penitentiary. As the months went by, he sank into a deep state of depression. It is rather surprising for those times that two medical men, Drs. George A. Waters and T. J. Nunnery, were concerned enough about an inmate's mental deterioration to recommend his parole. Wiley's condition is stated as part of his early release, and reads:

> WHEREAS, it is made to appear from letters of Dr. Geo.
> A. Waters and a statement and recommendation from Dr.
> T. J. Nunnery, Prison Physician at the Reformatory; that,

he is physically a perfect man, he is a submissive prisoner with an effort to be respectful to all officers of the Institution and to fellow prisoners, he is making an effort to make good and obedient to every order so far as he is capable; he is not given important duties to perform on account of the fact that he does not retain the order long enough in his mind to perform it although he makes every effort to make good. His case is diagnosed as a Melancholic state which cannot be improved by change of duty or good treatment and it is steadily growing worse and on account of his mental condition of the said Wiley Post, I have decided to parole him. . . .

On the fifth day of June 1922—a little over thirteen months after his conviction—Oklahoma's Governor J. B. A. Robertson signed the parole, imposing stringent terms and conditions:

That the said Wiley Post shall abstain from the use or handling of intoxicating liquor in any form; that the said Wiley Post shall not gamble or in any way conduct a game of chance; that the said Wiley Post shall not carry firearms in violation of the statutes of this State; that he shall industriously follow some useful occupation, avoid all evil associations, improper places of amusement, all pool and billiard halls, obey the laws and in all respects conduct himself as an upright citizen; that he shall faithfully aid and support those dependent upon him . . .

There followed conditions concerning monthly reports of whereabouts and occupation, and the threat of his return to the reformatory should he violate any of these terms. Wiley, brought up in a Missionary Baptist home, was penitent. For more than twelve years, he lived by the terms of his parole without anyone becoming aware of his secret. It was Governor "Alfalfa Bill" Murray who finally signed a full pardon, but by that time Wiley Post had performed deeds never before accomplished, and had become the great American hero of both young and old.

When the pardon arrived at their home, Wiley did not even want to see it. He asked Mae, his wife, to forward it to his mother. It was Wiley's way of apologizing to the family.

After his release from the reformatory we hear of Wiley next in 1924, showing up in Chickasha, some 35 miles northwest of Maysville. He sought out his old boss, Klingman, who was then drilling for Powell Briscoe. Wiley was put to work and for the next six months—still roughnecking—kept his eyes on the engines and pumps. He still talked very little, and saved his money. Whenever a stray plane would chance over the field, Wiley would take to the open ground and watch it. "He looked to me like he was just working to make enough money to do something else," Klingman remembered. "Maybe he was interested in aviation, but he never talked about it. He was a "natural" for working with machinery."

Later, now in the Seminole district, Wiley found work as a roughneck, roustabout, truck driver, and swamper at times. One day he saw a poster advertising Burrell Tibbs and his "Texas Topnotch Fliers," a flying circus, which was to appear at nearby Wewoka, Oklahoma. Nothing could keep Wiley away; when he learned that Peter Lewis, the group's regular parachute jumper had been injured, Wiley offered to jump in his place. Though Wiley had never jumped before, Tibbs, obligated to present the widely advertised attraction, agreed to let him jump.

The parachute used was carefully packed in a bag and attached to the right-wing strut. When the plane reached an altitude of 2,000 feet, the pilot cut the throttle to lessen the propeller blast. Wiley had to climb out of the open cockpit onto the wing, inching his way along while holding on to the struts. Buffeted by the rushing air, holding on precariously, he had to strap himself into the parachute harness, then jump. Wiley later reported that the jump was "one of the biggest thrills of my life."

When he was offered a job as a parachute jumper with the flying circus, Wiley accepted immediately. Along the tour, he managed to pick up bits of flight instruction. Imaginative and cool-headed as Wiley was, he saw even greater opportunities: Would he not earn far more money if he were to arrange his own exhibitions? An entertainment-starved hinterland would raise as much as two hundred dollars for a thrill-filled weekend—at a time when 71 percent of American families had an income of less than $50 a week. His only expense was rarely more than $25 to hire a local plane and pilot. Any flier was glad to pick up some extra money. About these days, Wiley said: "I was studying crowd psychology—

my desire to thwart the spectator's hope of witnessing my untimely end was so strong that I grew so reckless as to scare myself.''

Wiley began to add his own crowd-pleasing thrills, such as delayed openings and jumps with two parachutes. Only once did he have a slight mishap. It happened near Hugo, a small town in southeastern Oklahoma. Wiley had selected a meadow for his landing site and had taken off with a local pilot. Bailing out at about 2,000 feet, Wiley dropped until the gasping crowd thought he would fall to his death—then he pulled the rip-cord. As he floated toward the selected pasture, he noted a grazing mule, which had not been there earlier in the day. Though Wiley maneuvered as best he could, the chute fell on a surprised mule, covering its head. The terrified mule took off, dragging the parachute and Wiley, still attached, all over the field. It was several minutes before Wiley and the mule parted company. Fortunately, only Wiley's dignity was slightly bruised; in later years he would often tell of the incident to amuse his listeners. Paid an average of $25, Wiley made some 100 parachute jumps.

Taking the odd half-hour flying lesson wherever he could, Wiley attempted his first solo flight in 1926. The airplane he used on that occasion was a "Canuck"—a Curtiss JN-4 Jenny, built in Canada. The Jenny's owner blatantly demonstrated his total lack of faith in Wiley's solo-flying ability. While the Jenny was worth no more than $150, Wiley was asked to make a security deposit of $200 before he would be allowed to leave the ground. Wiley did admit afterwards that he was not yet really qualified to solo, and that in fact he nearly lost control a couple of times during the flight.

Wiley took a great liking to the old Jenny in which he had soloed. While working in the oil fields at Three Sands, about 15 miles southwest of Ponca City, he would drive into town in his old car, and hang around the airport. He declared to one and all within earshot that he was saving his money to buy a Jenny of his own. This dream for his own plane was not just an idle aspiration; since Wiley wanted to get into commercial aviation, he needed a plane to gain the necessary experience. But before he could do anything further, an accident happened.

On October 1, 1926, while on a drilling rig, a tiny steel chip flew from a spike struck by a co-worker's sledgehammer and lodged in Wiley's left eye. It became badly infected and grew steadily worse. Despite every effort then known to the attending physicians, the infection could not be contained, spreading rapidly to the other eye, a condition called sympathetic opthalmia. As a last step, to save the remaining eye, Wiley's left eye had to be removed.

It is easy to conjecture that the loss of an eye might be a crushing blow to anyone's dreams of fame and fortune as a flier. But Wiley was not an ordinary man. His determination, so obvious in all his efforts in later life, allowed him neither self-pity nor the abandonment of his self-set targets. He knew that he wanted a future in aviation, and nothing, not even the loss of an eye, was going to keep him from that goal.

Recovery took time, and Wiley used those weeks to train the vision and depth perception of his remaining eye. Ingeniously he would first gauge distances between two arbitrary points, then measure them to compare the accuracy of his estimation. Day after day, he would practice on an infinite variety of distances, first guessing, then measuring, until he became so precise that he could best all his fellow fliers.

While nothing would ever make up for the loss of his left eye, there was some redress which, in turn, had far-reaching consequences. The records of the Oklahoma State Industrial Court indicate that one Wiley H. Post was awarded workmen's compensation on October 30, 1926. The Oklahoma Industrial Commission records go into more detail and reveal that at the time of the injury, Post was earning an average wage of $7 per day. The specifics of the case, as published in the Commission's Journal, vol. 159, pp. 660-61, show that Wiley H. Post (claimant) "was in the employment of the respondent (Droppelman and Cuniff) and was engaged in a hazardous occupation covered by and subject to the provisions of the Workman's Compensation Law and that while in the course of such employment and arising out of the same the claimant sustained an accidental injury on the first day of October 1926. That as a result of said accident the claimant sustained the loss of the left eye." The Commission ruled that Post was to receive compensation at the rate of $18 per week for 100 weeks, beginning on the sixth day of October 1926.

Post had a different idea. He wanted the entire amount in a lump sum. The Commission considered the request favorably but decided to pay compensation for only 94 weeks. A check for $1,698.25 was then duly issued.

In 1927, using some of the compensation money, Wiley realized his dream. "I finally found a Canuck [Jenny] with an OX-5 motor which suited my purpose. It had been in a slight accident and the two fellows who owned it couldn't afford to repair it. I gave them $240 for the plane and spent $300 having it rebuilt throughout . . ." According to Aircraft Registration #1767, Wiley bought the plane from Arthur Oakley of Ardmore, Oklahoma. The same record indicates that Wiley sold the plane January 13, 1928, to J. B. Scott of Purcell, Oklahoma for $500.

Jack Baskin, one of Wiley's classmates from Sweeney's Auto and Aviation School days, recalls: "It wasn't very long until I heard he had lost his eye; and here he came, flying an old 'Jenny' like mine, jumped out of the cockpit, and said, 'Well Jack Baskin, I bought a plane like yours, but it cost me an eye.' I asked him how he flew with one eye, but he reminded me of Roland Pettet, a Three Sands flying farmer, who flew with one good eye, and said he guessed he could too. He did.

"One noon I was working on my ship at the Ponca City airport, and heard a plane drone. The motor cut out, and I saw it land in a field of wheat. I drove to where it had landed, and out stepped Wiley. 'Well, here I am in a wheat field, knee high to a tall Indian,' he said. 'Broke my oil line.'

"We taped the pipe and I cranked his motor for him, but in three or four runs across the field he could not lift from the wheat. Just then I saw Wiley stand up in the cockpit, shouting, 'Look, Jack, at the farmer with the long shotgun!' And there was a big Polack farmer coming with a whale of a gun. Wiley gave the bus the gun and lifted the wings above the wheat to catch the air. That farmer let go a couple of shells but was too far off. That's where Wiley learned to lift a ship from the ground with a short run. . . ."

In 1927 airplanes had to be licensed, but it was perfectly legal for Post to operate as a one-plane airline, transporting fare-paying passengers, or give flying lessons, without a pilot's license. Wiley must have wondered how long it would take the recently established U. S. Department of Commerce Aeronautical Branch to require all pilots to take both proficiency and physical fitness tests. Looking ahead, he must have realized that quite possibly his flying days were numbered. But for the moment he had another preoccupation; she was seventeen years old and her name was Mae Laine, a farmer's daughter from Sweetwater, Texas. Wiley, eleven years her senior, had met Mae while barnstorming. They discovered that their families had known each other years earlier, when they had both been at Grand Saline, Texas. But this slight contact did little to make Wiley acceptable to Mae's parents.

Even though Wiley and Mae were very much in love, Mr. and Mrs. Dave Laine made it quite clear that they opposed any thought of marriage. Not only was Mae far too young, but Wiley certainly did not represent their idea of a stable son-in-law, even should he happen to survive in his chosen profession long enough to attend his own wedding.

On June 27, 1927, Wiley and his bride-to-be decided to face her family with their decision to get married, and they climbed into the Jenny and took off. Though headed for the Laine home, fate intervened. Near Graham, Oklahoma, the engine sputtered and Wiley had to make an emergency landing in a farmer's open field. The cause, a faulty distributor rotor, was quickly found. There was no way to reach the Laine domicile that day, or even to alert either family. There was only one thing to do: find a minister. Fortunately the law in Oklahoma had no legal waiting period for impatient lovers. Once legally wedded, they spent the first two days of their married life sleeping on an oil rig's wooden platform and overhauling the distributor. For Wiley it was merely another mild mishap, but it was Mae's introduction to the vagaries of her new husband's occupation.

Because of their age difference, Wiley would often kid people by claiming that he had raised Mae. "It would embarrass me to death," Mae recalled, "I'd tell him to stop it because people might believe him."

Wiley continued to make good money with his barnstorming tour until the fall of 1927, when he critically damaged the plane in a ground roll. He could barely afford the cost of having the wrecked plane shipped back to Arthur Oakley's repair shop in Ardmore, Oklahoma. When he could not raise the money for the repairs, he sold the plane and again sought employment as a barnstormer and flight instructor. It was winter in Oklahoma, with the weather at its worst; there were no spectators willing to stand for a couple of hours in bare fields, nor were there students volunteering to freeze in open cockpits. Times became hard for the newlyweds.

Wiley's fortunes changed permanently when he applied for a job with Powell Briscoe and Florence C. ("F.C.") Hall, partners in Hall & Briscoe, Inc., dealers in oil-field leases. These two men had realized the importance of a plane in a business where speed often meant the difference between closing a deal and losing it. They had decided to buy a new three-seater, open-cockpit Travel Air biplane.

The partners were not exactly comfortable with the idea of trusting their lives to a one-eyed pilot, but Wiley was so persistent and sincere that the two oil men finally hired him. He became their personal pilot, chauffeur, and hunting companion, with a monthly salary of somewhere around $200. While it was not as much as Wiley had been able to earn at times as an independent barnstormer, it certainly was far more regular.

Now that he had steady employment piloting a commercial aircraft, it became mandatory that Wiley obtain a U. S. Department of Commerce, Aeronautical Branch pilot's license. He was convinced that his single eye would automatically disqualify him. To avoid detection, he employed a number of ruses, such as landing at out-of-the-way airports, or scheduling his departures and arrivals at times when he knew that official inspectors had left for the day.

Finally the issue could no longer be avoided, and Wiley's fears were confirmed. Ordinarily he would have been excluded from applying for a license because of the lost eye, but he learned to his relief that "waivers" in cases of trained and experienced aviators were possible. The Secretary of Commerce could grant waivers for physical defects which would otherwise disqualify an applicant, if in his opinion the experience of the pilot compensated for the defect. After a probationary period of seven hundred flying hours, Wiley received his air transport license, No. 3259, on September 16, 1928.

Powell Briscoe was quite impressed with the new pilot, even though Wiley had some unique traits. He recalled that given his first month's pay, Wiley went out and bought himself a high-powered hunting rifle, when it was obvious to all that his personal wardrobe stood in desperate need of complete overhaul.

"He apparently didn't have a nerve in his body," Briscoe is quoted as saying when asked about Wiley Post. "When other people were scared, Wiley just grinned." One friend said he was a "natural flier" who piloted with a sense of feel, frequently making cross-country hops without looking at either compass or map. But perhaps the most cogent description of Wiley, the pilot, came from one of his early students: "He didn't just fly an airplane, he put it on."

In 1928, having suffered enough of Oklahoma's numbing winter cold and broiling summer heat in an open cockpit, F.C. Hall sent Wiley with the Travel Air biplane to the Lockheed factory in Burbank, California, to buy a new cabin plane, a Vega.

This $20,240 plane was the newest and fastest aircraft Lockheed had yet built. Its Pratt and Whitney Wasp engine and its sleek lines brought together the latest advances in aeronautics. Its cruising speed ranged from 150 to 190 miles per hour. Lockheed's enviable record of usually placing several models among the top finishers in air races launched the slogan, "It takes a Lockheed to beat a Lockheed."

F.C. Hall named the new airplane after his daughter, *Winnie Mae*; this was the first of three consecutive Lockheed Vegas F.C. Hall was to own, each with the identical name. The stock market crash in October of 1929 and its effect on the American economy decided—or forced—Hall to lay off Wiley Post and sell the plane back to Lockheed.

Post was now thirty-one-years old. His air transport license showed that his height was 5 foot 5 inches, that he weighed 155 pounds, and that his hair and eye were brown. What the license did not show was that he was now unemployed.

At this time Joe Crosson' first entered Wiley Post's life. Joe had come to Oklahoma to ferry a plane back to the California coast, and Wiley, with no money, hitched a ride with Crosson from Oklahoma City to Los Angeles. This hitchhiking was a courtesy pilots extended to one another. Crosson, still single, always with a kind heart for his fellow man, took his new-found and broke friend to his parents' home in San Diego. It was a home where numerous pilots, penniless and between jobs, could find a temporary haven. Crosson even tried to get Wiley a job; Post, quite conscious of his lost eye, may have thought it charity and left—going his own way for a while. In the years to come, these two men would meet again several times and a strong friendship developed between them. But it was always Joe Crosson who would help Wiley Post.

Calling on Lockheed, Post talked himself into occasional assignments. He was not on Lockheed's payroll, but would, when needed, perform certain tasks on a contract basis. Usually he was asked to test new models, or determine needed repair or alteration in used planes brought for overhaul. It was a responsible job, requiring a pilot with mechanical ability.

His stay with Lockheed was brief, but Post acquired a good deal of technical knowledge about aircraft. He also added many flying hours to his pilot log, when he was asked to deliver Lockheed aircraft to cities in Washington and Oregon. (Wiley also ferried Lockheed Vegas between El Paso and Brownsville, Texas, and Mazatlan, Mexico, for the Detroit Aircraft Corporation, parent company of Lockheed.)

While Post was working at Lockheed, Amelia Earhart arrived from New York with a newly purchased, ill-used Vega "demonstrator." Earhart was about to enter the highly publicized "Powder-Puff derby," flying from Clover Field in Santa Monica, to Cleveland, Ohio, and she had come to the Lockheed strip in Burbank for a thorough check of her plane before the race.

It was Wiley Post's first meeting with Amelia Earhart. Earhart referred to her Vega as a "third-hand clunk." But after Lockheed's stocky new test-pilot, sporting an eye patch, had checked out the plane and had found it wanting, he had a far more derogatory name for it. Lockheed, wishing to protect its good reputation, replaced Miss Earhart's plane with a far superior demonstrator they had on hand.

On June 5, 1930, Wiley heard from F.C. Hall. It seemed that the company had ordered a new plane and would need his services again. Wiley agreed to return with the understanding that he would be free to use the new plane in some upcoming national races.

Still living in California, Wiley was permitted to supervise the construction of the latest Hall plane. This model 5B Vega—with a seven-seat cabin, powered by a Pratt & Whitney Wasp engine and bearing the registration number CN 105W—was destined to become the most famous plane of its day. Painted white with blue trim, it, too, was named *Winnie Mae*.

Wiley's first chance to test the new plane came in the fall, at one of the National Air Races of 1930, a non-stop flight from Los Angeles to Chicago. There were five competitors, four of them famous fliers: Roscoe Turner, Art Goebel, Lee Shoenhair, and Billy Brock. Of course there was this newcomer nobody had heard of before, what was his name again? Oh, yes, Wiley Post.

Nine hours and nine minutes after take-off, Wiley set his plane down at the Curtiss-Reynolds airport north of Chicago, the winner by seconds. Associated Press reported that when he "nonchalantly walked to check in, the judges had to consult their program to see who this portly, bushy-haired fellow was."

The result was a surprise to all but Wiley. Although he had lost three-quarters of an hour after take-off due to a malfunctioning magnetic compass, he never doubted that he would win.

Actually Wiley had started with a more ambitious plan in mind. After winning the non-stop race to Chicago—so his scheme went—he wanted to simply land, refuel, and be off on his way to New York to break the transcontinental speed record. To chart the best course, he had consulted an Australian-born navigator named Harold Gatty who had been recommended to him. But having lost the better part of an hour at the beginning of the race, there was no longer a chance to break the old record. Wiley stayed and accepted the first prize of $7,500.

The winning of the non-stop flight to Chicago was just the beginning. For their next exploit, F.C. Hall and Wiley Post wanted to do something bigger, much bigger. Something startling and attention-grabbing. And what could be more spectacular than, say, a flight around the world? In an interview, F.C. Hall told the Associated Press that his late wife[2] was the first to suggest the round-the-world flight.

True, there had been two earlier flights around the earth. The first in 1924, when the United States Army Air Service sent two Douglas World Cruisers to circle the globe. The planes, large open-cockpit biplanes, each had a crew of two, and the trip took almost six months. Five years later, in August 1929, the famous German airship *Graf Zeppelin*, took twenty-one days to float once around the earth.

Wiley Post now wanted to show the world just how fast a man could circle the world. If all went well, he thought, he could set a new record of ten days.

In January 1931, Post flew the *Winnie Mae* back to California in order for Lockheed to make modifications for the long-distance flight. He also met with Harold Gatty in San Diego.

Gatty, who was three years Post's junior, had studied at the Royal Australian Naval College with the idea of becoming a ship's navigator. He had emigrated to the United States in 1927, settling in California. There he established a school, teaching navigation to aviators; among his more famous pupils was Anne Morrow Lindbergh.

The course of navigation Gatty taught was essential to any pilot in an age of little, if any, ground control. Aircraft radio was still in its infancy and unusable by a lone pilot; weather information was usually unreliable, and maps were not always available or accurate.

At their meeting, Wiley suggested to Gatty that the two would make an ideal crew for a globe-circling flight. Gatty would attend to charting the route, arrange for ground support along the way, and navigate. Post, for his part, would attend to the preparation of the aircraft and pilot the plane.

The third, and certainly equally pivotal associate, was F.C. Hall. First of all, the *Winnie Mae* was his airplane; secondly, and equally important, he was the project's foremost financial backer, since his partner Powell Briscoe feared that the flight could only end in tragedy and wanted no part of the venture. Hall's attempts to raise funds elsewhere procured little.

Of course, there was the semi-realistic expectation that a successful flight could reap substantial financial rewards. In an interview, Hall mentioned amounts for personal appearances, endorsements, advertisements, and other sources, which could total close to half a million dollars. Most of this money—probably after repayment of Hall's outlay—would go to Post. Gatty had come aboard on a guarantee of $5,000, with the promise of a 25 percent interest in the anticipated earnings. What nobody seemed to have fully taken into account was the fact that this was the year 1931, and the country, indeed the world, was in a deep economic depression.

Leaving financial matters to Hall, Wiley concentrated on making the *Winnie Mae* safe and efficient. Pratt & Whitney's Wasp engine was completely overhauled. The electrical starter was removed to save weight, which meant that the plane would have to be started by hand. A special hatch with a folding windshield was installed in the top of the fuselage to make it possible for Gatty to make celestial sightings.

As this was the first flight of its kind, new problems had to be foreseen and solutions found. Wiley, with the aid of mechanics, carved out quarters for Gatty amid the additional fuel tanks cluttering the cabin. Since the distribution of weight would change considerably as fuel was consumed and tanks became empty, Gatty was provided with a sliding seat; moving forward or backward, his body weight could thus help balance the plane by keeping the center of gravity constant.

A system of communication between pilot and navigator—a simple tube through which pilot and navigator were supposed to speak to each other—suggested by Harold Gatty, was installed. It worked perfectly in the workshop, but once in flight, the roar of the engine drowned out their voices and the two men could barely hear each other.

The *Winnie Mae* had all the usual standard instruments, such as fuel gauges, fuel-pressure indicator, altimeter, airspeed indicator, tachometer, oil-temperature gauge, cylinder-head temperature indicator, artificial horizon, bank-and-turn indicator, rate-of-climb instruments, and outside air temperature indicator. Some of these gauges had to be duplicated in the cabin, so that Gatty received the same information as Post. In addition Gatty developed a wind-drift and ground-speed indicator specifically for the flight.

After all the structural additions and changes, the government rescinded the *Winnie Mae's* license NC 105W (the 'C' indicating Commercial) and issued a new license, NR 105W (the 'R' indicating Restricted). The difference is noteworthy. While under a ''restricted'' license, a plane may never carry passengers—only the pilot and crew members essential to the flight. As the *Winnie Mae* was now rated, even F.C. Hall, her owner and the chief backer of the venture, was not allowed to fly in it.

Another problem anticipated by an astute Post was the stress on the human system caused by moving constantly across time zones. The body, used to certain hours for sleep and meals, would be thrust into different sequences, where mornings became afternoons, and nights became days. He drastically shortened his daily rest times and arranged his sleeping schedule and meals for different hours each day, to break the long established pattern his body expected. He sought hour upon hour of solitude, to prepare himself for the days he expected to spend silently at the controls, staring at gauges and out of windows. He felt no need for a strenuous exercise program, as he expected to perform little physical activity. Only one concession to personal comfort did Wiley allow himself: He had the pilot's straight-backed, bucket seat removed, replacing it with a comfortable armchair.

A dilemma never once alluded to in the reports of the day was one of body waste disposal. Of course that was not a new problem; it affected all longer flights, and almost any flier faced the same difficulty. Post and Gatty ate only light meals to reduce excretion. In flight, they used lidded, waxed containers, which were then stored until the next stop. When they flew over water, the containers were simply thrown overboard.

The *Winnie Mae* and its two men crew left California, arriving at Roosevelt Field, Long Island, New York, on May 23, 1931. The plane and the men were ready. All that was needed now was for the weather to cooperate. Actually, it was not the weather in New York that needed to be favorable, but conditions over the Atlantic and in England. The science of forecasting weather conditions was still very young, and basic data for a huge area like the North Atlantic were especially difficult to obtain.

Dr. James K. Kimball, often called the guardian angel of transatlantic fliers, was the U.S. Weather Bureau's meteorologist in New York. Since 1927 he had advised every pilot attempting to fly the North Atlantic. It was Dr. Kimball who had sent Charles A. Lindbergh on his way to Paris, after first halting him for the better part of a week.

Dr. Kimball now had bad news for Post and Gatty, who conferred with him daily: weather conditions did not look promising for an early departure. The three men realized that the start of the globe-circling trip was of primary importance. If the very first leg—crossing of the North Atlantic—proved too fatiguing to Post, the rest of the trip was in jeopardy. If too much energy were to be expended at the outset, there would be no opportunity for Wiley to regain his stamina for the balance of the flight.

The days went by, but the weather reports remained unacceptable. On several occasions, Dr. Kimball saw improvements, and the plane was gassed and readied for take-off. On at least two occasions the two fliers had actually climbed into the plane, ready to leave, when new reports arrived of threatening squalls and fog. The *Winnie Mae* was returned to the hangar.

After midnight, June 23, 1931, a month to the day since Post and Gatty arrived in New York, Dr. Kimball seemed satisfied with weather conditions ahead.

While Post lifted the *Winnie Mae* into the pre-dawn sky, Gatty scribbled hastily in his log: "Took off at 4:55 daylight-saving time, set our course, visibility poor."

Six hours and 47 minutes later, Post set the plane down on the jagged, coarse landing field at Harbour Grace, Newfoundland. It was here that Gatty realized to his chagrin that he had forgotten his billfold and carried only a single dollar, which immediately went for food. As soon as the fuel tanks had been topped, Wiley took off for England. He was not about to dawdle anywhere.

About this moment Gatty wrote: "Wiley let the motor roar out its defiance to the 1,900 miles or more of open water which lay beyond the tranquil harbor. He cocked his one good ear to the tune of the exhaust, and his one good eye was glued to the tachometer."

Despite all the time lost in waiting in New York, and all the predictions of safe weather over the Atlantic, the fliers spent the next hours flying blind through heavy overcast and fog. When Gatty calculated that they must have crossed the ocean, Wiley broke through the clouds and landed at the first inviting airport he spotted. He found himself the guest of the Royal Air Force at the Sealand Aerodrome in Cheshire, barely a dozen miles from Liverpool. Post and Gatty had crossed the Atlantic in 16 hours and 17 minutes from Harbour Grace.

A quick snack, some refueling and the *Winnie Mae* was off for Berlin, Germany, where a cheering crowd awaited them. Having flown for twenty-four hours, and without sleep for almost two days, both men were near exhaustion. Post later conceded that he had been extremely weary and could barely keep a magnetic course.

Early the next morning, refreshed, with a refueled plane, they took off for Moscow, a distance of one thousand miles. It was Post's practice to use 87-octane fuel for take-off and then, once airborne, he would switch to any of the other tanks to cruise on ordinary 80-octane gasoline.

In near ceiling-zero conditions Post was forced to practically hedge-hop across eastern Europe into Russia. When they landed at October Airdrome, they found that only a handful of people had come to meet the plane. But later, at a festive gathering arranged by a cultural group in their honor, the Russians hailed the two men and continuously offered toasts. Post and Gatty drank only plain water. They refused to take chances on what alcohol might do to their digestion or judgment.

Since the June dawn in Moscow broke about 2 A.M. Post and Gatty had only two hours sleep before leaving Moscow for Novosibirsk in Siberia. At Novosibirsk, the Russians insisted on another gala reception, with more toasts, music, and dancing. At about 10 P.M., Post and Gatty made their excuses and retired to their hotel rooms. They got little rest that night, bothered by uncomfortable beds and bedbugs.

After barely three hours sleep, Wiley lifted the *Winnie Mae* off just before 5 A.M., with her next scheduled stop at Irkutsk. Six hours later, they landed safely. Wiley cabled his wife just two words: "Feeling fine." Harold felt fine too, except he suffered from a severe case of perpetual hunger.

After only 2 hours, 19 minutes on the ground for refuelling, the *Winnie Mae* took of for Blagoveshchensk, where problems awaited.

Cloudbursts had turned the Blagoveshchensk dirt landing strip into a quagmire, in which a couple of inches of water covered half a foot of mud. Wiley, seeing the mess below, instructed Gatty to crawl as far back in the tail as possible, and to "hang on like hell."[3] When Post landed, the plane barely rolled as the *Winnie Mae* gradually settled down into the Siberian mud. "It was the first mishap of the flight," noted the *Los Angeles Times*.

Tired and annoyed by the delay and frustrated by language barriers, Post tried to outline what he expected the Russians to do. He wanted a tractor brought from some nearby collective farm to pull the plane to some drier surface, if one could be found. At last, with the vague feeling that he had made himself understood, Wiley stretched out in a cabin, where he slept for four hours. Gatty, meanwhile, took off on foot for nearby Blagoveshchensk to buy something to eat. He not only found some hot food, but something even more welcome: his first bath since the Biltmore Hotel in New York City.

When it became quite obvious that no tractor was forthcoming, Post bowed to the Fates and, lowering his sights, asked for a team of horses. More time was lost waiting for the horses to arrive. The Russians were trying to be helpful but the horses were unable to budge the plane. Wiley went back to sleep; there was no sense wasting time when he could catch up on his rest.

Five hours went by before more horses finally freed the plane and the *Winnie Mae* could continue on her flight. Post and Gatty had lost half a day on the ground at Blagoveshchensk. Two-and-a-half hours later they reached their next stop, Khabarovsk, some 365 miles distant.

The Pratt & Whitney Wasp engine performed perfectly, never missing a stroke. Gatty, in the cabin, lulled by the steady rhythm, would become alarmed as the engine periodically sputtered and nearly stalled. It was some time before he realized that it was simply Wiley's habit of draining the very last drop of fuel from one tank, before switching to the next full one. Gatty never did get used to the sound of their single engine backfiring.

The *Winnie Mae* left Khabarovsk at 6:45 P.M., local time, with her tanks filled. Because of adverse reports received from a Japanese weather station, the two men decided to fly non-stop 2,500 miles, to Solomon, Alaska, by-passing the planned refueling stop at Petropavlovsk.

The Japanese weather report proved accurate. Wiley was forced to fly through, over and around storms, facing fog and icing conditions. Added to the dangers was the fact that they were flying over unfamiliar territory. The maps provided by the Russian government were useless. Mountains were not always in the locations indicated and their heights were understated; several times Post had to pull up sharply when a towering mountain suddenly loomed ahead through the fog. Post was often misled, and even taken out of his way by misplaced cities and incorrectly displayed rivers. The puzzled fliers never learned an explanation for these inaccurate maps. The truth came to light two generations later when, in the spirit of *glasnost*, the Russian government admitted that it had intentionally issued imprecise maps to mislead potential enemies.

Repeatedly Post had to climb to great altitudes, to get above clouds and storms, so that Gatty could get a fix on the sun or stars to correct their course.

With the fuel tanks near empty, Wiley landed on the beach at Solomon, Alaska. The *Winnie Mae* was back on American soil. At the small outpost they were able to secure some one hundred gallons of fuel, more than enough to get to Fairbanks, where they had planned to spend the night.

Since the engine had to be hand-started, Gatty, though unfamiliar with the chore, was called to duty. On the first attempt, the Wasp backfired and the propeller blade struck Harold on the shoulder, knocking him to the ground. Bruised and stunned, he picked himself up and was able to start the engine. But trying to get off the beach, the wheels stuck in the soft sand, the tail lifted up and Wiley nosed the plane over, bending the propeller tips. He managed to straighten the blades sufficiently with a broken hammer, an adjustable wrench, and a stone picked from the beach. Gatty started the engine without difficulty and Wiley was able to lift off.

In Fairbanks, Wiley's old friend Joe Crosson, now chief pilot for Pacific Alaska Airways, came to the rescue. His mechanics happened to have a spare propeller on hand. While the two fliers slept for three hours, the propeller was replaced and the tanks refuelled. Then it was off for Edmonton, Alberta, Canada. The *Winnie Mae* was on the homestretch.

By the time Wiley and Harold Gatty approached Blatchford Field at Edmonton, they were exhausted. A steady downpour had nearly turned the landing strip into another Blagoveshchensk-type morass. Not wanting to have the *Winnie Mae* stuck in mud again, Wiley made a soft landing and almost flew the plane to the concrete apron leading to the hangers.

The fliers were surprised at the world's press that had come to Edmonton to greet them. There were newspapermen, newsreel cameras, and radio reporters. Someone stuck a microphone in Post's face: "Say something, Wiley!" And to a world waiting for some profound statement, Post bluntly announced, "I'm tired of sitting down."

It soon became obvious that the plane could not take off from the soft airstrip. It was a Canadian airmail pilot who suggested that Post should use the paved surface of Portage Avenue, the road leading from the airport to downtown Edmonton, as his runway. Rapidly the city fathers adopted the plan, and while Wiley and Harold slept, Edmontonians labored. Crews took down telephone wires and restrung power lines so that no wire crossed the road. Then they washed the *Winnie Mae* until she gleamed. With just plain human muscle power, the plane was rolled to the head of Portage Avenue. There was civic pride involved; Edmonton wanted to be the best host possible for such an heroic pair of aviators.

At dawn, Wiley raced the now shiny white and blue trimmed plane down the road, past telephone and light poles, past hydrants, and perhaps half the population of Edmonton, and lifted skyward. "Curbstones and electric-light poles clipped by the wingtips so fast that I was just a little scared myself," Post recalled.

Gatty now routed them for Cleveland and on to New York City. The *Winnie Mae*'s wheels touched down at Roosevelt Field in the evening of July 1, 1931, at exactly 8:47 P.M., as recorded by the official timer of the National Aeronautic Association. The men had flown 15,474 miles in the total time of 207 hours and 51 minutes (eight days, 15 hours and 51 minutes).[4]

The reception in New York, though late in the evening, drew a huge crowd. The signed and notarized statement accounting for the gate receipts at Roosevelt Field, reports that after the expense of gate-men, ticket salesmen, etc., $835.25 was taken in, an amount which Roosevelt Field, Post and Gatty shared.

The ticker-tape parade up New York's Broadway rivaled the one given to Charles Lindbergh. During the reception, on the steps of the City Hall, Mayor Jimmy Walker quipped that Post's plane was "the 'Winnie May' before the flight started, the 'Winnie Must' while in progress, and the 'Winnie Did' now."

An invitation came from Washington, D.C., for a meeting with President Hoover at the White House, which was followed by luncheon given in honor of the two fliers by the Aeronautical Chamber of Commerce.

There followed a procession of innumerable interviews with newspapers, magazines, radio stations, and picture-taking sessions with wives, without wives, the two men together and singly, sitting, standing, waving, smiling, serious, bending over maps, looking at each other, both looking in the same direction. No end seemed in sight, it was always: "Just one more!"

Gatty surprised readers, saying that the radio equipment aboard proved "very nearly just so much dead weight. . . . We sent signals once or twice; once as we were nearing Ireland, then again over the Aleutians, but as far as I know, nobody heard them." Gatty explained further in an exclusive story to the *Los Angeles Times*:

As far as radio weather reports were concerned, we didn't receive any. Of course, we didn't have much time to listen and on a large part of our flight—the part where weather reports would have been of most value—if there were any they were sent in Russian and we wouldn't have been able to understand them if we had got them.

The weather reports are usually sent out on long waves and long wave equipment weighs too much at present to be desirable on an airplane that is making a long-distance flight and on which weight has to be conserved as far as possible in order to carry large stocks of fuel.

The firm of H. A. Bruno–R. R. Blythe quickly arranged a Post-and-Gatty speaking tour under the sponsorship of "Aviation Mobilgas Ethyl and Mobiloil Aero Oils." It was scheduled to run from July 18 until September 7, covering some twenty-five cities from coast to coast. The fee was to be in excess of $20,000, but as part of the tour was canceled, the two fliers shared only the guaranteed $15,000 minus expenses and agent commission.

There was some revenue from *The New York Times* and the National Broadcasting Corporation, and from endorsements, such as the Bulova Watch Company and the Sperry Gyroscope Company.

On the parade drive between Albany and Schenectady, New York, the state trooper assigned as an escort set too fast a pace. Post signalled to the trooper to slow down, "Please, don't go any faster than 30," he begged. Wiley was just as cautious when in the air. When motion picture producers wanted him to fly low over Manhattan, he objected because he did not think it safe. "That's silly," he said to Bennie Turner,[5] "I don't believe in taking chances just for publicity. It won't help aviation any and it won't prove anything." He amazed Boston once by declining to chance a scheduled flight to Providence, Rhode Island, because of drizzle.

Will Rogers made mention in his column that the two fliers would not be able to visit Claremore, Oklahoma, his adopted home town, because it had no airport. In five days the little town, located some twenty-five miles northeast of Tulsa, built an airport. Rogers flew to Tulsa, where he met Post and Gatty. Together the three flew to Claremore, even though Rogers was an illegal passenger aboard the *Winnie Mae*. In his newspaper column, Rogers told of his conversation with the two men:

> They had no parachutes, they would have taken up too much room, and been too hard to sit on, and besides if you had to use 'em, where would you been anyhow. They carried nothing at all of any precautionary nature, Post said, "it was make it or else." Now all you radio nuts get ready for a shock. Their radio was a flop. Gatty said they didn't expect to use it only on getting the weather at the place they were headed to land at, but that it was a fliv. He says no radio has been made that will fit those particular requirements, so radio played no part in their accomplishments. . . . They attributed their staying awake to their lack of food, as they said they always kept hungry.

Claremore acclaimed the two national heroes and Will Rogers, naturally, delivered the main address. As one of America's foremost aviation enthusiasts, he fully appreciated Post and Gatty's outstanding accomplishment.

When asked about their incredible endurance, Wiley explained: "I was in good condition when I started and I am now, except that my leg is still sore from kicking the rudder. We did not do any special training for our trip, but on the flight we took good care of ourselves as circumstances permitted. We drank plenty of water and ate very little food—not more than one meal a day. We ate hardly at all in the plane. That kept us fresh and we are not particularly hungry now."

What Wiley left unsaid was the fact that during that one week flight he lost so much weight that his belt had to be taken in five inches.

When asked about any humorous event of the flight, Wiley chuckled, "Here we've been around the world and have spent a tremendous day in New York and we literally haven't spent a cent. We had $35 when we left New York for incidental expenses. I had $34 of it and Gatty had the other dollar. And I've still got mine. Of course arrangements had been made in advance for our gasoline and oil. We never had a chance to buy anything—we were treated to such generous hospitality everywhere that we never got our hands near our pocketbooks.''

Post bought the *Winnie Mae* on July 8, 1931. He signed a contract with F.C. Hall, which set down the terms. Post would pay $3,000 in cash within thirty days, with the balance of $18,200 payable on a note, with interest at eight percent per annum. Harold Gatty signed as witness.

As the year progressed, Wiley became ever more discouraged and bitter. In a November 21 report, the North American Newspaper Alliance described Post as '' a little hard of hearing, plump, genial and disillusioned.'' The temporary deafness was due to the high noise level in a Vega cockpit. He had flown from Oklahoma City to Chicago only the night before the interview. Wiley described his 'round-the-world flight as a "stunt" which really "didn't advance the mechanics of aviation an inch," since only already proven equipment had been used. He admitted that he had some offers in aviation. But he complained that it was difficult to make money in aviation, that Lindbergh had been the big money maker, and he said that he might just write a book, looking *Behind the Scenes in Aviation*, intimating that it would be a real exposé.

It was a depressed Post who must have given that interview. He was about to reach his thirty-third birthday, and after four months, the cheering had begun to die down. He must have shared the disappointment of so many others who have learned that adulation is not the coin of the market place. Rent cannot be paid with the roar of crowds along a parade route.

In August 1931 Rand McNally & Co. published *Around the World in Eight Days*, Post and Gatty's own story, hastily put together by New York writer Leo Kieran.

There was more money for the pair from lectures in a number of American cities, but the Depression cut deeply into the optimistic estimates of sudden riches to be made from their exploit. Finally Gatty went back to San Diego and his navigation school.

Little is known of Post's activities during the next twelve months. Flight records show however, that between March 15, 1932 and September 15, 1932, he logged a mere fourteen hours of flight time. The assumption is that there was little money for fuel. In his solitude, Wiley had a new dream. He was determined to circle the world again, only this time he would do it much faster, and definitely alone. The principal reason for this second attempt was the emergence of malicious small talk.

There were voices who suggested that Gatty was the real "brains" of the operation and implied that all Post really had done was just to sit up front and "steer." This was, of course, absurd; the first one to so label it would have been Harold Gatty. Those opinions were voiced mostly by parties who in some way simply wished to belittle the feats of others. *Isvestia*, the Soviet news-paper, stated that the Soviet Union could easily produce a whole corps of airmen just as skilled in blind-flying techniques as this Wiley Post. As Joseph Stalin stated, there existed: "no fort which the Bolsheviki could not storm." *Outlook Magazine*, for another, had felt compelled to note the obvious, that the Post-Gatty flight only covered 15,000 miles while the earth's circumference is about 25,000. Perhaps in Wiley Post's mind, some of those barbs had caused a deep wound, which he wanted to heal, once and for all. A solo flight around-the-world would prove to all doubters that Wiley Post didn't need anyone else; he could do it all—alone.

On January 14, 1933, the semiannual inspection reminder for a Lockheed Vega, serial number 122, license NR 105W, the plane known across the country as *Winnie Mae*, was sent to Winnie Mae Fain in Oklahoma City. (Winnie Mae Hall, for whom the plane had originally been named, had in the mean time married Leslie Fain.) It would appear that the plane had passed out of Wiley Post's hands.

Three weeks later, on February 5, 1933, the same plane was listed on a record, transfer, and reassignment form as having been purchased from Winnie Mae Fain by a company calling itself the "Fain and Post Drilling Company," its office registered at 706 N.W. 29th Street, Oklahoma City, Oklahoma. Officers of this company were: Leslie Fain, president; Wiley Post and L. B. Thompson, directors. Wiley also appears as secretary-treasurer. The company now applied for a restricted license for its plane, to make appro-priate alterations preparatory to a solo around-the-world flight.

Although Wiley would fly alone, he could not finance the venture alone. Harry G. Frederickson, a young Oklahoma City businessman, undertook to help raise funds from a number of companies interested in furthering aviation. It was also arranged with several major companies to provide equipment and services free of charge. Thus Pratt & Whitney not only provided the spare parts needed to upgrade the Wasp engine, but also the services of a technical specialist, Lionel B. Clark, who attended the engine to the moment of take-off. The Sperry Gyroscope Company donated the automatic pilot, which Post dubbed "Mechanical Mike," as well as technicians; Socony-Vacuum (Mobil Oil) promised to supply gasoline and oil, Mobil-grease for the rocker arms, and compass-liquid and other light oils for lubrication. The Roosevelt Hotel in New York City, which was to be flight headquarters, would provide free-of-charge, a $35-per-day suite of rooms both before and after the flight as well as supply all meals at half price.

The need for more money was constant. Workmen had to be paid. Fuel tanks would arrive and needed to be installed, but a C.O.D. charge of $638 held them at the express office. Banks rejected a loan on so precarious a project, suppliers balked at extending further credit. Wiley's personal appeal to Oklahoma City's businessmen raised a few hundred dollars, but it was far from the needed sum. An unexpected benefactor appeared. He was John F. Kroutil of Yukon, a suburb of Oklahoma City. As president of the Yukon Mill and Elevator Company, he offered several thousand dollars to continue the project; he made only one request: "Mention Yukon, Oklahoma, sometime."

More delays: trouble with the wiring; fuselage gas tanks that were too large and could not be installed; parts that disappeared in transit; wrong instruments—there seemed to be no end to the variety of problems which arose.

Larger gasoline tanks were installed in the *Winnie Mae*'s wings. Since Post was going to fly solo, the airplane would be able to carry additional fuel. The cabin, formerly Harold Gatty's domain, was also filled with fuel tanks. Six fuselage fuel tanks could hold 405 gallons of fuel, while five wing tanks had a capacity of 240 gallons for a total of 645 gallons.

Since there was no longer a passenger to maintain a constant center of gravity by means of weight-shifting, a substitute would have to be found. As fuel was used and tanks became empty, a system of pumping gasoline from the fore to the aft tanks was devised. A radio mast, six feet in length, was installed. One of the lessons learned from the 1931 flight was the need for frequent lubrication of the rocker arms, which control the opening and closing of the engine's intake and exhaust valves. So that Wiley could attend to this while in flight, a special grease gun, inside the cockpit, was connected to eighteen pieces of copper tubing leading to the rocker boxes.

By mid-March, the *Winnie Mae* was in New York and had a Sperry automatic pilot installed. Invented by Lawrence Sperry, it would permit the pilot short periods of sleep or just rest, while dependably holding the plane on course. An Automatic Direction Finder (ADF), on loan from the U.S. Army Air Corps, was installed by the Signal Corps. One of the very first of its kind, it would indicate to the pilot the course toward the signal sent from a low frequency radio station. A pilot therefore, could now select a distant city's radio signal, and simply follow it to its source.

An accident at the airport south of Chickasha, Oklahoma, almost ended the *Winnie Mae*'s career. Post asked an old friend, Luther "Red" Gray, to test the automatic pilot. Though Gray pointed out that the fuel gauges indicated the tanks to be almost empty, Post felt certain that there was enough fuel for a short hop. The plane, with Post and two other passengers aboard, reached a height of about 50 feet when the engine ran out of fuel. The plane crashed with a minimum of damage, thanks to "Red" Gray's expertise. While Gray and another man were unharmed, and Post suffered no more than a cut finger, the fourth passenger cracked two ribs.

Post had the wrecked *Winnie Mae* hauled to Oklahoma City where a Braniff Airways crew began to rebuilt it. Finally, everything seemed in place and Braniff rendered its bill; Wiley's bank balance of $1,200 was $563.92 short.

Braniff was adamant. Unless full payment was received, the plane would not leave the hangar. Four old friends—Paul Braniff, Operating Manager of Braniff Airways, pilots "Red" Gray and Claud Seaton, and S. E. Perry, Superintendent of Maintenance of the Airline—came to Wiley's rescue. Each one of these men put up $140.98 in salary due them by Braniff, and the plane was released.[6]

Wiley planned to follow the identical route used on the 1931 flight, only this time he scheduled just five refueling stops: Berlin, Novosibirsk, Khabarovsk, Fairbanks, and Edmonton.

Fay Gillis, one of the early American women fliers, temporarily living in Moscow, was surpised to receive the following telegram:

NLT FAY GILLIS ANANEVSKY PER DOM 5 APT 26 MSK

LIKE YOU ARRIVE NOVOSIBIRSK BY JULY FIRST AR-
RANGE GAS PLANE IN TWO HOURS WHILLE [sic] I
SLEEP THEN FLY WITH ME KHABAROVSK TO DIRECT
SERVICE THERE GET ME BEST MAPS NOVOSIBIRSK
KHABAROVSK WILL PAY YOUR EXPENSES REGARDS
WILLEY [sic] POST

Fay began flying when she was only twenty, and one day
during her training was forced to bail out when her plane's tail
section separated from the rest of the fuselage. She thus became
the first woman member of the Caterpillar Club, whose membership is restricted to those who saved their lives by parachute
jumps. She now lived with her family in Russia. Her father had
gone there in 1930 to build two electrolytic zinc plants for the
Soviet government, one in the Caucasus, and one in the Ural
Mountains. Fay, a beautiful and charming young lady, had learned
to speak Russian and was fully accepted by Russian fliers as an
equal; even though she was an American she had been allowed to
solo over Moscow. In America, the community of young fliers
was a closely knit group. While they would compete against each
other, there was a camaraderie and they knew each other well.
That Wiley would telegraph her was not surprising, but Fay was
puzzled. How could Wiley suggest that she fly with him to
Khabarovsk? Was this not supposed to be a "solo" flight? But she
was prepared to assist her old friend. Following his instructions,
she left Moscow on June 25, 1933. As there was no regular
passenger service between Moscow and Novosibirsk she had
been given special permission to travel on a mail plane. It was the
first time a foreigner had been allowed to travel outside the
regular passenger lines. Arriving in Novosibirsk she began to
arrange everything for Wiley's arrival and prepared to wait.
    Dr. Kimball, again, was Wiley's advisor on weather condi-
tions over the North Atlantic. For four weeks, reports of inclement weather over the anticipated route grounded Wiley in New
York. An impatient Wiley could hardly be restrained. Finally, at
daybreak on July 15, after several false starts, Dr. Kimball's charts
looked encouraging. Wiley walked briskly toward the plane, Mae
hurrying at this side trying to keep up with him.

"Do be careful," was all Mae could think of saying.

Precisely at 5:10 A.M., Wiley took off from the Floyd Bennett runway. On the initial leg of this flight, through some fog and banks of heavy clouds, Wiley immediately made use of the Sperry auto-pilot and his radio compass and listened to St. John's, Newfoundland, radio for weather reports. Hours later, Wiley ran into a solid weather front. Climbing as high as 11,000 feet, he could still not fly over it. The only path led right through the rain-laden clouds. Still later, having passed the half-way mark across the Atlantic, Wiley was startled to pick up a British radio station, which greeted him with: "This is a special broadcast for Wiley Post. . . ."

Wiley immediately aligned his radio compass and set course for Berlin's Tempelhof airfield. He landed there after being aloft for 25 hours and 45 minutes. Among those welcoming Post to Berlin was Reichsminister Hermann Göring, recently appointed commissioner for air by Adolf Hitler.

Two hours and 15 minutes after arriving, the *Winnie Mae* had been refueled and was ready to leave on the next leg, destination Novosibirsk. An unscheduled stop at Königsberg, Germany, and another at Moscow, Russia, for maps and repairs, pushed Wiley a whole day behind his carefully crafted timetable.

But at least some preparations worked as planned. Arriving in Novosibirsk, he was met by Fay Gillis. She had been waiting for the past three weeks and had used the time to arrange everything perfectly. The Russians had repeatedly mowed the grass on the landing field, and put it in excellent shape. It was equipped for night operation and its weather bureau had plotted a specific forecast for Wiley's itinerary. A special room had been set aside where Post could rest at the airport. Even a menu of hot meals awaited Wiley, which he declined, in keeping with his practice of eating very little while on these flights. Fay had also arranged for numerous maps and detailed instructions on hazards along the way.

Fay, who was the New York *Herald Tribune*'s aviation correspondent in the Soviet Union, now took dictations from Wiley for his exclusive personal story to *The New York Times*. She had to cable Wiley's story before she could file her own coverage to the *Herald Tribune*; it was a matter of having to scoop her own *exclusive* story.

While she supervised the refueling, Wiley slept for two hours. The puzzle about accompanying Wiley was cleared up. It seemed that Wiley's New York agent had announced that Fay Gillis would be a passenger between Novosibirsk and Khabarovsk, to act as a translator for Wiley. He realized later that it would, of course, nullify the solo aspect of the flight. He made announcements canceling Fay's participation.

Post took off from Novosibirsk, but problems now seemed to pursue him. A malfunctioning automatic pilot caused another unscheduled landing at Irkutsk, and a reported storm to the east stayed Post for several additional hours. Steadily the hours he had so far gained on the trip were evaporating. By the time he made one more emergency stop at Rukhlovo, he was one hour behind his 1931 timetable.

It was here, at Rukhlovo, that Wiley had difficulties getting the idea across that he was thirsty and wanted a drink of water. Misinterpreting the sign language as the request for an alcoholic drink, a concerned Russian soldier first tried to dissuade Wiley from taking a strong drink, but seeing an adamant Post, obligingly trekked into town and returned with two bottles of Vodka.

Wiley never got his drink of water in Russia—he had to wait till he reached Flat, Alaska, 1,800 miles away. Rogers, commenting on it years later, quipped that Wiley Post, "Left two bottles of Vodka and flew 1800 miles for a drink of water. . . . 'Course," he carried the thought further, "if it had been me I would have poured one bottle in my engine and the other in me, and I would have been in New York by sundown."

But it was not that easy for Wiley. Mountains—some as high as 15,000 feet—lay hidden in heavy cloud banks, and Wiley flew "blind" for seven hours, depending entirely on his autopilot and instruments. Flying 1,800 miles non-stop would tax a rested man, and Wiley was close to exhaustion. Yet despite the effort and exertion, despite the ordeal and strain, Wiley and his plane worked as one, both performing without a flaw. The Signal Corps' WAMCATS (Washington–Alaska Military Cable and Telegraph System) stations at Nome, Teller, and Hot Springs transmitted signals to aid Post in checking his bearings on the flight from Khabarovsk, Siberia, to Fairbanks.

Starting in the north from Barrow (call letters WXB), where the U. S. Army Signal Corps' Sergeant Stanley Morgan kept watch, there were a number of official and private wireless stations all over the territory. These were not radio stations broadcasting entertainment; some of them were part of WAMCATS. Of course, being part of the United States Army, WAMCATS was primarily engaged in military traffic matters. But being the only communications network in Alaska it was also involved with the civil government and the population of the Territory.

Most WAMCATS stations were operated only during daylight business hours; others had prescribed broadcast times. Some were on the air twice daily for only a brief period, transmitting by morse code weather data, requests for medical assistance, or simply relating items of importance to Fairbanks and Anchorage. At other than broadcast times, some of these WAMCATS stations were not manned and consequently off the air. There was no way to contact them at other than their prescribed broadcast time, unless they had been alerted beforehand to man their station for continuous communication. Such unbroken contact with ground bases might be needed on an organized search for a lost pilot or trapper, or special vigils for flights on mercy missions or record attempts. When Wiley Post was expected to approach Alaska on his solo round-the-world flight, WAMCATS stations at Nome, Teller, Hot Springs, and Flat were of inestimable help. Without WAMCATS' assistance, Wiley Post would not have set a record, much less completed the flight.

Then, of course, Alaska had quite a number of private radio sets, operated by settlers, trappers, and Eskimos for their own means of contact with the outside world. Many of them were attended for several hours of the day, some even on a 24-hour basis. Notable among these independents was Joe Ulen, on the Koyukuk River, near Wiseman, who kept his set on day and night. When Joe was away, his Eskimo wife Tishu kept vigil. On several occasions his radio was the only one picking up distress signals, which he would then pass on at the appropriate times to a WAMCATS station. With dedicated men and women on alert, a sympathetic ear was usually available. As for actually flying in needed help when requested, weather could often delay it for days—and in winter storms—sometimes for weeks.

Transmissions by the American stations began eight hours after Wiley left Khabarovsk, and continued until the *Winnie Mae* had passed Nome. Hot Springs transmitted constantly for twelve hours until its batteries ran down.

In an article under his byline, Wiley reported this next phase of his flight through the worst weather ever, from Siberia toward his next goal: Fairbanks, Alaska.

"There were hours on end during all but one or two laps when I was forced to fly absolutely blind . . . out of sight of the ground." He also told of a dangerous brush with Alaskan weather, which unfortunately left no permanent impression:

> When mountains began to appear again above the clouds, I knew I had crossed Bering Strait and was above Alaska. I had crossed without even a fleeting glimpse of the surface. I flew to the north side of the mountains, where the wind had blown the clouds away, dropped down low, and flew back to the coast. I followed it around Cape Prince of Wales to Nome, where I circled the radio station and the airport, then headed for Fairbanks.
>
> The clouds were low and the visibility poor, and so I decided to climb back on top and, unable to pick up radio signals from Fairbanks which I expected would be broadcast for me, began what turned out to be a 1200-mile wandering around the central part of Alaska. For seven hours I dodged mountains, including 20,000 foot Mt. McKinley, and followed rivers to no avail. I was completely lost. I therefore headed back toward the coast of Nome, and on the way I spied what I later found was Flat. I landed at the airport there seven hours after I had circled the Nome radio station.

What Wiley described in his matter-of-fact style was the crisis that on this stretch his Automatic Direction Finder suddenly began to malfunction. He was unable to pick up the beam from Fairbanks' radio station to "home in," and, unfamiliar with the terrain, he started to drift off-course.

Noel Wien, famous Alaskan bush pilot, and his wife Ada were flying a Bellanca aircraft to Fairbanks, when they spotted Wiley's *Winnie Mae*—circling. It was a peculiar sight. Wiley was a man on a record-breaking attempt to circle the world, yet here he was, lazily flying in a large circle. At first the Wiens thought that Post might be lost, looking for a place to land. They tried to catch up with the faster plane, to alert him to the proper course to Fairbanks. But their Bellanca could not match the speed of the Vega. They continued to Fairbanks, fully expecting to find upon arrival that Wiley had found the right course and had landed ahead of them. But Fairbanks had not heard from Post. The Wiens now assumed that Wiley intentionally had set a circular course for the plane and was catching up on sleep.

What the Wiens did not know was that Wiley was indeed lost. And the landing at Flat was far more serious than Wiley reports. After circling the mining village of Flat, Wiley decided to land and ask for directions to Fairbanks. He discovered the airstrip which was little more than a small field, with a ditch at the end. He swung around into the wind and set the plane down, bumping over the bouncy terrain. He could not stop the plane quickly enough on the short, 700-foot field and the right landing gear support buckled, causing the engine cowling to dig deep into the ground. The propeller blades were bent beyond repair, and the tip of the right wing hit the ground. Wiley was unscathed. The accident was almost identical in character to the one at Solomon Beach, on the 1931 flight. This time, however, the damage was far more serious.

Wiley knew that he was ahead of his 1931 record; he had over thirty-one hours in hand. There was still a remote chance of setting a new record, if he could just find a new propeller, some landing gear and someone to make the needed repairs to the plane. And while he compiled a list of his needs, he added several hours of sound sleep. But here he was, in the tiny village of Flat, Alaska, hundreds of miles from any repair shop. Wiley Post saw his dream of a record fade. Aware that the WAMCATS radio operator had reported to Fairbanks, Wiley took care of one of the items on his list: he went to sleep. There was no sense in standing around and fretting. The WAMCATS station at Flat, Alaska, stayed on the air continuously from the time Post landed there until he left, all the time keeping in touch with Fairbanks, and the outside world.

The man who once again came to Post's assistance was Joe Crosson. At this Pacific Alaska Airways (PAA) office in Fairbanks, Crosson was apprised by radio of the accident and the extent of damage. He immediately rounded up Loren Fernald, PAA's chief mechanic, and mechanic Larry Davis. Needing a radio operator, Crosson next called Robert Gleason, PAA's communications superintendent and his most trusted friend. A new propeller, a temporary landing gear, jacks, and tools were loaded on a plane and the four men were ready to fly to Flat. Looking over the combined weight, and aware of the major shortcomings of the landing field at Flat, Crosson realized the plane was badly overweight. He had to make a difficult decision. He would have to risk flying without radio contact; Bob Gleason was left behind.

Since neither of the mechanics was able to operate a radio, Joe Crosson had to function as his own radio-telegraph operator. Holding communications down to the barest minimum, he kept Gleason at the Morse code key in Fairbanks, posted on his progress. Gleason then passed the information on to Flat.

At Flat, helpful townspeople had dug the *Winnie Mae's* front out of the soft earth and had righted her by the time Crosson and his crew arrived. Post and Crosson decided on what temporary repairs should be made at Flat, and which would have to wait for Fairbanks. While Crosson and his mechanics worked, Post went back to sleep.

By dawn the *Winnie Mae* was ready to take to the air. Post followed Crosson's plane, wing tip to wing tip, into Fairbanks. Crosson's plane was on floats and landed in the Chena Slough, while Post's plane, equipped with wheels, landed at Weeks Field, Fairbanks' small airport.

Once on the ground, Joe Crosson recruited every available mechanic in town. Post would need all the help he could get if he still wanted to break his own record. Jim Hutchison, a highly respected airplane mechanic, though not employed by Pacific Alaska Airways, was asked to build an entirely new right landing gear. Post asked Robert Gleason to check the faulty Automatic Direction Finder. Examining the ADF, Gleason determined that the right-left indicator was not working, and corrected it by simply replacing a defective tube. Wiley experienced no further trouble with it for the rest of his record flight.

Another eight hours were lost at Fairbanks, and when the *Winnie Mae* was finally ready for take-off, Post was rested. He needed to be. Ahead lay the almost 1,500 miles flight to Edmonton, and from there, more than 2,000 miles to New York City.

Post spend hours flying through heavy overcast which at times forced him to climb above 20,000 feet without oxygen, and still he arrived in Edmonton, Alberta, just 9 hours and 22 minutes after leaving Fairbanks. This time the field was dry, and after refueling, he took off without having to race down Edmonton's Portage Avenue. The final 2,000 miles were flown under perfect weather conditions. The sky was brilliantly clear, visibility unlimited, and Post was able to allow the Sperry autopilot to fly

the plane while he dozed. Sometime later Wiley explained how
he slept:

> I'll bet I fell asleep two hundred times before I reached
> New York City. Each time I actually got to sleep my
> muscles relaxed and my hand loosened its grasp on the
> stick. A finger was tied to the stick, and as the hand
> dropped I would be awakened.

This part of his dash around the world turned out to be
the easiest of all. As the afternoon wore on, Wiley picked up
radio broadcasts along the way. He especially enjoyed listening in
while announcers tried to speculate on his exact arrival time in
New York City.

On July 22nd, 1933, 7 days, 18 hours and 49½ minutes after
leaving Floyd Bennett Field, Wiley returned. He had broken his
and Gatty's two-year-old record by a surprising 21 hours, and he
had done it alone. A crowd of 50,000 spectators jammed into the
airport, and an estimated 5,000 cars clogged all approaches. Extra
editions of newspapers around the world told every major and
minor trivia of the flight; and what details editors did not know,
they could easily concoct. Wiley Post was the hero of the moment.
Even the usually restrained *London Times* was forced to unbend:
"Post definitely ushers in a new stage of long-distance aviation."

It was indeed a major achievement—to all but Wiley. He was
greatly disappointed that the trip was not accomplished in fewer
than seven days. He stated to the press that with the cooperation of
the weather, his flight could have been completed in five days.

When he returned, Mae Post recalled years later, "Wiley
said he understood what happened to pilots that started out and
were never heard from again. They, so Wiley said, became lost
from trusting only sight navigation, and just fly around in circles
until they run out of fuel." Mae paused, "He said, the hardest
thing he had to do was to learn to trust his instruments."

Again Wiley Post's financial rewards from the flight were
meager. A stage presentation in New York City was ill-conceived,
short-lived, and netted little gain. Although the Buick Company
presented Wiley with a new car, a few endorsements proved only
moderately lucrative.

Though he rarely smoked, he agreed to endorse Camel cigarettes. A picture showing him holding a cigarette, carried the message: "It takes steady nerves to fly around the world alone. Smoking Camels as I have for so long, I never worry about healthy nerves."

In September 1933, while on a two-month tour of the country under the sponsorship of Socony Vacuum, the oil company, Wiley nearly lost his life. After a speaking engagement in Quincy, Illinois, Wiley took off in the *Winnie Mae*. Barely a hundred feet off the ground, the engine quit and the plane fell into a small stand of trees. Investigation showed that someone had poured more than five gallons of water into the fuel tanks. It was neither the first time, nor would it be the last time, that sabotage nearly took Wiley Post's life.

During the next two years, the last of his life, Wiley Post performed his most valuable service to aviation by moving manned flight into a new direction toward high altitude. His service issued not so much from his accomplishments as from his failures; though calling his notable experiments "failures" is perhaps unfair. That they were unsuccessful is true; but that did not make their goals wrong. The experiments were unsuccessful only because Wiley was exploring a realm where hardly anyone had ventured before.

Every aspect concerning his project—plane, engine, even man himself—had to be adapted to new surroundings of oxygen-poor air and extremely low temperatures. But Wiley Post knew that if aviation was to advance, the pilot had to invade that hostile environment—space.

In his 'round-the-world journeys, Wiley had personally experienced the dramatic changes in flight that occurred once he was forced into high altitudes. Brief forays into heights of 20,000 feet and above clearly demonstrated to him that being above the strata that was permanently subject to the vagaries of weather was certainly preferable. He also observed another phenomenon: when traveling in an easterly direction, Post was certain that he had ridden strong air currents moving on an easterly track, and those "high winds" had added substantially to his ground speed. Post was probably the first to ride the "jet stream," though the words had yet to be added to the common vocabulary. Wiley Post now wanted to demonstrate these findings to the world.

The Post family home at Maysville, Oklahoma. (Photo: B. B. and F. N. Sterling.)

Above: Wiley's 1930 International Aeronautic Association license, signed by Orville Wright. (Photo: Archives & Manuscripts Division of the Oklahoma Historical Society.) *Right:* Wiley Post traces path of flight for his wife Mae. (Photo: University of Southern California.)

Above: Harold Gatty, Winnie Mae Hall Fain, (for whom the famous plane was named.), and Wiley Post. (Photo: NY Mirror Collection.) *Below:* The *Winnie Mae* after digging her nose into the ground while landing at Flat, Alaska, on Wiley's solo trip around the world, 1933. (Photo: Archives & Manuscripts Division of the Oklahoma Historical Society.)

Above left: Ticker-tape parade up New York's Broadway, after Wiley's solo flight around the world. (Photo: Archives & Manuscripts Division of the Oklahoma Historical Society.) *Right:* White House meeting with President Franklin D. Roosevelt, 1933. (Photo: Archives & Manuscripts Division of the Oklahoma Historical Society.) *Below:* Wiley Post and his famous *Winnie Mae*, after solo flight around the world. (Photo: Richard Sanders Allen Collection.)

Above left: Wiley and oil magnate Frank Phillips, after Post's successful flight into the stratosphere, December, 1934. (Photo: Archives & Manuscripts Division of the Oklahoma Historical Society.) *Above right:* Breakfast in New York City with aviatrix Fay Gillis, planning flight across Siberia. (Photo: C. Benedict Collection.) *Below: Winnie Mae's* 1935 during sub-stratosphere flight from Los Angeles to Cleveland, reaching 340 miles per hour. (Photo: Richard Sanders Allen Collection.)

During the following year, the *Winnie Mae* and the Wasp engine were rebuilt, adapted, modified, and subjected to all sorts of alterations, as each unsuccessful attempt at high-altitude flying taught new lessons. Perhaps the most difficult part of Post's experimentation was to accommodate the aviator to space. It was obvious to him that the *Winnie Mae*, with its wooden body, could in no way be adapted to protect the pilot in the inhospitable stratosphere. The flier, therefore, had to be encased in his own armor.

Early in 1934, Wiley Post conceived and patented specifications for a pressurized high-altitude flying suit. The design took its inspiration from existing deep-sea diving suits—with notable changes. Excess weight and any significant limitations on free movement, which were less troublesome to a person under water, were serious considerations in a plane that had to be controlled. An essential oxygen supply from tanks, too, was a fundamental modification from air usually pumped into diving suits. There were also protective measures against the extreme low temperatures that Wiley anticipated he would encounter at high altitudes. Post's brilliant concept became the prototype for space suits astronauts now take for granted.

Wiley took his drawings to the B. F. Goodrich Company in Akron, Ohio. They produced several models: a rubberized suit was fitted with pigskin gloves, rubber boots, and a three-pound aluminum helmet with a small glass window. The first suit ran immediately into trouble when it ruptured; a second model fared only slightly better. The third suit finally was successful; it used a double layer of rubberized material with the helmet now fitting snugly into a neck opening.

The months went by with minor progress and major frustrations. On December 3, 1934, Post, wearing a protective pressure suit, took the *Winnie Mae* to an altitude of 48,000 feet. A small, malfunctioning oxygen valve forced a premature descent. Four days later, on December 7, Wiley stayed aloft almost two-and-a-half hours, "heading into" as he later reported, "the wind which I estimated was blowing about 200 miles an hour." Though Wiley had climbed to 50,000 feet, he could not prove it; one of the two required barographs, supplied by the monitoring National Aeronautic Association, froze before registering the final altitude. But Wiley was not interested in annexing another record. He wanted to fly coast to coast and demonstrate the far greater speeds which could be achieved when using the fast current of air in the substratosphere. Frank Phillips, of Phillips Petroleum Company, Oklahoma, announced its sponsorship of Wiley Post's high-altitude flights. The company would supply the aviation fuel required. There was just one stipulation, Bennie Turner recalled: Wiley and Mae Post would both have to sign a release absolving Phillips of any blame in the event of a crash. Talking with Winnie Mae Fain and Frank Phillips afterwards, Wiley summed up his philosophy on safety measures for the proposed trip: "I know it's dangerous but if I get popped off that is the way I want to go. Doing the things I want to do."

"Wiley was a fatalist, totally unafraid, totally unaware that death might some day catch up with him," Bennie Turner explained. "Post never used the words 'killed,' or 'death,' or 'cracked up.' People to him 'popped off.' And there always was a human cause, airplanes just did not kill people because they were airplanes, someone was always to blame."

Convinced that Post's vision would materially influence its own and aviation's future, one airline, TWA, came forward with substantial support. As an indication of this patronage, the initials TWA, with the word "experimental" superimposed, were prominently displayed on both sides of the *Winnie Mae*'s fuselage. Under TWA's contract with the U.S. Post Office Department, the *Winnie Mae* would be allowed to carry 150 pounds of air mail across the continent. A special cancellation stamp, bearing Wiley Post's picture, would read: "First Air Mail Stratosphere Flight."

Wiley took twenty hours of additional training before applying for a Bureau of Air Commerce instrument rating. That meant that he would have to pass not only written tests in meteorology, instrument flying, and navigation, but that he also had to demonstrate—among numerous other skills—his radio proficiency while flying only on instruments.

Wiley obtained his rating from James E. Reed, an inspector for the Department of Commerce. This same James E. Reed, stationed at the Union Air Terminal in Burbank, California, would encounter Wiley again only a few months later and play an unfortunate, though unwitting, part in his death.

For the moment however, Post was not totally absorbed with his forthcoming coast-to-coast flight. He already looked beyond it; he was planning to go on an exploration trip. The current route to Asia was across the enormous, treacherous expanse of the Pacific Ocean. Wiley was going to prove that there was a more secure way for passengers and mail to reach Asia and Europe—over a safe land-bridge, via Alaska and Siberia.

Since he wanted this exploratory trip to be secret (lest someone beat him to it) Wiley invented a cover story of wanting to hunt tigers in Siberia. He even made a big show of exhibiting his rifles, which were of course for protection and obtaining a supply of meat should the plane be forced down in the wastes of Russia.

The *Winnie Mae* had to be retired soon, if not for profit, at least for his own safety. The *Winnie Mae* had been used—perhaps abused—excessively; it had been stood on its nose, landed on its belly, torn apart, altered, crashed, rebuilt, frozen, and broiled. Everything Post had demanded it had given; there was nothing the plane had not endured. As a plane, it was now of relatively little value; but as a remembrance of records made, and broken— as a memento of the first flight in the jet stream—as a trophy to human endurance and accomplishment, as a keepsake from the childhood of aviation, it would be worth a small fortune. The best solution would be a sale to the Smithsonian Institution or some other museum. But, Wiley must have realized that such a sale depended entirely on the *Winnie Mae* remaining in one piece. She had to be retired now, and he needed another plane.

On February 11, 1935, Wiley made a purchase from Charles H. Babb, whose principal place of business was located at the Grand Central Air Terminal, Glendale, California; Babb had branches in New York, Newark, Washington, Honolulu, Mexico City, and Montreal; St. John's, Newfoundland; Geneva, Switzerland; and Amsterdam, Holland. Charley, as he was called, was in a relatively new business; he was considered the world's foremost airplane broker, not only selling whole planes but dealing in parts as well. He claimed to have sold more Lockheed aircraft than the company ever manufactured. This, of course, was quite possible since he could—and would—at intervals, sell the same planes several times. His customers were airlines, air forces of nations great and small, dictators, executives, and private individuals. He supplied planes to the Spanish Civil War, and when approached, managed to locate and furnish 500 planes on a single order to China. His shops also rebuilt and refurbished planes and readied them for re-sale.

On that February day when Wiley Post went to see Charley Babb, he had, as usual, very little money. He bought a former TWA Lockheed Orion plane, and a wing from a Lockheed Explorer. Wiley planned to use the unrelated wing on the Orion. He had great hopes for the new plane he expected to construct for his exploratory journey.

Wiley, busy with his high-altitude flying tests with the *Winnie Mae*, needed assistance. He called on an old friend who had helped before, Fay Gillis. Fay had left Russia and had moved back to the United States, and was now associate editor of the magazine *Airwoman*. She was an excellent pilot, but she had proficiencies Wiley needed even more; she spoke fluent Russian, knew the Russian Ambassador, and was on excellent terms with the Soviet bureaucracy. Wiley was impressed with the way she had arranged the two refuelling stops on his solo 'round-the-world flight; he was certain she could make all the arrangements for this flight.

Wiley met Fay in New York City and the two discussed the plan; Fay was to obtain charts, visas, and special permissions to overfly Russian territory and make a number of stops. Wiley, foreseeing some snide remarks about the team of Post and Gillis, announced to the press that he would take his wife along.

Hoping to obtain needed financing, Post suggested this exploration to Pan America Airways, and hinted that after the had set the route he would expect to fly it as one of the airline's pilots. Pan Am showed interest in such a route to Russia and Europe, and indicated likely support for Wiley's survey.

In addition to Wiley's pressure suit and all the alterations to the *Winnie Mae* and its engine, there was the matter of rigging the landing gear so Wiley could drop it immediately after take-off, to reduce wind resistance. Arriving in New York City, he would land on a special skid, which had been attached to reinforce the belly of the fuselage.

Because of the new landing equipment, the aviation division of Phillips Petroleum approached the Contest Board of the National Aeronautic Association, for a special favor. Since Post would have to attempt landing without wheels, would the Contest Board confirm Wiley's arrival at New York's Floyd Bennett Field while he was *in flight*, rather than when he landed. The reason given was that Post might have to circle the field several times to look for the best landing area. The Contest Board agreed that crossing a "finish line perpendicular with the administration building *at a low altitude*" would constitute the finishing time for the transcontinental flight. "Starting time is taken when the plane leaves the ground on the take-off."

On February 22, 1935, in predawn hours, the *Winnie Mae* stood ready at the airport in Burbank. The time had come to put all the systems, including the pilot, to the test. Despite the early hour, a crowd of newspapermen and photographers were there to witness and record the historic event, since any new exploit by Wiley Post was news. There were also the official observers and timers from the National Aeronautic Association of the United States.

One interested spectator was Will Rogers, who had come from his Pacific Palisades home to see Wiley off. After helping Wiley into his patented pressure suit, Will wrote in his daily squib:

> Was out at daybreak to see Wiley Post take off. Was in the camera plane and we flew along with him for about thirty miles. We left him 8,000 feet right over the mountains. He soon after had to land. He brought her down on her stomach. That guy don't need wheels.

Barely twenty feet off the ground, Post dropped the detachable landing gear and virtually shot into the sky. Wiley took 35 minutes to reach an altitude of 24,000 feet. After having covered just 225 miles, the engine began to spew oil. Wiley assumed it to be caused by a leaking oil line. With three hundred gallons of aviation fuel still aboard, and no way to jettison them, Wiley shut off the engine and made a perfect dead-stick landing on Muroc Dry Lake, bending the propeller as it dug into the ground.

Without assistance Wiley managed to climb out of the plane and went looking for help. A hapless, unoffending motorist had stopped by the road, looking for the cause of engine trouble. His head buried under the hood, he felt a heavy hand on his shoulder. As he straightened up, "he screamed in terror." The *Los Angeles Chronicle* article explained: "before him stood a weird apparition with head encased in a huge helmet out of which stared a great glass eye." The motorist tried to flee, thinking he saw "a monster from Mars" but the apparition held him. This is Wiley Post's story:

"I had a time calming him down but I finally succeeded and he helped me out of my oxygen helmet." Together the two then went to the nearest telegraph office to summon help.

It was announced a few days later that the cause for the termination of the flight had not been a ruptured oil line, but rather two pounds of steel shavings and powdered emery which mechanics had found in the engine's intake pipe of the supercharger. Sucked into the engine, pistons and cylinders were severely scored, causing the engine to overheat. On March 3, it was announced that J. S. Marriott, supervising aeronautical inspector for the Department of Commerce, would press the investigation into the possible sabotage. As the plane had carried U. S. mail, the federal government was drawn into the case. Though no culprit was ever identified, Wiley was convinced that it was a deliberate act of sabotage. In an interview he said that he was no longer interested in finding the guilty party as much as he wanted to know the reason for the act.

By March 5, 1935, the engine had been extensively overhauled, and Wiley was once more ready for a transcontinental hop to New York. With half-hourly weather reports from major cities along the way, the flight went smoothly until Post was about 100 miles east of Cleveland, where he ran out of oxygen for his pressure suit. He turned around and landed the *Winnie Mae* safely on the skid. Post had flown from Los Angeles to Cleveland, a distance of over 2,000 miles in 7 hours and 19 minutes, for an average ground speed of 279 miles per hour; this was at least 100 miles faster than the plane's maximum speed capability in the atmosphere. Newpaper reports claimed that Post had reached ground speeds as high as 340 miles per hour.

On April 1, 1935, Fay Gillis and famous author, foreign correspondent, traveler, and aviator S. Linton Wells eloped and were married by a Justice of the Peace in Harrison, New York. This purely private act would certainly affect Will Rogers' life, possibly even Wiley Post's.

Twice more Wiley Post and his *Winnie Mae* would attempt transcontinental flights at high altitudes. On April 14, 1935, an external supercharger failed and Post had to land at Lafayette, Indiana, slightly more than eight hours after leaving Burbank, California. The Associated Press reported another reason for the aborted flight. It claimed that Wiley's nose was sore. Quoting

Post, AP reported that an automatic valve started pouring oxygen into his rubber suit faster than the release valve could carry it away and the inside of the windshield in his aluminum headpiece became constantly fogged. Unable to clear it with his hands, Wiley had to stretch his neck forward and wipe the moisture off with his nose.

"The oxygen made me feel goofy," Wiley said after landing safely, "I had a cold before I started and I didn't feel so darn well when I landed. I didn't see the ground from Denver until I landed in Lafayette."

On June 13, 1935, on Post's fourth attempt, engine trouble forced him to land dead-stick at Wichita, Kansas. Wiley decided that it was time to retire the *Winnie Mae*. "You're getting tired, old girl," he is quoted as saying.

Will Rogers commented:

> Wiley Post, just about king of 'em all, can't break records getting to New York in a six-year old plane, no matter if he takes it up so high that he coasts in. Equipment and engines change too fast. That *Winnie Mae* should be right in that Washington Museum along with all the other historic planes. It's already done more than any other plane in the world . . .

On June 24, 1935, Josh Lee, a congressman from Oklahoma, introduced House Resolution 8622, to authorize the Smithsonian Institution to purchase the *Winnie Mae*, with her original instruments, exactly as she had been on her round-the-world flights. The price was not to exceed $25,000.

Wiley was in Washington when the bill was introduced; it was said that he had come to see his Oklahoma congressman to push that sale, for he certainly could have used the money. True, there were some minor riches promised for the distant future in the shape of a motion picture contract calling for twenty-one days of actual shooting. David Weiss, vice president of an independent motion picture company, disclosed that he had placed Post under a $5,000 contract to star in fifteen serial episodes. Unfortunately the money was to be paid "in three weekly installments, commencing the first week when production commences, and weekly thereafter . . ." and "Shooting was to begin no earlier than September 1st, 1935," the contract read.

"Post will play the part of a Department of Justice agent, a G-man, operating largely by airplane. The famous plane, the *Winnie Mae*, will be featured in the pictures," Weiss said. He also made know that the agreement had been reached shortly before Post made his third transcontinental effort. "When Post failed," Weiss said, "he came back here and offered to abrogate the contract. He said he had no value to us in a picture having failed to set either a high altitude, or a speed record. He didn't want to hold us to something that hadn't turned out right. We told him we still wanted him."

Post was in Washington to apply in person at the Soviet embassy for authorization to fly across Siberia. "But I have no idea how long it will take to get the approval," he was quoted as saying. He hoped to be able to leave by mid-July.

Fay Gillis, now Mrs. Linton Wells, received the following letter from the Embassy of the Union of Soviet Socialist Republics, Washington, D.C., dated July 5, 1935:

Dear Mrs. Wells:

I should appreciate your informing Wiley Post that permission has been granted him, Mrs. Post, and yourself for the flight along the following route:

Whelan or Providence Bay—Nagaevo—Yakutsk—Irkutsk—Novosibirsk—Sverdlovsk—Moscow.

The plane may be landed in all these places and refuelled.

The Soviet authorities are suggesting that you postpone the flight until the end of July as the necessary maps for the flight will not reach the Embassy in time for you to start in the middle of July, as Mr. Post plans. The maps have already been sent and will be forwarded to you as soon as they are received by the Embassy.

It is necessary that we cable to Moscow the exact date of your departure and the kind of radio equipment you are carrying; also the exact coloring of the different parts of the plane. Mr. Post told me in general that it is red and silver but he did not go into detail as to which parts

are red and which silver. Please wire this information to
me as soon as possible.

Sincerely yours,

B. E. Skvirsky

BS/h   Counselor

The flight had now been postponed. It would have been
wiser to leave in July, as Wiley had planned. Winter comes so
early in the far north, and it is hard to count on the weather. But
they would have to wait for the Russian maps.

With the *Winnie Mae* safely now in Bartlesville, Oklahoma, Wiley and Mae set out by car for California. Married now
eight-and-a-half years, this was really the first time when they had
no deadlines, no obligations awaiting them.

"We had the best time in July," Mae Post remembered. "We
drove all the way to California. Every time we passed an airport
beacon, Wiley would say that he would just catch the next plane
and I could drive on and meet him there. I wouldn't take anything
for that trip." They sold their car in California.

Fay Gillis Wells obtained the Russian visas for herself,
Wiley, and Mae . . . though she was certain that Mae would never
come along.[7] As for the official maps, they could always be forwarded to California. Fay, on her way to California, had reached
Detroit when she heard from her husband that he had just been
retained by New York's *Herald Tribune* newspaper to cover the
Italian-Ethiopian war from the Abyssinian side. Fay had eloped
after Wiley had asked her to fly with him across the Soviet Union;
she and Linton had originally agreed that her commitment to
Wiley would have to be honored, but now Fay decided to cancel
her flight with Post and accompany her husband. "I figured
Wiley could always get somebody else to go along, but I didn't
want my husband to find anyone else."[8]

There was more bad news to follow. While Pan Am was
impressed with Wiley Post as a courageous pioneer, it did not feel
that he was the "steady pilot" who would perform any routine job
for very long. Pan Am had worked with Charles and Anne Lindbergh
on a similar exploration for an air route to South-East Asia in 1931;
but Wiley Post, ever restless, might easily be off tomorrow, pursuing
some new, more glamorous goal. Daring record breakers are great
for front-page news, but their hair-raising tales of near disasters

hardly instill great confidence in timid airline passengers. The year was 1935, and the public was still reluctant to accept the airplane as a medium for general transportation. Pan Am was not in favor of tying its image to Wiley Post, no matter how great his accomplishments. It fell to Lyman Peck, Pan Am's man in charge of Alaskan development, to tell Post that the company would not hire him.

To make the disappointment somewhat less painful, Lyman Peck referred Wiley to Will Rogers' weekly article of March 10, in which he had written: "I never have been to that Alaska. I am crazy to go up there some time." In the years that followed, Lyman Peck would feel responsible for Rogers' death, having steered Wiley Post into his path.[9]

Post made a mental note about Will Rogers' wish to see Alaska, but assigned it no immediate priority. It would just have to wait, pending his substratospheric, transcontinental flight.

Though Wiley Post was a hero to millions around the world, he was far from being everybody's hero. The fact that several acts of sabotage had been attempted against him is some proof of that. But there was more resentment, most of it below the surface, for Post had an explosive temper, a sharp tongue and a surly disposition against those he did not like.

And yet, there was another Post known to only few. He was a most loyal friend to his intimates. He was generous to those he liked. He was kind and considerate with youngsters; one of his major regrets was that he had no children of his own, although it was a topic he never wanted broached.

Bennie Turner, who, it is said, knew him better than anyone, wrote about his friend,

> We called him "Weeley" and he often had some personal name for his friend. . . . Wiley Post, in himself, was not particularly colorful—it was the things he did that were colorful, interesting, and because he was so much a part of everything he did that he became colorful and interesting.
>
> None ever knew Wiley. He was completely self-contained, so much so that few knew he was subject to moods that could change from blue to rose in a flash.
>
> It's little traits of personality that make a man, a man for friends to enjoy. Little traits like his habit of

waking in the middle of the night with a desire to go for a walk, and dressing in the dark so as not to disturb his companions; or his half-anger when anybody worried about him; or his dislike of liquor, yet always eager to mix drinks for others; his love for flying, yet his devotion to automobiles.

There was nothing sentimental about Post, except his love for children. He would never pass a ragged newsboy without buying a paper. He would swear until the rafters rang and memorize the name of a person mentioned in print in any child abuse stories: "Some day I may meet him. I like to beat the hell out of guys like that!" he would say.

He would sit on the floor for hours and play with a child. I can remember when he left his clothes behind and used the space in his old plane to bring a doll from California here for the daughter of old friends.

One of Post's amusements was caring for his watches. He had 42 of them that had been given him by civic clubs and admirers. Often, when idle, he would take them all out, wind each and set it to the split second. Then he would keep them going until he went off on some trip.

His guns were another passion, but unlike his watches, whenever he got a good gun, he wanted to give it away to a friend.

Post had another passion only friends knew—it was for baths. Four or five baths a day were not unusual.

Post disliked parades as much as he disliked to talk; but in parades he would often stop to tell police that they were not to chase the usual following of kids away from his car. "Leave 'em alone, someone should get some fun out of this," he would say.

Mae Post, who claimed that "I mainly let Wiley do the talking, and Wiley talks scarcely at all," granted an interview to the *Oklahoma City Times* which fortified the picture of her complex husband.

"He is in love with the out-of-doors. If he ever forsakes aviation, he's likely to turn to some other sort of life in the open—

perhaps mining in Alaska. Right now he's crazy about Alaska, he believes money can be made there in mining, and he might try it some time.

"His favorite recreation is hunting. . . . one of his proudest possessions, a double-barreled shotgun. . . . The breech is handsomely engraved and there is a miniature globe with his route traced in gold. . . .

"Next to hunting, Wiley likes fishing best . . .''

Asked about the prospects of settling down soon, Mae was pessimistic and claimed that home for the two would continue to be "largely where the hat is off. He is an easy man to cook for. He isn't a bit hard to please," she said. "I'm not much of a cook, but I can cook what Wiley likes."

What does Wiley like? "Everything," she said.

Mae pictured Wiley as a man whose one big desire was to do things. She liked reading, but he did very little of it, being definitely a man of action. She thought of her husband as a great flier and an experimenter, not particularly as a scientist. "I don't know that he's ever studied to the extent some men have," she explained. "He just seems to have a natural ability—but he did design that famous suit he used on his sub stratosphere flights."

As to any future plans, everything was "up to Wiley."

But in his contact with the outside world, especially newspapermen and officials, Wiley Post created an entirely different image. During the months of preparations for the stratospheric flights, Post had frequent confrontations. Perhaps it was the pressure, perhaps it was the usual habit of the man.

Letters from the files of the National Aeronautic Association of U.S.A., Inc., show constant friction between Wiley Post and officials. A letter, dated June 18, 1935, refers to Wiley's supposed swelled head: "I think by this time Wiley only needs a cane to scratch his ear."

Another, dated July 29, 1935, states:

> Wiley, as you no doubt have found out, is, we might say, a rather peculiar fellow when he gets the wrong idea of something. Personally I am not going to argue with him . . . In our experience we have found Wiley Post almost an impossible person to deal with.

A third letter, on official stationery of The Southern California Chapter of the National Aeronautic Association, and dated
August 3, 1935, states in part:

> Your opinion coincides with mine as to his big-
> headedness. The newspaper men out here have no use at
> all for him. This goes for the news cameramen as well. To
> show you what they think, one of them told Wiley that
> he wasn't out there to get any pictures of the take-off.
> Instead of that he was there in hopes that you crack up so
> I can get a picture of you frying on both sides, and
> knowing the fellow that said it I know he wasn't kidding.
> Well I guess we won't be bothered with him
> for awhile as I understand he is going to Siberia for
> awhile. . . .

It was true now, Wiley Post was indeed preparing to go to
Siberia—and even further; the *Winnie Mae* having made her
mark on history, was at last retired to a place of deserved honor;
and an improvised plane, "Wiley's Bastard," would take him the
rest of the way.

But Wiley was becoming desperate. Now that Pan Am had
turned down his proposal, there would be no funds coming in
from that source; Fay Gillis, who would have been such a great
help, had backed out. A mounting pile of bills would have to be
settled. There was only one last name left on his list—the one
given him by Lyman Peck.

The time had come for Wiley Post to go and talk to Will
Rogers about going to "that Alaska."

CHAPTER TWO

THE PASSENGER

The air is more interesting. You can just see everything while up there . . . you can just sit up there
in the middle of some cloud, or maybe fog, and
you don't even have to worry. That's the pilot's
business to do the worrying.
—Will Rogers, *Weekly Article,* July 21, 1935.

Neither before nor since has America produced another man like
Will Rogers. Star of vaudeville and films, the most widely read
newspaper columnist and the most listened-to radio commenta-
tor; he was among the best of ropers of all times, and surely, the
most popular American of his day. Will Rogers loved America and
its people, and that love was returned a million-fold. He could
have been elected to almost any office he wanted; his name was
placed in nomination for the presidency twice as a favorite son,
but Rogers wanted no part of a political career:

> There is no inducement that would make me foolish
> enough to ever run for any political office. I want to be
> on the outside where I can be friends and joke about all of
> them, even the president. As long as it's all right with
> him, why, my conscience is clear.

But efforts persisted to have Will Rogers officially represent
those for whom he had become a spokesman. Will again addressed the issue in order to settle it:

> If you see or hear of anybody proposing my name hu-
> morously, or semi-seriously, for any political office, will

you maim said party, and send me the bill. I not only
don't choose to run, I will say I won't run! No matter
how bad the country will need a comedian by that time.

He could fill Carnegie Hall in New York City by promising
to do nothing else but sit on the edge of the stage, his legs dangling
over it, and just "blather." He was one of the most popular after-
dinner speakers, commanding large fees, yet he would travel
thousands of miles at his own expense to raise money for charitable causes. Will was one of the largest individual contributors to
the Red Cross and the Salvation Army. Indigent actors could
always count on his liberal help, and he was as proud to participate at a benefit as to be invited to the White House. When
disaster struck, be it flood or earthquake, Will would be there, to
help with money and to buoy up spirits—usually beating the Red
Cross to the site.

In the Ziegfeld Follies at the New Amsterdam Theater, with
brilliant sets and dozens of glamorous beauties almost dressed in
the most expensive costumes, the appearance of a cowboy would
seem a sacrilege. Yet it was this cowboy, Will Rogers, who was
the star of the show. His radio broadcasts were eagerly anticipated
events. His films made big money at the depth of the Depression.
Yet he never claimed to be an actor; he was himself, just Will
Rogers from Oologah, a speck of a village along a railroad track,
in what was to become Oklahoma.

The Indian Territory in the late 1870s was peaceful and
quiet. The Civil War was over and the tribes of the Great Plains
were seemingly resigned to their new life, dominated by the
white man. Towns and villages began to spring up beside the
various treks leading westward, ever more infringing on the land
that was once exclusively Indian.

Before the war Clement Vann Rogers had come to the
Cooweescoowee District, so called after the Indian name of John
Ross, the famous Cherokee leader. On Rabb's Creek, Rogers had
laid out his ranch and built his house. Though educated in the
Baptist mission school and the Cherokee–run Male Seminary at
Tahlequah, Indian Territory, he was basically a self-made man.
Hard-working, tough, honorable and ambitious, he prospered.

It was to the house on Rabb's Creek that he had brought his
bride, Mary America (nee Schrimsher). She was a gentle, kind and

thoughtful woman. She had had a superior education for the time and place. She had attended an academy in Arkansas, and afterwards, the respected Cherokee Female Seminary at Tahlequah, where the leading Cherokee families sent their daughters. Religion meant much to her. She was disturbed that her husband insisted on working Sundays and that he made the hired help labor as well on the Lord's Day. She insisted that Clem say grace before meals, and he obliged her—though he raced through it.

It was here at Rabb's Creek that their first child, Elizabeth, was born in 1861. As cattleman and trader, Clem Rogers controlled some sixty-thousand acres of blue-stem grazing land and had acquired a sizable fortune when the Civil War broke out. Clem sent his wife and daughter to Texas for safety while he joined the cause of the Confederacy as a cavalry officer.

Four years later, the war over, Clem returned to his home on Rabb's Creek. His cattle had been driven off, the house was in ruins; little Elizabeth had died. Sallie, Robert, and Maud were born before Clem was able to move his wife into a new two-story house, now built on the Verdigris River. Clem had gone to work to restore his fortune. In the years that followed there were three more children, though two of them died in infancy.

As the years passed, Clem Vann Rogers became one of the most influential and successful men in the Territory. With wealth and respect came homage. He was a senator in the Cherokee Council and became a judge. He was chosen a member of the Constitutional Convention preparing Oklahoma for statehood, and the county of his residence was named Rogers County in his honor.

On Tuesday, November 4, 1879,—Election Day—William Penn Adair Rogers was born in the annex of the "White House on the Verdigris," as the Rogers home was known. Will later told the story, "Just before my birth my mother had them remove her into the log part of the house. She wanted me to be born in a log house. She had read the life of Lincoln. So I got the log house end of it OK. All I need now is the other qualifications."

Of Irish, Scottish, Welsh, English, either German or Dutch, and Cherokee ancestry on both his parents' sides, William Penn Adair Rogers was listed on the official Cherokee rolls as No: 11384.

At home the boy was simply called Willie. Clem Rogers wanted the boy, his last surviving son, to follow in his footsteps and someday take over the ranch. Mary America's ambition for her son was that he become a preacher. But Willie, unaware of either of his parents' ambitions for him, was happiest when riding his pony or practicing rope tricks taught him by "Uncle" Dan Walker, a freed slave working for the ranch.

Life became serious for Willie when he was sent to attend his first school. Days in a one-room schoolhouse were misery for the boy who had spent all his time outdoors, and he would volunteer to run errands or fetch water rather than be confined to the classroom. Most of his fellow pupils were full-blooded Indians. As Will put it later: "I had just enough *white* in me to make my honesty questionable."

He was well liked—at least by the students, if not by the teachers—but when the term ended, Will decided that school was not for him. He tried to persuade his father to let him stay at home, but "he sent me to about every school in that part of the country."

> . . . Willie Halsell School, and I went there awhile, in fact quite a while. I was four years in McGuffey's Fourth reader there, was in Ray's arithmetic three years and couldent get to fractions. Well, I saw they wasent running that school right. I could have taken it and made something out of it, so I just got out. That's the way I have always done with schools; the minute mine and their plans dident jibe, why, I would get out, or some- times they would ask me. I would generally always do it if they did. I was an accommodating boy.

When Will was ten years old, his mother died. Being the youngest child, he was sent to live with his oldest sister Sallie and her husband Tom McSpadden. It was from their home in Chelsea, some fifteen miles northeast overland from Oologah, that Will continued to go to school. When Will Rogers talked about his battles with formal education, he was partly joking.

His dislike of schools was real, but his progress was steady. In 1897 Clem sent his son to Boonville, Missouri, to attend the Kemper Military School. "I have my hard-to-manage son in a military school," he told a friend.

"I spent two years there," Will later reminisced, "one year in the fourth grade, and one year in the guard house. One was as bad as the other.'' The end came when he and the commandant didn't see eye to eye on school matters. Will left; he was through with schools for life.

After taking a job as a cowboy in Higgins, Texas, and driving steers to market, he returned home. His father gave him a spread and cattle with his own brand, and suggested he try ranching on his own. It kept Will busy for a while, but he much preferred racing horses, roping anything that moved, or going to dances and parties. To entertain his friends he sang tenor in a quartet. "I have what is called a fresh voice. It's got volume without control; it's got resonance without reason. It's got tone without tune. I got a voice that's got everything but a satisfied listener.''

It was in Oologah, now a small town of about three hundred, that Will met Betty Blake. He was almost twenty-one. Betty had come from her native Arkansas to visit her sister Cora, who was married to one Will Marshall, the local railroad station agent. Rogers fell in love with Betty immediately and courted her shyly and tenderly—and mostly by mail—for the next eight years. Many months would go by without either hearing from the other, for Will had left Oologah and was on his way around the world.

The restless curiosity which would drive him all of his days had to be obeyed. The horizon was always a barrier to be scaled; there were always other people to meet and talk to; there were always new things to see and learn.

Before he was twenty-five years old, Will Rogers had made his first 'round-the-world trip.

Actually, that trip started out as the fulfillment of Will's long-harbored interest to see the gauchos of the Argentine Pampas. In his early geography lessons, Will had come across pictures of those Argentineans, who were so much like—yet different from—the cowboys he knew. In 1902, Will decided to sell the small herd he owned, and use the money to travel to South America. For company on this adventure, Will asked Dick Parris, a boyhood friend, to come along.

The plan was perfectly simple and logical, although as it turned out, not feasible. Since Argentina was in South America, Will reasoned, all one had to do, was to go south to New Orleans and catch a boat for Buenos Aires. Early in March, Will and Dick packed their bags, took their saddles, and set out for Louisiana. On March 15th, Will, now at Hot Springs, Arkansas, received a letter from his father, Clem V. Rogers, stating that a draft for $1,300 had been sent to New Orleans. Probably that money came from the sale of Will's cattle. By the time Will collected the money, the two young men had learned that no boats were scheduled to leave New Orleans for the Argentine. To get to Buenos Aires, so they were told, they would have to start from New York City.

Three days later, March 18, Will wrote to his sisters, Sallie and Maud in Chelsea, "Leave in the morning for New York to get a boat to South America." On Wednesday, March 19th, 1902, Will and Dick were aboard the steamship *Comus* enroute to New York City, where they were expected to arrived on Monday, March 24.

New York was far less intimidating to the two young men from the Indian Territory than might be expected: they checked into a hotel, then walked around town and took in some of the sights. What turned out to be more disturbing was the news that no ships were scheduled to leave for the Argentine in the foreseeable future. The advice was to go to England, which maintained regular, scheduled traffic with South America. The two men, now practically seasoned travelers, booked passage for England aboard the *U.S.S. Philadelphia*. One thing Will had learned by this time; he was not a good sailor. Somehow riding a bucking horse was easier than handling a rough ocean, and he did not look forward to the long sea voyage.

Among the souvenirs from this trip is a draft (No. 55418), dated March 24, 1902, made out to W. P. Rogers. Drawn on the London and River Plate Bank Ltd., Buenos Aires, it calls for 100 Pounds Sterling. Since the date coincides with Will Rogers' arrival in New York City, it is safe to assume that Will converted some of the money, rather than carry so much cash on his person.

The Times of London reported the arrival of the *U.S.S. Philadelphia* on April 3. Since Will and Dick left England aboard the *Danube* on April 10, the two young men had a week to explore London. They visited the Houses of Parliament and Westminster Abbey; they stood outside Buckingham Palace and went through the Tower of London. It was all part of their great adventure.

"Steaming along the west coast of Africa . . . 9th day out," Will wrote to his father in a letter mailed when the ship stopped briefly at St. Vincent, Cape Verde Islands.

By April 24th—two weeks after leaving England—Will and Dick were in the province of Pernambuco, Brazil. Reporting faithfully to his family back home, Will wrote that the ship was scheduled to "get to Rio de Janeiro in 4 days."

On May 5, Will and Dick landed in Buenos Aires and checked into the Phoenix Hotel. In less than three weeks, Will would be faced with a hard decision that would affect his entire future and clearly show his character.

The two friends had been away from home for two months. They had seen New Orleans and New York City, they had been to London; they had crossed the Equator and traveled by ship for thousands of miles; they had experienced more adventures, seen more sights and met more people than their homefolk could imagine. There would be much to tell when they returned to the Indian Territory.

Walking around Buenos Aires, hearing only a foreign tongue, home seemed far away and Dick Parris was homesick. He suggested that they return to Oologah, for they had seen enough for two lifetimes. Will tried to persuade his buddy to stay, to think of all they had yet to see and experience, but Dick was adamant. Feeling responsible for his friend, Will paid for Dick's passage home. He also asked him to take along some presents for "Papa" and his sisters.

On May 24, Dick Parris left for home. Will, now almost without money, remained alone in the Argentine. It would have been easy for Will to give in. He could have claimed that he was practically broke; he could have used his friend's return as an excuse to go back with him; he could have argued that he did not wish to continue alone.

Will stayed behind, saw the gauchos, and admired their exceptional skills. He ran out of money, and sold his saddle—the last item any cowboy will sell. He looked for work, did odd jobs and often went hungry. There were benefits: "Years and years and years ago I spent six months in the Argentine republic and inhaled enough Spanish to ask for something to eat and to cuss," he recalled some twenty years later.

When he was offered a job aboard a ship bound for South Africa, he briefly weighed the expected attendant seasickness against the wages, and decided in favor of the salary.

He was to "chaperon mules and she-cows." The thirty-two day trip proved a horrible experience. Will was seasick almost the entire time and could do little work, but "they couldn't fire me."

From Durban, Natal, Will helped drive the herd 150 miles inland, worked for a while on the ranch, but soon became restless again and left. To earn a living, he saddle-broke horses for the British Army, then signed up for a cattle drive to Johannesburg. There he met the man who gave him his second introduction to show business. The first one had come some years earlier. As Will recalled:

> It was a little Fourth of July celebration at Claremore on July 4, 1899, they had a steer roping, and I went into it. It was the first one I ever was in; the very first thing I ever did in the way of appearing before an audience in my life. Well, as I look back on it now, I know that that had quite an influence on my little career, for I kinder got to running around to 'em, and the first thing I knew, I was just plum "honery" and fit for nothing but show business. Once you are a showman, you are plum ruined for manual labor again.

The man Will met in Johannesburg was Texas Jack, owner and principal star of a wild west show. Will's preoccupation and constant practice with the lariat paid off. He could do all the tricks Texas Jack performed nightly, and had an additional array of spectacular stunts. He was immediately hired as the new roping star of the show at the liberal salary of $20 a week, and billed as the "Cherokee Kid." Will learned a lot about showmanship from Texas Jack: "It was him who gave me the idea for my original act with a pony . . . and from him I learned the great secret of show business—I learned when to get off!"

From South Africa, Will sailed to Australia where he joined the Wirth Brothers' Circus. When the company moved to New Zealand, Will went along. At the end of the tour Will had just enough money left to book a third-class passage back to America.

He reached San Francisco broke and traveled the rest of the way by freight train. He had circled the world and had proven to himself—and his father—that he could earn his own way.

"I left home first class," he later wrote, "and it took me two years and nine months to get back third class. That's what a clever lad I was, and had to go all the way around the world to do it." But Will Rogers had accomplished what he had set out to do, and he had done it all by himself. He had seen how other people lived, for he had lived among them. He had learned to understand that "it was their country, and they had a right to run it as they saw fit." He never remonstrated or complained. Will Rogers would continue to travel extensively throughout his life, and he would retain his understanding of others. He saw more of the world than almost any observer of his day, and when he wrote or spoke of other lands, it was based on personal knowledge. And when Americans returning from abroad would complain or protest a real, or imagined violation of "their rights," Will would tend to side with the other country:

> I left home as a kid and traveled and worked my way all through Argentine, South Africa, Australia and New Zealand . . . But I never found it necessary to have my AMERICAN rights protected. Nobody invited me into those countries and I always acted as their guest, not their advisor.

But Will Rogers was not ready yet to settle down and be a rancher. When Colonel Zach Mulhall formed a wild west group to perform at the St. Louis World's Fair in 1904, Will joined him. He also went with the Colonel the following year to perform in New York's Madison Square Garden as an additional attraction in conjunction with the Horse Fair. During one evening's exhibition of roping, a Texas Longhorn steer became so terrified by the thousands of applauding and cheering spectators that it jumped a low barrier and raced up a stairway leading past ringside boxes. Everybody scattered in terror. Will, who had not been part of this act, grabbed his rope and pursued the frightened animal into the stands. This is what the *New York Herald* of April 28, 1905, reported:

> Will Rogers, a Cherokee Indian, and three other cowboys had joined in the chase, and Rogers got a rope over the steer's horns as it turned to run down into the arena. Rogers clung to the rope, but was dragged over seats and down the stairs.

A man on foot can not restrain a runaway steer. As it was, Will at least caught the animal with his lasso and slowed it down, while Tom Mix, another member of the group and not yet world-famous, missed the steer, but caught an usher instead.

When the Colonel left to return to Oklahoma, Will stayed behind in New York City. He was determined to break into vaudeville, and this was the place to do it. Remembering Texas Jack's advice, he developed an act to display his roping skills. He made the rounds of theatrical agents until the manager of Keith's Union Square on 14th Street hired him for a single performance. On the same bill was the Keaton Family: Joe, Myra and ten-year-old Buster. "He was the hickiest guy you ever laid eyes on," the elder Keaton recalled. "One day, he was out there twirling his rope and getting madder and madder. He'd missed making a knot five times. Up to then he had never spoken a world. Finally, Will got so exasperated, he dropped his lariat and said: 'It's kinda hard working out here, 'cause when a feller makes a mistake he ain't allowed to cuss.' "'

The audience liked the unusual act, and Will remained for the balance of the week. From there Will was booked to appear at Hammerstein's Paradise Roof, where he proved such a remarkable hit that he was asked to stay for the rest of the summer. "We played on the roof at nights and downstairs at Matinee," Will would recall years later.

An extended tour of European capitals followed. In London, Will appeared before King Edward VII, whom he had last seen when he and Dick Parris were on their way to the Argentine. Appearing at the Palace in London, the *Times* critic wrote:

> Another new turn is that of Will Rogers, who is a genuine cowboy and an expert lassoist. This is one of those strange exotic entertainments, like the pelicans at the Hippodrome, which occasionally appear, and are very welcome on the Music Hall stage. The skill with which this man can make a bit of rope do his bidding is incredible; he can throw two lassoes at once, catching a horse with one and the rider with the other. And that, though the most difficult, is not the most showy of his tricks.[2]

Will enjoyed Paris, but he loved Berlin. Since he was still corresponding with Betty Blake, Will sent her clippings and reports.

He also tried to make Betty jealous by writing what a simply wonderful time he was having in the night spots of Europe.

As Will Rogers had planned the act, it was "dumb," which is show business talk for "silent." Will would simply perform his rope tricks, either by himself, or having Buck McKee of Pawnee County, Oklahoma, ride a pony across the stage at a run. Without saying a word he would rope both, or any part of either. While the audience liked what they saw Will do with such seeming ease, they did not realize the art involved. A fellow performer finally suggested that Will better introduce and explain each trick. The shyness and sincerity of the Westerner came across the footlights and improved the act. Will then prepared a few "ad libs" just in case he missed a trick, which was rare. "Swinging a rope is all right," he would say as he retrieved his lariat, "provided your neck ain't in it!" Or on another occasion: "Well, I got all my feet through—but one!" Laughter greeted these little asides, and Will began missing his throws on purpose, so he could use his special gags. As the weeks went by he would add comments about other acts on the program.

Now that Will Rogers changed from being a silent performer to one who made audiences laugh, he kept looking for new material. Soon references about his fellow performers were not enough, and he began to joke about topics he felt would be of interest to theater patrons. People came to see Will as much for the rope tricks as to listen to the man. Even Betty finally listened and on November 25, 1908, they were married. Their honeymoon started with a two-week booking in New York City, and continued all along the Orpheum vaudeville circuit. The marriage proved to be ideal, for Betty was not only his wife, and mother of his children, but his adviser, his critic, and in many ways, perhaps, even his patient, indulgent mother. Will needed someone to love, someone who gave stability to his life, someone who was there when he needed her, yet would not stand in his way or compete with him. In all honesty Will could say on their twenty-fifth wedding anniversary: "The day I roped Betty, I did the star performance of my life."

Will and Betty were living in New York City on Manhattan's Upper West Side when their first child, Will Jr., was born in 1911. Early the following year, Will opened in his first regular Broadway show, *The Wall Street Girl*, starring Blanche Ring. Will received excellent reviews but the show played only fifty-six performances. Will went back to the vaudeville circuit.

Another child was expected, and since he had to be on tour, little Will, Jr. and Betty went to stay with her mother in Arkansas. When Mary Amelia, named after her two grandmothers, was born in 1913, Will was appearing in Houston, Texas.

The following year Will wired Betty to leave the children in the good care of her mother and to meet him in Atlantic City, New Jersey. When Betty arrived, expecting problems, Will surprised her with tickets for a trip to Europe. Betty had to buy clothes and accessories in a hurry. Will had no engagements planned in Europe, but since he had performed there before, he was known. Within a few days he was booked at London's Empire Theatre on Leicester Square, at $400 per week, appearing on the same bill with Nora Bayes. While Will was busy in a show, Betty and some of her friends went to the Continent to take in the sights and do some shopping.

Will felt uneasy about the political situation in Europe. Despite protestations from their friends that there would be no war, Will left the show and booked passage for their return to the United States on the next available ship, the Hamburg American Line's *Imperator*. Before the ship docked in New York, war had been declared in Europe.

Again Will returned to vaudeville. Though he was working he was becoming discouraged. His career had not advanced as he had hoped, and he seriously considered returning to Oklahoma and life on a ranch.

Fred Stone, the famous star of many Broadway hits and Will's closest friend, persuaded him to stay. Will rented a house in Amityville, Long Island, across the road from Fred's home. Here the family spent the summer of 1915, the summer of the Rogers' household's newest addition—a son, James Blake. Here, too, occurred an accident that could well have ended Will Rogers' career.

One exceptionally hot morning, Fred Stone, his brother-in-law, the renowned novelist Rex Beach, and Will decided to go swimming in the ocean inlet near Stone's house. Not realizing that the tide was out, Will dived into the now shallow water. His head hit a submerged rock. His companions dragged him from the ocean semiconscious.

As his friends attended the bleeding head wound, Rex wondered: "Didn't you see that the tide was out?"

"Tide?" Rogers was reported to have countered, "Tide? We didn't have no tide on the Verdigris River, where I learned to swim."

The head wound proved superficial, but when Will tried to move, he found that his right arm was paralyzed; he could not lift it or control his fingers. He had engagements lined up in various theaters in nearby states; how would he be able to fulfill his commitments? He was supposed to perform rope tricks, but his arm hung useless. He had less than two weeks before his next booking. There was no possibility he could teach his left arm the dexterity it had taken his right arm a lifetime to learn. But he started to practice hour after hour, day after day. His good arm learned to perform some of the simpler feats by opening day, but a "new" Will Rogers stepped on that stage—one who performed only a few simple rope tricks with his left arm, and "I sho' did me a mess of tall gabbing on anything that I could think of and you know—they never missed the rope tricks."

After weeks of practice sessions, Rogers became proficient with his left arm. In time, as the full use of his right arm returned, he would astonish audiences by performing difficult rope tricks equally well with either hand. He could, for example, toss three lassoes at once, catching a galloping horse by the neck, while the other two ropes would hobble the horse's fore and rear feet, respectively.

But by the fall of 1915, Will's virtuosity with lariats had become secondary; people now came to listen to what he had to say. In 1915, too, Will Rogers took his first airplane ride. He and Betty were in Atlantic City, where an enterprising flier offered $5-rides in an open Curtiss sea plane. They passed the plane every day, with Will vowing to take a spin; but it was not until the very last day of their stay that Will actually made up his mind to fly. A man had to carry him piggy-back through the shallow surf to the plane. A picture taken at the time shows a "nervous, but vastly pleased" Will. It was the beginning of a lifelong enthusiasm for aviation.

Once again Broadway beckoned. Will appeared in two short-lived shows: in *Hands Up* where he received good personal notices (while the show did not) and in Ned Wayburn's *Town Topics*, which had an even shorter run.

Gene Buck, Florenz Ziegfeld's right-hand man, changed the path of Will's life. Buck had seen a performance of *Hands Up* and felt that this unusual cowboy would bring a brand-new type of humor to the *Midnight Frolic*. Ziegfeld had two separate productions: The *Follies* in the New Amsterdam Theatre on West 42nd Street, and the *Midnight Frolic*, upstairs, on the theater roof. The top floor of the theater building had been transformed into an ultra-fashionable nightclub, serving food and liquor. The *Follies* was a regular musical revue, with famous stars set in lavish production numbers, original music by top composers, scenic splendor and comic sketches. The *Frolic* was an entirely separate variety show that began at midnight and catered to the late crowd. It was the most lavish nightclub production ever attempted, having more than fifty cast members.

Ziegfeld, who did not particularly like comics or humorists, was not convinced that some "crude" cowboy could add anything to his extravagant presentation. Buck finally persuaded Ziegfeld to give Rogers a chance.

The difference between vaudeville and the *Frolic* became immediately obvious to Will. In vaudeville, audiences would change nightly and towns would change weekly—sometimes twice a week. A performer would perfect his act and then play it again and again, year after year, without a single change, all along the circuit. But *Frolic* audiences consisted of many repeaters, patrons who would return night after night to eat, drink and watch the show. While it was no hardship to look at Ann Pennington's famous knees several nights in a row, a humorist could not expect audiences to laugh at the same jokes twice; he needed a fresh act at every performance. Betty came up with the solution. Will, she suggested, should talk about the day's news. His habit of reading every available newspaper from front page to back would provide all the background he needed.

Nightly, Will kidded public figures, their actions or inactions, the events of the moment. Because of the war in Europe, Americans had become more aware of the importance of the time and the men who were shaping their present and future. With his good-natured humor, Will talked sense to the audience while he made them laugh. He was convinced that the war would eventually involve America, and he pointed out her unpreparedness. At a special performance for President Wilson he voiced that thought: "There is some talk about getting a machine gun—if we can borrow one." When Will saw the president lead the laughter, he pushed further. "We're going to have an army of 250,000 men," he said as he started to spin his rope idly, as if in thought; "Mr. Ford makes 300,000 cars a year." With another whirl of the lasso, Will quipped "I think, Mr. President, we ought to at least have a man to every car."

In January 1916, a call came from Florenz Ziegfeld: could Will perform in the *Follies* as well as the *Frolic*—starting at once? Will did not hesitate to accept. That evening he used the material he had prepared for the midnight show. Around eleven o'clock he sent out for the first editions of the morning newspapers and prepared an entirely different act for the *Frolic*. Two different routines every day remained the practice as long as Will Rogers stayed in both Ziegfeld productions. Will never used a writer, but prepared all his own material. He did, however, have inestimable help; as he would say years later, "I watch the government and report the facts, that is all I do, and I don't even find it necessary to exaggerate."

Acclaimed by critics, Will Rogers became Ziegfeld's greatest star. His words were repeated by those who heard him, and even President Wilson quoted him. Will Rogers had become a prominent voice.

As the rich, the famous, and near-famous came to the *Follies* or the *Frolic*, Will would introduce them in the audience, ask them to stand up and be applauded. Sometimes he would ask celebrities to come on stage and say a few words. During the time Will Rogers was with the *Follies*, there was just one single surprise:

> Best Edison joke I know was on me. He and Mrs. Edison used to always come to the *Ziegfeld Follies* and I played directly to him with my little jokes for four years, before I knew he was deaf.

Will Rogers' importance can best be judged by Ziegfeld's dramatic concession in the following letter:

> My Dear Bill:
>
> I tried everywhere to get you on the telephone today before leaving for Easthampton, but it was impossible to find you.

Gene Buck tells me he had a long talk with you and we are to see the new skit Tuesday at 3 p.m.

Gene also told me you insisted on being away three matinees during the Polo Games—that your heart and soul are set upon seeing those games. You know Bill, there isn't anything in the world I would not do for you, but you must realize we have an enormous organization, enormous expenses, and with the production necessary now for the *Follies*, it takes a year to get our production back. To give matinees without you in them *would be absolutely impossible*.

There is only one thing to do. Of course it is going to entail a great loss, because unquestionably our matinees will be greatly hurt. There is only one solution— give the matinee on Friday instead of Saturday, and on Monday instead of Wednesday. Mr. Holzman will see you about this, and I think we can get a good story through the dramatic column so we will be able to have them; owing to your desire to see the Games I agreed to this, so you know in what high esteem I hold you.

What the result will be Bill, we will only have to wait to determine, but I want to please you in every way I possibly can. I would like to talk with you, so if you can call me at 115M Easthampton when you get this, I will be glad to talk with you.

Very sincerely yours,
(signed) Flo

Will was not overly impressed with the letter or the unparalleled matinee arrangements. He crossed out the typing with a soft pencil, wrote the word *over* in brackets at the bottom of the page and used the reverse side to make notes for a never completed biography.

In 1917 America went to war. At first Will Rogers was hesitant about continuing his special type of humor, but he found that people were eager to hear him put the news into his own individual perspective. His oft-quoted chides that "the airplane program turned out more air than planes" resulted in a Senate investigation. His comment that "the guy who makes the bullets was paid $5 a day, and the man who stopped them got $15 a month" was an indictment that he strengthened by adding, "Of course, stopping bullets comes under the heading of unskilled labor!"

When Will spoke, America's political and industrial leaders listened. The cowboy from Oologah—or Claremore, as he preferred to be known as he felt that "only an Indian can pronounce Oologah"—became their friend and adviser; he met the great and the near great, but he remained what he had always been, sincere and unaffected: "I joked about every prominent man of my time, but I never met a man I didn't like."

Peace came and when questions arose why American doughboys were still kept in Europe now that the war was over, Will offered an explanation: "Would have brought them back sooner, but we didn't have anybody in Washington who knew where they were. We had to leave them over there so they could get the mail that was sent to them during the war. Had to leave them over there, anyway, two of them hadn't married yet."

At last the soldiers returned. A huge parade was planned for New York's Fifth Avenue. "If we really want to honor our Boys," Will Rogers asked innocently, "why don't we let *them* sit in the reviewing stands and have the people march by?"

Theodore Roosevelt, too, realized the impact Will made on his countrymen. In 1918, speaking to advertising executive Albert D. Lasker, he said:

> This man Rogers has such a keen insight into the American panorama and the American people that I feel he is bound, in the course of time, to be a potent factor in the political life of the nation.[3]

It was also in 1918 that Will made his first motion picture, *Laughing Bill Hyde*, based on a book written by Rex Beach. In fact, it was Edith Beach, Rex's wife, who suggested that Will would be ideal for the part of Bill Hyde:

> The part was that of a crook, who received money under false pretenses. Mrs. Beach had seen my little act in the *Follies*, so naturally she decided that I was the one to do the crook who obtained money under false pretenses.[4]

Making movies was a new experience for Will Rogers. Each day was spent at the Goldwyn Company's studios in Fort Lee,

New Jersey. Evenings he appeared at the New Amsterdam Theatre. When Will saw the film, he was aghast. "I'm the world's worst actor!" he said, crestfallen. The critics disagreed and Sam Goldwyn offered Rogers a one-year contract at an inviting $2,250 per week, fifty-two weeks a year; the contract contained an option for a one-year renewal at an even more lavish weekly salary of $3,000. There was just one stipulation: Will would have to move to California. After years in New York City, the wide-open spaces of the West Coast were tempting. The family had now grown to three boys—Fred Rogers was born in 1918—and a girl. Will and Betty felt that California would offer more of the life they themselves had known as youngsters; it would certainly be good for the children. It was therefore decided to leave the East and see what the movies would bring. On November 30, 1918, Will and Sam Goldfish (he had not yet changed his name to Goldwyn) signed the contract.

Will went ahead to Los Angeles and rented a large house on Van Ness Avenue. The family followed, bringing everything they had at their home on Long Island, including the ponies. During a nationwide diphtheria epidemic, the three boys became sick. Will was away, making a motion picture on location. He was notified and:

> I rushed 600 miles by a relay of automobiles in less than 10 hours . . . to arrive and see this . . . anti-toxin was administered too late, and to also see what it saved when it was given on time.

The two older boys, Will Jr. and Jimmy recovered, but Fred could not be saved. Will grieved over the loss of his little boy for the rest of his life, but stoically refused to display his sorrow publicly.

Before going to work at the Goldwyn Studio, Will published *The Cowboy Philosopher on the Peace Conference*, and *The Cowboy Philosopher on Prohibition*, two collections of quips he had used on those subjects during his stay with Ziegfeld.

During the two years of his Hollywood association with Goldwyn, Will made twelve films. When the contract expired, the studio did not negotiate for a new one. Several of the films won awards and some made lists of special merit, but they were not the great financial successes Goldwyn had hoped they would be.

Will tried to produce his own motion pictures. Of these *The Ropin' Fool* is truly outstanding. Here Will Rogers preserved a permanent record of his matchless roping skill. Using slow-motion photography, Will captured the movement of ropes whitened with shoe polish. The loops seem alive as they unerringly seek their targets. Incredible tricks are performed with such seeming ease, proof of the untold hours Will practiced. But even a master like Will Rogers had his occasional failures. You can still see those times when the ropes fell short, or the horse pulled its head back, because Will Rogers saved the "outtakes," those scenes which were not used in the finished motion picture. Perhaps he should have, as he sometimes "ad-libbed" in vaudeville, "put some glue on the horse's nose."

But Will learned a most expensive lesson: there was more to film making than just putting a story on celluloid. Financial problems arose, especially because he lacked distribution. Will was forced to mortgage his home, borrow against life insurance policies, and liquidate most of his assets. When all this was still not enough, he signed a contract with Hal Roach, to star in a dozen two-reel comedies. Still deprived of his voice—the films were silent—comedy films had to reduce everything to slapstick and sight gags. This was not what he wanted to do. He finally left the family in California and went back to New York, to star once again in the *Ziegfeld Follies*.

Will embarked on two new phases in his career. He began to write a series of weekly articles for the McNaught Syndicate. The column was Will Rogers as his fans saw him: the reporter, the social observer, and critic; the voice of the people. These weekly articles proved immediately popular and he continued them until 1935. Will next struck out in an entirely new direction when he broadcast his first monologue over radio station KDKA, Pittsburgh, Pennsylvania. He also continued in great demand as an after-dinner speaker. Over the period of several years, Will Rogers repaid every dollar of indebtedness his expensive venture into film production had incurred. He began to invest some of the money in real estate. As the son of a rancher, he knew the value of land. Even though the stock market was booming and "fortunes" were made on paper, Rogers felt that speculation on the stock exchange was not quite ethical. At Eddie Cantor's persistent urging, however, Will did make a single second-hand fling.

Having made some substantial gain without actually investing a dollar, Will sent the profit from the brief Wall Street speculation to Cantor's favorite charity. He wanted no part of it, and stuck to real estate.

One would assume that Will Rogers' waking hours were filled to capacity. He appeared nightly in the *Follies*, he wrote weekly articles, read stacks of newspapers, practiced roping for hours, and addressed innumerable functions. This would have taxed any ordinary man, but Will was not an ordinary man. His habits were uncomplicated, his demands were few. He rarely slept more than four or five hours at night. He might take short naps during the day, if an opportunity presented itself. Five minutes in a chair, or in a car, and he would be as refreshed as another man after eight hours sleep. He could eat anywhere, for his tastes were simple. A bowl of chili or beans would be his favorite dish. His taste in clothing was equally unpretentious—a plain white shirt and a simple suit.

Will rarely stayed long enough in any place to send laundry out. It was simpler to abandon used clothing than to carry the soiled articles along. When it was time to buy a new tie—he would walk into a store, reach for a dark one on a rack, take off the old one, put on the new one, pay for it, and walk out leaving the old tie behind. When he traveled he would often take his bath while sending a bellboy to buy another set of underwear, socks, and a shirt.

In 1924 he began to take on even more work. Having published the *Illiterate Digest*, a summary of earlier weekly articles, he prepared to leave the *Follies* and embark on a nation-wide lecture tour the following year.

In 1925, on his way to California, Will stopped at the "National Joke Factory" (Will's name for the U.S. Congress) in Washington, D.C. He was to be the guest speaker at the annual Gridiron Dinner. There he met General Billy Mitchell, who invited Will to join him on a flight the following day. Will accepted. Though he had been aloft in a plane before, it was this particular flight that made Will a firm believer in the future of aviation. When the plane landed, Billy Mitchell told Will:

> You have been with me on the last flight I will make as a Brigadier General. Tonight at 12 o'clock I am to be

demoted to a Colonel, and sent to a faraway post, where
instead of having the entire Air Force at my command,
there will be seven planes.

Brigadier General William "Billy" Mitchell, the foremost U.S. combat air commander of World War I, was a strong proponent of an independent U.S. air force and of unified control of air power. Opposed by the army general staff and the navy, he was demoted and sent to a post in Texas. Continuing his public advocacy of a strong air force, he was court-martialled for insubordination. Sentenced to suspension from rank and duty for five years, he resigned from the army.

Will not only attended Mitchell's court-martial, but took up his cause for a strong United States Army Air Corps, and advocated it for the rest of his life.

Will's decision to tour America on a lecture circuit was really not unusual. He had been asked to speak in almost every major city, but his commitments in either New York City or California had never allowed him to go "meetin' the regular bird." Now Will was free to go and speak in hundreds of cities and towns, as well as address conventions. "I faced men," Will wrote "who made every known and unknown commodity that the American people could very well get along without. I even got so low one time that I talked to real estate men." He told them what no other speaker would have dared, and the closer to the truth he came, the better they liked it. "Loan Sharks and Interest Hounds," was his opening salutation to the National Bankers' Convention. "The Robbing Hoods of America," were the advertising men, and when he spoke to the automobile dealers, he called them "The Old Time Horse-Trading Gyps with White Collars On."

In the spring of 1926, Will Rogers planned an extended trip to Europe from where he had contracted to write a series of articles for the *Saturday Evening Post*. In them he pretended that he was really going as the "self-appointed unofficial ambassador" and that his articles were reports to President Coolidge. These "confidential" communications were gems of penetrating insight and observation, truth and humor. "Will Rogers' analysis of affairs abroad was not only more interesting but proved to be more accurate than anything I had heard," wrote Franklin Delano Roosevelt.

In New York City, Will ran into Adolph S. Ochs, publisher of *The New York Times*. They spoke for a few moments, as they knew each other well. When they parted, Ochs casually remarked "If you run across anything worth while, cable it to us. We'll pay the tolls."

Will left aboard the Leviathan on May 1. Whether he gave serious concern to Ochs' offer at that time is not known. The fact is that Will did not send his first cable until the end of July, almost three months later. By that time he had been to England, France, Spain, Italy, Germany, Switzerland, and Russia. He had met with the Prince of Wales, Pope Pious XI, Mussolini; the Spanish dictator Miguel Primo de Rivera, and the King of Spain. Yet none of them apparently was important enough to warrant a cable to the *Times*. After being entertained by Lady Astor, Will sent this:

> LONDON. NANCY ASTOR, WHICH IS THE NOM DE PLUM OF LADY ASTOR, IS ARRIVING ON YOUR SIDE ABOUT NOW. SHE IS THE BEST FRIEND AMERICA HAS HERE. PLEASE ASK MY FRIEND [MAYOR] JIMMY WALKER, TO HAVE NEW YORK TAKE GOOD CARE OF HER. SHE IS THE ONLY ONE OVER HERE THAT DON'T THROW ROCKS AT AMERICAN TOURISTS. YOURS RESPECTFULLY, WILL ROGERS.

The New York Times printed it on the first page of its second section on July 30. Other cables followed. On August 2, Will explained further the open animosity against American tourists in Europe:

> A BUNCH OF AMERICAN TOURISTS WERE HISSED AND STONED YESTERDAY IN FRANCE, BUT NOT UNTIL THEY HAD FINISHED BUYING. YOURS, WILL ROGERS.

The New York Times continued to publish Will's cables as they arrived in a steady stream now, seven days a week. Not only did the regular readers of the *Times* enjoy Rogers' cables, but other newspapers around the country wanted to feature them also. Lawrence Winship of the *Boston Globe*, an old admirer of Rogers' wit, approached the *Times*. But Ochs would have none of it. Those were cables exclusively to the *Times*, he maintained, and exclusive they would remain; this despite the fact that Rogers was not on the *Times* payroll, nor was there any written or implied contract.

Rogers, in Europe, knew nothing about the interest in his squibs on this side of the Atlantic. He had no thought of continuing these contributions after his return to America, where a strenuous lecture tour awaited him.

On his travels around Europe Will had a camera crew follow him, filming his visits to a number of countries. These films were later released as travelogues, giving Rogers' unique slant on customs, sights, and scenery.

After covering Europe, Will decided to fly to Russia. Unlike others of his time, he was not ready to dismiss that huge country as simply being "in the grips of an experiment." Will always had to see for himself. He returned with a far deeper understanding of Communism than most of his contemporaries. "To me," he wrote, "Communism is one-third practice and two-thirds explanation . . . but these people are going somewhere and we better watch out while they are on their way."

Back in London, Will stepped into a faltering revue produced by a man named Charles Cochran. Called England's Ziegfeld, Cochran was an old friend, and Will was happy to help him. With Will in the cast, the show was sold out nightly. Will Rogers, ever himself, showed his ability to transcend cultures. The cowboy from Oologah, could walk onto a stage in London's West End and delight the staid British critics. Wrote the *London Times*:

> Mr. Will Rogers, the American comedian and film actor, appeared on Friday night in Cochran's Revue at the London Pavilion. He is presenting each night for a season of at least six weeks the "turn" that has earned him such popularity in America. He walks on the stage in an ordinary shabby suit—and just talks. At the first performance on Monday night, he talked a little too much, but that mistake can soon be rectified. At the beginning Mr. Rogers seemed a little timid. He need not have been. Humour of the kind in which he delights, is international and, in a very few days he will be attracting all London to the Pavilion.

And James Agate, Britain's foremost critic, did not spare compliments, either. He wrote of Will Rogers, "A superior power had seen fit to fling into the world, for once, a truly fine specimen—fine in body, fine in soul, fine in intellect."

Will eventually had to leave the show to honor a commitment to make a motion picture, *Tip Toes*, with Dorothy Gish and Nelson (Bunch) Keyes. Charles Cochran, recalled Will's modesty in their deal over salary: "When he appeared for me at the London Pavilion he refused to name his price, saying: 'Pay me what I am worth' . . . I sent him a check for $1,000 at the end of the week, and he sent it back with the remark, 'I'm not worth it.' "

A special act of generosity by Will Rogers endeared him to his new British fans. It was the kind of assistance Rogers would provide without a moment's hesitation in his native country, but the fact that an American, a foreigner, should help the Irish, especially the very poor, touched the British.

It was a tragedy in which forty-seven men, women and children burned to death; a ghastly fire in Dromcolliher, a village in County Limerick, about thirty-six miles southwest of Limerick City, on the border of County Cork. According to the *London Times*, it started at a rare treat called a "Cinematograph Entertainment"—a motion picture showing:

> Since there is no public hall in the village, the films were shown in a large loft over a garage—the upstairs portion of a wooden building [which] had one door, reached by an ordinary ladder from the floor of the garage.
>
> About 200 people, including many women and children, were packed into this room. The program had just started when a film burst into flames. As the projecting machine was placed near the doorway, escape from the room would have been difficult. Only those near the door had a chance in the panic to get away in safety. Many women and children were trampled under foot and it was not long before the ladder, which formed the only means of egress, collapsed, leaving the people trapped within the loft. The room by this time was a mass of flames. . . .
>
> The fire is believed to have been caused by the carelessness of a cigarette smoker or by the presence of a lighted candle near the operating box.

The next day, William T. Cosgrave, president of the Irish Freestate, opened a fund for the relief of Dromcolliher. Will not only contributed substantially to the fund, but appeared in a benefit which had been organized on short notice. There were no fanfares for Will Rogers, just a handful of lines in the newspaper, hidden away on an inside page. But he had not gone to Dublin for publicity; it was the right, the decent thing to do, and Will did it.

When Rogers landed back in New York on September 27, Ochs persuaded him to carry on his short telegrams to the *Times*. Then the McNaught Syndicate, already handling Will's weekly column, took over the management of the daily feature as well. Almost 600 newspapers eventually highlighted Will's squibs.

It is almost impossible to overestimate the impact and significance of Will Rogers' daily column. In an age when news coverage was almost entirely through newspapers—radio was still the new kid on the block—Will's observations brought not only commentary and understanding, but above all perspective, to his readers. In the years that followed, it was his column, rarely more than three hundred words, that was first read by almost forty million Americans, including the president of the United States. The column made Will Rogers one of the most talked-about and important voices in the country.

On December 21, 1926, when Rogers interrupted his lecture tour to return home for Christmas, a surprise awaited him. During his absence he had been "elected" Mayor of Beverly Hills, and a large crowd came to greet him at the railroad station. Will addressed the crowd: "It don't speak well for your town when this many of you haven't got anything to do but come to meet me." He was proud to have been chosen by his friends and neighbors, and signed his daily columns as *"Mayor Rogers."* He summed up Beverly Hills: "My constituents, I don't claim that they are all good, but the most of them is at least slick." Will's "reign" is riddled with beneficial acts, paid for by His Honor out of his own pocket; among his gifts was a gymnasium Rogers built for the local police department, and a handball court.

The mayor's position was mostly ceremonial, as the city of Beverly Hills was administered by a board of trustees. A few months later, the California legislature decreed that in any town of the sixth class governed by a board of trustees, the chairman of the board of trustees had to be known as the mayor. Will was out of office. As usual, he had the last word:

> There is only one thing that makes me sore about the whole thing and that is this. This new law applied to cities of the sixth class only. My Lord, if I had known that I was ruling in a city of the sixth class, I would never have taken the thing in the first place. Mayor of a sixth-class city—why, I will be years living that down.

Ether and Me was written after Will's famous gallstone operation in 1927. He wrote it, he said, to pay the doctor bills. He had suffered slight attacks and occasional discomfort over the years, but this time acute pain struck him at a tour stop in Bluefield, West Virginia. Despite the severity of the attack, Will continued his tour, which was about to recess. When he reached his home in California, he developed jaundice and Betty sent for the doctor. After a thorough examination and consultation with a specialist, it was decided to operate.

After the operation, Will's condition was far more serious than his doctors anticipated, and for some time it was doubtful that he would survive. The hospital issued frequent bulletins on his condition, and the news media reported them as if he were a head of state. Thousands of letters, telegrams and bouquets flooded the hospital.

In 1927, still recovering from the operation, Will was in Washington, D.C., for the filming of *A Texas Steer*. While there, the National Press Club elected Will Rogers "Congressman-at-Large" and invited him to a formal installation dinner. After he had been "officially" commissioned by Senator Ashurst of Arizona, Will delivered his inauguration speech:

> I certainly regret the disgrace that's been thrust on me here tonight . . . I certainly have lived, or tried to live my life so that I would never become a congressman, and I am just as ashamed of the fact that I have failed as you are. And to have the commission presented by a senator is adding insult to injury.

One of Will's first "official" acts as Congressman-at-Large was on the international level. Relations with Mexico had deteriorated and were approaching the breaking point. President Cool-idge had appointed Dwight Morrow as the new ambassador to Mexico, hoping that this able man would help re-cement rela-tions. One of Morrow's first acts was to invite Will Rogers and Charles Lindbergh to Mexico City. Just a few months earlier, Lindbergh had electrified the entire world with his daring solo crossing of the Atlantic. By asking Rogers, America's foremost private citizen, and Lindbergh, the world's current hero, to come to Mexico, Morrow created precisely the feeling toward the United States he had hoped for. Will joked with President Calles as he would have with President Coolidge or, for that matter, with any other man. The Mexican appreciated the obviously genuine friendship Will exuded. This, in turn, gave Morrow the opening to discuss diplomacy on a far more personal basis. Will's visit to Mexico was an unqualified success, and Lindbergh's natural charm and youthful openness captivated his Mexican hosts.

The Mississippi floods of 1927 caused enormous damage. Again Will was on his way, flying from town to town, giving benefit performances and raising funds. He would start each town's drive with a sizable sum out of his own pocket.

In January 1928, Will was master of ceremonies for an important "first" in radio history—a national coast-to-coast hook-up, emanating from five cities. Will was to broadcast from his home in California, Fred Stone would be in Chicago, Paul White-man and his orchestra in New York, and Al Jolson, stage and film star, in New Orleans. There was also a brief statement by Edward George Wilmer, president and chairman of the board of Dodge Brothers Motor Car Company.

After Will Rogers opened the show, he announced that he had a great surprise for his listeners: "It's Mr. Coolidge, who wants to take this opportunity to deliver a short message to America."

The next sounds heard over the eighty radio stations, seemed to be the nasal, New England–accented voice of President Coolidge:

> Ladies and Gentlemen, it's the duty of the president
> to deliver a message to the people on the condition of
> the country. I am proud to report that the condition of
> the country as a whole is prosperous. I don't mean that

the whole country is prosperous, but as a hole it's prosperous. That is, it's prosperous for a hole. A hole is not
supposed to be prosperous, and this country is certainly
[in] a hole. There is not a whole lot of doubt about
that. . . .

There was more to this mock State of the Union speech. It
was incredible that the dignified Mr. Coolidge would say such
things, but it was his voice—or was it? Few people knew of Will's
uncanny ability to imitate voices. Will's friends were quite familiar with his imitations of important politicians and movie stars but
this was the first time the country heard it. Will was upset to find
that his imitation had fooled many listeners. As he explained after
the broadcast: "The idea that anyone could image that it was him
uttering this nonsense—it struck me that it would be an insult to
anyone's sense of humor to announce that it was not him." Will
immediately sent a letter to the president explaining the incident.
President Coolidge returned a hand-written note saying that Will
should not give it a moment's worry.

Grace Coolidge, the president's wife, later recalled the
incident to Will and proved that she could imitate the president's
voice better than Will. Replied Will, "Yes, but look what you had
to go through to learn it."

Will planned to attend the two national conventions that
summer to report on the "National Follies." The Republicans met
in Kansas City, Missouri. Will, now traveling by air whenever he
could, took a plane from Los Angeles. Landing in Las Vegas,
Nevada, his plane broke a wheel and flipped over. Still stunned,
Will changed planes. Later, taking off near Cheyenne, Wyoming,
he crashed again. Undismayed, Will waited for a replacement
plane to be flown in. He finally arrived in Kansas City.

The airplane was still in its infancy, and accidents, both
minor and major, were part of the growing-up process. Dorothy
Stone, Fred Stone' daughter and a Broadway star in her own right,
recalls one morning at the family house in New York, when
"Uncle" Will arrived, ashen and disheveled. He had flown into
town and his plane had crashed on landing. Could Will clean up
before going to his own home so that Betty needn't know about
the accident. "She would never let me fly again if she knew,"
Will groaned.

It was a plane mishap which brought Will Rogers back to Broadway. Fred Stone had been taking flying lesson when his plane crashed in Connecticut. His broken body was rushed to the hospital, where doctors worked desperately to save his life. Their prognosis finally was that Fred Stone would live, but his legs were too severely crushed from him to ever walk or dance again. Will raced to his friend's bedside to comfort him. He reassured him that he would be back on the stage, greater than he had been in his original hits as the scarecrow in *The Wizard of Oz,* and the lead in *The Red Mill*. When Will left his injured friend he had succeeded in buoying up Fred's spirit. He had given him hope. A few minutes later Dorothy Stone walked into the corridor and found Will, his head resting against the wall, sobbing over the tragedy that had befallen his best friend.

Before the accident, Fred Stone had been in rehearsal for the Broadway-bound musical *Three Cheers*. Dorothy was to co-star. Will offered to take his disabled friend's place.

Charles Dillingham, the producer, was delighted. Will Rogers' offer promised to save the show, for if anyone could help audiences forget the absence of Fred Stone's artistry, it would be Will Rogers. This act of friendship touched America, and especially Broadway, where acts of sentiment are rare. Few people ever knew that Will Rogers had to cancel a fully booked lecture tour that would have grossed close to half a million dollars. Will felt honor-bound to reimburse promoters for expenses incurred and lost profits.

Three Cheers was not a very good show, the critics agreed, but Will Rogers made it a hit. Though he had rehearsed—in his own fashion—he made no attempt to learn his lines. He simply carried the script in his hip pocket and consulted it from time to time, more for the story-line than the dialogue. He would make up his own lines. He would deviate from the plot and do what he had done in the *Follies*. Dorothy Stone's talent and charm were a perfect foil for Will. Together they presented a show unlike any New York had ever seen, or would ever see again. No two performances were ever the same. The audiences loved it.

After a performance, Will, who used no makeup, was the first to leave the theater. Usually there were a number of indigent actors and beggars waiting at the stage door. Will was prepared; he had a roll of dollar bills that he distributed. Soon the rumor of this windfall spread round town, and a crowd would gather nightly to take part in the bountiful handout. The crowd grew so large that eventually police had to be on hand to help the other actors get to their cars.

There is just one footnote to this episode: Fred Stone recovered almost completely. He not only walked again, but danced in many Broadway performances and began a film career.

During the fierce presidential campaign of 1928 fought between Republic Herbert Hoover and Democrat Al Smith, the humor magazine *Life* nominated Will as its candidate on the "Bunkless" ticket. Will entered into the jest by paraphrasing Calvin Coolidge's famous statement: "I chews to run!" Will waged his campaign solely in the pages of *Life* magazine, his only campaign promise being that if elected, he would resign. This mock campaign, simply a series of articles commenting on the real campaign going on, was endorsed by Henry Ford, Nicholas Murray Butler, Judge Ben B. Lindsey, Charles Dana Gibson, Reverend Francis J. Duffy, Glenn H. Curtis, Harold Lloyd, William Allen White, Grantland Rice, Ring Lardner, General Billy Mitchell, and Babe Ruth, among many others.

On November 2, 1928, Election Day, *Life* declared Will Rogers the winner on the vote by the great silent majority, and called Will "Unofficial President of the United States."

Motion pictures had discovered sound and on March 22, 1929, Fox Film Corporation and Will Rogers signed a contract. It called for Will to make four motion pictures "during the period commencing June 1, 1929 and ending September 30, 1930. . . . In full payment for your services hereunder we agree to pay you the sum of $600,000." Will's first talking picture, *They Had to See Paris,* premiered September 18, 1929 at the Fox-Carthay in Los Angeles. It created an immediate demand for more Will Rogers pictures. (Will, playing himself, became a major movie star, and by 1933 he was America's top male box-office attraction.)

The Twenties had less than ten weeks to roar when the house of stock certificates collapsed. Will had warned: "You will try to show us that we are prosperous, because we have more. I will show you where we are not prosperous, because we haven't paid for it yet." The time to pay had arrived, and America was to pay dearly.

Will Rogers changed his tone. He realized what the country needed most was confidence. "Of course," he kidded, "I haven't been buying any stock myself. I wanted to give the other fellow a chance to have confidence first." Will traveled throughout the country, raising morale, contributing huge sums to relief, and playing benefits. Though his sentiments were with the Democrats, Will quickly came to the defense of President Hoover: "You'd think Hoover got up one morning, looked out the window, and said, 'This looks like a nice day for ruining the country, I think I'll do it today.' "

The impact of the Depression reached into every corner of the American economy; yet for Will Rogers, those years were quite lucrative. On October 27, 1930, he signed a new contract with Fox Film Corporation. It called for Rogers to appear in an additional six motion pictures, for which Fox would pay Will Rogers $1,250,000.

Also in 1930, Will signed a contract with E. R. Squibb & Sons to go on a coast-to-coast radio network for fourteen Sunday talks. They would last fifteen minutes each, and he would receive a salary of over $70,000. Will Rogers never saw the check. He stipulated that the entire amount be divided between his two favorite charities, the Red Cross and Salvation Army. His reasoning was simple:

> The most unemployed or the hungriest man in America has contributed in some way to the wealth of every millionaire in America. . . . A few years ago we were so afraid that the poor people were liable to take a drink, and now we have it fixed so that they can't even get something to eat.

Millions of Americans would find excuses not to attend their houses of worship on a Sunday morning, but to miss Will Rogers' radio talk on a Sunday evening was unthinkable. And yet his 'little jokes and digs' were more penetrating and thought provoking and inspiring than most sermons. Will spoke *with* America and *for* America. Will did not preach or lecture in the accepted way. With a twinkle in his eye, an infectious grin, his Oklahoma drawl, and a wad of chewing gum to chomp on, he would use his perceptive humor to make Americans laugh—at themselves. And each would think he had, all by himself, discovered the deeper hidden meaning. Instead of pointing an accusing finger at his countrymen for mental and moral laziness, Will just chuckled: "I reckon some folks figure it a compliment to be called 'broad-minded.' Back home, broad-minded is just another way of saying a feller is too lazy to form an opinion." Those who did not read his daily columns or his weekly articles, who did not attend his lectures, his stage performances or his films, were now lassoed by his radio talks.

Will's astute observations, his ability to put into simple words what his generation believed, raised him to a level of influence unparalleled in the history of America. Since he was unencumbered by political ties, his observations and reproaches were not open to charges of partisanship. His talks were always in the language of the people, accurately understanding their thoughts and fears; he was their man and they listened. Such power in the hands of a lesser man could have been dangerous. But Will Rogers never changed, neither did he ever abuse the trust. He simply went on doing what he had always done better than anyone else: serving as the official conscience of his country.

Lightnin', a motion picture made in 1930, featured as a juvenile lead a handsome, tall newcomer just out of the ranks of the extras. His name was Joel McCrea. According to McCrea, Will helped him that first day on the set. The scene was to take place in a buggy, the two men sitting side by side. Will had some lines to say, then McCrea was to answer. As they were running through the dialogue, McCrea couldn't hear his cue. Finally Will, famous for making up his own lines, turned to him and said: "You know, Joe, I fix up my own dialogue. Sometimes I make it better, sometimes I don't. But when I think I've said enough, I'll poke you. Then it's your turn." Will would call McCrea 'Joe' from then onward.

His film commitments fulfilled for the moment, Will decided to take a closer look at the Far East, and when Will Rogers had a thought, it had to be executed at once.

He took the S. S. *Express of Russia* and arrived in Japan on December 6, 1931. He toured Japan and visited Korea, then he went on to China where he was presented to the Emperor. From Malaya, Will traveled by plane to Iraq, Palestine, and Egypt. In London he met Betty, who had come over directly from America, and together they attended the Geneva Disarmament Conference. Will had been through the same formalities before, in London. With eternal hope and an open mind, he took another look. His conclusion: "There is nothing to prevent their succeeding—but human nature."

Betty and Will returned to America. Will was under contract to Fox Film Corporation and their biggest star. Films like *A Connecticut Yankee, State Fair, David Harum,* and *Steamboat Round the Bend* are classics of a budding film industry. Much of what is seen and heard in those films is purely Will Rogers'. He rarely left dialogue as he found it and he constantly added "business" and gags the writers and directors never imagined.

This was the era of the glamorous dressing rooms on motion picture sets. To keep a star happy, the studio would build what was called a dressing room, but was actually a bungalow consisting of living room, bedroom, kitchen, bathroom, *and* dressing room. Land was still cheap and plentiful. When Will Rogers signed with Fox Film Corporation, the studio decided to build a desert home for him, complete with cactus garden. It was to be a great surprise for Will Rogers, but it turned out to be a bigger surprise to the studio, for Will rarely went near it. Old timers only remember him using it once, to offer visiting Calvin and Grace Coolidge a place to sit down in private. What Will usually did was to park his car close to the camera, change his clothes or stretch out for a nap in the back seat, or sit in it to type his column— pecked with one finger on each hand. The Buick was his traveling dressing-room and office, his home away from home.

After having made a number of films for Fox, Will went to see Winfield Sheehan, who was the head of the studio. McCrea remembers:

> "Winnie," he said, "I think I ought to pick the parts I want to do myself. I have done all right so far. I'd like to choose some of my own roles. Irvin Cobb has written lots of things, and some of my friends have written stories." And Winnie said: "But Mr. Rogers, in running a studio we have tremendous investments in properties, we have bought scripts, we have stories submitted to us, and we have to build a program. That's sort of our department and we would like to control it."
>
> Well, Will, said: "I would like to pick a couple of things I would like to do. I know the kind of part I can play. I won't pick anything I can't do."

There was nothing for Winfield Sheehan to say. He apparently spent a great deal of time thinking about it, not wanting to offend Will, not wanting to shake up his biggest star, and he finally got an idea. He got a five-ton truck with every script, every property, every book, every synopsis that Fox ever had, and he sent it to Will's ranch, with an inter-office communication, saying, 'Dear Mr. Rogers, these are a few of Fox's properties. Will you read these and tell us which ones you want to do.'

Will just turned the memo over and wrote on the back: "You win, Winnie!" and sent the whole truck back.

Will Rogers was the least temperamental star Fox ever had. He would help another star as much as he would help the smallest bit player. If a picture came in ahead of schedule, Will would feel sorry for the extras, bit players and crew, and pay their lost salaries out of his own pocket.

Will's contract stipulated that he make three or four films a year, and Will liked to work continuously. Just as soon as he had finished one picture, Will asked to start a new one. He wanted no time off in between. That way he would complete his obligation to the studio and could take the rest of the year off, to do the things he wanted to do. This was 1932, an election year, and Will wanted to be at the conventions. Both parties met in Chicago. The Republicans renominated Herbert Hoover.

Then the Democrats took over. On the first ballot Oklahoma nominated Will Rogers as the favorite-son candidate, with all twenty-two votes going to him. "I made the mistake," he kidded afterward, "of going to sleep, and when I woke up, my votes had been stolen. I not only lost my twenty-two delegates but I woke up without even as much as an alternate." The Democrats chose Franklin Delano Roosevelt.

Early in 1933 Will signed with Gulf Oil to broadcast seven radio talks coast to coast. When he had fulfilled his commitment, he told reporters that he had decided not to broadcast again. Shortly after that news reached the newspapers, a most unusual petition was delivered to Will. It asked Will Rogers that he reconsider his decision to abandon radio. It was signed by almost every member of the United States Senate, as well as by the secretary and the sergeant-at-arms. Will was touched: "The next fellow that knocks the Senate will have to answer to me. . . . that's my privilege and nobody else's." Will did return to radio, again for Gulf Oil.

Will had his numerous obligations, but whenever time allowed, he could be found in Washington at the "National Joke Factory." Improved air service made it easier for Will to travel. He also had an important letter which he carried with him:

In reply refer to
file: 54   DEPARTMENT OF COMMERCE
                   AERONAUTICS BRANCH
                   WASHINGTON

Mr. Will Rogers   October 25, 1933.
Beverly Hills, Calif.

Dear Mr. Rogers:

This will constitute authorization for any scheduled airline to carry you as passenger in any aircraft operated on the line, provided that while utilizing aircraft not on regular passenger runs you are equipped with a parachute, and that the authorized loading as shown on the license for the plane is not exceeded.

Very truly yours,
(signed)
Eugene L. Vidal,
Director of Aeronautics.

Will Rogers wrote in the top right corner by hand: "Very Important, save." This special permission from the Department of Commerce was the least the government could do for its unofficial president.

No trip to Washington was complete without a visit with Alice Roosevelt Longworth. President Theodore Roosevelt's eldest daughter was married to Nicholas Longworth, congressman from Ohio, who was also the speaker of the House. To Will, Alice was the most politically astute person in Washington, and Alice, in turn, was very partial to Will Rogers. "Will," she recalled years later, " . . . was always sheer fun, incapable of bad taste, incapable of an error of any sort in his relation with people . . . What an extraordinary character he was, and, you know, everyone had affection for him—affection in the truest sense of the word."

There was still one form of show business—outside of grand opera—Will had not attempted, and that was the legitimate theater. In 1934 he agreed to star in the West Coast production of Eugene O'Neill's play *Ah, Wilderness!* George M. Cohan had originated the role of Nat Miller on Broadway to rave reviews and producer Henry Duffy had urged Rogers for months to play the part in California. When Will finally agreed to appear in the play, there was no written agreement between him and Henry Duffy, just "a word-of-mouth agreement."[5]

It would be the first time Will would be required to study a script without changing a single word. For the first time he would have to sustain a character, for unlike the movies, there would be no cuts, no retakes. With his friend Fred Stone as adviser, Will rehearsed the first straight role of his career.

Will Rogers opened the limited engagement of *Ah, Wilderness!* on April 30, 1934, at the Curran Theatre, in San Francisco. On opening night the applause that greeted Rogers' first appearance lasted several minutes. *News-Week* reported that "the shrewd, simple philosophy of Nat Miller might have been written for Mr. Rogers, so easily does he slip into the part and make it his own." And the prestigious *New York Times* added: "He [Will Rogers] made Nat Miller a delightful personage, and in the father's scene with his adolescent son, Richard, he played with a simple sincerity that brought out handkerchiefs and made tears and smiles mingle."

During the first few performances in San Francisco, Rogers took his time giving and responding to cues, just as he was used to doing in motion pictures. The shows ran too long and audiences got out late. But in a matter of days, as Will picked up the tempo, the play lost 30 minutes without a word having been cut.[6]

In fact, during the entire run of the play, Will Rogers deviated only a single time from the script. It happened in Los Angeles. In the afternoon, Will played a game of polo, his favorite sport. Will was an accomplished player who played with great enthusiasm and abandon. Jimmy Rogers, Will's youngest son, played on the opposing team. In one collision between the highly competitive father and his son, as Jim recalled, "I bumped him so hard I knocked his horse down and he landed on the sideboards. He lay there motionless, and as I jumped from my horse and ran to him, all I could think of was that I had killed him. As I got to his side, he moved and tried to sit up. Still stunned and groggy, his first words were: 'Is the horse all right?' "

Will seemed to recover and prepared to go to the theater that evening, even though Betty wanted him to rest. But Will would not hear of it. Betty finally insisted that as a precaution, Jim drive his father to the theater, wait for him and bring him back.

During the performance, without warning, Will suddenly left the script and went into a ten-minute monologue on current affairs, much as he had done in his lecture days. Anne Shoemaker, the fine actress and Will's co-star as his wife, Essie, ad-libbed her lines, slowly guiding Will back to O'Neill's script and the show continued without further incident. The audience laughed and applauded during Will's digression, believing it part of every performance. The next day, Will could not even recall having gone to the theater. There were no after-effects of the concussion.

It had been understood from the very beginning that there would be a three-week run in San Francisco and that the show would then play three weeks at the El Capitan Theatre in Los Angeles. Advance sales in Los Angeles were extremely heavy, however, and the attendance figures set records for West Coast theater audiences. The El Capitan Theatre had 1,571 seats, with top prices for matinees $1.65 and for evenings $2. To accommodate the crowds in Los Angeles during the third—and supposed last—week, Will Rogers agreed to an additional matinee show, thus giving nine performances in one week, for a gross revenue of $18,500. When approached by the producer, Will agreed to a fourth week; the revenue was $22,000 for ten performances, the extra show being given on Sunday. But still more people wanted to see the show. Will agreed to extend the run to a fifth week, with nine performances. And then there was still another week, the sixth. In all, some 72,000 people came to the El Capitan Theatre. Will Rogers could have stayed with the play, as seen in *Variety*: "[This show] could have continued indefinitely." But Will wanted out and Eddie Cantor told this story:

. . . during the play's run something happened which, I feel sure, indirectly led to his death. Will received a letter from a clergyman: "Relying on you to give the public nothing that could bring the blush of shame to the cheeks of a Christian, I attended your performance with my 14-year old daughter. But when you did the scene in which the father lectures the son on the subject of his relations with an immoral woman, I took my daughter by the hand and we left the theater. I have not been able to look her in the eye since."

This so disturbed Rogers that he finally withdrew from the play. He also asked to be released from his commitment to do the screen version for Metro-Goldwyn-Mayer, promising to do another film in its place as soon as a suitable script was found. While waiting Will accepted an invitation from the famous pilot Wiley Post, to fly around the world—the trip which ended in the death of both men.

It would seem that with three extensions—doubling the length of the planned run—Will Rogers was not exactly anxious to leave the show. It would therefore appear that if such an accusing letter arrived, it came during the sixth and final week, and it was then that Rogers would not extend the run any further.

For the three weeks in San Francisco and the six weeks in Los Angeles, the show grossed $190,000—according to *Variety*—a record total. When the play closed, *Variety* gave the explanation as "picture work of Rogers' at Fox prevented his continuing doubling for screen and stage."

This was definitely the official version issued by the producer. However, *Ah, Wilderness*! closed Saturday night, June 30, 1934. Ten days later, Will was in Texas, visiting, and by the twenty-second of July he was aboard the *S.S. Malolo*, on his way to Honolulu and a trip around the world. Rogers did not return to America until the last week of September, 1934.

So it would seem that the story released to the press, that the play's closing was due to pressing "picture work of Rogers' at Fox," was not the true reason. There was nothing he had to do at Fox, as his picture commitments for the year had been completed. If, however, Will Rogers did receive the letter mentioned by

Eddie Cantor, his reaction in closing the play and refusing to appear in the film is consistent with his character. According to Louella O. Parsons, Will had told her months before: "His own studio knew it last fall, that he would not appear for Metro-Goldwyn-Mayer in 'Ah! Wilderness,' [sic] the play in which he won triumphant success on the stage."

As for the film version of *Ah, Wilderness!*, scheduled for production in 1935 by Metro-Goldwyn-Mayer and starring Will Rogers (on loan from Fox), Will Hays, czar of the movie industry, recalled talking to Rogers about it. Without mentioning the title, it is obvious that the reference is to this O'Neill play:

> Rogers told me he was going to reject the story. "I know it is a fine play by a great writer," said Will [Rogers], "but it is for grown-ups. It will make a fine picture, but when I play in a picture, folks always bring their children to see it. Most of the story is great, but there is one scene in it that people wouldn't want their children to see. You can't leave that scene out without spoiling the story. It should not be left out, but I just don't want to play in any picture where folks may think they shouldn't have brought their children."

Having closed the play and with no further obligations scheduled for several months, Will, Betty, and the boys Will Jr., and Jimmy, started a trip around the world. (Mary had decided to stay behind and study acting in a summer stock theater in Maine.) The family's first stop was Honolulu, Hawaii, where the Rogers received an invitation from a vacationing President Roosevelt. Referring to the meeting, Will quoted, "The President told me, 'Will, don't jump on Japan. Just keep them from jumping on us."

Leaving the Hawaiian Islands, Will commented, "You don't have to be warlike to get a real kick out of our greatest army post, Schofield Barracks, and the navy at Pearl Harbor. If war was declared with some Pacific nation we would lose the Philippines before lunch, but if we lost these it would be our fault."[7]

Of course there could be no doubt in anyone's mind as to which "Pacific nation" could possibly be meant. There was only one capable of aggression by sea and air, Japan.

Above: "The White House on the Verdigris," Will's boyhood home near Oologah. (Photo: B. B. and F. N. Sterling.) *Far top right:* The Will Rogers family at mealtime, from left Betty, Mary, Jimmy, Will, and Will, Jr. (Photo: Rogers Family Collection.) *Far bottom right:* On Goldwyn set of *An Unwilling Hero*, Will tries to teach Charlie Chaplin the finer points of handling a lasso. (Photo: Academy of Motion Picture Arts and Sciences.) *Lower left:* Young Will in Kemper Military School uniform. (Photo: C. Benedict Collection.)

Far top left: Betty and Will Rogers returning from Europe aboard *Ile de France*, September 25, 1934. (Photo: Collection of Library of Congress.) *Center:* Will and General Billy Mitchell in 1925. (Photo: Collection of Library of Congress.) *Top:* Will Rogers' relaxation—roping calves. (Photo: Fox Film Collection.) *Near left:* Fox Film Corporation's top stars: Will, Janet Gaynor, and Shirley Temple. (Photo: Academy of Motion Picture Arts and Sciences.) *Far left:* The Rogers family ranch home in Pacific Palisades, CA. (Photo: George Spota Collection.)

The family traveled on to Tokyo, where they stayed several days; then by boat to Korea, across Manchuria to Harbin, where they stopped for a few days before taking the Chinese Eastern Railway to Manchouli. At that point they changed to the Trans-Siberian Railroad "train de luxe" for what seemed an interminable journey. Before leaving Tokyo, the Soviet government's local representative had faithfully promised Will that the family would be met at Novosibirsk by a Russian plane, which would fly them all to Moscow. But there was no plane waiting in Novosibirsk, nor indeed, was there a message of either regret, or explanation. Nothing! Will, Betty, and the two young men spent six days and nights wedged into a tiny, uncomfortable compartment, jammed with the luggage for four people, some fresh and canned food bought just before boarding, and a small canned-heat outfit to brew tea.

After Moscow came a visit to Leningrad, then the Scandinavian countries; then on to England and finally, back home aboard the *Ile de France*.

Will was back in the United States in time to see some of the World Series games between St. Louis and Detroit. The contest became so exciting that Will, an enthusiastic baseball fan, hired a plane and pilot to be in Detroit on October 8, for the final game in which "Dizzy" Dean pitched the St. Louis Cardinals to an 11-0 win over the Detroit Tigers.

On November 30, Will began *The County Chairman*, directed by John G. Blystone, with beautiful Evelyn Venable, Kent Taylor, Louise Dresser and a young Mickey Rooney. The film was scheduled to be released in 1935.

The demands on Will Rogers' time were now massive. On January 15, he delivered a speech at Notre Dame University, which was broadcast. The following night in Washington D.C. he appeared at a joint, nationwide broadcast with Helen Keller, the famous blind and deaf author and lecturer, to raise funds for the production of "talking books." On the 17th, a night later, he was in Philadelphia, where he spoke before the Poor Richard Club. On the 18th, he was in Indianapolis at a benefit for the James Whitcomb Riley Hospital. On the 19th, Will Rogers was again in Washington, to appear for the Alfalfa Club. On the 22nd—after a Sunday and Monday off at last—Will spoke in Austin, Texas, at a benefit for crippled children. On the 30th, he was in New York

City at the Baseball banquet. While in New York, he also appeared at a number of benefits for charities.

Still on the roster for the first part of 1935 were speaking engagements carefully spaced around his film schedule. On June 15, Will was to speak to the Bar Association in Los Angeles; in July, he was master of ceremonies at the dedication of the *Los Angeles Times* building; and for a Fourth of July celebration, he wanted to fly to Stamford, Texas, to attend a cowboy reunion and a small-town rodeo. As the weeks went by, additional pledges to appear for worthy causes would be added to the list.

Then, of course, there were the films for 1935: *Life Begins at Forty*, directed by George Marshall, with Rochelle Hudson and Richard Cromwell; *Doubting Thomas*, directed by David Butler, with old friend Billie Burke (Florenz Ziegfeld's widow), Alison Skipworth, and Sterling Holloway; *In Old Kentucky*, directed by George Marshall, with Dorothy Wilson, Russell Hardie and Bill "Bojangles" Robinson; and *Steamboat Round the Bend*, directed by John Ford, with Anne Shirley and Irvin S. Cobb.

In addition, and by this time routine, were the daily columns and the weekly articles; then for the weekend, in segments of fifteen weeks, there were the nationwide Sunday radio broadcasts for Gulf Oil Company.

Looking at such a busy schedule, it is not surprising that Will's children often felt that they had to share their father with a whole country, and that perhaps the country was getting the bigger share. But as much as Will traveled for work, or even for pleasure, his thoughts were never far from Betty and the children. Perhaps his Indian ancestry made him less demonstrative, but he was a loving, involved family man. He tried to keep his family and their lives private, rarely referring to them in his column or radio talks. They were another part of his life, one he kept as much as possible separated from the public man. When he was away from fans, he wanted Betty and the children around him, sharing his good time. He assumed that they, too, enjoyed all the things he did. When they lived in Beverly Hills and had a swimming pool, Will was in the water, teaching the children to dive. Later, at the ranch in Pacific Palisades, they had enough land for a polo field and bridle paths. Betty rode, and every one of the children had learned at the age of two; not just riding enough to stay on a horse, no! Will taught them trick-riding. They all learned to play polo, which included long hours in a practice cage he had built at the ranch. There they would sit on a wooden form representing a horse; suspended from four corners, the "horse" would pitch and roll freely, teaching the rider to keep his seat while learning to swing the mallet at a ball. The inward sloping floor of the cage always returned the ball to the player from different directions, developing reflex and an accurate eye. Though the children, including Mary, went through this learning process, only son Jim pursued the sport in later years and remained a well-known player. Will was proudest when he and his sons were on the same team.

Picnics were another family activity. Will loved eating outdoors, and for the slightest reason—or none at all—he would suggest a picnic. Huge baskets would be prepared and the family headed off for the beach or the nearby mountains. Years later, Jimmy Rogers, the youngest in the group, would joke that he was twelve years old before he realized that "the sand did not come with the hot dogs."

Perhaps Will enjoyed those hours with the family so intensely because in the early years there had never been enough time he could spend at home. He had missed so much of their growing up years, kept busy and far away by demanding schedules. There had been vaudeville, the Ziegfeld Follies, season after season of lecture tours, and then the many trips. Now that he was in motion pictures, and at home more, the children were grown up and all he could do was watch as they took off in different directions. There was no going back in time; no making up for missed occasions. Will knew it; the children, too, knew it. They were the ones who had to share their father with the country. But Will still felt himself the loving father, and he wanted to keep close to them.

Holidays meant a lot to Will. Even on his demanding lecture tours, he would break his routine and return home to California for the Christmas season. The year 1931 was one of the few times Will spent Christmas away from the family. On a round-the-world trip, he was in Shanghai on Christmas Day, and absolutely wretched.

Christmastime 1934, his last, was just not complete without daughter Mary at home. She was in the east, appearing in the play *On to Fortune*, starring Ilka Chase. Dad was proud of her, of course, but he would have preferred having her at the ranch for the holidays. He wrote her, putting into words how much he missed her, which he tried to hide behind an all-inclusive "we":

"We are all broke up at not being able to see you Xmas, we had planned a big time, and you not being here is going to knock it into about half what it was to be . . . " There is more to the letter, all of it private, all of it exposing Will's deep love for his family.

His was a strenuous life; Rogers would be the first one on a movie set, but he would usually take off about 4 P.M. with a war cry of "Santa Monica Canyon," which could be heard on adjacent sets. It was his public announcement that as far as he was concerned, the working day had ended, and that he was departing for the hills of home to fulfill any of his many public and private obligations or simply to rope some cattle or ride the trails of his ranch. If asked, on special occasions, he was always cooperative when the director required late work. Of course, there was the matter of the daily column which Will usually filed around noon. Should the assistant to the assistant director call him to the set, the honing of the column often had priority. And once it was written, Will would stop any passerby, whether grip or star, and read it out loud, to see the reaction. Almost everyone on the set knew what would appear the next morning under the heading of "Will Rogers Says." And if all the assistant directors kept persisting, Will at last—reluctantly—would come to the set. He had years of experience in these matters. First hurrying when the director's call came and then having to wait while still one more light had to be moved, or a camera angle needed changing. He had developed this philosophy which he passed on to co-star Lew Ayres: "No matter how late you are, you're never too late for pictures."

Film-star Peggy Wood said of Will that he had a habit not emulated by other stars:

> When Will Rogers and I appeared in the movie *Handy Andy*, we finished ahead of time, ahead of schedule, and that last day he stalled and stalled. In one scene he had to lie in bed, and he wouldn't get up . . . Only when he was assured that the crew would get their full pay, did he get off that bed. He was going to get them their full money—and he did.

In a weekly article, published in most newspapers March 10, 1935, Will expressed a thought he had carried with him for years. He wrote in part: "I never have been to that Alaska. I am crazy to go up there some time.'' Some who read this would remember it.

While Betty mentioned to friends that she thought Will, now in his mid-fifties, showed signs of slowing down, others, who did not know him as well, envied his energy. John Ford, who was directing Will's current film, *Steamboat Round the Bend*, complained that Will always beat him to the set in the morning. He tried to reason with Will:

> Once I said to him, ''look, I'm a late sleeper. I have to get up and stand in the shower bath for ten minutes, a cold shower. Then I have a cup of coffee, and dash down here, and I'm always a little late. But I'm down here at eight-thirty.''
>
> Will said, ''I'm an early riser. You know my cowboy training.'' So I told him, ''Well, will you hang out in your dressing room until I get on the set? You're making a bum out of me!''
>
> But he didn't. He wanted to visit with the grips and the cameraman and the rest of the cast, and whiz around and chat and talk, making jokes. I'd sneak on the set and he'd spot me, ''Ah, there he is! The late sleeper!''

True, Will had taken on a multitude of tasks which kept him busy much of the time, but none of them seemed a chore to him. He enjoyed what he was doing; but perhaps ''The Restless One'' had become even more restless. He, who never liked making plans a long way ahead, but rather moved as the spirit dictated, was already thinking where he would want to go once the film was completed. He talked of flying to Rio de Janeiro and from there taking one of the regular rides on the German Zeppelin leaving for the coast of Africa. But Will never made his reservation. And a few days later he had surprise visitors, Wiley and Mae Post.

Post had accomplished great feats as a flier, yet he had little to show for it. Will felt that Wiley deserved better; he had followed Wiley's exploits and tried to boost his fellow Oklahoman's sputtering career whenever he could. Wiley had fine ideas, but at times the fates—and perhaps his impatient, abrupt personality—shattered those plans.

Somehow a reporter, who must have overheard a private conversation, wrote a story about Will Rogers and Wiley Post planning a trip to Siberia. There was truth to it, but neither Wiley nor Will wanted any public talk about it. When a reporter posed the direct question whether Will was going tiger hunting with Wiley in Siberia, Rogers laughed it off: ''I can get as close to a tiger in the Los Angeles zoo as I want to.''

Three days later Wiley and Mae Post were ready to test the new plane Wiley had assembled by going on a long weekend. As they waited at the airport, surrounded by reporters, there was an unexpected development: Will Rogers arrived. He purchased a magazine and a pack of chewing gum, and to the reporters' surprise, climbed aboard. The trio flew to Albuquerque, New Mexico.

They visited with Waite Phillips, co-founder of Phillips Petroleum Co., at his famous Philmont ranch near Cimarron and Vermejo Park near Raton, both in New Mexico. Then the three flew over Bryce and Zion Canyons in Utah, set down on convenient spots long enough for Post to do some trout fishing, and then flew back via the Grand Canyon and the new Hoover Dam.

Filing his daily columns from New Mexico and Colorado, Will would not lie, nor could he make people forget what had been written; so he made light of it in his daily column:

> Wiley Post and I been blathering about flying over to a ranch in New Mexico and some guy with a poor slant on geography got it mixed up with Siberia in Russia. Looks like New Mexico has got a suit.

The plane was back at Burbank's Union Air Terminal by Monday, July 29. It is safe to assume that Wiley spoke to Will about his plans for a trip to Alaska and across Siberia, but Will did not make up his mind to go along—not yet. It was just another one of those ''future'' commitments he would rather not make. Whether Wiley told Will the whole story about the trip to Siberia and beyond shall never be known. If Will knew it, he never mentioned it.

But before there was any decision to be made, there was a film to be finished. And Will ran into his old friend Hal Roach. They had played polo together over the years, and whenever Will

needed to fly anywhere, he would rent Hal's plane and pilot. Will
was adamant about paying the going, regular rental fee. Because
of their close association, Hal felt ill at ease charging his friend for
a plane which stood idly at the airport, and a pilot who had
nothing to do. Hal tried to assess Will a small fraction of the actual
cost. Will saw through that, and would have none of it. The next
time Will came to ask Hal about renting his plane, he stopped off
at a plane rental concern first, found out the cost and confronted
Hal Roach with a check drawn for the full amount: "If you don't
want my check, forget the whole thing and I'll rent a plane
elsewhere!"

Hal, a committed polo player, had been invited to take a
polo team to Hawaii for a series of games against local teams. His
first thought had been to invite Will Rogers, Hollywood's foremost polo enthusiast. Then he had second thoughts:

> In the first place, we would rather have had Will than
> anybody else. But I never dreamed that he would want to
> go away for four weeks. Yet when he heard about the
> trip, he came up to me and expressed his desire to go. I
> said, "My God, Will, why didn't you let me know?" He
> sort of criticized me for not inviting him. I told him,
> "The Hawaiian people invited us to come over and play
> polo, and I've been having the damndest time trying to
> get a team together—I had no idea you'd want to go."
> Will said "Oh, Glory, I would have liked to go." So I said,
> "Well, you're in!" He looked down for a moment, then
> he said, "I promised Post that I'd go on a trip with him."
> I asked him, "Well, can't you change that and come with
> us?" So Will said, "Let me think about it." A day or so
> later he told me, "I don't think it's right for me to call this
> trip off; Wiley's got it all set up." So I said, "If by any
> chance you change your mind, please let me know.

John Ford owned a yacht, the *Araner*, which he had docked
a stone's throw from Rogers' ranch at Santa Monica. He gave a
party for Rogers and Post. Having now directed Will in three
motion pictures, he kept trying to persuade Will that they should
make another film together—perhaps in Hawaii. He was heading
there right after their current film was "in the can;" Ward Bond,

the actor and Ford's friend, was coming along and the three of them could have a great time in Hawaii. John Ford tried his best to induce Will to come along on the yacht. Will was tempted, but made a decision: "You keep your duck and go on the water, I'll take my eagle and fly."

Though Rogers is quoted as if he had made his decision to go with Post, he still had reservations. As Wiley was about to fly his new plane to Seattle to have pontoons attached, Will was supposed to have said, "When you get to Seattle, call me. I'll give you my decision then."

Wiley and Mae Post needed passports, the Russians insisted. Wiley had with him an expired and canceled passport; in his haste, he had apparently picked up his old passport, leaving the new one in Oklahoma City. Mae had never needed a passport before and did not own one.

On Monday, July 29, 1935, Wiley appeared before Robert Zimmerman, chief clerk of the United States District Court, in Los Angeles, seeking renewal of his canceled passport.

"When do you want it?" Zimmerman asked.

"I'd like it right away," Post answered. "I've planned to take off tomorrow at noon on a flight to Siberia."

But the chief clerk could not issue a renewal on a canceled passport. Wiley mentioned that he had another passport of later date, but that it was in a safety deposit box in Oklahoma City.

"Why don't you fly there and get it?" Zimmerman suggested.

Post, impatient to be on his way to Siberia, vetoed the idea. Zimmerman then sent a letter to the main passport office in San Francisco, requesting to be notified by telegram whether the Posts could pick up new passports there with a minimum of delay.

Fame had its advantages, and Wiley obtained the passports in San Francisco. When informed that Wiley Post would call, passport agent S. A. Owen kept his office open twenty minutes after regular closing time.

Then there was also the matter of Russian visas. Fortunately Alexander Troyanovsky, the Soviet Union's ambassador to the United States, though stationed in Washington, D.C., happened to be in San Francisco. He had come to be on hand for what was hoped to be a triumphal welcome for three Soviet fliers attempting to reach the United States non-stop from Moscow, via the North Pole.

Pilot Sigismund Levanevsky, co-pilot Boris Maidukoff, and navigator Victor Levchenko left Sholkovsky airport in Moscow on August 3. It was announced a few days later that a damaged oil feed line had forced the plane to turn back and land in Leningrad.

Ambassador Troyanovsky, being quite familiar with Wiley's plans through Fay Gillis Wells' correspondence with the Soviet embassy, granted the visas immediately. He also extended his warmest wishes for a successful flight.

Wiley and Mae arrived in Seattle at 6:30 P.M., August 1, 1935. Having checked into their room at the Olympic Hotel, Wiley Post picked up the telephone and called Will Rogers in Pacific Palisades, California, to learn his decision.

CHAPTER THREE

THE PLANE

It didn't do my nerve any good when they pointed
our plane out to me, for it had only one engine.
You know, there is some confidence attached
when you know there is a sort of bevy of engines,
and if one goes wrong, why, some of the others
will keep percolating. But I looked at this one and
thought: "Sister, if you stop on us, we are just
smeared over the landscape. . . ."
—Will Rogers, *Saturday Evening Post*,
October 23, 1926.

Wiley Post's new plane had no name. As if to stress its ignoble end
as a pile of debris in two feet of brackish water at the top of the
world—and its dubious origin in a warehouse containing second-
hand plane parts—it has been remembered as "that plane," and
much, much worse.

It was the practice of the time to personalize planes by
giving them names, which were painted in good-sized letters
along the fuselage or tail section. Sometimes this was done to
advertise a company or product, or to obtain popular financial
support; sometimes owners would try to transfer to a plan their
own, distinctive personality, or endow it with a superstitious
protection. Some of the best-known planes of the era included
Charles Lindbergh's *Spirit of St. Louis*, Jimmy Doolittle's *Super
Solution* (for Shell Petroleum), and Sir Charles Kingsford-Smith's
Lady Southern Cross. There seemed no end to the ingenuity, for
there were names beginning with almost every letter of the
alphabet, from *Akita* through *Black Hornet, City of New York,
Doctor Brinkley III, Early Bird, Fort Worth, Gilmore Lion,* all
the way past *Viking*, Post's own *Winnie Mae*, to *Yankee Doodle*.
Will Rogers referred to Post's new plane in his columns as "the
little red bus," and "Post's Toasty;" Wiley was heard to call it
"Aurora Borealis" a few times. But those were polite nicknames,

thought up on the spur of the moment. No name for the plane was ever registered.

Experienced pilots and mechanics took one look at the "unusual-looking" plane, which was easily identifiable as the only one of its kind, and dubbed it "Wiley's Orphan"; or still more to the point, alluding to its illegitimate origin, "Wiley's Bastard." Lockheed, as registered manufacturer of some of the parts, turned a corporate back on its hybrid stepchild:

> Officials of the Lockheed plant at Burbank yesterday said the craft had not borne the official, factory stamp of approval since it was not a product of the concern. The ship, it was said, incorporated two entirely different engineering designs and was regarded therefore, more or less as a freak.

Unfortunately, whether "Orphan," "Bastard," or "Freak," they were all right. The plane was conceived in Wiley's mind on February 11, 1935. On that date he entered into a purchase agreement with Charley Babb, the famous west coast plane broker, to buy a second-hand plane, a Lockheed Orion 9-E Special, U.S. License No. NC 12283; and the wing from a long departed Lockheed Explorer, U.S. License No. NR 101W, "as is" and "where is." The price paid for the Orion is not known; the bill of sale between Babb and Post simply used the standard phrase: " . . . for and in consideration of the sum of ten ($10.00) dollars to me in hand . . ." Depression prices for used Orions went from $17,500 down to $10,000, depending on equipment and condition. The plane and the unrelated wing were to be wed to form a new plane. There was perhaps a certain logic to this strange union, but none advanced by any engineer or aerodynamic authority; it was a merger solely devised by Wiley Post and happenstance: Post needed a plane, and the Orion and the unattached wing just chanced to be available at the same place, at the same time.

A Lockheed Orion had retractable landing gear, which folded neatly into "wells" on the underside of its low wing. Wiley bought the Explorer wing because he knew that a solid wing would be needed as a base for the mounting of first wheels, and then pontoons—or floats, as they are called by bush pilots. The *Los Angeles Examiner* reported:

"Post said he wanted a wing with a large lifting surface,"
Babb said, "I assumed that he knew what he was about
and it seemed logical when he explained that he was
going to put a Lockheed Sirius wing on a Lockheed
Orion fuselage, saying this combination would give him
greater visibility. The Sirius wing is more practical for
pontoons and skis; also wheels, and 'since there are more
lakes in the northern country on which to land than
there are landing fields, I'll do most of my flying up there
with pontoons,' Post told me."

Each piece—plane and wing—had its own story; each, completely separate from the other, had found its way to Babb's
warehouse. The plane had been there only three days, the wing
had come a long time ago. Lockheed's Orion was one of America's
superior aircraft. It was a natural progression from Lockheed's
famous "Vega" series; its great popularity had established the
company's name. The Orion, with a "low wing," as opposed to
Vega's high wing, offered greater speed and a more profitable
operation to passenger carriers. It could carry up to six passengers,
though with such a load, quarters were somewhat confined.

During its production run, 1931 to 1934, a total of 35
Orions were built. Transcontinental and Western Air, Inc. (TWA)
bought two Orions and incorporated them into its passenger line.
So efficient were the Orions that TWA purchased a third one on
May 28, 1933 (U.S. License No. NC-12283). It was part of a relay
system between Newark, New Jersey, and Los Angeles, California,
on regular schedules well into 1934. Originally equipped with a
450-hp Pratt & Whitney Wasp engine, TWA exchanged it in late
1933 for a 550-hp Wasp. This made the plane even faster and
allowed it to carry additional weight. Then, a ruling by the Civil
Aeronautics Authority mandated that henceforth all passenger
planes carry a pilot and a co-pilot for safety reasons. It made the
Orion obsolete for passenger flights. There was no way to fit a co-
pilot into the small cockpit. The plane was sold to Charley Babb.
While owned by TWA, the plane sustained two minor accidents:
on June 10, 1933, damage in Amarillo was so slight that no major
repair was required and the plane was inspected and approved for
service just two weeks later; on February 5, 1934, the plane was
returned to Lockheed for rear spar and wing tip repairs, damages

that were caused in another minor mishap. The plane was almost immediately put back into service, and no further accidents were reported.

Unfounded stories circulating at the time—and ever since— tell that the plane had been in an accident just prior to the sale to Babb. In fact such a nonexistent accident was advanced as the reason for the sale. The truth is that the plane was in perfect flying condition when TWA sold it on February 8, 1935.

The wing had its own history: it came from a limited production series—a handful of Lockheed planes, called "Explorer." The prototype was specially designed for the famous polar explorer, Sir George Hubert Wilkins, and named in his honor. Wilkins (he had not yet been knighted when he placed the order) never took possession of the plane. An affliction known to many visionaries prevented him from consummating the deal— his funds ran out. In April 1930, the third plane in this series was built for Colonel Arthur C. Goebel, a veteran pilot of record transcontinental flights. Goebel planned a Paris-to-New York Flight in his new plane. The Lockheed Explorer, now painted blue and yellow, was named *Yankee Doodle*. Testing the plane in California, he was not satisfied with its performance and refused to take delivery.

Yankee Doodle, ordered, painted, named, and now abandoned, was eventually purchased by the Pure Oil Company of Chicago, to be used in an advertising campaign. Repainted blue with white lettering and renamed *Blue Flash*, the plane was to be flown by pilot Roy W. Ammel. Almost from the beginning, ill-fortune haunted this plane. Ammel took possession of the plane at the Lockheed factory in Burbank, California. On the way east, engine trouble forced him to land at Gila Bend, Arizona, where fire damaged the *Blue Flash*. A Lockheed crew came from California, disassembled the Explorer and shipped it back to the plant for repair.

In September 1930, Roy Ammel and the plane finally reached New York City. Restless after weeks of delays, Ammel suggested a non-stop flight from New York to Panama. It had never been done and would get a lot of publicity. And so, on November 9, 1930, Ammel left Floyd Bennett Field and headed south. He faced strong head winds and claimed he had to fly an extra one thousand miles, just to make up for being blown off-course. After 24 hours and 35 minutes in the air, a very tired Ammel set the plane down on the runway at France Field in the Canal Zone.

Preparing the return trip via Chicago, Ammel had the plane transferred to the longer, but as yet unfinished, runway at Ancon. With fuel tanks topped, Pure Oil's *Blue Flash* raced down the uneven runway, skidded, dug her nose into the ground, flipped her tail up and crashed on her back. Fearing that gasoline spilling out of damaged tanks over the hot engine would cause a fire, rescuers quickly chopped an unconscious Ammel out of the fuselage. Luckily there was no fire, but the plane was a loss. Only the wing was salvaged, and somehow it found its way to Charley Babb's warehouse and began to gather dust—until Post discovered it more than four years later.

Wiley had plane and wing immediately transferred to Jack Waterhouse's hangar at Pacific Airmotive, Ltd., at Union Air Terminal, Burbank. By February 15, the plane had been checked out. Pacific Airmotive then sent the following list, detailing parts needed and work required, to Wiley Post, who was still at Bartlesville, Oklahoma:

The following equipment will be needed as soon as possible:

Wasp motor	Bypass valve
Fuel pump	Vacuum pump
Battery	Vacuum pump regulator valve
Navigation lights	Venturi tubes
Pitot tube	Propellor [sic]
Ignition switch	

Instruments:

Oil pressure	Compass
Fuel pressure	Turn and bank
Oil temperature	Gyro
Altimeter	Artificial horizon
Rate of climb	Thermocouple
Clock	Airspeed
Manifold pressure gauge	

Above: W.C. Fields, Wiley Post, and Will Rogers at the Los Angeles premiere of *David Copperfield*, in which Fields starred. (Photo: Academy of Motion Picture Arts and Sciences.) *Left:* Will and Wiley visit with Joe Crosson at his gold mine. It was here that Will heard the adventure of Mickey and the bear, the story found in his typewriter. (Photo: Pan Am Airways.)

Top: The Lockheed Explorer, restricted license number NR 101 W *Yankee Doodle,* being fine-tuned. Found unsatisfactory, the plane was sold. *Middle:* The same plane, now repainted and named *Blue Flash,* being readied for its flight to the Canal Zone, where it would crash. The only remaining part, the wing, was bought in 1935 by Wiley for use on his newly acquired Lockheed Orion. *Bottom:* The Lockheed Orion, as passenger plane still owned by TWA before it was sold to Charles H. Babb, February 8, 1935. Three days later Wiley bought it. (All photos: Richard Sanders Allen.)

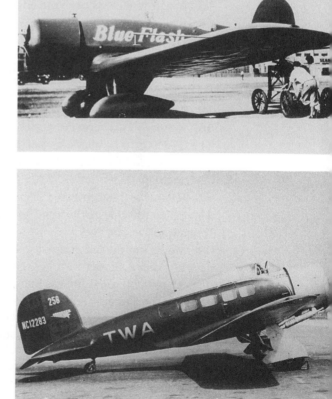

Make all shipments of parts to the Attention of, or notify
Otto Santoff, 331 N. Lima St., Burbank, California.

The following work to be done on fuselage:

1. Remove linen on fuselage and drive down all nails,
   recover fuselage and paint as per your specifications
   or best practice.
2. Remove paint on tail surfaces and repaint, install on
   ship.
3. Replace plywood on wing nose leading edge, install
   cabin floor in wing. Place all pulleys and necessary
   compression tubes from Orion wing to Sirius [sic]
   wing for adaption on Orion fuselage.
4. Install leading edge landing lights.
5. Make necessary landing gear changes for Orion fuselage hook-up.
6. Install wheels as per your instructions as to kind of
   wheels.
7. Fireshield to be adaptable to new series H Wasp
   engine.
8. New instrument board as per your instruments and
   layout.
9. New Aileron hook-up.
10. New cables wherever needed.
11. Cowling to be made as per latest engineering data
    furnished by J. Gerschler [assistant chief engineer at
    Lockheed].
12. Seats to be installed as per Orion setup as formerly used.
13. Collector ring to be used as is unless changes are
    authorized by you.
14. Motor mount and controls to be used as installed by
    Lockheed factory.
15. All plumbing, oil and gas lines to be of annealled [sic]
    copper tubing.
16. If new fittings for wing are necessary, to be designed
    by Lockheed Engineers and made by Lockheed, parts
    to be furnished by you.
17. All instruments, motor and accessories to be fur-
    nished by you as per separate list.

18. Cabin to be weather proofed as much as possible.
19. Cockpit to have heater as per your suggestion.
20. Ship to near NR license and be licensed by Department of Commerce.
21. Ship to be painted as per your color scheme.
22. All parts and accessories to be rushed as fast as possible so as not to delay ship assembly.
23. All cockpit accessories for Orion landing gear to be removed and held until shipping orders received from you as to disposition of same.
24. Any and all changes to be in writting [sic] unless you personally are at hangar at time any changes are to be made.

Wiley's instructions were to have the plane painted "Waco Red" with silver trim.

On April 10, 1935, Pratt & Whitney shipped a 550-hp Wasp engine #5778, model S 3H1-G. The company agreed to lend Wiley this brand-new engine on "rental" terms, even though it was listed as being worth $3,500. Actually, they were not in the rental business, nor did they expect any money in this transaction. But corporate wisdom felt that helping a man like Wiley Post would receive a lot of free publicity. After all, he had already circled the world twice in a plane powered by a Pratt & Whitney engine.

The Wasp was a very powerful engine that could develop 600 horsepower for take-off; correspondingly, it used a lot of fuel. For that brief period at take-off it would guzzle gasoline at the staggering rate of 68 gallons per hour; on climb, consumption was an excessive 43 gallons. Even when gently cruising, the expected fuel use was still a high 32 gallons per hour.

In addition to the items mentioned earlier, the plane was to be equipped with an overpowered Pratt & Whitney engine weighing 145 pounds more than the original, a borrowed propeller adding an extra 50 pounds, De-icers, 45 pounds; tools and rations, 19 pounds; engine cowel, 50 pounds; electric starter, 35 pounds; battery, 65 pounds; generator, 50 pounds; flares and holders, 50 pounds; radio, 135 pounds; heater, 22 pounds; 2 landing lights, 15 pounds; fire extinguisher, 8 pounds; and a

non-retractable landing gear moved the center of gravity even
further forward. Most seats were removed to increase the storage
area. Then Wiley installed more fuel tanks; just the smaller, new
30-gallon tank under the pilot's seat, weighed 32 pounds empty,
and 212 pounds when full. In all, Post increased the plane's fuel
load by 110 gallons, extending the plane's range by roughly three
hours flying time.

The propeller presented a problem at first. As the Orion
had originally been designed, it was a land plane on wheels; thus
the appropriate propeller blades easily cleared the ground. Since
Wiley intended to exchange the wheels for pontoons, the front of
the plane would sit much lower and the original blade tips would
impact the water. Wiley switched to a Hamilton Standard constant-
speed type, controllable pitch, three-bladed, aluminum-alloy propeller; its blades were shorter and easily cleared the water.

While work on the plane was going on, Wiley was still busy
preparing the *Winnie Mae* for stratospheric flights. James E.
Reed, the U.S. Department of Commerce Inspector stationed at
the Union Air Terminal in Burbank, came by daily to inspect the
quality of workmanship on Wiley Post's new plane. That plane
was not "re-designed," it was a plane that had never been
"designed." Wiley started with the basic concepts that a plane
needs a body, a wing, an engine, a propeller, and an under-
carriage—and simply went out and found one of each. The parts
he found were first class—no doubt about that—but they did not
belong together. In August, 1935, the Associated Press claimed
with hindsight:

> Post's resolve to build his own ship instead of buying a
> new standard plane caused considerable comment among
> fliers, who believed limited financial resources influ-
> enced the noted pilot in going ahead with his plans. . . .
> When the plane was finished, Post expressed approval of
> the job, airport mechanics recalled.
> "It's the same type construction as the *Winnie
> Mae*," he said,. "That's a Vega. This is a specially built
> low wing job. It is two planes in one."

Of course the new plane was not a Vega, anyone could see
that. And Wiley must have realized it more than anyone, for when

work on the new plane was completed, Wiley Post was the only one to take it up for a test flight. The *Los Angeles Times* of August 17, 1935, reported that "Post expressed his own approval of the job . . . the fuselage is twenty-eight feet long; the wing spread forty-three feet. The tanks hold 220 gallons of gasoline. . . . "

It is surprising that all data given in this interview with the *Times* reporter are misstatements. The correct fuselage length was 27 feet, 6 inches, while the wing span was 48 feet, 6 inches (five-and-a-half feet wider than Post had claimed); the tanks could hold 270 gallons, not the 220 gallons claimed. Did Wiley really not know those facts?

What Wiley had learned on his test flight, but had not told anyone, least of all Inspector Reed, was that his new creation was seriously nose-heavy. According to General James Doolittle, this was no small consideration:

> There are forgiving airplanes, and there are unforgiving airplanes. An airplane—which, if you make a mistake—corrects that mistake, is a forgiving aeroplane; an aeroplane which amplifies a mistake, is an unforgiving aeroplane. Some aeroplanes, if you take your hands off the stick, will fly along by themselves; some have to be controlled at all times."

Wiley, an experienced pilot, must have had no doubt that there was too much weight forward of the center of gravity. In flight, this nose-heaviness would cause the plane to assume a diving attitude.

The nose-heaviness of an airplane, or indeed any temporary imbalance to a point, can be counteracted by the pilot. He simply has to compensate for the plane's inclination to deviate from the norm. What the pilot's counteraction does, however, is to limit the plane's remaining maneuverability. Every plane can only be controlled so far; if part of that control is needed just to keep the plane on an even course, less maneuverability is left to control the plane. In this particular case, the plane would constantly tend to dive. Wiley would have had to put the plane into a climb attitude to overcome that downward drive—just to stay level. Using part of the plane's ability to climb for the purpose of just staying level would then leave less capability to climb in an emergency. A valid simile might be an automobile that pulls to the right. It can only be driven by over-steering to the left, so that a straight course is achieved. Later, when a left turn is needed, the driver finds that since he has been steering left all along, he now has a much smaller turning capability left.

As any seasoned pilot could, so Wiley believed that he could fly the plane; he would just have to be exceedingly alert. Wiley must have known that should he ever lose engine power to provide the essential lift, the plane's built-in dive would add to the earth's gravitational pull. If the power failed at a high altitude, the plane would dive earthward, but could—after a substantial drop—be induced into a glide. Then a dead-stick landing might be possible, if the terrain allowed it. Should power be lost at low altitude, however, there would be no margin for error in which to regain control.

From interviews and newly discovered records it is clear that the plane was already critically nose-heavy before floats were attached. Lockheed had correctly predicted the problem: an assistant chief engineer, Jimmy Gerschler, claimed that Post's suggested additions would alter the aerodynamic integrity of the ship and that "You'll be in trouble if there's just a slight power loss on takeoff." The warning went unheeded. The conversion to seaplane added considerably to the plane's instability. Such a lack of stability, however, could have been counter-balanced had Post only taken the time, money, and trouble to do so. Of course, such counter-balancing would have meant to add weight to the tail section, which would have reduced the cargo capacity. But Wiley simply kept the plane's imbalance a secret when he applied for an aircraft license on July 23, 1935.

On the application, Wiley again made several misstatements of fact: fuel capacity is now stated as 260 gallons, instead of the 270 gallons; and it is declared that a Sirius wing had been added, when in fact, the much larger wing from an Explorer had been substituted.

Under Point #9 of this application, Wiley applied for a *restricted* license, defining the aircraft's purpose as: "Long Cross Country Flights and special Test Work."

Not everything seemed to have gone well at Pacific Airmotive Corporation. Wiley and Mae had originally planned to leave July 22 for Seattle, but their departure was delayed. The plane, so the company announced, was "not quite ready" for a long flight. The Posts were "in seclusion."

After an additional hold-up for passports and visas in San Francisco, Wiley and Mae Post finally reached Bryn Mawr field at Renton, Washington, at 6:30 P.M. on August 1, 1935. The flight from San Francisco had taken five and a half hours. The *Seattle Post-Intelligencer* reported: "A dog, a small boy and a woman wiping her hands on her kitchen apron. That was the entire 'crowd' and reception committee." Indeed, when the plane set down on the suburban airstrip, twelve miles south of Seattle, only Marian (wife of Field Manager Ashley Bridgham), their son Jimmy, and the family dog were on hand. It was young Jimmy who first realized that Wiley Post had landed at his front door. Mrs. Bridgham, who had come to the door of her residence, would not believe it. "No," she said, "the plane's too little, Jimmy." But seconds later she had to agree with her son. "When they got out of the plane, I invited Mrs. Post into the house. She said she was certainly thrilled about making the trip with her husband. William Lindsley and Jack Waley, attendants at the field, took charge of the plane."

Though the Posts had been expected, the explanation for the small reception committee was simple; an eager crowd was waiting for Post at Boeing Field, a dozen miles away. But Wiley had flown to the smaller airport, because it was at Renton's Northwest Air Service that the wheels were to be exchanged for floats.

Now that the final part of the plane was about to be added, it would at last be exactly as Wiley envisioned it. But all along its path of assembly, most people shook their heads and clucked their tongues, but no one told Wiley that he should not fly it.

Nobody, that is, until Joe Crosson said it to him in Fairbanks. But Wiley flew anyway, because by that time he had convinced himself that he had mastered the "Bastard."

CHAPTER FOUR

THE DAYS OF AUGUST

Rain is not so bad; it's how low the clouds are—
"visibility," I think, is the term.
      —Will Rogers, *Saturday Evening Post*,
          Jan. 28, 1928.

The Great Depression continues to grip nations around the globe. In 1935 not only does unemployment seem incurable as hunger ravages populations everywhere, but unrest—domestic and international—threatens once stable governments.

A plebiscite in the Saar advocates a return to Hitler's Third Reich by a margin of nine to one. The German Führer then unilaterally abrogates the Versailles Treaty: specifically rejecting the clauses limiting German military power, while openly proclaiming the establishment of a new German Army, Navy, and Air Force. Full conscription is instituted once again. Berlin signs an agreement with London, promising not to expand the German navy to a size larger than thirty-five percent of the Royal Navy.

Germany, now dominated by the National Socialist (*Nazi*) Party, introduces the infamous Nüremberg Laws, depriving native German Jews of their citizenship. The state-controlled news and propaganda bureau begins its drive to force the non-Nazi press out of existence, effectively regulating all information and garroting any other source.

Heinrich Himmler, the son of a secondary schoolmaster and once briefly employed by a fertilizer manufacturer, has swiftly risen in the Nazi Party. Named police chief of Munich, he had established the first concentration camp at Dachau, a suburb.

This is the prototype for scores of concentration and extermination camps to follow. Appointed leader of the *SS* (Black Shirts), he initiates project *Lebensborn* (Life Source), to produce a pure Aryan race of blond, blue-eyed Nordic beings to carry on the "thousand-year Reich."

Alarmed by the rapidly growing German military might in central Europe, the nations of Britain, France, and Italy convene a conference at Stresa, Italy. There they attempt to forge a defensive union in an effort to display a common front—at least on paper. Little is done by either Britain or France. Italy arms, but for a different purpose: dictator Benito Mussolini, like his counterpart in Germany, is bent on military adventurism.

Emperor Haile Selassie of Ethiopia, fearing for the safety of his country, desperately appeals to President Franklin D. Roosevelt for support. The president rejects his request, saying "The U.S. is loath to believe that either Italy, or Ethiopia, would use other than pacific means to settle the dispute." In October Italy invades Ethiopia.

Northern Ireland's Belfast has anti-Catholic riots and a number of Catholic families are expelled to the Free State. Naturally there are reprisals in the south. Ireland also amends its criminal code; henceforth it will be a felony to advertise, sell, or import any form of birth control device or method.

In Russia, basic essentials are desperately in short supply and many people take the law into their own hands. Conditions can best be judged by Stalin's severe edicts: Soviet children, so the new laws proclaim, will be subject to the identical punishment as adults: eight years in a labor camp for the theft of corn or potatoes, five years for stealing cucumbers.

But in a world plagued by unemployment, paradoxically, one-half feverishly prepares for war while diplomatic deception still works full time. In addition to the naval limitation agreement between Germany and Britain, which Hitler has no intention of observing, there are other, equally weak accords. France and Russia now sign a five-year treaty of mutual assistance, but in the fourth year of that pact, Russia will sign a far more advantageous treaty with Germany. Later, France will be attacked by Germany, while Russia will sit idly by, ignoring its vowed assistance. When, however, Russia is attacked by Germany, Stalin immediately asks for help from the Allies. Russia and Czechoslovakia sign a mutual-assistance pact, which Russia will later use to help herself to Czechoslovakia. The Soviet Union and the United States sign a trade pact.

Fabled Persia changes its name to Iran, by order of Reza Shah Pahlevi, who has ruled the country for ten years.

There is serious trouble in the United States. At a time of catastrophic unemployment, there is disunity in Labor's ranks. A new labor organization is formed when a group of dissidents walk out of the American Federation of Labor (AFL). This new splinter unit, the Committee for Industrial Organization (CIO), elects John L. Lewis, former head of the United Mine Workers, as their new president.

Louisiana citizenry demonstrates against the "dictatorship" of Senator Huey Long. This general unrest threatens to get out of hand after 500 national guardsmen force 100 demonstrators to surrender, and then fire tear gas into a group of unarmed sympathizers. Martial law is declared. In September, Huey Long, the "Kingfish," will be assassinated in Baton Rouge.

A killer hurricane wipes out the Florida East Coast Railroad line between Florida City and Key West and sweeps across the Keys, killing 400 people.

Dust storms in the Southwest continue to blow away precious top soil, leaving barren fields. Highway traffic is stopped, schools close, and business is at a standstill, as the sun is obliterated and day is turned into night. The Dust Bowl, extending primarily from Texas across Oklahoma to Nebraska and Colorado, becomes an open wound of devastation in the landscape of America; it will take decades to heal.

Bruno Richard Hauptmann is tried for the kidnap-slaying of Charles and Anne Lindbergh's baby. After thirty-two days of court procedures, during which every phase of the crime is recreated in the nation's newspapers, the verdict is rendered. The jury of eight men and four women find Hauptmann guilty. Still protesting his innocence, he will be executed.

Fred and "Ma" Barker, members of the notorious Karpis-Barker gang, are gunned down by federal agents near Ocklawaha, Florida. In Newark, New Jersey gangster "Dutch" Schultz is "rubbed out" by a newly formed New York City crime syndicate.

But all is not wrong with the world. A German chemist, Gerhard Domagk, discovers the first sulpha drug, named prontosil.

It will be used to combat streptococcal infections. British inventor A. Edwin Stevens manufacturers an electronic hearing aid, the first wearable model, though it weighs two-and-a-half pounds.

Congress passes the Social Security Act, providing old-age benefits and unemployment insurance. At Geneva, the League of Nations, founded to end all conflicts for ever, moves into a gleaming white palace, costing six million dollars. In Washington, D.C., the U.S. Supreme Court, too, moves into its own Vermont marble quarters.

In American homes, fifty million chickens are consumed, even though they cost more per pound than red meat. The first hot meal on a plane in flight is served aboard a Pan Am Clipper. And while this is the year Alcoholics Anonymous is founded, it is also the year in which beer in cans is first introduced.

English inventor Robert Watson-Watt builds the first practical radar defense system for detecting aircraft. The French liner *S.S. Normandie* wins the symbolic "Blue Ribbon" for the speediest transatlantic crossing, taking 107 hours and 33 minutes. Renowned flier Amelia Earhart solos from Honolulu to California in eighteen-and-a-half hours, locating Oakland's landing strip in a typical Bay Area fog.

On America's stages, the big hits are George Gershwin's *Porgy and Bess*; Robert Sherwood's *The Petrified Forest*; Emlyn Williams' *Night Must Fall*; and Maxwell Anderson's *Winterset*.

The most popular songs hummed, strummed, or whistled are: "Begin the Beguine," "Red Sails in the Sunset," "The Music Goes 'Round and 'Round," "Just One of Those Things," and, from *Porgy and Bess*, the theme song of the era, "I Got Plenty o' Nuthin'."

With money scarce, a few pennies still buy escape at the movies; and Hollywood makes better and more spectacular films. *Mutiny on the Bounty* with Clark Gable and Charles Laughton will win the Academy Award as best picture of the year. *A Midsummer Night's Dream*, with James Cagney, Olivia de Havilland, Joe E. Brown, and a young Mickey Rooney, will win for Hal Mohr, a write-in candidate, the Academy Award as the best director of photography. Other outstanding films: *The Story of Louis Pasteur* with Paul Muni; *Anna Karenina* with Greta Garbo and Frederick March; *The Thirty-Nine Steps* with Robert Donat and Madeleine Carroll; and *The Informer*, directed by John Ford, which will win its star, Victor McLaglen, an Academy Award as best actor.

And when the magazine Motion Picture Herald publishes the list of the top ten box-office stars of the past year, plain, folksy Will Rogers leads such timeless greats as: Clark Gable, Janet Gaynor, Wallace Beery, Mae West, Joan Crawford, Bing Crosby, Shirley Temple, Marie Dressler, and Norma Shearer, in that order. This surprises no one, except Will Rogers. At fifty-five years of age, he finds himself the nation's father image, its spokesman, its conscience. Pleased but unimpressed with the honor, Will is looking forward to a vacation. The question is: where to go? He has several offers, and several plans of his own—and then, there is Wiley Post with his flight to Alaska and west, to Europe.

Only at the moment Wiley Post telephoned the ranch in Pacific Palisades on August 1, 1935, did Will Rogers make his decision: he was going to join Wiley in Seattle! In his heart, Rogers had wanted to go to Alaska all along. However, there had been several personal considerations that must have caused him to delay that final commitment as long as possible. Betty Rogers had been present when Wiley and Mae Post had first approached Will about it, and she was immediately troubled by the idea. Flying around Alaska seemed safe enough, but she had seen parts of Siberia. She knew its enormity of space and distances, its inhospitality. It was not that she had premonitions of a crash; what she envisioned was Will and Wiley lost somewhere in that immense, featureless North. Once forced to set down, a tiny plane would be difficult, if not impossible, to find. In her mind she saw them missing, exposed to the elements, hungry, unable to communicate with the outside world. Hers was a reasonable concern.

Will tried to calm her. He assured her that he had not yet decided to fly with Wiley all the way across Siberia; quite probably he would return home from Alaska, while Wiley and Mae would continue without him. The decision about Siberia, he soothed Betty, would be made only after he had seen Alaska. Then, Will offered a brand-new suggestion.

As Will was going to be away in Alaska for some weeks, Betty had planned to leave California also, flying to New York and then taking the train for Skowhegan, Maine, where their daughter Mary, was a member of the cast at the Lakewood Theatre. A young actress, with Broadway appearances to her credit, Mary now had a motion picture contract, earning it under the assumed name of Mary Howard, so that she would not capitalize on her father's fame. Will was immensely proud of his daughter, but knowing the vagaries of the acting profession, he wanted Mary to have sound training in all the facets of her chosen field. He had suggested summer stock for the experience it would provide. Mary, chaperoned by Betty's sister Theda, affectionately called "Aunt Dick" by everyone, had been in Maine since the season started. As actor Keenan Wynn described her: "Aunt Dick was the duenna of all times. You know, she didn't carry a .44, but she sure gave you that impression."

Will now offered Betty his new plan. Should he—mind you, should he—decide to accompany Wiley across Siberia to Europe, would Betty join him in Europe and the two of them would see the sights and then come back together? Betty agreed, though she was not too anxious to travel alone to Europe; she would much prefer for Will to return directly from Alaska. Somehow, she knew better; she remembered how just the year before, in 1934, Will, she and the boys had ridden that tedious train across Siberia. It had been such a monotonous journey; she recalled only too well how restless Will had been; how he wanted to be up in the air, looking over the landscape from a plane. If only the Russians had kept their word last year, and provided the plane at Novosibirsk, as they had promised; she was almost certain that Will would now want to fly with Wiley to see Siberia from the air.

Yet, she could also see the joy on Will's face when he talked about Alaska. He looked tired, she noticed; for the first time in his life his heavy schedule had begun to wear him down. He looked forward to a vacation. Possibly, she thought, a leisurely trip would do him a lot of good; perhaps she worried unnecessarily.

Northwest Air Service, located in Renton, Washington, at the southern end of Lake Washington, was the only government-approved shop in the Northwest specializing in airplane conversion. Probably every pontoon-or ski-equipped plane between Seattle, Pt. Barrow, Alaska, and northwestern Canada had work done by this company at some time. Owner Alan Blum zealously guarded the excellent reputation his company had earned; Johnny Blum, Alan's brother—while also active in the firm—was better known as a courageous pilot who would fly anywhere at any time.

Here, at Northwest Air Service, veteran workmen began work on Wiley's plane. They replaced the wheels with used EDO J-5300 floats and rudders. There had been problems with the electrical system and an overhauled generator and a new electric starter were installed. It was routine work for the experienced crew.

Over the years more myths have developed around the floats than for any other part of Wiley's plane. The most popular story claims that the floats were wrong for an Orion/Explorer, and originally had belonged on a Fokker. That particular legend is easy to disprove since the records of all Fokkers built in America show not a single one that had been on floats at that time.

Another legend has it that the floats were too large, and thus caused the crash. Alan Blum explained that the EDO factory had issued charts that prescribed the correct size and displacement of floats for specific weights. For Post's plane, the EDO J-5300 was the correct size.

Lloyd Jarman, veteran Alaskan mechanic and plane authority, tells an interesting tale: pilot Alex Holden, and Jarman (as his mechanic) were flying a Pacific Alaska Airways' (PAA) Fairchild 71 from Juneau to Funter Bay, on Admiralty Island. Coasting after a landing the plane struck a submerged log, which severely damaged the plane's left float. The set was shipped back to Edo Corporation, at College Point, Queens, New York, for repairs. As Jarman tells the story, it seemed that those same floats—now repaired— were on hand when Post brought his plane in for conversion. Joe Crosson, speaking for PAA, made arrangements to lend the floats to his friend Wiley. Proof is provided by a Seattle reporter who filed a story that stated: "A four-inch riveted aluminum square covered a tell-tale patch on one pontoon." Furthermore, photographs clearly show that the left float on Wiley's plane had been repaired. This, however, would have had no effect on the pontoons' performance.

If still further proof is needed, the original Work Order #1006 by Northwest Air Service—dated August 6, 1935—shows as its first item: PICK UP FLOATS AT ALASKA STEAMSHIP COMPANY, and as its second item: PICK UP ACCESSORIES FROM PACIFIC AIRWAYS. It is obvious from this invoice that the floats used came from PAA, as there is no charge for "floats" on this invoice. This is a most detailed invoice, listing such minute parts as "4½ inch nuts—12 cents," and "8⅝ steel washers, 16 cents."

Surely Northwest Air Service would not overlook such large charges as "floats" and "accessories." Thus both came from PAA.

The electrical replacements are properly itemized:

1 - M2101 Solenoid switch	$13.50
Rebuild Armature	15.00
Overhaul Generator	26.00

Cornered by reporters, Wiley announced that he and his wife would not be accompanied by Fay Gillis Wells, the aviatrix, as originally planned, but that he "may pick up" another passenger at Seattle. "I expect to hunt a little and fish a little—and look around a little, too. I hope to get a chance at a Siberian tiger."

Here in Seattle, Wiley Post had problems, too. What had upset him in the early morning of August 2 is not known, but when he walked into Northwest Air Service, he was in a foul mood. He snarled at reporters, shouted at workmen, and "switched on no-sunshine charm for the curious youngsters, airport mechanics and interviewers who saw him." Post behaved unlike the shy, unassuming man he had been portrayed. When a local newspaperman asked him when he and Mrs. Post planned to leave Seattle, Wiley turned abruptly and thundered: "I don't even know if Mrs. Post will go all the way with me. Why don't you ask her." It was this remark that started malicious rumors that eventually found their way into print.

The *Seattle Post-Intelligencer's* headlines read, "WILEY POST, IT SEEMS, WAS JUST A LITTLE ANNOYED!" and described Wiley as "sour and glum." Nothing at Northwest Air Service seemed to be going as Wiley thought it should. Wiley "gave a first-rate demonstration of annoyance this forenoon," wrote the observer.

> "Who's in charge around here?" Post wanted to know when he learned the deck plates were set a fraction of an inch to one side of where they should have been set. Bustling mechanics gulped.
>
> "Let's get some action." Post demanded. The mechanics hurried to get some action. Angrily he strode about the hangar where the crimson mono-plane lay, picking up parts and tossing them down.

Flying, not glad-handing, is Wiley Post's business, he figures. That was why he stood with hands thrust in the pockets of his unpressed suit, wisps of blond hair blowing down over his forehead, a squint in his uncovered right eye, and gave his splendid performance as a celebrity 'with a mad on.'

When questioned about Post's display of annoyance, Alan Blum, owner of Northwest Air Service, recalled:

I honestly believe the reporter who wrote that piece was either dreaming or was at the Renton Airport (Bryn Mawr) on an off day (either for him or for Wiley), we all have them, of course.

I can't believe the reporter's statement that deck plates were off center. If they were off center they were made that way on purpose by the factory. And further, this was Post's first experience with floats and I doubt he would have known if such plates should or should not be centered.

I discount entirely the quote "Who's in charge around here" etc., as he knew full well who was when he made the request for us to do the work and certainly none of my men would "gulp". We had a justifiable reputation of years of excellence and I don't believe anyone ever questioned our competence.

More than a thousand miles to the south, at the Rogers household in Pacific Palisades, California, everything was falling into place. Betty reminded Will that there were some letters to be answered: there were also other things beginning to pile up on his desk. Amon Carter, Fort Worth newspaper publisher, politician, and Will's old friend, had sent his grandchildren's autograph books. Betty suggested that Will at least sign them so she could return them. But Will settled the matter with the promise to take care of all of it when he returned.

Now that Will Rogers had made his decision to fly with Wiley, there were things to do, and to be done swiftly. Until the very last moment, finishing touches on his latest film, *Steamboat Round the Bend*, kept him busy.

Will thought he needed to have his passport validated and, of course, he would have to obtain a Russian visa. He decided to take care of both of those chores in San Francisco, on Monday morning, on the way to Seattle.

Saturday morning, August 3, Will went to the Bank of America, where he kept an account. He wrote out a check for $7,540, covering a $5,000 letter of credit, $2,040 worth of traveler's checks, and $500 in cash.

Then there was the matter of a testament; that Saturday afternoon, having some guests at the ranch, Will asked Ewing Halsell and Ed Vail, two old and close friends, to witness his signature. The document was simple, a one-page statement, leaving everything to Betty. There was the stipulation that should Betty not survive her husband, his assets should be divided "share and share alike," among his three children, Will Jr., Mary, and James, or their issue, should one of the children not survive their father.

In Seattle, Wiley Post did not show up at Northwest Air Service all day long; he had gone to Puget Sound to fish with Seattle sportsman Ben Paris. Wiley was after salmon. Early in the morning he caught an 18½ pound king salmon off Hermosa Beach, near the mouth of the Snohomish River. Actually Wiley caught several fish that morning, but some were too small to keep, and two managed to get off the hook. Newspaper reports claim that the two "escapees" "crowded the forty pound mark." When interviewed, Wiley grinned: "I'm going out again," he said, "after the big ones that got away."

The rumors that Will Rogers would now accompany the Posts had somehow reached Seattle. Probably the wire services had sent out questions to be asked of Wiley, but he kept up the pretense and played the surprised party:

> "I don't see what basis they have for starting that story in Hollywood that Rogers will go with us," he said. "he isn't here, is he? If Rogers said he was going and I said so, there would be something to go on. I am not ready yet to make any further announcements as to who will be accompanying me."

At 8 o'clock that evening, Wiley spoke at the Sportsmen's Show at Civic Auditorium.

Reporters in Seattle still were probing whether Will Rogers was coming to join Post; they followed Post wherever he went and hounded him with the same, now routine questions.

"No!" Wiley kept insisting, "I won't be leaving today," when pressed when he and Mrs. Post would be leaving. He only indicated that he would be testing the plane, now that it had been equipped with floats.

The weather had not been cooperative; there had been rain and fog. Wiley, having driven a rented Oldsmobile to the little Bryn Mawr airport, stood dripping and forlorn in the penetrating wetness. Hands deep in his pockets, he could only look at his plane, tethered to the ramp sloping down toward Lake Washington, its engine and cockpit covered with a protective canvas. A few hardy, curious spectators had come to see the famous man and his plane. Someone snapped a fuzzy picture in the semi-darkness of the depressing day.

According to the *Seattle Post–Intelligencer* (August 17, 1935), one of the mechanics asked Wiley about flying float planes in the Northland. "I don't know much about Alaska," Post said. "I haven't had much experience flying planes with pontoons. I wonder how it's going to work out."

Talking to a reporter, Wiley said that he planned to equip the *Winnie Mae* with retractable landing gear on his return from his northern pleasure trip. He wanted to continue his exploits in the stratosphere and was tired of having to drop the wheels to reduce wind resistance, then bringing her down "on her belly."

Sunday morning, August 4, Will and Betty went for a long ride along the trails of their Pacific Palisades ranch. They talked of laying out new trails and making some improvements Will had planned. They rode down into the canyon, where a small log cabin—a retreat—had been finished just a few days earlier. Will regretted not having had an opportunity to spend some time there, away from the bustle of the main house. Betty, trying to postpone his departure, suggested that he delay his trip and spend the night there. "No," Will is quoted as saying, "Let's wait till I get back."

The packing was usually taken care of by either Betty or Emil Sandmeier, the major domo in the Rogers household. Except this time Emil was not available; a serious accident on the ranch had shattered his left leg, and he had been rushed to the hospital. Will, greatly upset, had called in several specialists and orthopaedic surgeons. Emil was treated like the member of the family he had become.

Betty had neatly set out the clothes she thought Will would need in Alaska; and then, just in case he decided to go on to Europe, there was an additional assortment. When Will saw the piles of clothing, he "discarded nine-tenth of the things laid out for him." Will always wanted to travel light with no more than the barest necessities.

As he stowed his clothing into the bags, Betty walked in and out of the room several times. Once he stopped her, "Say, Blake, you know what I just did?" Will always called Betty by her maiden name when he was in an impish mood. "I flipped a coin."

Betty realized immediately that her husband was still trying to persuade her to give her wholehearted approval to his trip. He always felt happier about any new venture if he thought that Betty wanted him to do it; he wished she would feel as excited about this vacation, as he was. But Betty still had her reservations. "I hope it came tails," she said.

Will laughed, "No, it didn't. It's heads. See, I win.'"

A United Airlines plane reservation to Seattle via San Francisco was made under the assumed name of Mr. Williams. Then, with two bags packed and all the chores done, Betty and Will went to see the last part of a polo game at the Uplifters Ranch. Later, back home, Will and Buddy Sterling roped calves until it was time for supper. Will Jr. was home for the meal and afterwards drove with his parents to Gilmore Stadium, where they attended a rodeo. Some of the contestants came over to where Will and Betty sat, and paid their respects; after all, Will had been one of them. He felt he had grown too old for all of it, but he still loved to watch the performers and think of the days when he was down there in an arena.

Someone gave him a wooden trick puzzle. Will played with it for a few moments, then slipped it into his pocket.

It was getting near midnight, time to go to the airport. On the way they stopped and ate a sandwich at a little open-air restaurant.

The airport lounge was crowded. Betty and Will stayed outside until it was time to board. He kissed her goodbye, and with his raincoat slung over his arm made his way to the newspaper stand where he bought several late editions. There was another wave of the hand to Betty and a quick boyish grin, then he disappeared into a group of passengers.

The next day, Will telephoned Betty from San Francisco. He had no difficulty with his passport, which, it turned out, was still valid from the previous year's trip. The Russian consulate was most cooperative and issued the necessary visa. Will was able to get aboard the 11 A.M. plane for Seattle. After a brief stop at Sacramento, the plane landed in Medford, Oregon. He was recognized and reporters bombarded him with questions. Still trying to cover the ultimate trip, Will stated: "I see by the papers that I am supposed to make some kind of a hop with Wiley Post, but you can say right now that I am not." But the reporters persisted. Will feigned confusion: "Wiley Post?" he scratched his ear, trying to look bewildered, "let's see, now. He's that flier fellow, isn't he?"

But the secret was out. Rogers arrived at Seattle's Boeing Field in late afternoon. Wearing a brown hat, grey suit, blue shirt and tan shoes, Will was met by Mayor Charles L. Smith, Lieutenant Governor Victor A. Meyers, W. W. Conner, district governor of the National Aeronautical Association, and officers of the Boeing Airplane Company.

"I know all about you," Rogers said when introduced to Meyers.

"Yes," the Lieutenant Governor reminded him, "You once called me Washington's 'trick lieutenant-governor.'"

"Yes," replied Rogers, "but I also said some nice things about you." Then they had their picture taken for the *Seattle Times*. In his August 6 column, Will noted: "The Lieut. Governor of the State is a fiddle player, the only politician in America with a legitimate profession."

As movie and still cameras clicked and whirred, Will drawled, "I'd like to see that new Boeing bomber I've heard so much about." Boeing was then constructing a new, huge plane, an early XB-17, the prototype for what would become known as the B-17, the Flying Fortress. Escorted by C. L. Egtvedt, president and general manager of the Boeing Airplane Company, and C. B. Monteith, vice-president and chief engineer, he was shown through the giant plane. Emerging, Will commented: "Gosh, that's a buster! It's the biggest plane I've ever seen, and I've seen a lot of them. Well, if we don't want it, Abyssinia will take it."

Autograph-seekers besieged Rogers when he emerged from the Boeing plant. A small boy held forth a book for Will's signature. "I don't autograph books, sonny," Will told him.

"But it's a good book," the boy insisted. "You wrote it— it's *Letters of a Self-Made Diplomat to His President*."

"That's different," grinned Rogers. "Sure I'll autograph it."

Another young boy held up a card for the autograph. "No," joked Rogers. "You didn't buy my book." But he gave his autograph all the same.

The official reception over, Will checked into the Olympic Hotel where Wiley and Mae Post were staying.

Now that the last cover had been lifted from the not-so-carefully concealed plan to fly to Alaska, Will was the constant subject of reporters' questions. He became the spokesman for the three. Asked whether he and the Posts would leave in the morning, Will announced: "Wiley wants to make a few minor adjustments and test out the ship again. Then the weather is not so good beyond 400 miles north of Seattle, according to the latest reports. We plan to make Juneau the first day. I've never been in Alaska and this is a good opportunity. I expect I will take a look at the Matanuska colony while I'm up north. I want to see what the Democrats have done to the Republicans."

There were interminable questions about the plane. Obviously eyebrows had been raised at the strange-looking craft Wiley had assembled. There was something not right about the way the low-wing craft sitting on pontoons looked; no wonder everybody had questions. But Will Rogers' said, "I don't know anything about the plane Wiley has, but if he is the pilot, I don't care. He is a marvelous flier." Even though he had already flown in Wiley's plane, Will actually knew very little about the plane, its engine, its characteristics, or any part of it. In fact, Will knew little of machinery in general. Though he drove cars, Betty doubted that Will knew how to change a tire. Aware of his lack of mechanical knowledge, Will had written:

> I had to make a speech to the Automotive Engineers' Association. Can you imagine me talking to a lot of technical mechanics? . . . Out of 110 million people in America, there couldn't possibly be one that knew less about machinery. I never raised the hood of any car I

ever had. If the thing stopped, I'd just get out, kick it in
the shins, and wait there till one of the things came that's
going to pick me up and take me somewhere.

   If I raised up the hood and a rabbit jumped out, I
wouldent know but what it belonged in there. I drive
'em, but sho don't try to fix 'em.

Asked whether he would hunt and fish with Wiley, Will
quipped: "I'll just sit on the plane and keep the wolves away while
Wiley is out killing game."
   Of the two men, Wiley was more of interest to pilots and
mechanics, and of course, the young men and boys. To them
he was a hero who had conquered space and distance—and even
time. He had done what others only dreamed about. Aviation
was young and exciting; it was the future. The land had been
mastered; the air was yet to be subdued and Wiley Post had
done it twice. But to the average man and woman in the street,
Will Rogers was the man to see. To reporters, Will Rogers was
far better copy; his quips made news. How often could Wiley's
past achievements—great as they were—be retold? While Post
was ill at ease with reporters or crowds, Will was used to
them. He explained, "Wiley is kinder of a Calvin Coolidge
on answers; none of 'em are going to bother you with being
too long."
   Will had been to Seattle a number of times before. There
had been 1909, when he was in vaudeville and appeared at the
Orpheum at 3rd and Madison Street. Bill Burton, who had been
the stage manager, remembered Will telling him, "Next time I'm
back, I'm going to get rid of some of these horses. They're kicking
about too much."
   Bill Burton recollected that he had answered Will, "Get rid
of those horses, Will, and you'll have no act!" Burton admitted
that he never was much of a prognosticator.
   Sure enough, in 1912 Will Rogers was back in Seattle. "He
had gotten rid of the horses—all except one. He seemed to like
that horse and hated to give it up. He didn't wisecrack much in
those days on the stage. He was too shy. But across the street after
the show, he'd sit down and tell stories about Oklahoma and then
he really did keep you chuckling." In his mind Burton could still
hear Will Rogers tell those stories, and he smiled to himself.

A few years after that, Will Rogers was again back in Seattle. He played the Alhambra at Fifth Avenue and Pine Street. Burton remembered that this time Will had no horses, but he now had put those Oklahoma stories into his act. Burton shook his head, "I made a bad guess about those horses. It was Will that made the show." When Burton read about Will Rogers being back in town, he thought of going to see him. He didn't.

That morning, Wiley, too, was up early. In Seattle, the day broke brilliantly clear, just a few billowing white clouds, floating in a dazzling sky. Now that the pontoons had been installed, Blum recalled Post asking, "What's the technique of flying these?" Blum, also a pilot, told him: "The old tried and true—give her the gun, rock her up on step and fly off. Well, his plane had so much power that when he first took off he pulled back and he got it up there and just took off."

At the Renton airport that day, there were more aviation enthusiasts standing around, gawking admiringly at Post and his strange-looking plane. Wiley was checking over the engine and then, looking around dockside, he spotted a few now familiar teenagers, equipped with cameras. Gordon Williams from nearby Clyde Hill, and his friend Bob McLarren (called Mac), visiting from Los Angeles, had been daily observers. They had come to look at the conversion progress and to snap pictures. They had besieged the famous pilot with their questions every day; Wiley had been friendly to the young men, and easy to talk to. But now he was about to take off for the new sea plane's first test flight. After a brief conference with a mechanic, Wiley turned to Gordon and Mac and said, "Hey, you kids! Want to go up for a ride? I need some ballast." The two didn't have to be invited twice. A mechanic handed them life jackets, while Post ordered the young men to position themselves as far back in the plane as possible: "I don't have much load on board," he explained. Gordon and Mac sat on the only seat left in the interior, the very aft, two-seat bench, and fastened their seat belts. Gordon had the window seat, and his older brother, George, who had also come to Renton this day, took a photograph from dockside of his kid brother looking out.

Wiley climbed into the cockpit, slid the overhead cover shut, and turned around to face the teenagers. "Ready to go?" he asked. The boys assured him they were. The engine started and

Wiley taxied slowly, warming the engine and experimenting with floats and rudders; then full throttle and the plane took off into the strong north wind. For almost three-quarters of an hour they flew over fifty-mile-long Lake Washington, doing shallow banks, climbs, dives, and generally testing the controls. During the flight, Gordon Williams took the only existing picture of the plane's interior. It clearly shows Wiley Post's back and the cockpit's door pockets stuffed with maps and charts. It was a thrilling adventure for the two young aviation fans; but veteran Wiley Post should have been seriously concerned.

The work at Northwest Air Service was completed, there was nothing more to be done but pay the bill and be off. As Alan Blum recalled:

> At the conclusion of the work that we did, I presented a bill to Wiley Post; the airplane was his, he had ordered the work. He wrote out a check. And few minutes later, well . . . what caused the few minutes delay, why, Will Rogers was busy handing out $20 bills to the men that worked on the plane. And then, when he got through with that, he said [to me] did you take that man's money? I said, "Sure!"
>
> "Here, let me have it," he said and he tore Wiley's check up. And then he said: "How much is it?" And he got his check book out. I started to tell him, and he says "Oh, you know these things better than I do," and he just signed his name to a blank check and handed it to me: "You fill it out!" The bill was, oh, something like $500, which in those days was a lot of money."

On August 6, the weather in Seattle was good, but reports from "the Gulf of Alaska" were discouraging, and departure for Mae and Wiley Post and Will Rogers was delayed. Spending the day in Seattle, Will decided to see how "this new ship" performed. Near noon, Rogers and Mae and Wiley Post drove the twelve miles south to Renton but only the two men took off on a short test flight over Lake Washington. When they returned, after swooping low over the airport, Will praised Wiley to the ever-present reporters: "He's sure a marvelous flier; I'll fly anywhere with him, if he'll take me along."

Post, who had listened to this, added, "I'll take him as far as he wants to go."

Rogers motored back to town. At the Pacific Marine Supply Company, located at Western and University, Will bought rope for a lariat. This store was one of the few in the Seattle area selling suitable spotted rope. Will also bought some life preservers. Having such a famous customer in the store disrupted the orderly conduct of business. Sales help and customers alike wanted to shake Rogers' hand, or get his autograph. John M. Gerard, a clerk at the store, was disappointed that he did not get to wait on Will, but he shook his hand and would remember it the rest of his life.

Rogers spent the afternoon playing polo at the Olympic Riding and Driving Club's new Polo Field. He cut an astounding picture, racing along the field, "clad in a garish red shirt and a pair of bibless overalls." The strange ensemble must have been hastily borrowed at the Club, as Will carried no such items in his luggage.

After the game, in the shower, Will spoke to Royal Brougham, noted sports columnist for the *Seattle Post-Intelligencer*, and said, "Polo [is] a great game, because even old guys like me can play it . . . I tell you-all, polo is a dog-eat-dog sport, and no sissies are playing it."

That evening, Will was guest at the polo dinner of the Washington Athletic Club. Addressing several hundred members for a half-hour, he told them that he was going north to "get a polo team going on the Matanuska project," as that was about the "only thing the Democrats haven't done for the colony." When the laughter died down, he continued, "That isn't any funnier than a lot of the things this present administration has been doing."

Ad-libbing his talk, he stood at the head table, tracing patterns on the table cloth with his knife, while he raked Republicans and fired a few salvos at the Democrats. When the Toastmaster kidded, "Will! Even the Republicans join me in thanking you for coming here tonight," Rogers had an answer. "You see, he said, "it's like this. I'm certainly glad to hear that, because you know, them fellers is likely to be in power again some day. And I want to keep on the good side of 'em, because I might have to sorta have to go on relief if things start breaking tough."

Asked about the flight to the Northland, Will explained, "I told my wife I wanted to mess around with Post and do a bit of hunting and she said, 'Go ahead. As long as you're with Wiley, you're all right.' ''

Will called Betty several times from Seattle; the last time they spoke was Friday, August 7, just before he and Post left Seattle. Will had not yet made his decision about accompanying Wiley across Siberia. A few days later Betty flew to New York, and continued on to Maine.

In his weekly article mailed from Seattle and published August 20, Will Rogers enumerated some of the things Wiley had prepared for the trip:

> He has got a rubber boat and a canoe paddle, some life vests, or protectors. Oh yes and his gun case, I don't know what kind it is, I don't hunt or shoot; It's a long looking thing. I expect there is a Springfield rifle in there. Oh, yes, and his fishing rod and 80 reels. Oh yes! and two or three coils of rope, (and they are not mine). They are to tie the ship up and pull it up to the banks. That will be my job to get out first and tie the rope and then vault ashore and haul it in. I will have to have a card from the "Longshoreman's Union."
>
> What no camera? No that's what we are going on this trip for to get away from cameras, then too, I don't know nothing about 'em, and can't work 'em. We may see some fine sights but you can always lie about a thing better than you can prove it. Then you always have to explain that "this picture don't near do the scene justice." Oh yes, and some sleeping bags, Wiley got them; said they was great to sleep in. I never was in one of 'em. You zip 'em up around you after you get in 'em some way. I always have trouble with those zippers, so I can see myself walking around in one of those things all day.

After Will's brief test flight in the new plane, there appeared the first stories about Mae Post possibly not accompanying the men to Alaska. There were even some allusions to a rift in the Post family. It was remembered that Wiley had snapped at a reporter, telling him to ask Mrs. Post directly whether she would come along to Alaska. Different stories were quoted. The *Los Angeles Herald and Express* cited a wire story, reporting "friends" had disclosed that Rogers "kidded" Mrs. Post about the hunting and fishing they planned on isolated Alaskan lakes, saying that it was "no place for a lady." The wire story said, "The 'kidding' in which Post joined, finally convinced Mrs. Post not to make the trip with them."

Will, writing about this change of plan, simply said, "Mrs. Post decided at the last minute to go up to Alaska a few days later by boat, so it's only Wiley and I that are taking off." Indicating no hard feelings, Rogers quotes Mae as asking that he "take good care of Wiley. I said, 'Of course you mean in the air, after we get on the ground he is able to look after himself.' "

In a syndicated news story by Universal Service, May Post spoke about her husband: "He's so erratic. I've always sworn that the next time I'd go with him, because at least we'd be together if anything happened." Explaining further, she said:

> Will Rogers wanted to go to Alaska so badly. He'd planned it for weeks, way back to the time Fay Gillis thought she might come along, too. Will wanted to pay my passage to Alaska, after he joined us in Seattle and took my place in the plane with Wiley.
>
> But I couldn't let him do that. Wiley wouldn't have been comfortable. And I'd have spoiled their party, once in Alaska, with my bum appendix and the three of us crowded into the plane for eight or nine hours at a stretch.

There would be further variations of the reasons why Mae Post did not accompany her husband, but for the moment, it was pretended that Mae would join the two men in Alaska. A decision, however, had already been made for her to return to Oklahoma, while Wiley and Will would fly on alone.

In the early morning hours of Wednesday, August 7, everything was ready for Will and Wiley to begin their trip. There was some last-minute excitement which caused a delay. The evening before, Ash Bridgham, manager of the Northwest Air Service airport, had pumped six drums of gas into the plane's fuel tanks. Each of those drums held fifty gallons, for a total of three hundred. In the cool of the night, when fuel contracts somewhat, it might have been possible to get 300 gallons of gasoline into tanks

which were supposed to hold a total of 270 gallons. Post's instructions had been to fill the tanks "right to the top." But in the
morning, as the warm sun of the clear day began to heat up the
plane, the gasoline expanded and began pouring out of the tanks.
The fumes and smell of gas were everywhere. The plane and the
area had to be thoroughly washed down before anybody would
even consider starting an engine.

There were the usual reporters and photographers, the
usual questions, the usual requests for "one more picture." Wiley
was all business, while Rogers said he might have to "get a fish
dinner at Ketchikan." He carried on a bantering conversation
with the newsmen. Occasionally he aimed a good-natured barb at
Post, who retorted in kind.

Post showed Rogers a khaki-colored life jacket, to be used
in case the plane was forced down on water. Post held the jackets
up and said: "You know, we have to take these along."

Will suddenly became solemn. "I don't like to think about
that," he said, "I'm going for a good time."

The moment to leave had almost come. Mae Post watched
as sandwiches and coffee were stowed aboard. Fourteen-year old
Earlene Paddock, holding on to her five-year-old brother Franklin, observed the scene. Her family lived just off the Renton
airport, and she had come to take photographs with her box
camera and to get autographs from the two famous men. Wiley
Post looked "just spiffy," she thought, exactly the way she
had seen him in the newspapers. But she was disillusioned with
Will Rogers. Being a 14-year-old young lady, she had certain
rigid standards and ideas of just how people ought to look. Will's
gray suit, she thought, was rumpled as if he had slept in it for
two weeks; and his tie was askew. "A movie star," she believed,
"ought to look as if he had just stepped out of a fashion magazine." The hat too, crushed and perspiration-stained, she found
objectionable. But she had come to take pictures and get autographs and she was not going to let her disappointment keep
her from that goal. The paper she had brought with her for
the autographs was a pad from the Renton Variety Store, with
its name and three-digit telephone number clearly printed at
the top.

Wiley signed the paper, kissed Mae good-bye and climbed
into the cockpit. He started the engine to warm it up. Will signed

Earlene's pad, then, tousling Franklin's blond locks, he bent down and spoke to the little boy. Who could tell at that moment the thoughts of a loving father who had lost a little son?

Rogers climbed on the wing and before entering the plane he turned to the assembled reporters: "Say good-bye to that fiddle-playing Lieutenant-Governor of yours for us!" he shouted over the roar of the engine.

The fact that Wiley Post decided to leave Seattle on a day when the Weather Bureau still reported inclement weather along the northern British Columbia coast and southeastern Alaska is surprising. The 8 o'clock Associated Press report from Ketchikan told of a light rain falling, while a ship dispatch said there was rain at Juneau. The forecast for the entire flight route did not sound promising, especially for a supposedly careful flier. The Associate Press wire story, datelined Seattle, August 7, records, "Ignoring reports of storms on their route, Wiley Post and Will Rogers took off here today in Mr. Post's new plane for Alaska."

Finally, at 9:15 A.M., Wiley's little red plane lifted off Lake Washington, heading toward Ketchikan, Alaska. Films still exist of Post's take-off. As Will described it, "Well, she took off like a bird, with an awful short run . . . we had pretty weather for about the first 300 miles, then it begin to kinder close in."

Indeed, rain and low-lying clouds lay along the route they now traveled; it was not a day to be flying over unknown terrain. Bob Ellis, well-known Ketchikan pilot, was asked whether Post would stop in Ketchikan. Bob was quoted as saying, "The weather is so bad that even the locals are not flying." Then in about an hour after he made that statement, Post went flying by, no more than fifty feet over the water, and did not stop.

Will Rogers shed light on this, writing that "We had expected to stop in Ketchikan, our first city in Alaska, but Wiley I guess figured that if he stopped there he would get closed in and wouldent get any further up the coast. So he flew low over the very pretty little city right along the water's edge with the high mountains to the back of it."

Post and Rogers landed on Juneau's Gastineau Channel at 5:30 P.M. It was raining. The nearly thousand-mile hop had taken eight-and-a-quarter hours. They had been expected, as throngs lined even the adjacent docks as the plane taxied to its berth at the PAA hangar. Wiley was the first to emerge, coming out in his shirt sleeves. Will, seeing Alaska for the first time from ground level, stepped from the plane, smiling. He now wore his topcoat over the gray suit; he shivered and said, "It was cold in the plane, but warm in the motor room."

They were greeted by Joe Crosson, Wiley's old friend and rescuer on both round-the-world flights. Joe Crosson had a present for Rogers. It was copy of *Arctic Village*. Joe believed that this book would give Will a good introduction to life in an Alaskan village. Will thanked him and promised to read it.

Walt Woodward, cub reporter for Juneau's *The Empire*, was not only the first radio newscaster in Alaska, but covered the waterfront and new arrivals as well. He recalled, "I had no chance to even get close to them at the floats. I do remember, however, that many of the bush pilots, after looking at the plane, were shaking their heads in doubt—not at Wiley Post's skills, but at the plane. They apparently did not approve of it."

While Woodward could not get to interview either Rogers or Post, he was close enough to plainly see how tired both men appeared. He hoped that Will Rogers would recover enough to be able to appear on his 10 P.M. newscast over station KINY.

Later, asked by reporters how long he intended to stay in Juneau, Post snapped: "We're going to stay here until we get ready to take off for somewhere!" The crowd kept Post and Rogers at dockside for half an hour before Crosson finally took the two men in tow and drove them to the Gastineau Hotel. After they had checked in, they attended a banquet given in their honor at the Territorial Mansion, home of Governor John W. Troy. Everybody liked Governor Troy; Will did too. When speaking about him. he used a favorite line: "The Governor is a nice fellow, a Democrat but a Gentleman."

Waiting at the governor's mansion, Walt Woodward could hear governor Troy ask Will Rogers whether he was up to driving over to the radio station for a short talk. The governor pointed out that the local station, KINY, had announced all day that Will Rogers would appear at 10 P.M. Of course, the governor maintained, that there was absolutely no obligation on Rogers' part. "Will Rogers hesitated for a long time, and then, in a very tired voice, said he'd make the broadcast."

Rogers and Post were delivered to the studio in the governor's car. The hour of the broadcast arrived. The visitors' gallery at the station was packed by fans who wanted to see the famous men. Wiley, who was first to speak, said in part:

> I have just had a very good evening. I like Alaska, like its Governor, and like the dinner I had at the Governor's house. We ate a lot of Matanuska cantaloupes and salmon and stuff like that. Our plans are very vague; We have a lot of friends here in Alaska and I hope I will get to see all of them, but if I don't I'll be back sometime. I've always liked this country and always had a good time here, except when I broke down and got lost on my trip around the world, and even then there was a good friend to come along and pull me out of it. We plan to sort of wander around in the interior and see a lot, and hunt and fish and just sort of wander around.

Then Walt Woodward said, "Here he is! Will Rogers!" At that the kindly, tired man squared his shoulders and suddenly was transformed into the brilliant humorist he was."

Will Rogers spoke at greater length:

> I have never been here before and I ought to be ashamed of myself. It ought to be in the Constitution that everybody had to come here.
>
> I am not up here on any commission. Wiley and I are like a couple of country boys in an old Ford—we don't know where we are going and we don't care.
>
> Amelia Earhart was out to my place a couple of Sundays ago. She ought to be an authority on that sort of thing and she said she thinks Post is the greatest pilot in the world.
>
> I expect to be here a while. I will have to buy an awful lot of rain coats and rubber boots—it will take me all morning to buy all those things.
>
> I think Roosevelt will be elected by a bigger majority than before.
>
> People wonder where I get all my jokes. I just listen to the government and report the facts. I have 96 senators working for me and all I got to do is write down what they say.

I expect we will go up to this Matanuska Valley and see where the Democrats are feeding the Republicans. I think it is a good idea. I think it would be swell if they brought all the Republicans up here and put them in a valley. It wouldn't take a very big valley to hold them all.

I think Roosevelt would like to have been along on this hop. He'd rather like to get away from down there. Everyone who has any money has it in for Roosevelt. Funny thing about the Republicans; they'd rather make their money under a Republican but if they can't do that they will take what they can get.

The next morning, August 8, Rogers and Post awoke to the same steady rainfall, and "not a plane mushed out of Juneau," as Rogers put it. The Gastineau was a comfortable, fine hotel and the two men had spent a good night. Will went downstairs for breakfast.

Warren Tilman, one of PAA's mechanics, came in for his breakfast and immediately spotted Will Rogers. He lived in Fairbanks but had flown into town on one of PAA's regular flights, as each plane carried a mechanic. Seeing Will read *Arctic Village*, Tilman bragged that he was mentioned in the book, though his identity had been protected by a change of name. The two men talked and they found that they came from the same part of the country, with Warren born in the Ozarks. Tilman had even been to Claremore, Will's adopted hometown. When Rogers heard that Tilman also had Indian blood, he dubbed him "Chief," a name that stuck.

The two men were still sitting at the counter, eating their breakfast and talking, when a mother and her two very young children came into the small restaurant. The little boy might have been six, the little girl perhaps a year younger. Their slickers and boots were dripping from the heavy rain. The mother took a table right behind Will Rogers. Tilman caught the little boy standing to the side of Will Rogers, staring at his profile. "Somebody's watchin' ya!" he told Will.

Will turned. "Hi, Pop!" the boy said; his little sister had now come to stand beside him.

"Hi, you guys!" Will greeted them.

The mother tried to explain, "They saw you in a picture with Louise Dresser, you know, and they wanted to see you."

Will shook hands with them, "I see you're all decked out for rain, it looks like we're goin' to have some today." Outside the downpour continued. Will used this little episode in his weekly article, poking fun at himself:

> Fellow comes up and says, "I see all your pictures" and I ask him which ones, and he can't name a one. Woman brings a little 5-year-old girl up and says, "Tillie wants to meet you, she reads all your little articles in the papers and enjoys 'em," Tillie says, "Who is he, ma?"

After waiting out a down pour that dropped almost three-quarters-of-an inch of rain, Will finally rushed to a nearby store and bought some rubbers and a couple of raincoats, quipping, "With this weather I'll need lots of them. If I was going to stay in Juneau, I would buy at least one more outfit." Then he picked out a pair of trousers which were definitely too large around the waist,: "If there is as much fish in Alaska as I hear there is, I will gain a couple of inches around the middle when Wiley gets to catching them."

Whenever Will or Wiley stepped outside the Gastineau Hotel, a crowd of admirers were waiting either for autographs or photos. Dozens of times the two men were asked to pose; they could not walk down the street without admirers following from a deferential distance.

When friends suggested strip-fishing to Rogers, he inquired, "What is that? Something like poker? Who strips? The fish or the fishermen?" He was told that "strip-fishing" was fishing husky salmon with lines from a rowboat.

Learning that Representative C. Elmer Dietrich, Democrat from Pennsylvania, a member of the House territorial committee, and Frank T. Bell, United States commissioner of fisheries, were at Anchorage, Rogers said, "I want it distinctly understood I'm not one of them. I am paying my own expenses."

Invited by the Juneau Chamber of Commerce to address their luncheon at Bailey's Cafe at noon, Will spoke to them for twenty-five minutes on a variety of subjects, ranging from his impression of Alaska to President Roosevelt, and from politics to aviation:

I sent a little dispatch to 650 newspapers in the United States after my arrival here. I told 'em what a swell place you got . . .

We—Wiley Post and I—did sorta figure on taking a hop to Skagway today. But the weather grounded us. So Wiley and Joe Crosson went down to tinker on the engine and I come up here to talk to you fellows.

. . . Speaking of pilots, you've got a great bunch here. They have to be good. They don't need no Government tests up in these tough channels. Just send a new pilot out. If he comes back, he's okay.

You know, Roosevelt is like a magician in a vaudeville show. He's arrived at the theatre, only his special properties and luggage ain't arrived yet. So he's got to borrow somebody else's magic hat. Well, he goes ahead and does his tricks. But when he reaches in the hat to draw out a rabbit, he doesn't know himself whether he is drawing out a rabbit or skunk. That's like most of these New Deal schemes. He's got to hold 'em up for public view, regardless how the idea turns out. But he's a great guy, Roosevelt is.

I understand you've got a Senate with eight members, and a House with 16. All the Senators are Democrats, and so are 15 of the House members. That's all right. I'll get [Jim] Farley to workin' on that other guy . . .

. . . Well, folks, I just want to tell you how much I enjoy your Alaska and your Juneau. As a traveling committee of one, representing the Democratic Party—and I'm paying my own ticket—I'll go back and report to President Roosevelt about Alaska. When he asks me, ''Will, what's wrong with 'em up there?'' I'll tell him, 'Not a damn thing!'

Rex Beach arrived in Juneau that day by boat. As he took a taxi from the ship to the Gastineau Hotel, he learned that Will and Wiley were in town; he found them eating dinner with Joe Crosson in the cafe. Rex and Will had been friends for more than twenty years. They had last seen each other a year earlier, in New York City's Dinty Moore's, a Broadway restaurant famous for its chili. They had much to tell each other, especially since Will had seen Fred Stone's first Hollywood motion picture, and Rex wanted to hear all about his brother-in-law's new career.

"How come you can take time out to hitch-hike up here?" Rex wanted to know.

"I have got three pictures ahead and I always wanted to see Alaska. Wiley is crazy about it and wants to live up here."

Wiley smiled and half chidingly complained, "I want to go fishing, too, but Will won't give me a chance."

"Say, I've heard nothing but fishing since I got here," Will defended himself. "All these boys do is brag about who caught the biggest salmon. Last night an oilman brought one weighing fifty pounds into my room and wanted to put it in bed with me. Yea, the oil business is so bad that all the executives come here fishing. Wiley's as bad as the rest, and I can't see the use of catching salmon when they crawl out of the water to meet you. The first handshake I got when I stepped ashore was from a big cohoe. A cohoe, they tell me, is a king salmon that's on relief."

A group of eager autograph collectors descended on the celebrities. Will, who disliked signing autographs, grumbled at first but then signed any piece of paper held in front of him. Soon it was discovered that he had signed his name as Tom Mix and Ben Turpin. He was persuaded to sign his own name, but neither Wiley Post nor Joe Crosson were asked for their autographs at first. Rogers spoke up: "This is Wiley Post," he said to the group around their table, "he flew around the world with Gatty and broke the record, then circled the globe alone and broke it again. Both times he had trouble here in Alaska and Joe Crosson pulled him out. Their autographs are really worth having."

When the last fan left satisfied, having all his questions answered and clutching the signatures of four famous personalities, the men went back to their stories and talked.

"What are your plans?" Rex asked.

Wiley grinned and said nothing.

Will confessed, "We haven't any. We're just on a vacation. We want to see Dawson and Fairbanks and those farmer colonists at Matanuska of course, and we would like to see the Mackenzie River, too. We might even hop across to Siberia and go home that way. When Wiley was flying around the world those Russians laid out his course and told him exactly where to head in at and made him stick to it. Now they have given him permission to fly anywhere and stop anywhere as long as he wants. We have the maps and it would make a swell trip to go by way of Iceland and Greenland. The longest water jump is only 1,000 miles.''

The men gabbed there until midnight, until Wiley went to sleep with his head on his forearms. "He never had a word to say," Will said. "I do the talking for the team and it works out fine.''

They had to waken Wiley when they at last decided to retire for the night. Will had taken a two-room suite, one room for Wiley and one for himself. But Wiley shared his room with Joe Crosson.[2]

While Will and Wiley were occupied about town, Joe Crosson had left orders with the PAA crew to check the plane carefully, and to make it ready for departure. Bob Ames, a fine mechanic, thoroughly examined the engine, cleaned the plane, checked the battery, added oil and filled the gas tanks. Everything seemed in perfect order. There was only one discovery that surprised him. Although Wiley had six gas tanks, he had only one fuel gauge. Ames recognized it. It had come from an old Ford automobile. Wiley had it installed above the instrument panel, right in front of his face; it provided a reading for the thirty-gallon tank that was stowed under the pilot's seat. Many small planes had no fuel gauges, as pilots would know how long they had flown on a full tank, and how much fuel their plane consumed per hour. But it seemed strange to Bob Ames, that with so many tanks, Wiley would want to rely on his memory to accurately recall how much gas remained in any one of those tanks, and which tanks were empty and which were full.

Charley Goldstein, the mayor of Juneau, came to visit with Rogers, Post, Crosson, and Beach, and naturally pictures were taken. Goldstein was a fur trader who had his purchasing agents all over Alaska, so Will dropped into Charley's store and picked out a red fox fur for Betty. He had it wrapped, then he addressed it in his own hand and took it to the post office.

Will spent some time looking over a map of Alaska; he had always been fascinated by atlases and maps and read them well. This day the *Associated Press* reported a mild disagreement between Will and Wiley over plans for resuming their flight:

Post yearned for salmon fishing with light tackle. Rogers urged a quick take-off for Nome so he could "lasso a

reindeer.'' Inasmuch as weather forecasts were unfavorable, Rogers said he would compromise and ''let Wiley
do his fishing.''

Turning to an ever-present reporter he commented, ''I
guess Wiley and me'll have to flip a coin to see where we are going
next. Wiley's the very best man on this trip. He fills the gas tank
and then we're off.''

But through several remarks he made to reporters, Post
gave the impression that take-off and routes were a matter which
Post would decide and that Rogers was a passenger on the ''pleasure jaunt.''

When Will came to the dock the next afternoon, he handed
out five-dollar bills to the PAA employees. After several days of
rain, a bright sun gave promise of ideal flying conditions. The plan
was to fly to Dawson City, with a couple of sightseeing stops
along the way. Wrote Will Rogers, ''We are going to Skagway now
and see the famous Chilkoot Pass. We will do it in ten minutes and
it took the pioneers two and three months.''

At the dock, Wiley bought an anchor so they could moor
the plane should they set down to either fish or spend the night on
a lake or river. While Post and Crosson were once more going
over charts and telephoning for the latest weather reports, Rex
Beach, Mayor Goldstein, and Will loaded the personal belongings
aboard. Will clowned with the crowd that had once again gathered. It was 1:25 P.M. when Rogers and Post finally climbed
aboard, and the door and hatch were closed; there was a good-
bye cheer from the hundreds who lined the wharves on Juneau's
waterfront as the red plane ''took off in a smother of foam.''
Wiley circled over the city, then laid course up Lynn Canal towards Skagway.

Standing at the float, Lloyd Jarman, a mechanic for PAA,
took motion pictures of Wiley's take-off. He shook his head; he
had flown thousands of miles in pontoon planes, and he knew
their dangers. He thought that ''Wiley Post was not a good seaplane pilot, he was too abrupt on take-off and pulled up too
steep—you do not make this kind of action and stay alive. I have
movies of him when he left Juneau and it was too quick and nose
high. I have flown with many pilots and the few that did this type
of flying were quickly eliminated.''

Rex Beach stood and watched the little red plane disappear in the distance. Writing in his newspaper account about it, he reported that as the plane vanished into the mist down Gastineau Channel, Joe Crosson turned to him and said, "There's a ship to go anywhere with. With that engine Wiley could lift her out off a frog pond."

Three hours and five minutes later, Wiley Post set the plane down at Dawson City, Yukon Territory, Canada, 475 miles from his starting point. He had not stopped at either Skagway or Whitehorse.

Getting out of the plane at Dawson, Will found that a crowd had collected. The news of their planned arrival had caused excitement in the community and hundreds of miners had swarmed into town to greet the celebrities. Looking the crowd over, Will shouted, "Hello folks! I always stop places that look pretty on the map!"

Harriet Malstrom reported his arrival in Dawson for her uncle's newspaper, the *Dawson News*. This was the biggest story she had ever covered, and that evening she had dinner with Rogers and Post, interviewing the celebrities. Suddenly Will leaned over to her and said, "No riding in any railway contraption for me. What if the thing jumped the track? I prefer an honorable death in a plane, or falling off a horse." Harriet was stunned and marked down the words; she did not want to get them wrong.

There was talk that Post and Rogers would fly to Aklavik, North West Territory, to visit with Nicholas Sokoloff, a Russian. As vice president of Amtorg, Inc., the Soviet government trading company, Sokoloff was there to establish radio contact and report weather data to Sigismund Levanevsky and his two Russian companions, who were still planning to fly from Moscow to San Francisco by crossing over the North Pole.

Checking on his plane, Wiley slipped while stepping from one float to another and fell into the Yukon River; he disappeared in the ice-cold water right up to his neck. Scrambling out of it in a hurry he seemed to be none the worse for the dunking.

In the afternoon, the two "vacationers" moved on. Will reported,

Aklavik, North West Territory.
    Get your map out and look this up. The mouth of
the Mackenzie River, right on the Arctic Ocean. Eskimos

are thicker then rich men at a Save-The-Constitution convention. This is sent from one of the most northerly posts of the Northwest Mounted Police. A great body of men, like the G-men.

We are headed for famous Herschel Island in the Arctic. Old Wiley had to duck his head to keep from bumping it as we flew under the Arctic circle. What, no night? It's all day up here.

Will was shivering in the 40-degree cold at Aklavik. It was not just the temperature, it was the addition of those steady, penetrating winds that cut through ordinary clothing right to the skin like a thousand scalpels and numbed it in seconds. Will had bought a pair of gumboots in Dawson and he trekked around, trying to persuade the Eskimos that they were as good as genuine *mukluks*. The natives just laughed good-naturedly but remained unpersuaded; they persisted in what they knew to be fact: seal skin was better.

Will dropped into All Saints Hospital in Aklavik to cheer up the patients. Alice Brown, who worked at the hospital, led him to the bedside of a young boy, who had his foot crushed when two boats had collided, tossed against each other by the sea. Will spent some time with the lad and when he left, he pressed a "substantial check" into the boy's hand.

While in Aklavik, Rogers and Post met Alan Sullivan, an Anglo-Canadian writer. The three men talked Sunday and again Monday, and Will must have confided his plans to Sullivan. Probably he felt that anything said in the isolation of that northern outpost would remain secret long enough until events would make it a secret no longer. Sullivan, arriving in Edmonton, Alberta, on August 19, told reporters that Rogers and Post "wanted to see Alaska first and then both definitely intended making the flight across Siberia. They planned to go from Nome across the Bering Strait.

On the same day on which Wiley and Will told their plan to Alan Sullivan, the Associated Press carried an "exclusive" story. It claimed to have the "solution" to the mystery whether Will Rogers would accompany Wiley Post on that "hunting trip" to Siberia. Referring to an interview with Mrs. Will Rogers at the Los Angeles airport, leaving "for a visit with relatives in Boston," Betty was quoted that Will "would join her there, after Post has left Alaska."

Top left: Monday, August 5th, 1935. Wiley's plane leaves Northwest Air Service's protective hangar on its way down the ramp into Lake Washington. (Photo: Museum of Industry, Seattle, WA.) *Middle left:* Tuesday, August 6th, 1935. Equipped now with floats, Wiley takes the plane on a test flight. Gordon Williams and his friend Bob McLarren are "ballast" visible through the last window. Note restricted license indicated by the letter "R." (Photo: Gordon Williams.) *Bottom left:* Tuesday, August 6th, 1935. The first test flight completed, "Wiley's Orphan" presents an odd silhouette as an unusual low-wing float plane. (Photo: Lockheed-California Company.) *Top right:* Sunday, August 11, 1935. At Aklavik, North West Territory, Canada, Will visits with Nicholas Sokoloff, vice president of Amtorg, Inc., the Soviet government trading company. Sokoloff is there to establish radio contact and report weather data to Sigismund Levanevsky and his two Russian companions planning to fly from Moscow to San Francisco by crossing over the North Pole. (Photo: Archives & Manuscripts Division of the Oklahoma Historical Society.) *Bottom right:* The flight path of the final voyage of Rogers & Post during the days of August, 1935. (Map: Arlene Goldberg.)

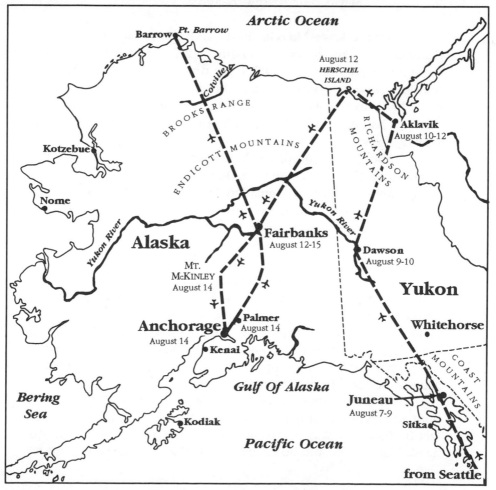

Walking about the village of Aklavik, as Rogers would do, he picked up all sorts of stories his readers in the forty-eight states would find interesting. Alaska, after all, was still a huge, unknown, unexplored land mass to most Americans of the Thirties.

> Was you ever driving around in a car and not knowing or caring where you went? Well, that's what Wiley and I are doing. We are sure having a great time. If we hear of whales or a big herd of caribou or reindeer, we fly over and see it. Friday and Saturday we visited the old Klondike district, Dawson City, Bonanza, El Dorado. Say, there is a horse here; the furthest north of any horse, and he eats fish and travels on snowshoes.
>
> Maybe Point Barrow today.

About to leave Aklavik, Post had to purchase fuel from the Canadian Airways depot. Air engineer Frank Hartley was up on the wing, busy filling the tanks. He turned to Rogers, who was standing close by, "What's the fuel capacity of this plane?"

Will, to whom details relating to engines were a life-long mystery, had no idea. "How much does that crate of yours hold, Wiley?" he yelled.

"About 260 gallons in all seven tanks," Post yelled back. It'll take about eighty more to fill her up. . . ."

Captain Farrell, of Canadian Airways, was standing next to Will. "And you say this gas is costing us $1.16 a gallon?" Rogers asked, surprised at the high price. "Well, you just go right ahead and fill'er up! I ain't never ridden on no $1.16 gas before and I want to enjoy everything you got up here in the Arctic."

When Hartley had topped the tanks, Rogers shoved a ten-dollar bill into his pocket. Hartley was reluctant to accept it and tried to return it. Rogers would have none of it; "You just take my picture and we'll call that a fee," he insisted, as he stepped on the wing of the plane. He posed a second, Frank Hartley took the picture and Rogers entered the plane, moving to his now-accustomed seat in the very rear.

This conversation is revealing. Why would an experienced pilot like Wiley Post say he had seven gasoline tanks, when in fact he had only six? He would have to keep a lot of facts in his head. Not only would he have to control a difficult plane, but he would have to remember the time he had spent in the air, the gasoline consumed, and which tanks were empty and which were full.

Then, too, Post's habit of draining the last drop of fuel out of each tank, before switching to a full one, looms now even more ominous. It had startled Gatty every time. Without gauges, how would Wiley remember which tanks were full, and which he had emptied today—not to be confused with the pattern of yesterday's flight. As the engine began to sputter, could he not easily switch from a just emptied tank to a tank which was already empty? And if his altitude was low at the time—say, only 200 feet—he would have no chance to restart a stalled engine before the plane would hit the ground; especially a plane which was hazardously nose-heavy. The facts as they emerge show that Wiley did not know exactly how much fuel he carried, nor how many fuel tanks were on his plane.

Rogers, unaware of any of this, was in his element. This was why he had wanted to come to Alaska: Everywhere he looked he found something he had never seen before. Perhaps it reminded him, in its own way, of the land of his youth, when the Indian Territory was the frontier and pioneers still pitted themselves against nature. He literally burst with excitement as he recounted this part of the trip to his readers:

> It was interesting to be flying where the trip took us over where the head of one river went to the Arctic Ocean, and a few miles over a divide, the water of the other would be headed for the Pacific.
>
> That happened coming out of Herschel Island in the Arctic, we couldn't land there on account of the ice in the water, but we circled it a time or so.
>
> . . . it's a noted place, it's where the old whalers, the real old sailing boats used to land and spend the winter. They would come up from America or the various Scandinavian countries in one summer, get in there, and winter and then that would give them an early start the next summer when the ice went out. Then they would hunt all that summer which was about three months, then back into Herschel for the second winter and then out with the whalebone the next summer.

Before leaving Aklavik, Will sent Betty a telegram to reassure her. He knew, of course, that his daily columns in the newspapers would let her know exactly where he was, but he wanted to hear some news about the family:

S13 15 = AKLAVIK 4NWT AUG 10 800P (stamped) 1935
AUG 11 AM 8 14

MRS WILL ROGERS =
BEVERLYHILLS CALIF

MOST MARVELOUS TRIP NO DANGER WITH THIS
GUY WIRE ME ALL NEWS FAIRBANKS ALASKA LOVE =
                                    DAD

Betty, packed and ready to leave California that Sunday, August 11, for Maine, replied immediately. Either Betty, or someone at the ranch typed the text, as carbon copies are still on hand:

WILL ROGERS, FAIRBAMKS [sic], ALASKA

LEAVING NOW ARRIVING TUESDAY. JIM AT HERBS
LEAVING TUESDAY FOR EAST. BILL GETTING BOAT
WEDNESDAY FOR PHILLIPHINES [sic]. SHEEHAN JER-
ITZA MARRIED TOMORROW AND GOING TO EUROPE.
ALL FINE, GOOD TO HEAR FROM YOU. LOVE,
                                    BETTY

Though several words on the original telegram form are crossed out to save transmission charges on superfluous words, the message was perfectly clear to Will; Betty was leaving California and would arrive in Maine on Tuesday; son Jim would leave Oklahoma on Tuesday, where he was currently visiting with Herb McSpadden (Will's nephew, who ran the Rogers family ranch near Oologah); and Jim would be coming east to join Betty and Mary and Aunt Dick in Maine. Son Bill would get his wish and spend part of his summer vacation working aboard a tanker, going to the Philippines. Winfield Sheehan, the boss at Will's studio, Fox Film Corporation, was about to marry Maria Jeritza, the famous opera diva, and they would honeymoon in Europe. It certainly was a lot of news compressed into few words.

Will would get to read the telegram late in the next afternoon, August 12, when he landed in Fairbanks. By that time
Sheehan and Jeritza had already been married in the old California
mission at Santa Barbara.

Betty also sent a telegram to Mary:

NIGHTLETTER TELEGRAM: Aug. 11, 5:46 PM, Beverly
Hills:

MARY ROGERS, LAKEWOOD PLAYERS, SKOWHEGAN,
MAINE

LEAVING NOW, WILL WIRE YOU TOMORROW FROM
N.Y. BILL LEAVES WEDNESDAY ON BOAT FOR PHIL-
LIPINES [sic], JIM IS IN OKLAHOMA BUT WILL LEAVE
THERE TUESDAY FOR SKOWHEGAN. WIRE FROM
DAD, HE IS HAVING A GRAND TRIP. LOADS OF LOVE
TO YOU BOTH AND WILL SEE YOU TUESDAY. GOOD
LUCK AND LOVE,

BETTY

Then she had a thought. Perhaps she should purchase additional flight insurance on Will. What if the plane went down and a
lengthy, expensive search would have to be instituted? It was still
a somewhat unusual matter to insure against losses and she instructed her brother, ''Sandy'' Blake, to make inquiries. He was to
wire the information to her New York hotel.

In New York that evening, August 12, Sandy Blake's wired
response to Betty's inquiry arrived. It was sent from California at
1:45 P.M. local time, or 4:45 P.M. New York time:

MRS. W. P. ROGERS   BILTMORE HOTEL   NEW YORK

LLOYDS COVERS ALL ACCIDENTS INCLUDING POLO
AND AVIATION ANYWHERE IN THE WORLD AMOUNT
FORTYSEVEN THOUSAND FIVE HUNDRED PREMIUM
SIX HUNDRED TWELVE WIRE TODAY

SANDY

Whether Betty Rogers received this telegram on August 12,
or only the following morning, is not known. What is known

is the fact that she did not respond to it until Wednesday the fourteenth.

On August 12, at 3:40 P.M., Wiley's red plane was sighted over Fairbanks. For days it had been expected, and now it was finally here. When the sound of the engine was first heard overhead, several hundred men and women in about seventy-five automobiles and on foot, rushed to Chet Spencer's homestead, where float planes usually tied up. The dock, appropriately named Spencer's Float, was situated on the Chena River (referred to locally as Chena Slough) some three miles from the center of town. The Chena Slough was a tributary of the Tanana River, which in turn joined the Yukon River some 120 miles further west. A small stream, the Chena Slough wends its serpentine path through Fairbanks from east to west, dividing the city into two sections. Fairbanks was an old gold-mining town, which managed to survive when the "yellow" ran out. In 1935, it was still a small community of under five thousand inhabitants; yet it believed that its destiny was to become the economic and cultural capital of Alaska. It was a town on the move and one could almost feel it flex its muscles. There were ambitious plans that would make Fairbanks the northern American hub of air traffic to Asia, and possibly Europe beyond. Very few of those dreams would materialize over the years, but that day, August 12, 1935, they were still very much alive and no one had any doubts about the future.

Wiley made a perfect landing on the river and the plane taxied slowly up the stream, past a wooded area of birch and stunted spruce. Joe Crosson, who stood on the floating dock, directed his friend Wiley by means of hand signals. Wiley did not know his way around the dock; the previous times he had flown into Fairbanks, it had been aboard the *Winnie Mae*, a land plane, and he had set down at the local airport, Weeks Field.

As Will crawled out of the plane, he spotted Crosson. "Want a rope, Joe?" he called out, then tossed a line. The plane was tied to the dock. Will got his first good look of the relatively narrow Chena Slough. Having just visited the wide Mackenzie River, and flown over the broad Yukon, Will drawled, "Is this all the river you got? Gotta have more river than that for an airplane."

Someone in the crowd called out, "Mr. Rogers, we're glad you're here!"

Will looked in the direction of the voice and shouted back, "Well, I'm glad I'm here too; I like these gold mining towns. Been having a great time in Dawson talking with the oldtimers."

Fairbanks' Mayor E. B. Collins was on hand to welcome the famous guests. Among those presented were Mr. and Mrs. Noel Wien, who had spotted the *Winnie Mae* circling back in 1933, when Wiley was on his solo trip. Noel was famous for having pioneered the Anchorage-to-Fairbanks mail flights in 1924.

Getting onto firm ground, Post answered questions. "We flew from Aklavik by way of Herschel and Porcupine River. I don't know how long we'll be here or where we'll go from here. No, I haven't got any program." Post also told the reporter for the *News-Miner* (Fairbanks' newspaper) that he would have some work done on the plane, though he did not go into specifics.

Once through the milling crowd, Wiley and Will loaded what little luggage they carried into the Crossons' Chrysler, which bore the Alaskan license plate #13. Here Will met Lillian Crosson, Joe's wife, and their two children, Joe Jr. and Don. Will, who loved all children, seemed especially taken with little Joe, who was generally called Jody.

When everything was stowed in the car, an impromptu parade formed. With the Crossons' car in the lead, all the automobiles that had come to see the plane land now followed in one long column. The procession did not break up until the celebrities lead car reached the Pioneer Hotel. Managed by the Gibbs family, the Pioneer stood proudly on Front Street—facing the Chena Slough—and a couple of blocks east of the only bridge. It had the distinction of being one of those rare hotels which had no lobby; as one entered, one turned left sharply, entered the bar, and, with one foot up on the brass rail, signed the guest register. Will Rogers found it hilarious that he had to go to the bar to get his room key.

Once registered and cleaned from the flight, Wiley spent the afternoon with his old friends, the Crossons. Will was off on a sightseeing tour on his own. The northern latitude of Fairbanks was a big help on his one-man exploration tour; in mid-August, it would stay light until close to midnight.

Will strolled the streets of Fairbanks, talking to residents. He made a lot of new friends, signing autographs, posing for pictures and shaking hands with everyone he met. Will dropped into stores and markets, learning all he could about the city. Wherever he went, he had a cluster of little boys and girls follow him.

For dinner, Wiley and Will were the guests of Lillian and Joe Crosson. Lillian prepared the recipe she usually served important guests. It was a dish she called "Chicken Legs." Will enjoyed it greatly and wanted to know more about it. Lillian admitted that the name was quite misleading—there was no chicken in it:

> It was veal and pork and I had my butcher cut it for me so that I then could roll it in something like bread crumbs, and the only reason I recall this is because Will Rogers was teasing me about my chicken legs;
>
> I don't know what else I cooked with it—oh, yes, mashed potatoes. I had a young girl living with us; her name was Virginia Rothaker, and as part of her rent she helped out. Will wandered into the kitchen, and he assisted her by mashing those potatoes. I think I had a frozen dessert—but the chicken legs were something that he teased me about.

Virginia also had a full-time job: She was the operator of Fairbanks' only elevator. Located in the Federal Building at 2nd and Cushman, that elevator was Virginia's pride—as if she had built it herself. While Will was mashing potatoes, Virginia kept pressuring him to come downtown and ride in her elevator. Finally Will could resist no longer; he promised faithfully to come and see it before he left town.

It was at Lillian and Joe Crosson's dinner table that the plan to go to Barrow originated. It was Joe Crosson's account of that interesting man, Charles Brower, that convinced Will he had to fly there. He wanted to meet the "King of the Arctic," as Brower was called.

For close to half a century, Brower had been operating a whaling station and trading post; he held the position of Commissioner, representing the U.S. government and the local law. He was administrator, policeman, judge, and arbiter. He had seen a world change and he would be able to tell many a story Will's readers would enjoy. "I'd rather see him than Greta Garbo," Will would tell the press.

After dinner, Will, who was a Shriner, was off to the Nile Temple ceremonial at the Masonic Temple. The next morning he said, "It was the first time I had seen an initiation in a long time; we had a lot of fun. It was pretty rough." Then changing the subject: "Everybody prowls around here at night in this town. At midnight there are more people on the street than at any other time. But I was the first one down to eat this morning, though."

A newspaper reporter asked Post (who so far had not entered the conversation) what time he got up. Post admitted that Rogers was the earlier riser. To illustrate the point, he told of Dawson City, where he went to bed at 3 o'clock in the morning, the same time as Rogers did; when he got up three hours later, at 6 o'clock, Rogers was already walking around town.

"While in Fairbanks," Will announced, "I want to get a lot of books. That's all I can do in the plane, is read. Post won't tell you where he is going or anything. He'd have gone to Point Barrow yesterday if he hadn't hit a head wind."

That seems a startling revelation. Any pilot flies into head winds. Being already on the Arctic Ocean, all Post would have had to do to reach Point Barrow was to fly due west; instead Wiley headed south and returned to the Alaskan interior. Of course, the weather could have been far worse than just "head winds," perhaps as bad as it was for the next few days, including August 15, the day Post and Rogers did set out for Barrow. But if the weather deterred Post on the twelfth, why did it not deter him three days later? Or had he reached the end of his patience by that time? The facts are that on the twelfth of August there were head winds and Post did not fly to Barrow; on the fifteenth of August, the weather bureau reported *no visibility, no ceiling*, yet Wiley did go.

The rest of the morning Will spent in his hotel room, pecking out a weekly article on his portable typewriter. He also found time for "typing out answers to 15 or 20 very nice telegrams which I have received."

Betty Rogers was, of course, in New York. But son Jimmy and his cousin Jimmy Blake had been working on the *Mashed O* ranch of Ewing Halsell, at Amherst, Texas. They were now in their small car driving half across the country to join Betty in Maine and had just reached Hagerstown, Maryland. Jimmy thought he ought to let his sister know where he was, and he sent a night-message telegram:

MARY ROGERS, LAKEWOOD, SKOWHEGAN, MAINE

HOPE TO GET TO NEW YORK TONIGHT BE IN MAINE
SATURDAY OR SUNDAY LOVE TO ALL
                                                    JIM

As most young fellows, even Will Rogers' son, Jimmy was a
little short of money; he sent the telegram collect and the next
morning, Tuesday, August 13, his sister had to pay the toll—35
cents. Later in the day, when Betty arrived at Skowhegan, Mary
was able to calm a worried mother with the news that her youngest was quite safe.

Will Rogers, walking around Fairbanks, was asked about his
further plans. He avoided any direct answer with a simple "we're
just bumming around." But the Fairbanks Chamber of Commerce
felt obligated to keep him busy. It appointed a committee to talk to
the distinguished visitors, and find out just what they wanted to see
and do in town. On the committee were the mayor, E.B. Collins;
Paul Rickert, president of the Chamber of Commerce; Don Adler,
manager of the Empress Theatre; and W. J. (Joe) Barrows, Pacific
Alaska Airways' Divisional Engineer.

Will hoped to avoid that type of organized touring. "I don't
want to be shown around while I'm in Fairbanks," he said. "I'll
show myself around. I know pretty nearly everybody here already." The strong hint not to arrange anything for him seemed
to have worked. When he left Fairbanks, Will was able to tell
reporters, "You have a lovely Chamber of Commerce. They
didn't annoy me at all while I was here and I think I bluffed your
mayor out."

They visited the experimental farm of the University of
Alaska at Fairbanks, where they were shown agricultural experiments and results. Will learned that almost all kinds of hardy
vegetables and berries, and even some grains, could be raised
south of the Arctic Circle. It was surprising to Rogers that despite such a short growing season—the late spring and the early
winter—such gratifying crops could be raised. It was explained
that daylight in the Northland was so much longer than in the 48
states, that it made up for the shorter growing seasons.

While the two men toured the University facilities, Taylor,
Ortman, Eagan, and Tilman (having returned from Anchorage),

all members of Loren Fernald's PAA maintenance crew, inspected Wiley's plane and went through "general routine servicing of motor, plane and pontoons." What was needed was one two-pole master switch, a Wasp Generator cover plate (used), 4 AN Spec. copper soldering lugs, and one 30 Amp. 'BUSS' fuse.

Actually Tilman didn't like the plane. A low-wing plane has more lift and is speedier, but putting floats on it defeated the purpose of making it faster. Besides, Post was not his idea of a safe pilot. "I never liked his flying—he was always taking a chance."

Lillian Crosson again invited Will and Wiley for dinner, but Will extended an invitation of his own. Reminding her that she had cooked for him the night before, he said he didn't want her to have all that kitchen work again on his account, and would she and Joe join him and Wiley at the Model Cafe?

At about 6:30 that evening the four of them sat in one of the old-fashioned booths, Will and Lillian on one side, and Wiley and Joe on the other; of course the two pilots on their side of the table talked about aviation, while Will and Lillian talked "well, mostly about his family." He showed her a picture and an article about Mary. "Will was so proud of her and her effort in the theater back in Maine—very proud of that."

To Lillian, Will looked old. He was twice her years and youth has a one-sided view of age. In deference she only called him "Mr. Rogers. "Course, Wiley was "Wiley" to us."

Pete and Alma Despot, part-owners of the Model Cafe, were both at the restaurant when Will and his party entered. Alma remembered that Will was surprised about the high Fairbanks prices. Walking to the cash register, manned by her husband, she told of Will putting a five-dollar bill on the counter. In Los Angeles, or New York, that would have covered the price of a meal for four, but in Fairbanks it was different. As Alma Despot tells the story, her husband looked at the five-dollar bill and laughed, "Hit it again, Will!"

Rogers looked a little puzzled; he was familiar with the phrase used in poker when an additional card is wanted, but he had never heard it in connection with a restaurant meal. Pete Despot asked, "Do you play blackjack?"

Rogers admitted, "Well, I'm not much of a gambler but I've played it on occasion."

"Well, then hit it again!"

Now Will understood; he took out a couple of silver dollars and placed them on the counter, "Here, are these any good? I just can't get used to these high prices."

Pete Despot explained that the reason for the huge cost of every item was that almost everything had to travel nearly three thousand miles, usually by boat from Seattle, then by train or plane.

After the meal, Lillian went home and Will, Wiley, and Joe went to a meeting of the Q.B. (the Quiet Birdmen), a pilots' organization.

Will was having a great time in Alaska; he loved every minute of it, and he was glad he had come. On Tuesday the thirteenth, he sent the following daily column:

> This Alaska is a great country. If they can just keep from being taken over by the U.S. they got a great future. . . .
>
> There may be some doubt about the Louisiana Purchase being a mistake, but when Seward in '68 bought Alaska for $7,000,000 he even made up for what we had overpaid the Indians for Manhattan Island.

August 14 promised to be a beautiful day in Fairbanks. As usual, Will was up early, having his breakfast at the Pioneer Hotel. It was shortly after 6:30 A.M. when he was joined by Warren Tilman. Warren lived next door at the Northern Hotel, which had no restaurant, so he came to the Pioneer. The two men talked while Nellie Norris, the waitress, served them more coffee. Suddenly the old cook came out of the kitchen. He was at least seventy-five-years-old; neither he nor anyone else could remember when he was born. He was a great Will Rogers fan and had seen every one of Will's films; when he heard that his favorite film star was sitting in the dining room, he had to come out and shake Will's hand.

"Boy," he said to Rogers, "you sure can shoot!"

Will seemed puzzled.

"You know, I seen you shoot in the movies."

"Anybody can shoot in the movies," Will tried to explain. "I probably couldn't hit the side of a barn."

"Boy," the cook insisted, "you can't tell me that. I seen you shoot in the movies, and you sure can shoot." Will thought it wiser not to disillusion the fan.

After breakfast, Will spent the early morning doing exactly what he had done the day before: he walked about town and chatted with all he met. Strolling north on Cushman in the direction of the Chena Slough, Will saw two ladies approaching. Naturally they recognized the visitor to their town and they smiled. One seemed to have Indian features. As they came close, Will, with his Cherokee ancestry, addressed her, "Oh, here comes one of my relatives."

The two ladies stopped, shook hands with Will and introductions were made. Mrs. Jessie Anderson was indeed part Indian; her companion's name was Mrs. Ted LaFon. Not at all intimidated by the famous man, Jessie told Will that she was about to buy some last-minute items for a small party she and her husband Carl, were having that evening; they were celebrating their tenth wedding anniversary, and would Will please come? Actually, Jessie went on to explain, their anniversary was really on the fifteenth, but there were other plans afoot for that date, and so they decided to have this little party on the fourteenth.

Rogers wanted to know where she lived. Jessie pointed out that, standing on Cushman Street, they could look straight north, across the Chena River bridge to the Anderson house at Driveway Street. Will said he still had some work to do, but if he had time, he would certainly try to show up. Later, Jessie told her husband about the meeting with Will Rogers, and that she had invited him. Carl held out little hope that so busy a man as Will Rogers would actually come to unimportant people's homes.

Walking past the post office, Will mailed the weekly article he had typed the day before, to the newspaper syndicate in New York City. It contained some newly acquired inside information about Alaska:

> An Eskimo dog from the time he is just a half-sized pup is never untied. He is always tied with a chain, and he don't bark at all, he howls. They call all Eskimos "Huskies." I always thought it was the dogs that were called "Huskies" but it's the Eskimos themselves.
>
> That's enough northern knowledge for one lesson, especially when some of it maybe ain't so.

The morning report from Point Barrow's weather station, however, ruled out any trip in that direction. But there were other things to do. Will wanted to visit the colony Franklin Roosevelt's Federal Emergency Relief Administration had only recently settled in the extremely fertile valley of the Matanuska River. It was a plan to give some two hundred impoverished farm families of the forty-eight states a new start, while at the same time developing and settling Alaska. Rumors of some discontent about governmental mismanagement had reached the newspapers, and there was talk that not enough housing would be ready before the winter weather arrived. Will had to see for himself.

At 10:45 A.M. Joe Crosson drove Rogers, Post, and Joe Barrows (PAA's Divisional Engineer) to Weeks Field. Warren Tilman was there as Will climbed into a Pacific Alaska Airways Lockheed Electra. Warren explained to him, "You just sit anywhere and taking off or landing, you buckle that belt; then after you get in the air, just unbuckle it and you can walk all around."

Will settled into his seat and began to tighten the belt. "With me and Wiley it's different," he told Tilman. "In his airplane I walk around only when he's landed." Post shot Will a quick look, as if he wished Will had not mentioned it.[3]

Almost ready for take-off, Joe Crosson, Operations Manager for PAA, was asked by a reporter where they were going. Crosson, who was to pilot the plane, shrugged his shoulders mischievously. "I don't know!" he claimed, smiling broadly.

The plane arrived at Savage Camp, McKinley Park, at noon. The party stayed only five minutes on the ground before taking off and flying around the peak of Mt. McKinley, viewing the monolith from all sides. Then they headed toward Palmer, the small town in the Matanuska Valley. Arriving over Palmer's still-primitive airstrip, Joe Crosson looked it over carefully. Circling it several times he thought the surface too rough and unsuitable for the large Electra, and decided instead to land in Anchorage, only minutes away. Before heading in that direction, Crosson flew over the valley for about fifteen minutes to give his guests a perfect aerial view of the terrain and building activity of the entire area. They saw the mountains surrounding the delta basin, where a dozen streams had deposited rich topsoil for centuries. With virgin soil and unlimited water, plentiful harvests seemed assured.

The four men landed at Anchorage's Merrill Field at 1:30 P.M. Anchorage had expected a visit by Rogers and Post, and everyone was on the lookout for Wiley's red float plane. When the big silver Electra with wheels arrived, no one connected it with Post and Rogers. However, the moment Rogers stepped from the plane, wearing an "infectious grin; his grey rough shirt was open at the throat and yellow corduroys were splattered with airplane grease," the news spread through the city. Residents came from all parts of town to see the two celebrities. By this time Rogers, Post, Crosson, and Barrows had gone to the Anchorage Grill counter for lunch. Settling themselves in a row on individual seats at the counter, Will ordered roast leg of lamb. When an *Anchorage Times* reporter asked Wiley whether he would be accompanied by Rogers on his contemplated flight to Moscow, Post evaded an answer by saying: "Go, ask him!"

To the reporter, Rogers was indefinite about his future plans:

> "I don't know whether I will accompany Post to Russia. But this" said Will, as he took a deep breath and a bite of the lamb, "this is a great country, and I'm glad I came. Never saw anything to equal Mt. McKinley . . . I'm telling them Outside all about it in my daily short message to a syndicate of 650 newspapers which get my service.
>
> Will paused long enough to take another bite. "Yep," he said as he reached for a Matanuska radish, "I want to get up there this afternoon, and see the whole works."

Then Rogers wanted some answers: how many were there in the colony, how many had quit, how many men were working up there and how did things look; he clearly indicated to those gathered around him that he realized the importance of the colonization project. Everybody chimed in at once, trying to tell all they knew. Then Will, having finished his meal, reached for a piece of pie. "How's the tourist business—lots of people coming this way?" he wanted to know.

Someone in the crowd told him that ships coming up the coast were crowded to capacity and that hundreds weekly were going over the Alaska Railroad.

"Yes, and there will be more every year," Rogers predicted. "They will get their money's worth. Alaska's scenic charms and

climate are a permanent lure and asset. Hope she works it for all
its worth. It will bring fortunes to the country. Alaska has something the others haven't.''

"Will you go fishing for one of Alaska's famous rainbow
trout or try to get a bear while you are here?'' someone asked.

"Nope—don't fish—don't hunt—wouldn't know what to
use for bait or how to shoot or what to do with the victims. Just
don't have the urge,'' Rogers answered.

Having heard about the huge Alaskan mosquitoes Will
stated his suspicions. "About these mosquitoes,'' he said, sound-
ing almost disappointed, "why, I haven't seen any mosquitoes.
That seems to be a big piece of bunk about the country being
eaten up by the mosquitoes.''

At the airport Will made arrangements with Oscar Winch-
ell, "flying cowboy'' of the Star Air Service, for a flight in a small
plane to Palmer. Their pilot would be Chet McLean, a well-known
Alaskan pilot. But Wiley, a great pilot, was a poor passenger. He
kept looking for problems, and when he saw the landing field at
Palmer, he exclaimed, "Jees! that field looks rough.''

Rogers, on the other hand, with not a care in the world,
took a short after-lunch nap on the flight.

They arrived at 3:15 P.M. The visit to Palmer and the Matanuska colony was rewarding. To the transplanted farmers, Will
Rogers was a welcome reminder of home. His weekly radio
broadcasts had been such a reassuring voice during these years of
the Depression; but here in Alaska, the broadcasts could not be
heard. Now Will Rogers had come to them, and they all wanted to
see him, hear him in person, talk to him, touch him.

Before Rogers could even squeeze out of the plane, questions abounded. "How do you feel, Mr. Rogers?''

"Why, uh, why—wait'll I get out, will you?'' He drawled
kindly. "I came to look around, not to report on my health.
Where you boys from?'' He asked, pressing into the crowd.
"Anybody here from Claremore?'' Everybody thought that one
funny. There was no one from that part of Oklahoma. Wiley
looked over the scene; he stood, almost overlooked and forgotten
on the edge of the crowd.

After a motor tour of several of the camps and a few of the
new homes, guided by the administrator, L. P. Hunt, Will was
impressed with what he had seen. "The valley looks great, you

have a mighty fine place here and the crops look good," was his verdict. Then they returned to the small plane. Just as Rogers was about to close the door, the construction gang's cook rushed up with a handful of brown, fat cookies. Rogers took a bite, brushed off the crumbs. "Very good!" he announced, "but I'll toss them out if we can't get off the ground!" were his last words, as pilot McLean inched the plane forward. Will had left them laughing.

They were back in Fairbanks by 7:30 P.M. Joe Crosson drove his two guests to his home. Lillian had prepared some hors d'oeuvres, and she served some cooling drinks. She urged Will to stay for dinner, but Will was off, he had a call to make.

The Anderson's anniversary party was in full swing, with everyone having a good time, when there was a knock at the door. Will Rogers had come to call. A taxi driver had driven him to the Anderson house, and was patiently waiting outside. Will stayed for about half an hour, then he left. He had enjoyed himself and he had given the guests and Jessie Anderson a memory none of them would ever forget.

Way back east, in Skowhegan, Maine, the Lakewood Theatre would be dark now, the performance long over. In Maine, where Betty, Mary and Aunt Dick were, it was past midnight, but in California the sun was just setting. But unless he worked exceptionally long hours in his office in Beverly Hills, Sandy Blake did not receive a telegram, dated August 14; it was time-stamped in California at 7:58 P.M. Not until the following day did he act upon the instructions:

J K BLAKE
BANK OF AMERICA BLDG BV

INSURANCE OK TAKE EXTRA FORTY SEVEN =

BETTY.

Thursday, August 15, Will was up early, as usual. He ate breakfast at the Pioneer Hotel, Warren Tilman joining him again. Afterwards Will went out for his morning walk, visiting with the folks of Fairbanks. He stopped to buy a book telling of the purchase of Alaska from Russia. With a grin Will explained to the salesgirl that he wanted "to learn how the Russians swindled us." Speaking with the reporter from the Fairbanks *News-Miner*, Will told him that one of the statements he would send to newspapers in the States was: 'Don't let the United States take over Alaska; leave it as it is, an independent republic. Alaska,'' he continued, ''is much different from the States and more interesting. And Fairbanks is the busiest city in Alaska. I like Fairbanks very much and when the Sunday newspapers for which I will write my report of Fairbanks reach here, you will see that I speak well of your city.''

The reporter wanted to know whether the two famous men would be on hand for the Gold Discovery celebration set for the next day, Friday, August 16? Will wanted to know more about it. When told that the Fairbanks baseball team was scheduled to play against Dawson, Will wrote a check for $100 that he wanted presented to the Fairbanks team.

On his way back to the hotel—he had yet to finish some work for his syndicate—he ran into the famous musher, Leonhard Seppala. Will had looked forward to meeting him. Seppala had gained international acclaim in 1925, when he and his dog team trekked diphtheria serum to gravely ill Eskimo children in Nome, averting a major tragedy.

While Will was walking about town, Wiley Post and Joe Crosson went—of all things—house hunting. Wiley had fallen in love with Alaska, and he decided that he would settle down in Fairbanks. There were so many things he could do here. Having seen the Crosson's gold mine, Post wanted to prospect for gold and find his own mine. Then he wanted to go wolf-hunting. For years Post had dreamed of hunting wolves in Alaska. In fact, on his last visit home he had shown Bennie Turner, his old friend, and Billy Parker, head of Phillips Petroleum Co. aviation division, a design for his ''Arctic hunting plane.'' It was a Pusher-type plane, equipped with skids and a swivel, high-powered gun in the front cockpit.

''It's a cinch,'' he had told Bennie, ''you just sit up there until you see a pack of wolves and then pick 'em off. They will scatter from a plane and all you have to do is land on the snow and pick up the pelts. It would be lots of fun, profitable, and you would reduce those hounds.''

Wiley and Joe Crosson went out in the morning of August 15, to look for a home in Fairbanks, where Wiley could settle down with Mae; and Wiley found just what he wanted. On Cushman

Street, near the school, he found a suitable house. Without hesitation, Wiley Post rented it.

Then the two friends drove to the airport, Weeks Field. There Crosson went once more over charts, explaining to Wiley the various routes, the passes and landmarks; then he selected a pile of maps and shoved them at Wiley. "Here, you may need them." Crosson again pointed out the dangers facing a pilot in the Arctic region. "Both Post and Rogers discussed with Crosson and others their proposed flights, and . . . Post remarked that in their flying about Alaska, under no circumstances would he fly with Rogers in or above any cloud or fog bank. His plan was to travel as safely as possible by so-called 'contact flying,' turning back and landing in lake or river at any time when the weather made it dangerous to proceed."

Wiley believed that he could lift off from Chena Slough with a fully laden aircraft, but wiser counsel prevailed. It was decided that Wiley and Will would take off from Fairbanks with minimally filled fuel tanks, fly to Harding Lake, some forty miles southeast of the city, and have the tanks topped there. With an entire lake as his "runway," Wiley would have little difficulty lifting a nose-heavy craft off the surface.

When Pan American Airways' bill for maintenance work was presented, Will Rogers signed a check, not bothering to fill in the amount nor checking the items listed. If he had, he would have seen that there was a charge of $187.50 for the charter of the Lockheed Electra, used the previous day for the trip to Anchorage. There was an item of $15 for "our truck, taking gas to lake" which had later been crossed out. Then there were charges for 106 gallons of gasoline 73 Octane aviation gasoline, and 106 gallons of 87 Octane aviation gasoline, both identified "(to lake)". The 73 Octane was obviously intended for cruising, while the 87 Octane gasoline was for take-offs, climbing and whenever extra power would be needed. Will paid for the fuel as billed.

The weather in Fairbanks was fine. At noon the thermometer had reached 60 degrees, with a gentle three-mile-an-hour breeze. But the first of two daily radio reports from Barrow was discouraging. The early morning temperature, so Sergeant Stanley Morgan of the U.S. Signal Corps manning the WAMCATS station at Barrow reported, was 40 degrees and conditions were "Dense fog, nil, nil, S9," indicating *nil* ceiling, *nil* visibility, with a southerly wind of nine miles. It was the kind of weather report every pilot dreaded. Having no view of the ground meant that a plane could not land.

Will finished a weekly column, slipped it into the envelope and addressed it. Then he decided to send a telegram to Mary:

FAIRBANKS, ALASKA, AUGUST 15,1935

MARY ROGERS, SKOWHEGAN MAINE

GREAT TRIP. WISH YOU WERE ALONG. HOW'S YOUR ACTING? YOU AND MAMA WIRE ME ALL THE NEWS TO NOME. GOING TO POINT BARROW TODAY. FUR-THEST POINT OF LAND ON WHOLE AMERICAN CON-TINENT. LOTS OF LOVE. DON'T WORRY.

DAD

Then he dashed off the daily column, which would have to be telegraphed to the McNaught syndicate in New York City. Just before 11 A.M. Lillian and her two small children drove to the Pioneer Hotel, to pick up Will and his luggage. With young Jody now relegated to the back seat, Will climbed into the Chrysler next to Lillian, holding one-year-old Don on his lap. In fact, Will carried the baby almost until it was time to leave. Rogers asked Lillian to stop at Lavery Bailey's grocery store at Cushman and Second. Here Will loaded up on chili cans. Happily grinning, he carried them to the car. Then, as Lillian waited some more, Will walked across to Vic Brown's Jewelry store to pick up a wrist-watch left for repair.⁴ Since Will did not wear such a watch, it had to belong to Wiley.

This should settle an old dispute once and for all time. During investigations of the crash, certain puzzling time inconsis-tencies about the day's activities had been glossed over by the claim that Wiley's wristwatch was set on Oklahoma time. There was really no rational reason why that should be so, as Wiley had not been in Oklahoma in some time; yet that theory was offered and widely accepted. But since the watch now came directly from a Fairbanks jewelery store, it seems reasonable to assume that Mr. Brown, the jeweller, like his colleagues everywhere else, wound and set the watch before turning it over to Will. He would obviously set it to local time.

When Will finally got back into the car, Lillian handed him little Don again for safekeeping, before she started the engine. There was, however, one more stop Will wanted to make.

Having promised Virginia Rothaker that he would come and ride in her elevator, Will stopped at the Federal Building, dutifully rode to the second floor and back down, and shook hands with Virginia. Then he was off to the dock.

When they reached Spencer's Float, Joe and Wiley had already arrived from Weeks Field. Joe was still trying to dissuade his friend from leaving Fairbanks in the face of the threatening morning weather report. Wiley was intent on moving on. Joe even offered to pilot Will and Wiley to Barrow in one of the PAA's Fairchild 71s—but not this day. Wiley wanted none of it: "We might as well go, anyway," he said. And Will supported him: "There's lots of lakes we can land on."

The best compromise Joe could reach with Post was the promise that Wiley would telephone from Harding Lake to learn the afternoon weather report, which was expected before 2 P.M.

At dockside Will handed Joe Crosson the column to be mailed and the telegram to Mary. When Betty later received the telegram, the phrase "YOU AND MAMA WIRE ME ALL THE NEWS TO NOME" was a clear indication that Will had made his decision: he would go on with Wiley to Russia. Gone was the plan they had made about his joining her in Skowhegan after his return from Alaska. They had spoken of leisurely motoring through the Cape Cod country. She had so looked forward to that: just the two of them, away from the film studio and the stream of visitors at the ranch. Now she would have to fly back to their California home, pack, and get ready to meet Will somewhere in Europe, perhaps even Moscow.

The two men climbed into the plane, the door was closed. The time was 11:30 A.M. The engine was warm; it had been idling with the plane tied to the float. Joe Crosson unhitched the ropes. Wiley taxied away from shore.

On the morning of August 15, Wiley would take-off downriver where in that direction the river curved to the right. When using this stretch of the river for take-off, PAA pilots always made the turn first and then got off the water. In fact, some experienced pilots had developed the technique of lifting one float out of the water as they entered the curve of the river and then took off in the turn.

For Wiley Post this would be the first time he had ever taken off from the Chena River. It is safe to assume that Joe Crosson had told Wiley the usual technique employed by Alaskan pilots in take-off from the river.

Once in the center of the river, Post turned to face into the wind and started down-river, quickly on the step, then very quickly off the water and climbing very steeply. He was in the air well before the bend in the river and climbed steeply over the trees. Robert J. Gleason, Communications Superintendent for Pacific Alaska Airways, watching the take-off heard pilots standing near him remark that "with a take-off like that, if the engine quit, he's a goner."

Everett W. Patton, watching the plane leave, was surprised to see Wiley as he "pulled it up into a very spectacular climbing turn and he went out of that and swung around over the city, came back and waggled his wings and then took off for Harding Lake. This type of flying with a float plane is a complete no-no. You just don't do these things with a float plane and survive very long."

One thing was obvious: the plane was "over-powered," which allowed Wiley to literally jump the plane out of the water. Pilots and mechanics remembered how carefully, by comparison, Post had taken off two years earlier. On his solo flight around the world, when Wiley had flown the *Winnie Mae*, he had taken the whole field before lifting off in a very slow climb.

Harding Lake was a cool, scenic refuge, away from the sometimes stifling summer heat of Fairbanks; there were a few year-round residents, but mostly the houses dotting the shore were used during the hot months of the year. The arrival of a plane at the lake always drew a crowd of children, and even some adults. Rogers and Post had not been expected at the summer colony. In fact, when the plane was first heard, one Forbes Baker thought it was "another airplane that used to land out there every once in a while. So whenever an airplane came over, we always ran down to the landing, that's where the airplanes came in. And that's why we were there. There were my two sisters and some other kids."

The dock at Harding Lake was simple, without facilities; just some planks built on a few piles, jutting a few feet over the edge of the shore. Joe Crosson had made arrangements for aviation fuel to be driven from Fairbanks. Hours earlier a little blue 1931 Chevrolet pickup truck with mechanic Ron Taylor, four men and some drums of gasoline had rattled off on its way to the lake. The highway, leading from Fairbanks to Tok, Whitehorse, and further south, was a rough dirt road. Usually the trip from Fairbanks to the lake would take at least an hour and a half. Warren Tilman claims to have held the record for the fastest time from Harding Lake to Fairbanks. He made it in "a little over an hour, but that's the fastest ride that I ever went on." The reason: Mrs. Tilman had gone into labor and "my twins were almost born there."

When Wiley's plane arrived at Harding Lake, the PAA crew Crosson had sent went to work immediately. The plane was first pulled partly onto shore and gasoline was then hand-pumped to top all tanks. Their task was finished shortly after 1:00 P.M. Wiley had promised Crosson to call from the lake to learn the afternoon Barrow weather report. But there was no public telephone at the lake. In the area, however, along the dirt highway there were two saloons, mostly frequented by miners, which had telephones. It would have been a short ride, had Wiley asked for a lift in the pickup truck to either tavern. The *18 miles Roadhouse* was, as the name suggested, at the 18-mile marker outside of Fairbanks, some twenty miles back toward town; driving only a very short distance in the opposite direction, at mile 52, Post could have reached the *Silver Fox Roadhouse*. Wiley Post went to neither.

At 1:30 P.M., the expected weather report from Barrow was received in Fairbanks. It had changed little from the morning summary: "BARROW ONE THIRTY PM DENSE FOG ZERO ZERO FORTY FIVE SOUTH NINE." The message was unmistakable: at 1:30 P.M. there was dense fog, no ceiling, no visibility, 45 degrees and a south wind of nine miles per hour. When Crosson realized that contrary to the arrangement, Wiley was not about to telephone Fairbanks, he hastily dispatched a copy of the weather report by automobile to Harding Lake.

Wiley took off from the lake close to 2:00 P.M., a half-hour after the weather report and been received from Barrow. There would have been sufficient time for him to learn the weather conditions at his destination, had he but telephoned. Yet Wiley showed no interest in that information and by the time the automobile from Fairbanks labored up to the dock at Harding Lake, Wiley Post and Will Rogers had left long ago. Without an operational radio aboard, there was no way now to alert the pilot.

Wiley Post, unaware of what lay ahead, had forgotten his pledge that "under no circumstances would he fly with Rogers in or above any cloud or fog bank."[5] Wiley Post had taken off, "making his own weather."

The Days of August, 1935

August 1 (Thursday)	Wiley and Mae Post arrive in Seattle.
August 2 (Friday	Conversion of plane begins.
August 3 (Saturday)	Wiley Post goes fishing; Will Rogers is in Los Angeles.
August 4 (Sunday)	Rogers takes a late flight to San Francisco.
August 5 (Monday)	Rogers arrives in Seattle.
August 6 (Tuesday)	Rogers plays polo; Post tests the plane.
August 7 (Wednesday)	Rogers and Post leave Seattle, and arrive in Juneau.
August 8 (Thursday)	It rains in Juneau; departure is delayed.
August 9 (Friday)	Rogers & Post leave Juneau for Dawson.
August 10 (Saturday)	Rogers & Post leave Dawson for Aklavik.
August 11 (Sunday)	The day is spent in Aklavik.
August 12 (Monday)	Rogers & Post depart Aklavik for Fairbanks via Herschel Islands.
August 13 (Tuesday)	Rogers & Post spend the day in Fairbanks.
August 14 (Wednesday)	Rogers, Post & Joe Crosson take a day trip to Mount McKinley, Anchorage, Palmer, and Matanuska, then return to Fairbanks.
August 15 (Thursday)	Rogers & Post leave Fairbanks for Point Barrow; the plane crashes in Walakpa Lagoon.
August 16 (Friday)	Crosson & Gleason leave Fairbanks for Barrow. Mae Post leaves Ponca City, OK, for Maysville, OK.
August 17 (Saturday)	The bodies are returned to Fairbanks.
August 18 (Sunday)	The bodies arrive in Vancouver, BC. The Rogers family begins trip west to Los Angeles.
August 19 (Monday)	The bodies are flown from Vancouver to Seattle, Alameda, and Burbank.
August 20 (Tuesday)	Post's body is taken to Oklahoma City.
August 21 (Wednesday)	Rogers family reaches Los Angeles.
August 22 (Thursday)	Funeral services are held in Glendale and Oklahoma City.

CHAPTER FIVE

THE CRASH

> You know, this radio has made it mighty fine to
> find out what's ahead. You see, it's never the
> weather you take off in, it's the weather where
> you have to go through after you take off. I re-
> member one trip on our late tour with Captain
> Frank Hawks when we took off one day in a snow
> storm in New Mexico, when you just couldn't see
> a thing, not two hundred feet, and it was that way
> flying blind for the next hour, but he had heard
> before that it was clear in Albuquerque, where we
> were going. So it's how is the weather ahead of
> you, [rather] than how is it where you are.
> —Will Rogers, *Weekly Article*, April 19, 1931.

Wiley Post's gold wristwatch, showing the elapsed time since he
left Harding Lake, must have told him that he should have reached
the north coast of Alaska a long time ago. But Wiley Post was lost.

Being lost was no cause for alarm—not yet. He had been
lost before, many times. Pilots frequently became lost when
flying over unfamiliar territory with few or no identifying landmarks. There were certain procedures to follow. A pilot could fly
a straight line until he would find a river, railroad tracks, a
mountain, or a town, which would provide a point of reference.
Or, if the pilot thought that he had perhaps passed his target, he
would begin flying ever larger circles until he discovered his goal.
But Wiley Post knew that this was different; quite different.

Wiley's float plane was circling over northern Alaska's
thousands of square miles of unchanging, level tundra, dotted
with a myriad of shallow lakes. During the short summer months
in flat northern Alaska, ice and permafrost minimally melt, creating meandering rivulets and creeks that will find each other and
combine. Following twisted courses they flow slowly first this
way, then that way, then part to create islands, then unite once
again. Over centuries, these flowing bodies of water have cut into

the tundra and washed away some of the loose surface soil, creating shallow lakes. During the severe winter months the frozen surfaces make ideal landing places for ski-equipped planes; in the summertime, every lake becomes a harbor for a float plane.

Ordinarily Post could easily have set the plane down near a trapper's cabin or an Eskimo's hunting camp on any one of those bodies of water, except that he could not see a single one of them. Below the plane, from horizon to horizon, stretched the continuous layer of dense fog and thick clouds.

Wiley had violated the most basic of all Alaskan flight rules: "Never make your own weather!" Old-time pilots learned the wisdom long ago, to never make themselves believe that the weather will be different than reported. "Never make your own weather!" was an axiom based on experience, gained at the cost of many a lost life and wrecked plane. Before taking off from Fairbanks, Wiley knew the dangerous weather conditions north of the Brooks Range. The morning report from Barrow, Wiley's goal for the day, could not have been more explicit; it had warned: dense fog, nil, nil—meaning, zero ceiling, zero visibility. At Barrow, so the report translated, the fog was shrouding the ground and one could not see through it. In 1935, any pilot knew that under such conditions at his destination, he could not land. But Post was not just "any" pilot. He thought of himself as indestructible, and that he could control any situation—that he always had in the past and would always be able to do so in the future.

He and Rogers knew the morning report from Point Barrow, but they had already lost several days because of rain; they were impatient to get going. Winter comes early in the Arctic; ice floes drifting southward had already been reported in the Chukchi Sea off Barrow. And the two men still planned to go across Siberia to Europe. Wiley had suggested that just in case they should run into a little bad weather, they could always set down on one of the lakes, "open some of that chili and throw a party."

Wiley had been well-briefed. In Fairbanks, Joe Crosson had poured over maps with Wiley. The two old friends were in their element, talking flying, planning routes, exchanging technical information. But Joe had worried. It was one thing explaining the hazards of northern Alaskan flying to someone, and quite another to learn them through personal experience. How could Joe successfully transfer the knowledge gained by years of actually flying the Arctic? But then, Wiley was no novice. He had flown through almost any weather. He had even been briefly in the Arctic before. Still, Joe Crosson worried; against his explicit warnings, Wiley had decided to take off for the Eskimo village of Barrow, at the northern-most point of land on the American continent.

Separating the North Slope area of Alaska from the rest of the state, sprawling from east to west across the entire width of the land, lie the formidable Endicott Mountains, part of which is the Brooks Range. It is a rugged and barren chain of mountains, about eighty miles deep, their highest peak reaching 9,239 feet. Pilots flying to the north, or returning, never flew over the ranges, but through the lowest passes. It took experience and daring to negotiate the unexpected turns and sudden twists encountered while flying between walls of towering mountainsides at speeds exceeding one hundred miles per hour.

Even under the most ideal conditions, a flight from Fairbanks to Barrow was considered "hazardous as hell." A traveler's account of such hazards, published in the Point Barrow *Settlement Quarterly*, later provided *New York Herald Tribune* readers with background:

> From Fairbanks to Barrow—Ah! There's the rub. Only about 650 miles in an airplane, but over the precipitous Endicott Range. The saw-toothed mountains of the range leave no place in which to "sit down" in case of mishap and no way in which to get out, even if a forced landing could be made, and a region, too, particularly subject to storm and fog.
>
> I had questioned the seemingly exorbitant rate as established, $750 for the trip, and was told that the trip is of such hazardous and uncertain character by reason of the terrain and the weather that the airways cannot risk the plane and the life of the pilot for any ordinary commercial fare, and that any contract for passage is subject to reservation: "God willing and the weather permitting."
>
> I now concede the reasonableness of the charge.

Barrow, a tiny Eskimo village of fewer than four hundred inhabitants, sprawled around a lagoon along the west coast of a

triangular peninsula jutting into the Arctic Ocean. A narrow finger of land extends about twelve miles further northward, ending
in Pt. Barrow.

Flying from Fairbanks to Barrow, so Joe Crosson had told
Wiley, pilots usually headed due north until they touched the
coast near Cape Halket to the southeast of Barrow at the edge of
the continent at the Beaufort Sea, a part of the Arctic Ocean. From
there they would fly along the water's edge towards the northwest, or "up coast," to reach Barrow. Reaching Barrow by flying
west along the up-coast eliminated any possible chance of missing
it. It was a longer, but far safer route than trying to set course
straight for the village. Aiming directly for Barrow held one major
drawback. When reaching the coastline, a pilot's quandary was to
decide whether to turn left or right to reach Barrow. With few
identifiable landmarks along either coast, valuable fuel and time
could be wasted. Wiley had followed Crosson's advice, and had
flown due north to the Beaufort Sea.

The natives at Barrow could tell the place of origin of an
approaching plane long before it landed. They would listen carefully for the direction of the sound. If the motor noise came from
the up-coast the plane was from Fairbanks or Wiseman; if the
sound came from the down-coast the plane was from Nome,
Kotzebue, or Wainwright.

It had been an easy trip for Wiley to fly through the passes
on the way north, just as Joe Crosson had marked on the maps.
But then he had entered the North Slope, the basin north of the
mountains, which held the fog and the low-lying clouds. Perhaps
Wiley should have turned around then and sought the safety of
the fair weather. Even now, though he could not see the mountain
passes, he could still climb above the highest peak and fly back
some two hundred miles. There was still fuel enough for a retreat.

But Wiley was not a man who gave up easily—ever. He was,
as Will Rogers had written, "tough as a boot physically, and as
determined as a bull." There was time to turn back, later.

Wiley could not be certain whether he was still over land,
or having left the coast behind, he was now north of it, or west of
it, over open sea. He could see nothing. He kept to his plan of
covering a huge area again and again, searching for that one break
in the overcast which would show him the ground. The plane's
single engine droned on steadily. Wiley was circling, ever further

westward. Slowly the plane banked; there was no wisdom in speed now. It only used more fuel. Wiley could not foresee how long he might have to stay aloft. The more fuel he had, the longer he could fly, and the better his chances of finding a clearing. Somewhere, for one brief moment, there had to be an opening. Once he could see the ground, he could land and wait for the fog to lift. But his vision was not only limited by the oversized engine cowl directly in front, but by the fact that he had only sight in his right eye.

Wiley could have used an extra pair of eyes in the cockpit. While he stared out the right side, that single, life-saving opening in the overcast could slip by on his blind side and he would never know it. But there was no space for another person in the cockpit, and besides, he could not ask Rogers to come forward from his seat in the rear section. The plane was too nose-heavy now.

Natives tending a reindeer herd on the tundra some ninety miles from Barrow heard the sound of the plane flying overhead three different times. Obviously it was a circling plane, for it would approach from the east, fly off towards the west and then—later—reappear from the east.

Gus Massick, a trader from Demarcation Point, was en route to Barrow in an open motor boat that late afternoon, crossing Smith's Bay, some sixty miles east of Barrow. He distinctly heard a plane overhead and once even caught sight of it. He heard the plane leave for the tundra and after a while return, circling once again, evidently seeking some landmark. Finally, the plane seemed to leave for the West along the up-coast. Gus, a veteran of the Arctic who had accompanied the famous explorer Vilhjalmur Stefansson on his northern expeditions, was surprised to hear a plane aloft with the weather "very thick." Massick felt certain that the plane had missed Barrow because of the fog: "It was flying low and evidently looking for a place to settle." An Eskimo reported hearing the plane above Point Tangent, some fifty miles from Barrow.

Thomas P. Brower, who had a reindeer ranch some seventy air-miles out of Barrow, learned that his men at the ranch had not only heard but spotted the plane circling. Since they could see the plane, they felt certain that the pilot had seen them too, and they were disappointed when he did not land on their nearby lake. They confirmed that "we had a dense fog and it came out about ten or twelve miles north of my ranch and it was right down to the bottom, . . . you couldn't cut it with a knife to go through.'' The ranch was well-stocked with provisions and drums of gasoline. Wiley did not see them. He would not have passed up a chance to set the plane down near habitation.

Of course there was a radio aboard the plane, and Wiley was capable of operating a radio. He had taken instruction courses and passed an examination. But while he was in the pilot seat, his radio was merely 135 pounds of dead weight. The bulky radio could never be operated by a pilot fully occupied with keeping a difficult plane level and on course; it needed a radio operator, or at least a co-pilot. It might have been life saving had Wiley been able to establish radio contact.

On and on, the same drone of the engine; the constant, monotonous noise numbing the senses. Will Rogers, unless he was napping, must have been aware that the plane was circling. Consulting his watch, he, too, must have wondered why the trip to Barrow, which was to have taken at most four hours, was now almost six hours long. But he had supreme confidence in Wiley's ability. Still, for the gregarious Rogers, it must have been a trying time; he had no one to talk to. Once, on his 1926 flying trip into Russia, he had been the only passenger with a Soviet pilot and his mechanic, neither able to speak English. Rogers remarked then that what concerned him most during the long flight "was keeping my mouth shut a whole day." In addition, Rogers' quarters were confining for his 5-foot, 11-inch frame, and there was little he could do. Being a restless man, the act of sitting lazily and daydreaming was alien to him. His foremost pleasure was physical activity: riding, roping calves, and playing polo.

Yet even while pursuing those diversions, his mind was working on other projects. It has been said that he wrote his entire weekly article of some 1,500 words in his head. Then, when he sat down to type it, it was only an act of transferring the finished story to paper. Therefore he never had to rewrite it, or make corrections. In fact, he never re-read his own finished script. "I'm getting writing wages, not reading wages," was his explanation; but the fact was that he had done all the re-writing in his mind, before he ever faced the typewriter.

Relegated to the confining aft-section, he had typed most of his next weekly article. It was the story of Mickey, the wirehaired fox terrier belonging to the Crossons. The anecdote had been told him by Don Gustafson who, with his wife Inez, managed the Crosson's gold mine, named Hi Yu, near Fairbanks. One day, little Mickey had sniffed out a bear that had ventured too close to camp, and "attacked" him.

Will gave Don Gustafson the pseudonym Ernest. The third page of the article was still in the typewriter:

> . . . well, as a matter of fact Mickey went out and the bear chased him in, and Ernest had to shoot the bear to keep him from running Mickey under the bed. They say there is more fellows been caught by a bear just that way. An old pet dog jumps the bear and then they hike straight to you, and the bear after 'em, and the first thing you know you have a bear in your lap, and a dog between your feet.
> So there is two kinds of bear dogs; the ones that drive 'em away and the ones that bring 'em in. Little Mickey thought he had done it; As Ernest said, he chewed all the hair off the bear, after death, . . .

Will would never end it, stopping here, the last word being "death." For some reason Will had put the typewriter aside. Perhaps later, he would finish the column and send it from Barrow to his syndicate in New York City. He had leafed through a copy of the News-Miner, the Fairbanks newspaper; he had also read parts of *Arctic Village*, the book Joe Crosson had given him when they first met in Juneau. There was nothing to see looking out the windows. It was the steady cottony sameness outside for the past couple of hours.

Wiley, checking his instrument panel to keep his circling course, must have done some calculations. He had started from Harding Lake, some forty miles southeast of Fairbanks, with his fuel tanks topped. His four wing tanks held fifty-six gallons each; there was a thirty-gallon tank under his seat, and a sixteen-gallon head tank for a total of 270 gallons of gasoline in his six fuel tanks. Wiley was not quite sure how much the tanks held but he was certain that his Pratt & Whitney Wasp engine consumed thirty-two gallons an hour just to keep a steady cruising speed of 125 miles per hour. The plane was capable of a maximum speed of 180 mph. Wiley must have estimated that he had used close to two hundred gallons since leaving Harding Lake; he could not be positive, as five of his tanks had no gauges; only the thirty-gallon tank under his seat had the old Ford gauge.

It seems reasonable to assume that Wiley planned to use up the fuel in all other tanks first, before switching to the one with the gauge. That tank would be his final reserve. Then, knowing that he had less than one hour's fuel supply left, he could watch his reserve dwindle and make some plan for an emergency landing.

Wiley would have consulted the clock on the instrument panel and compared it with his watch. If his calculations were correct, and he had indeed used about two hundred gallons, there would be enough fuel left to stay aloft for about two more hours. There was no need to worry about darkness. At this latitude the mid-August sun would not set until quite close to midnight—long after the last drop of fuel would have been used up.

It was just after 7:30 P.M. that Wiley thought he saw something below. He dropped lower and banked. He could not be sure. He dropped lower still until he was barely twenty feet above the tundra. He now took in the hazy picture. It was an Eskimo summer hunting camp along a wide river outlet to the sea. He saw people moving about, with a lone figure standing by the water's edge.

Along most of the western Alaska shoreline on the Chukchi Sea runs a narrow beach from which an abrupt embankment rises about twenty feet, forming a palisade-like barrier. Over time, the force of the water has cut through these plateaus, lowering the river bed to sea level. Such a river is the Walakpa. When it eventually joins the Chukchi Sea, some ten miles southwest of Barrow, it first creates a sizable lagoon. The Walakpa River, too, had cut deep into the tundra plateau and carved a break into the embankment. At high tide, the ocean and the river are one. However, the shoreline was still elevated enough so that at low tide only the occasional wave would wash over the land barrier; the estuary basin held the river's water, forming a small, very shallow lagoon.

Wiley circled the water and noted a long sandbank dividing the lagoon. He could see smoke wafting from the fire where dinner had been prepared. Instinctively he must have registered that it was an on-shore breeze. He circled one more time. He had to be sure of his landing site, for in seconds a submerged rock could slash open a pontoon. Wiley could see that the lagoon was quite shallow, and he planned to keep his coasting to a minimum. He lined up the plane and dropped, touching water quite close to shore. He taxied till he heard the floats scrape sand, then he cut the motor and shut off the line leading to the fuel tank. They had made it.

Wiley got out of his seat and Will Rogers walked forward; both men stepped on the wing, down onto the floats, and waded through a few feet of shallow water to the shore. The cold water did not bother them as both men wore rubber boots. Will Rogers walked about, stretching his legs, inhaling the fresh air. Approaching the plane from the Eskimo encampment came forty-four-year-old Clair Okpeaha. It was his adopted son, Patrick, whom Wiley had spotted from the air, standing on the water's edge.

The Okpeaha family had been hunting on that site all summer. At first there had been more families, more tents, but the others had left once August had come. Now that summer was almost past, they had been alone at Walakpa Lagoon. Even the Okpeaha family had made arrangements to leave. When they first heard the faint hum of a distant motor, they rushed out of their tent. Supper had just been finished. Stella, Clair's wife, who taught Sunday school at Barrow, was cleaning up after dinner. Helping her was eleven-year-old Rose, while two younger boys— Robert, age eight, and Fred, age five—played. Patrick, at fourteen, was the oldest of the children; Sadie, the youngest, was still too small to take notice of events.

None of them thought that it could be a plane. "It was cold that day and it was foggy and drizzle little bit. We were waiting for the boats to come and pick us up. My uncle sent a message through somebody that he was going to come with two boats. We were waiting then."

They were surprised when out of the fog came this circling plane that finally landed so close to shore. The family, watching from the tent, could not hear what was said at the edge of the lagoon. But Post told Clair and Patrick that he was lost. Then he asked the direction to Barrow, and how far away it was. Clair Okpeaha, who spoke broken English, shrugged his shoulders and merely pointed toward the north and said, "twenty miles, maybe thirty miles." "Miles" was a white man's measure and had little meaning to Clair. Patrick just stood by and studied the two men.

His English was about as limited as his father's, but he understood every word. He left the talking to his father. Will Rogers wanted to know what Clair had been hunting, and was told that the hunt had been very good and that they had laid by walrus, seal and caribou for their winter food supply.

When Clair indicated that Barrow lay toward the north, Wiley would have realized that he was on the down-coast. He must have appreciated his good fortune in spotting this camp on the very edge of the continent. Had he continued in his search westward above the overcast, he would have been shortly over the open sea, with nothing below but the vast Arctic Ocean; he would not have known whether he had flown too far north off the continent, or too far to the west toward Siberia.

Rogers and Post walked around, about fifty feet away and back again, stretching muscles that had been cramped for more than six hours. They were the object of close study by the rest of the Okpeaha family, but no one else approached them.

The entire area was enveloped in fog, but shapes could be made out as the mist wafted in and out, becoming more dense one minute, thinning somewhat the next. Wiley and Will must have discussed their next move. It had taken long enough to find a break in the overcast and land here; why risk taking off again, only to be faced with the same problem further north along the coast? But, Wiley might have argued, Barrow was only ''twenty or thirty miles'' up the coast, or so Clair had said; they could be there in a matter of minutes; now that they were on the edge of the ocean, he could fly just off the coastline, and never go higher than, say, a couple of hundred feet, maybe less; it would be difficult to lose sight of the ground at that height.

Staying at Walakpa Lagoon would have meant safety, but also the loss of yet another day, maybe more; one could never tell about Alaskan weather. After all, northern pilots had a saying about accepting delays by the weather: ''Well, what's another day in Alaska?'' But Rogers and Post had a long trip ahead. While New York City or Washington, D.C., might be sweltering in mid-summer heat and humidity, in the Arctic, winter was already on its way. Just off-shore, they could see a mass of ice floes. Had they asked, they would have been told that this year, winter was coming earlier than usual. The men were heard discussing their next step. Clair told of their decision: ''They were in a hurry to go to Barrow.''

Rose Okpeaha, too, had her thoughts. "The fog was going in and out—maybe, if my father would have asked them to wait for a clear sky, maybe they would have . . . I think my father was regretting about that." But the right words were never said.

Post waded back to the plane and climbed in. Rogers thanked the Eskimos, stepped onto the float, turned and waved to Clair and Patrick on shore, and to the family by the tent; everyone waved back. Then Will, too, scrambled back into the plane. Wiley turned on the cock on the fuel line leading to the gas tanks he had been using and started the engine. Will arranged himself in the very rear of the cabin. There was no need to warm up the engine. It had been shut off for barely ten or twelve minutes. Though it was air-cooled, the oil would have kept it warm for quite a while longer.

Wiley pulled away from shore and taxied eastward, trying to avoid the gravel bank, which in places broke the surface of the water. About a quarter-mile from shore, he turned the plane. He was ready to take off.

Habits, whether good ones or bad ones, are hard to break. Once acquired they become part of everyday behavior and are performed so routinely that they seem the norm. Wiley, too, had acquired habits. For most of his flying career he had piloted a single type plane, a high-wing Vega, the *Winnie Mae*. It was a land plane equipped with wheels. The past ten days, for the first time in his life, he was at the control of a low-wing, pontoon-equipped plane. So far he had taken off and landed this plane only some seven or eight times, yet in that short time he had changed his take-off technique. When taking off with the *Winnie Mae*, Wiley was always known to take her up gently in a graceful slow climb. Not so with the float plane. Provided with an extremely powerful engine, Wiley now practically forced the plane to jump out of the water in an excessively steep climb. Bush pilots described it as "hanging by the propeller," which is unsafe. The aerodynamic function of a propeller is to cause air to flow over and under the wing, thus providing "lift."

Why Post developed this new practice with the float plane is a mystery; the fact is that on every one of his observed take-offs he forced the plane out of the water and climbed steeply. He did so at Walakpa Lagoon. And here he added one other breach of the pilots' rules: while climbing steeply, he banked sharply; dipping the right wing low and raising the left one, Wiley turned north toward Barrow. Wiley must have turned very sharply: "I thought they were going turn around . . ." Rose remembered.

At a height of approximately two hundred feet, witnesses heard the explosion of a back-fire, "like the sound of a shotgun," and the engine stopped. For the merest fraction of a second the red plane seemed to hang in midair, its upward drive halted. Then, being in a turning motion, it continued to somersault, tumbling side over side downward. It hit the shallow water head on, shearing off the right wing, breaking the floats and falling onto its back.

Clair and Patrick were back at their tent, barely three hundred feet away. Little Rose stood beside the tent. "We watched them in the fog, but we can see the plane there and we see my dad and my brother walking toward us, and after they took off, they were coming; right after they reach our tent. . . ." the plane crashed into the lagoon. Almost all of the plane remained visible. It had fallen into two or three feet of water.

"Was fog, was misty, foggy, and my father just started running toward the plane, he didn't want us to move from the tent; he told us not to move from there; and we stayed there and when he reached that plane—he on the shore, he said: Halloo! Halloo—many times. There was no answer. And he come back to the tent start changing his boots; he tell us not to touch it, go near it any more, no, just to watch it from there. Maybe he thought it might explode. And he told us to tell people whenever they came—tell them not to touch that plane unless the people from Barrow had seen it that way; but some of the people came—my mom told them not to—but they didn't do what my father said; they just start trying to take out the people inside the plane. After they take them—after they wrapped them up, we did go down there, we children go down there, see them there."

Clair had changed his boots to "knee-high boots. He don't have rubber boots; *muklucks*!" Rose would remember. Then Clair took his kayak and began paddling along the coast toward Barrow. Whether it was the threat of the early ice floes, or the eastward wind, which would have forced him constantly into shore, or the dense fog, is not known. But after "half a mile, maybe quarter mile," maybe even more, Clair beached the small boat and began to run along the coast toward Barrow.

It was not an easy trek. Many times Clair had to climb the almost vertical embankment, then descend it again, cross rivulets and small streams, circle around deeper lakes or traverse shallow ones. He was not a powerful man, but a hardy one. Squat and wiry, long hours of mushing behind a dogsled had hardened his muscles and he did not find the running gait too exhausting. As he passed other hunting camps, he quickly told the story of the crash he had witnessed and a number of Eskimos, perhaps hoping to be of help, perhaps just curious, made their way south to Walakpa Lagoon.

But Clair Okpeaha continued his run to Barrow. He did not know the names of the two men who had spoken to him. There had been no introductions. Even if he had been told their names, it would have meant nothing to him. He had never heard of either of them.

CHAPTER SIX

TO BARROW AND BACK

If I was backing an . . . airplane flight I would
certainly think enough of the people's lives . . . to
put a radio sending apparatus on there for them
the first thing. Then, if I had any more money left,
I would get some gas and a propeller for it.
—Will Rogers, *Daily Column*, August 19, 1927.

Clair Okpeaha continued his run north along the shore. At Barrow
it was still daylight, but in the east, the Lakewood Summer Playhouse at Skowhegan, Maine, was dark. It had concluded its
evening performance some time ago. The audience, consisting
mostly of seasonal residents and vacationers, had gone to their
homes and cottages.

Nightlife in Skowhegan was limited. The long-established
Lakewood Summer Playhouse was well known in theatrical circles for having produced more future Broadway successes than
any similar organization in the country. The theater presented
fine plays in stock. This week's presentation was a revival of an
exciting aviation drama, *Ceiling Zero*; the plot revolved around
"a daredevil pilot whose reckless flying enlivens the three act
play. He becomes lost in fog en route into Newark, and from that
point the action is thrillingly traced by the crackling voices on a
two-way radio as he asks and receives his bearings. Suddenly the
audience hears the roar of his plane over the airport and seconds
later, a terrible crash off-stage."

The play had been quite successful on Broadway, starring
Osgood Perkins as the airline's owner. At Lakewood, that part was
played by a young, promising actor named Humphrey Bogart.
The cast, in addition to Mary Rogers as the ingenue and nineteen-

year-old Keenan Wynn as the flight controller, also included Grant Mills, as the gallant flier who dies in the wreck.

In Maine, Betty Rogers, her daughter Mary, and "Aunt Dick" were asleep. But beside the Arctic Ocean, Clair Okeapha raced along the beach with news which would change their lives forever. He trotted steadily on the hard, wet sand. On his right was the coastal embankment that raised the tundra abruptly about twenty feet above the Chukchi Sea. The ocean, on his left, teemed with ice floes. Clair Okpeaha could not remember another summer when so much ice had come this early. He did not know it, but even the Coast Guard cutter *Northland*, which had been at anchor off Barrow, had earlier that day put to sea and moved some fifty miles further south, off Wainwright. Its captain, Commander W. K. Scammell, decided to pull out of Barrow, as the wind was changing and heavy ice floes began to float back toward shore, threatening to surround the ship and render it icebound.

The resident doctor, head of the Barrow Presbyterian medical mission since 1921, was Henry Greist. An elderly man, originally from Crawfordville, Indiana, he had given up a private practice to work for the church in Alaska. His second wife, Mollie, was a registered nurse. She liked her life among the Eskimos and had come to terms with Alaska—all, except the summer, which she regarded as "something awful. The weather is mostly drizzle, rain, mist, fog, fog, fog, clouds and wind and we dread it so much worse than 20 below. We all agree that 10 below is just fine."

Okpeaha followed the narrow shore line. It was safer and easier than running across the tundra. Clair knew that by keeping to the water's edge he was headed straight into Barrow. On the other hand, traversing the tundra—with its thick, spongy miniature overgrowth acting like soft matting underfoot—would be tiring and dangerous. Heavy patchy fog wafting across the featureless plateau could make any man lose his direction in minutes, and once lost in the fog, there was little chance of finding one's course again. But even running along the beach was not an easy path to follow. Driving a dogsled, Clair could have reached Barrow in an hour, perhaps even sooner; but running alone, with only the cold Siberian wind as companion, was different. Of course, he had his thoughts to occupy him as his legs moved steadily. What would he tell them when he got to Barrow? Would he know enough words of the white man's language to explain

Clockwise, from top left: Friday, August 16, 1935. Walakpa Lagoon, with the Clair Okpeaha family in the foreground; the crashed plane lies in two feet of water in the background. (Photo: David Brower Collection.) At Barrow. The radio room of United States Army Signal Corps Staff Sergeant Stanley Morgan, who first sent news of the fatal accident. Note Mrs. Morgan's mixing bowl on the wall. (Photo: Stanley Morgan Collection.) Friday, August 16, 1935. The scene of the accident with the bodies wrapped in sleeping bags for transfer to Barrow. (Photo: Stanley Morgan Collection.) Close-up of engine section of the fallen plane. (Photo: Smithsonian Institution.) Close-up of fuselage. (Photo: Smithsonian Institution.) Clair and Stella Okpeaha. It was Clair who brought the news of the crash to Barrow. (Photo: University of Southern California.)

what he had seen? Perhaps he should have looked into the wrecked plane, to see whether he could help? No! Nobody could have lived through that crash. But what if one of the men . . . ?

Clair Okpeaha had little worry of being overtaken by darkness before he could reach his goal. Starting on the tenth day of May, the sun had risen but once and not set; it made a complete circle of the sky every day and came near the horizon, but it would not leave. Now, since the second day August, just thirteen days ago, the sun had once again begun to dip below the sea; nights had returned to the land of the midnight sun. The first night had been only a quarter-hour long; but each succeeding night lengthened by twelve to fifteen minutes and after November 18, the sun would not come above the horizon at all for almost seventy days. This night, the night of August 15, would last close to three hours, though between afterglow and first light it would not get too dark at any time.

Barrow was a small village built around a circular lagoon. Running north along the "down coast," Clair reached the village about 9:40 in the evening. He had covered almost eleven miles of difficult terrain in about an hour and a half.

It has been unacceptable for many to believe that a man, dressed in heavy clothing, can cross such an exhausting topography in so short a time. All sorts of mathematical gymnastics have been invented to stretch the time; one researcher presented a theory which made Clair take five hours to reach Barrow. Forgotten was the fact that Clair Okpeaha knew but two methods of locomotion: the kayak, or his legs. His children found nothing surprising in the fact that their father would negotiate the distance between Walakpa Lagoon and Barrow in less than two hours. "One hour, 45 minutes, no more," Patrick Okpeaha insisted.

What has added to the confusion is the mistaken belief that Wiley's gold wristwatch, its crystal broken—having stopped at 8:18—indicated the exact time of the crash. When found, Rogers' dollar pocket was still merrily ticking and reading the correct time of 3:30 A.M., thus giving no clues to the time of the accident.

A statement by Staff Sergeant Stanley R. Morgan of the United States army signal corps has been overlooked. Arriving at the crash site with the first boat from Barrow, he suggested that the crash occurred about 7:30 P.M., and that Wiley's wristwatch did not stop until Post's arm either slipped into the water at 8:18 P.M., or the incoming tide, spilling over the sandbank into the lagoon, made the water rise to cover the watch. Sergeant Morgan's theory corroborates the Okpeaha family claim about the time the plane landed. Rose Okpeaha Leavitt, remembered: "After we have our supper, the plane arrived around seven o'clock, something like that."

At Barrow, just before 10 P.M., Thomas P. Brower was loading his boat, right near his father's trading post. Thomas, thirty-one years of age, was the oldest son of Charles D. Brower by his second wife. Charles, referred to as "King of the Arctic," was a veteran of half a century as an Arctic trader, whaler, and trapper; he had settled at Barrow and taken an Eskimo wife; when she died, he married another Eskimo. Charley, as he was known, was respected because he was honest and dealt fairly. He worked hard for his new people and they trusted him. He became a leader among the Eskimos and when he was appointed U. S. Commissioner, he represented both the Eskimos and the federal government. He was both chief of police and magistrate; he could even perform civil wedding ceremonies. He had raised his children to abide by his standards and principles.

Thomas stopped his work. "I saw a man running along on the beach and he came up to me and it was old man Clair Okpeaha, stomping down the coast." Speaking in Inupiak, the language of the local Eskimos, Clair blurted out the story: "Tom, an accident happened down at Walakpa, there is two men landed . . . they didn't tell me their names; they taxied over to where—close to where my kid was on the lagoon side. They asked me: Which way is it to Barrow? He said, I told them up the coast. And they thanked me, went back to their plane and taxied to take off—over towards the ocean. And they were just right over the stream that emptied out to the ocean, when—roughly hundred feet," he said, "they just—their motor conked off—and they just turned over and they dived right straight down into that stream."

As Clair recounted the events to Thomas Brower, Eskimos started to come out of their homes, drawn by the loud voice. Ever more men pressed in on the small group, eager to hear the details. It was then that Sergeant Morgan hearing the commotion, came from his radio hut to join the group. Clair Okpeaha reported to him in broken English "airplane she blew up."

Sergeant Morgan summed up Okpeaha's account: "The native explained in pidgin English that the plane, flying very low, suddenly appeared from the south and, apparently sighting the tents, circled several times and finally settled down on the small river near the camp. Two men climbed out, calling the native to the water's edge and asking the direction and distance to Point Barrow. The direction given, the men then climbed back into the plane and taxied off to the far side of the river for the take-off into the wind. After a short run the plane slowly lifted from the water to a height of about fifty feet, banking slightly to the right, when evidently the motor stalled. The plane slipped off on the right wing and nosed down into the water, turning completely over, and the native said a dull explosion occurred and most of the right wing dropped off and a film of gasoline and oil soon covered the water.''

Despite some obvious differences, the stories basically agree. Tom Brower and Sergeant Morgan rushed off to set rescue plans into action. Tom immediately sent Clair to notify Charles Brower, the civil authority in charge. Later, Charles Brower would recall that it was 9 o'clock when ''there came a sharp knock followed immediately by the headlong entrance of a panting Eskimo named Clair Okpeaha.'' Sergeant Morgan remembered it as being about 10 P.M. Dr. Henry Greist found out about Okpeaha's arrival later, second-hand, and recorded it as being 8 P.M. Hearing the account of a tragedy, it is not surprising that nobody bothered to fix the exact time of Clair's arrival in Barrow. Since it would be daylight at 8, 9 or even 10 o'clock, the confusion is easy to explain; the 10 o'clock time appearing in all of Sergeant Morgan's communications seems the most logical, fitting into the overall schedule. Whether the accident happened at 7:30 P.M., as Sergeant Morgan suggest, or 8:18 P.M., as Wiley's stopped wristwatch implies, it would be impossible for Clair Okpeaha to arrive in Barrow by 8 or 9 P.M. Morgan's time estimates seem more acceptable, especially when one considers that his life was regulated by the clock. As the army's communicator, he had to adhere to a rigid transmission schedule, making weather observations and reports at prescribed times. It seems natural that he would check his own watch frequently. To Charles Brower, on the other hand, the precise time of day was of lesser importance. To bolster this last conjecture, Charles Brower introduced a still different time in a letter: ''That evening, the 15th, about *eleven o'clock*, Claire [sic] Okpeaha an eskimo came to the village on the run and reported that a plane had crashed. . . .''[1]

While Okpeaha reported to Commissioner Brower, Sergeant Morgan sent word to Frank Daugherty, the government school teacher and local reindeer superintendent. Daugherty was also a "stringer" for United Press while Charles Brower was a stringer for Associated Press. All major news services maintained contacts in places which ordinarily would not warrant a reporter. These contacts, or stringers, would from time to time submit accounts of local events they thought might be of interest to a nationwide readership. Only if their stories were used would the news service pay them.

Mollie Greist and one of her helpers, Helen Surber, were on "the second floor of the hospital at the window sorting out mission boxes, when we heard the men of the village calling and we saw Mr. Morgan running and putting his coat on as he ran and his camera flying in the air from a strap around his neck. Helen said: 'Oh, Mrs. Greist, something has happened.' She ran down to see and I followed and we met Mr. Daugherty on the walk, running to tell us."[2]

By the time Daugherty arrived on the beach, Morgan had already chartered a launch from Bert Panigeo, a local Eskimo. It was an open whaleboat powered by a small gasoline motor. Morgan had also hired fourteen Eskimos as crew, and was ready to leave for Walakpa Lagoon to see what could be done.

Tom Brower had to look after his partially laden boat; the breeze was coming up, swinging the boat toward land. He would have to shelter it before it beached. He spoke to his younger brother David and his father: "Dad, you have any recollection of somebody coming up?"

Of course Charles Brower knew that Post and Rogers were in Fairbanks and had plans to come to Barrow to visit him, and he looked forward to their stay. In fact, the village had been alerted and festivities had been planned with a special culinary feast, featuring

the choicest reindeer roasts to be had anywhere, infinitely more juicy and tasty than anything Fairbanks or Nome can produce. And we are by common consent permitted to shoot fat wild geese when we can, for our own consumption, since, if the game laws were observed by us we would never secure such game. And we had

hoped to place before these noted travelers such a feast
by way of venison and wild fowl as would prove worth.

But all their plans for the reception of the visitors were delayed:

> When a spell of particularly bad weather followed, with
> snow and sleet and no visibility whatever, we resigned
> ourselves to an indefinite postponement. On the morn-
> ing of the fifteenth Morgan got another message. The
> men, still at Fairbanks, asked again for weather at Bar-
> row. There was nothing surprising about this. You never
> can tell what is happening in one place from conditions
> in another. But it was lucky, we told ourselves, that they
> checked up in case they'd had any idea of taking off
> today. We'd seldom experienced a meaner storm. At
> times you couldn't see fifty yards.
>   So Morgan sent the information warning them of
> what was going on in the Barrow district. After which all
> hands dropped back into the routine work of a nasty day.

Specifically, just how "nasty" a day was it? Charles knew
that Alaskan pilots would never fly in weather that was: "vile. No
visibility and no ceiling—just dense fog that one had to shove
aside to get through it." Who could those men be who crashed at
Walakpa, trying to come to Barrow on a day like this? In a letter
Charles never thought would see the light of day, he allowed
himself a guess: "We did not . . . know that it was Rodgers [sic]
and Post for they had weather reports that morning and weather
here was rotten Rain [sic] Fog [sic] and at times snow squalls. We
imagined it was some dam [sic] fool from the south trying to get
here before they arrived for newspaper work."
    Well, it was not just some "dam fool" representing a news-
paper and trying to get the story of Rogers' and Post's arrival in
Barrow. Yet whether it was some "dam fool" reporter or a
famous flier like Wiley Post, Charles Brower had his opinion that
he was a "dam fool."
    With Thomas Brower busy sheltering his boat, and Charles
having to make local preparation for the reception of the injured
fliers—whoever they were—it was up to David to hurry south.
Tom gave him instructions:

"Dave," I said, "you take a power boat, a dory—flat bottom dory—so you can go up that stream and from what I gather Clair remarked both those men never got out. They are probably pinned underneath there just broken—be prepared and take some of the utility blankets and some kind of a stretcher—canvass—if you have to move them out." So they took blocks and tackles and everything, they just zoomed down these 12 to 15 miles, and went into the inlet—there were five or six of them— I have a picture of them somewhere.

In their haste to reach the crash site and bring possible help to the fliers, both David Brower and Stanley Morgan overlooked the most important member of any rescue mission: They forgot to notify Dr. Greist. In a mimeographed newsletter, which Dr. Greist published "just across the ice from the North Pole, three or four times per annum . . . sometimes not at all," he allowed free rein to his displeasure at such heedless haste:

. . . the Doctor was not even notified of the accident that he might attend with emergency kit and stretchers and other first aid apparatus. They merely wished to get there, little knowing or considering what they would or could do on arrival. The Doctor accidentally learned of the wreck after all the boats had gone, ran to the beach with first aid necessities, but could not secure a boat, not even a skiff or canoe, man or lad.

Left behind, Dr. Henry Greist and his wife, known by all as "Aunt Mollie," prepared everything for emergency procedures. Instruments were sterilized, bandages and braces for broken limbs laid out, the operating table was scrubbed again, and beds were prepared; Aunt Mollie called in all the native girls who regularly assisted at the hospital.

When Aunt Mollie had first arrived at Barrow, her principal project had been to start a baby clinic. She wanted to teach both pre- and post-natal care and she recorded the events of the initial meeting with the Eskimo mothers. Shyly they came in and sat down, as she began to talk to them. After several minutes she asked them why they were sitting here, wearing their warm parkas. She suggested that they take them off while indoors. She could not understand the women's embarrassment until she was made aware that they had no clothing on underneath. It was then that Aunt Mollie started also sewing classes, with the first project: women's underwear. Thus she began both a women's club and a baby's club—classic missionary projects.

Now Mollie and her staff made a boiler of reindeer stew, gallons of coffee and hard bread for the men when they returned. Charles Brower sent blankets, jugs of hot water and bottles of brandy to the hospital, then he came over to offer his services. It was a good thing he did; his help would be needed that night. But for the moment, there was nothing to do. They would just have to sit and wait and talk and eat for hours with ears strained for the sound of the returning motors.

David Brower, with a much faster launch, towed an *oomiak*, a native skin-covered wooden frame boat. The shallow-keel boat would be needed to enter and exit the shoal water of Walakpa lagoon. David, though having started later, soon overtook Morgan and reached the crash site first. But it was Morgan who first knew the full truth—that the plane had carried Wiley Post and Will Rogers. He quizzed Clair Okpeaha who rode in his boat. Asked how he knew that there had been two men in the crashed plane, Clair replied: "Me talked with mans." Morgan asked: "When, after they fell?" "No," answered Clair, "before they fell, when they come down on water and ask me how to go to Barrow, where Barrow is, how far."

Morgan kept digging: "Did they tell you their names?"

"No," Clair replied, "Mans no tell names, but big mans, two mans, one sore eye with bandage on eye, he and other man then go inside plane, and man with sore eye start engine and go up, maybe ten fathoms [sixty feet] and then engine spit, start, then stop, start some more little, then plane fall just so—" and imitating a plane he indicated with his hands a bank, then a fall off the right wing and a nose dive into the water, with a complete somersault forwards. When Morgan wanted to know whether he waded out to the plane after the crash, Clair admitted that he had only stood on a sand spit some forty feet away and had hollered. There had been no answer and so he had hurried quickly to Barrow to summon officials.

Hampered by fog, mist and a strong adverse current, avoiding ice floes and slowed by the semi-darkness, the powerboat trip took three hours; it appears excessive when compared with Clair Okpeaha's run of less than two hours.

It was close to six hours since the accident when David Brower's boat rounded the embankment into Walakpa Lagoon. The sight greeting him was eerie. Barely a quarter-mile ahead, shrouded by heavy fog, lay the tangled debris of the plane; it was now a haphazard heap of splintered wood and misshaped metal. The plane rested on its back; one wing, which had been torn off, lay across the pile; and a pontoon stuck heavenward.

Some of the Eskimos Clair had alerted on his run to Barrow had walked south to Walakpa Lagoon. Before the boats from Barrow finally arrived, those natives had already smashed a hole into the cabin and removed Will Rogers' body. It had been carefully placed into one of the eiderdown sleeping bags found in the debris and now rested on the edge of the lagoon. All the baggage had been taken out and piled on the beach. Will's typewriter was twisted out of shape, Wiley's rifle was broken, fishing rods snapped. In fact, almost everything in the plane was smashed or splintered, except items of small size. Some of the woman began to salvage the papers, charts and personal effects scattered all around the place. There were several Russian dictionaries and translations. Among the books, searchers found one which Will must have been reading just before the landing on the lagoon. Tucked inside, as a bookmark, were Will's reading glasses— miraculously unbroken. Most of these items were floating in the brackish water, soggy. The Eskimos collected them and laid them in neat stacks on the shore.

The only problem was the removal of Wiley Post's body from the plane. The Eskimos had already tried, but without success. David Brower took a flashlight and entered the cabin. The plane's nose had struck with such impact, that it had forced the engine well back into the cabin, pinning Post's body solidly against the back of his seat, with the weight of one of the pontoons holding the body firmly in place. There was only one solution; the plane would have to be broken apart to give up the body.

First David attached the tackle to the pontoon and had it pulled off the plane. By this time about thirty Eskimo men had assembled, all eager to assist. Stella Walook Okpeaha, Clair's wife, having just earlier finished with meals for the day, now found herself with a new chore. Rose Okpeaha Leavitt remembers "helping my mom cooking for people to eat, getting ready for them to eat. Those people who were working on the thing."

David Brower next attached a rope to the side of the plane; it broke. David reattached the rope and the men on shore pulled. This time the plane, already cracked, split open. With great difficulty, David was able to free Wiley's body and pass it to his helpers. Like Rogers, Post was put into an eiderdown sleeping bag.

Sergeant Stanley Morgan took a series of photographs in the half light of the new day. He photographed the wreck from all sides and took close-ups of the engine as it hung from the debris. His is the only picture showing the lagoon with the split plane, while in the foreground rest the carefully wrapped bodies of the two fliers. Morgan was an accomplished photographer, who owned a Graflex camera with all the latest equipment; he was especially proud of his modern darkroom, where he did all his own processing.

David, too, must have taken photographs which Charles Brower later sent to Seattle. Though sitting on the biggest American news story of the year he felt troubled by the thought of benefiting from so sad a time. As he explained his feelings, "To make it worse for me Rodgers [sic] was on his way to pay me a visit and that rather broke me up for a while." Brower would send those photographs to *Associated Press*, but refused any further participation.

When all the personal belongings had been salvaged and stowed in boats, both bodies were placed into the *oomiak*. Slowly the caravan left the lagoon and began its trek back to Barrow. There was no need for speed now. As the boats turned toward Barrow, Morgan could see fragments of the shattered plane float seaward.

The Eskimos had no idea who the two victims were. Their names were completely unfamiliar, yet Brower's and Morgan's attitude indicated that they were important men. Somehow the loss was also felt by those who had just helped to recover the two victims. As the boats began their slow way northward, Morgan noted that "one of the Eskimo boys began to sing a hymn in Eskimo and soon all the voices joined in his singing until our arrival at Barrow." (Mollie Greist, too, referred to the Eskimo's sad chant, but called it a "funeral dirge.")

At the Presbyterian hospital in Barrow, the cruising hum of the motors could be heard a long way off as the little convoy made its way along the "down coast." The fact that the engines were not approaching at full power announced the sad news a long time before words were actually spoken; had there been injured men to attend, Charles Brower knew, his son would have raced at full throttle to bring them to needed attention. Henry and Mollie Greist, too, reasoned that way and relaxed; they could not foresee how they would spend the coming hours.

During the beaching of the boat, an Eskimo fell between the heavy rollers being used and was badly hurt. It was about 3 A.M. Alaska time when the Eskimos carried the bodies to the hospital, where Dr. Greist, Mollie, Charles Brower, and the hospital staff took over. Having given the bodies into the proper hands, Sergeant Morgan hurried to his home to check whether his superiors had been notified. When the news of a crash had first reached Barrow, Sergeant Morgan had immediately attempted to raise any station down the line which was on the air, hoping that the message would then be passed on. The late hour, however, found nobody listening and he had to leave for the site of the accident.

During their years in Barrow, Stanley Morgan had taught his wife Beverly how to operate a Morse code key. Her official job was that of government meteorologist, but those duties did not really constitute a full-time occupation. So thoroughly did Stanley teach his wife that she had acquired many of his idiosyncrasies; most listeners could barely tell whether it was Stanley or Beverly sending a message. Usually, experienced radio operators could immediately recognize a sender's "hand," but Stanley and Beverly were able to fool many a listener.

During the hours Sergeant Morgan had been away at the wreck, Beverly had sat at the key in the stark radio shack, trying to raise just one responsive voice on land or at sea. The southern U.S. Signal Corps stations did not respond. Beverly had spent hours operating the key and looking at the wall in front of her in the crammed room. It was filled with sending and receiving equipment, mostly government issue. But Beverly would never lose her annoyance when she looked at her steel mixing bowls, which her husband had imperiously expropriated and tacked on the wall to serve as insulators for the transmitting antenna lead-in.

Now that Sergeant Stanley Morgan was back at Barrow, he took his seat at the key. It was now up to him to tell the world that two of its best-known citizens lay dead at the top of the world.

At the Presbyterian hospital, Dr. Henry Greist and his wife began their gruesome task. The bodies were placed on the operating tables.

When the small plane had crashed into the shallow lagoon and broken apart, sand and gravel had been forced with great pressure into the clothing of the two fliers. The first thing Dr. Greist had to do was to cut those clothes off. They were so soiled with sand, gravel, and blood that everything—except the cut rubber boots, which were thrown away—would be washed before being returned to the widows. Carefully emptying the pockets, the Greists found that Will Rogers had about $770 in cash, $2,040 in travelers' checks, a newspaper picture of his daughter Mary, and a trick puzzle in his pocket. Will also had a pocketknife, a reading glass and two watches; one was an inexpensive Pocket Ben-Westclox watch, attached by a string to his vest; the other, a much larger watch—a St. Regis—he used as an alarm clock when he traveled. The pocket knife, Dr. Greist noted, was the kind a "Boy Scout might use for trading purposes. In all it was a strange assortment." It is also curious that none of the accounts of the accident recorded the contents of Wiley Post's pockets.

Though Dr. Henry Greist never mentioned it, an *Associated Press* report in the *Seattle Times* of August 17, 1935 refers to another item in Will's pocket. It was a Washington sales tax token given Will in Seattle as a good luck charm by Ralph Rogers, a third cousin.

Once the clothes and boots had been cut off, Dr. Greist examined the bodies. The injuries were massive. In the abrupt nosedive and subsequent impact of the crash, Will Rogers, who was not strapped into his seat, was obviously tossed about, striking sharp projections in the cabin. He had suffered a fracture of the frontal bone over the nasal region; his scalp had been partly detached and was hanging forward over his face, while one ear hung by a thread. There was a star wound on his right cheek. The nose, one eyebrow, and one lip were cut to the bone, as though dissected by a surgeon. His chest was crushed and a chunk of flesh as big as a man's fist was missing from one hip. His left arm was broken. Despite the fact that Will Rogers had worn boots, both legs were broken, and the tibia, the larger bone of the lower right leg, had a compound fracture, with a section of it thrust several inches through trouser-leg and boot. It was, they agreed, "a ghastly sight even to one who has seen many terrible sights."

Dr. Greist, with Mollie's assistance, worked feverishly on Will Rogers. It was all quicker and easier because asepsis was not necessary. Since there was no electricity, Helen Surber had to hold a flashlight. Dr. Greist made under-sutures, repaired all surface cuts, replaced a six-inch section of the tibia, that was broken off, and restored the body as best he could.

Wiley Post had sustained a massive abdominal wound, compound fractures of both legs and arms, and lacerations of the trunk and face. With Frank Daugherty holding the flashlight for hours, Charles Brower sewed up the many cuts on Post's body. But Dr. Greist had to close the gaping one "where some part of the plane had punctured his lower abdomen and emptied it of all intestines. Their wounds were frightful."[3]

For five hours Dr. Greist, Mollie, Charles Brower, Helen Surber and Frank Daughterty worked on the two bodies; then they "rouged and fixed the faces as best we could."

There still remained the matter of usable clothes. The few white men at Barrow had no spare suits to donate; they wore Eskimo clothing. The solution was the "missionary barrel"— clothes collected and sent by charitable organizations from the States for distribution by missionaries. Mrs. Greist found two old-fashioned long nightgowns, and Rogers and Post were carefully placed into them. Then, according to Dr. Greist, both bodies were "wrapped in white, freshly laundered sheets, taken to the new warehouse and put on the floor under lock and key. There are no morticians on this coast, no caskets to be had, and we did all we could under the circumstances."

During the hours of surgery, some sixty or seventy men who had returned with the bodies were fed and warmed at the hospital. Most of them sat patiently like mourners at a wake in the hall of the hospital, talking among themselves in low voices. There was a reverence, a respect among the Eskimos, as if Will Rogers or Wiley Post had been honored citizens of the community.

Mollie's squad of four Eskimo girl–helpers and the janitor at the hospital were all busy; it took hours to clean up the two operating rooms and the halls, laundry, and kitchen.

A year later, Henry and Mollie Greist were Betty Rogers' guests in the beautiful Rogers ranch home in Pacific Palisades, California. Will Jr., Mary, and Jimmy Rogers were present. Then, after the meal, the boys put on a polo game, while the others sat high above the field and watched. Suddenly Betty leaned forward, changing the topic of conversation abruptly and broaching a subject obviously close to her thoughts. She said that viewing Will's body before the funeral service, she had been unable to see anything that could have caused his death. Then she asked outright: "I wish you'd tell me the condition Will's body was in—do not spare me."

Dr. Greist, a most sensitive man, did not know how to reply. Should he really tell her? Would Betty be better off by knowing? At last he said, "He was badly broken." He never told her.

At Barrow, neither embalming nor an autopsy could be performed. In the Alaskan Territory doctors were not allowed to embalm; and as for an autopsy, that was, according to Dr. Greist,

> denied the doctor by the U.S. Commissioner as allegedly unnecessary (autopsies are with very great difficulty had anywhere in Alaska, all but regardless as to conditions, owing to the excessive zeal with which the authorities make a show of economy)—short of an autopsy, it proved impossible to determine whether the two victims had died instantly from their fearful injuries, or from drowning. In any event, the abdominal wound of the one and the crushed chest of Mr. Rogers together with his fractured skull, would in the aggregate as to each have likely proved fatal sooner or later, and possible at once. Certain it is that both men lost consciousness instantly with the accident and suffered no pain, that death was sure and certain and quickly had, in the position of the bodies when found.

Perhaps Charles Brower, the U.S. Commissioner referred to in this grievance, must have felt certain that death was due to the crash, and that any further mutilation of bodies already badly mangled would be insensitive. The question of whether the actual causes of death were the injuries or possible drowning could have been settled forever by an autopsy. To this day there is no consensus on the actual causes of death. The fact remains that the faces of both men were found below the water level. Both Dr. Greist and undertaker Hosea H. Ross in Fairbanks confirmed the fact that the faces of both men had been submerged for a considerable time. Mr. Ross claimed that all indications pointed to Will Rogers definitely having drowned; however, as Dr. Greist stated, there is little doubt that both men would have quickly succumbed to the massive injuries received in the crash.

The hospital was not the only busy place in Barrow. Sergeant Stanley Morgan, awake for almost twenty-four hours, was fully absorbed. At long last there was response to his search for a connection. Day had come to the west coast, and he reached his WAMCATS relay contacts. Morgan's message was also picked up by Joe Ulen near Wiseman on the Koyukuk River. Tishu Ulen, Joe's wife, remembered that day: "Joe acted as a relay station . . . and we felt as if we were sitting on top of the world with the news."

The account of the crash raced through Fairbanks, Anchorage and Palmer. Men, women, and children, who only a day ago had seen both Rogers and Post walk though their towns, could not believe the tragedy. Was there no mistake? Maybe an error in transmission? Nothing could happen to men like Will Rogers and Wiley Post!

In Fairbanks, without a doubt, the man most affected by the news was Joe Crosson. Wiley had been an old, dear friend, a hunting companion, a fellow flier; only hours ago they had made plans for the future. Perhaps, Joe accused himself, he had not been too insistent on keeping Wiley from flying to Barrow; perhaps if had he been more assertive—but who could keep Wiley from flying? Still, Joe Crosson must have felt guilt, that perhaps there had been something he could have said, or done, or suggested that would have saved those two lives. Now all he could do was to see that their bodies would be returned to their families. Without waiting for PAA's approval, he made up his mind to fly to Barrow and bring back the bodies of his friends.

First, he hurried home to break the news to his wife. Lillian was stunned. How did it happen, she wanted to know. Where?

When? It could not be. It was unreal. Will Rogers and Wiley Post had sat right there, at her kitchen table. Here the plan to fly to Barrow had been born; here they had eaten their last home-cooked meal. Here they had felt at ease, away from the towns-people who asked for autographs and just stood and stared at them. Here, too, the plan for Will Rogers to fly with Wiley across Siberia had been resolved. She had only to close her eyes and see them all sitting there at her table, eating and laughing; there were Wiley and Joe poring over maps; there was the spot where Will had stood in her kitchen, helping Virginia Rothaker mash potatoes.

But when Joe Crosson told Lillian of his decision to fly to Barrow, she became frantic. She could see the anguish and heart-ache in his eyes; she could tell how tormented he was by the loss of his friend Wiley. She knew full well that flying to Barrow needed a fully alert, clear-minded pilot. It was a hazardous trip even on a clear, sunny day; but this day, the sixteenth of August, weather conditions were identical to those existing the day before—and Joe Crosson was shaken and preoccupied by the tragedy. Only yester-day he had tried repeatedly to persuade his friend Wiley Post not to tempt fate by flying into the foul weather of the North Slope; his friend had not listened and now he lay dead at the top of world. At this moment, barely twenty-four hours later, Joe Crosson himself was about to fly into precisely the same weather. But every argu-ment that came to her mind, every entreaty could not change Joe's stubborn resolve. His sentiment overruled logic; perhaps it was not even sentiment but a man's duty to his comrade. He knew his capabilities and he was "the kind of guy who liked the challenge. He liked to fly when the weather was bad, very bad, and he liked to challenge it, getting through."

Lillian, the loving, worried wife, at last realized that there were no words which would change her husband's resolution. Joe Crosson was determined to go. It was the very least—the very last—he still could do for his friends Wiley and Will.

But Joe was an old hand at Arctic flying. He was not about to venture into the dangers of a fog-bound North Slope without a top-rated radio operator. He selected Robert J. Gleason. Even though Bob was barely twenty-nine-years-old, he was already Communications Superintendent for Pacific Alaska Airways.

The two men had met for the first time in 1929. Gleason was the radio operator aboard the *Nanuk*, a three-masted, 261-

ton schooner scheduled to pick up furs from Russian Arctic Ocean villages and return to the United States before winter set in. After many ports of call and heavily laden, the *Nanuk* became icebound at North Cape in the Arctic Ocean on October 4, 1929. Packed in solid ice, the schooner was forced to wait in place until July 8 of the following year. During all this time, young Bob Gleason was the sole contact with the outside world.

The famous flier Carl Ben Eielson, an Alaskan Airways pilot, was one of the men hired to locate the *Nanuk* and bring out furs and some of the men. But he and his mechanic, Earl Borland, failed to check in at Teller, Alaska. The *Nanuk*, being stationary, became the center in the effort to find the two missing men. Joe Crosson flew from Fairbanks to conduct a search. And it was aboard the *Nanuk*, in the frozen Arctic Ocean, that Crosson and Gleason first met.

Joe Crosson found the two frozen bodies. In a sudden, severe snowstorm, so typical of weather above the Arctic Circle, Eielson's plane had crashed killing both pilot and mechanic. It was Bob Gleason's key that kept the world apprised of the search efforts and that ultimately tapped out the sad news.

The rapport that had started on the Siberian ice grew into a close friendship, as Bob Gleason came to work for PAA, married one of the local belles, and settled down in Fairbanks. The Crossons and Gleasons spent much time together.

Joe and Bob were easy to spot in any crowd. Joe was six feet tall, with the physique of an athlete; Bob was several inches taller, but as thin as one of his antenna poles. The two knew each other's strengths, and that they could depend on each other completely. Those were qualities most needed in the Arctic, where the slightest miscalculation could be disaster. It was no surprise then, that on the mission Joe Crosson planned, he wanted the best man for the job, his friend Bob Gleason.

It was early morning, and Bob was still at home with his wife when a telephone call came from the PAA office. It was John White calling, the division accountant. His message was cryptic; it simply said: "Joe wants you to go with him to Barrow. He called by telephone. He'll pick you up in a half an hour." Thirty minutes later, Joe Crosson came by Gleason's house and picked him up by car; it was only then that Bob learned about the crash.

If Gleason had any reservations about flying to Barrow under prevailing weather conditions, he did not voice them. Joe

Crosson's job was to fly the plane, Bob's was communication. The thought to back out never occurred to him.

Bobbing in the water of the Chena Slough were several Fairchild 71 cabin mono-planes on floats, owned by Pacific Alaska Airways. Crosson had telephoned ahead to have Number NC 10623 made ready for take-off. He was eminently familiar with this type of plane, and felt completely at ease at its controls. In this case "making ready for take-off" meant more than the usual check of engine and filling of tanks. Joe ordered all passenger seats to be removed; he would need a flat space for the bodies.

When Joe Crosson and Bob Gleason arrived at the float, a small crowd of townspeople had already collected. Stunned by the first words of the disaster at Walakpa Lagoon, they had come to Spencer's Float when they heard about Crosson's planned flight to pick up his friends. Like the initial news, the report of Crosson's projected mercy trip had rapidly spread around Fairbanks. One of the men waiting for the fliers was Murray Hall, who was the area's inspector for the Department of Commerce, Bureau of Air Commerce. The accident had occurred in his jurisdiction and it was now up to him to investigate. Indeed, earlier that morning, he had received instructions from Washington, D.C.:

REPORT RECEIVED POST AND ROGERS KILLED THIS MORNING ENROUTE NORTH FROM ANCHORAGE OR FAIRBANKS STOP RADIO AVAILABLE INFORMATION IMMEDIATELY STOP USE ARMY RADIO IN CODE IF THIS DOES NOT CAUSE DELAY OTHERWISE REGULAR CHANNELS.

The telegram was signed J. Carroll Cone, Assistant Director of Air Commerce (Air Regulations).

Signal corps officers estimate that it takes an average of two hours to relay a message from Point Barrow to Seattle. It took far longer for this telegram to reach Betty Rogers:

1935 AUG 16 AM 7 10

MRS. WILL ROGERS   SEATTLE WASHINGTON VIA LAKEWOOD SKOWHEGAN MAINE
                                    BEVERLY HILLS CALIF

IT IS REGRETTED THAT I MUST NOTIFY YOU OF RE-
CEIPT FOLLOWING MESSAGE FROM SIGNAL CORPS
OPERATOR AT POINT BARROW

"POST AND ROGERS CRASHED FIFTEEN MILES SOUTH
HERE FIVE P.M. LAST NIGHT. BOTH KILLED. HAVE
RECOVERED BODIES AND PLACED CARE DOCTOR
GREIST."

KUMPKE, [sic] COLONEL
SIGNAL CORPS

Another, more detailed telegram was sent almost four hours later to the Rogers ranch in Pacific Palisades:

S38 148 GOVT RUSH RC 5 EXTRA PUR
FORTMACARTHUR SANPEDRO CALIF

MRS WILL ROGERS =   16 1037A
LOSANGELES CALIF OR FORWARD
                              1935 AUG 16 AM 10.53
          [Handwritten: Skowhegan Maine]

FOLLOWING FROM POINTBARROW DATE QUOTE
TEN PM NATIVE RUNNER REPORTED PLANE CRASHED
FIFTEEN MILES SOUTH BARROW STOP IMMEDIATELY
HIRED FAST LAUNCH PROCEEDED TO SCENE FOUND
PLANE COMPLETE WRECK PARTLY SUBMERGED TWO
FEET WATER STOP RECOVERED BODY ROGERS THEN
NECESSARY TEAR PLANE APART EXTRACT BODY
POST FROM WATER STOP BROUGHT BODIES BARROW
TURNED OVER DOCTOR GREIST ALSO SALVAGED PER-
SONAL EFFECTS WHICH AM HOLDING ADVISE RELA-
TIVES AND INSTRUCT THIS STATION FULLY AS TO
PROCEDURE STOP NATIVES CAMPING SMALL RIVER
FIFTEEN MILES SOUTH HERE CLAIM POST ROGERS
LANDED ASKED WAY BARROW STOP TAKING OFF
ENGINE MISFIRED ON RIGHT BANK WHILE ONLY
FIFTY FEET OFF WATER STOP PLANE OUT OF CON-
TROL CRASHED NOSE ON TEARING RIGHT WING
OFF AND NOSING OVER FORCING ENGINE BACK

THROUGH BODY OF PLANE STOP BOTH APPARENTLY
KILLED INSTANTLY STOP BODIES BADLY BRUISED
STOP POST WRISTWATCH BROKEN STOPPED EIGHT
EIGHTEEN PM UNQUOTE

                    KUMPE SEATTLE WASHINGTON.

The telegram was eventually forwarded, but this was the
age of radio and telephone. News, especially bad news, traveled
much faster than a hand-delivered telegram. Of course, the newspapers had their own way of getting the story. And there were the
eager reporters.

Therefore the whole family, scattered in different cities,
would learn of the tragedy long before the telegram reached
them. Youngest son Jimmy and his cousin Jimmy Blake, in their
trek across the country, had reached New York City, where they
learned the news. The oldest son, Will Jr., had signed on as an
engine room helper aboard the Standard Oil tanker *H.M. Storey*.
(Will Sr. had to send his consent by wireless for his son's employment as a lowly "wiper." But young Will was proud to have the
job, and did not want to appear the privileged son of a "super-
star" among his new co-workers.)

TELEGRAM, RECEIVED SKOWHEGAN, MAINE. NIGHT-
LETTER, FROM SANTA MONICA, CALIFORNIA, AU-
GUST 15, 1935.

MRS WILL ROGERS, LAKEWOOD

GOT ON BOAT TUESDAY BUT IN DRY DOCK. LEAVING
FRIDAY FOR FRISCO, THEN UP AND DOWN COAST
RUN . . . DON'T WIRE OR RADIO NOW PLEASE. DON'T
EMBARRASS ME BY TELEGRAPHING. HOPE JIM HAD A
GOOD TRIP. GIVE MY BEST TO MARY. HOPE SHE HAS
BEEN WOW-ING THEM. LOVE & LOVE.

                                        BILL

Bill hoped to work his way across to the Philippine Islands
and had reported aboard his ship this Friday morning at 5 A.M..
According to an account in the *Los Angeles Examiner*, he was
brought news of his father's death by a:

plainly shaken Standard Oil Company official [who] shouldered his way through sailors on the deck of the company's tanker, the SS *H.M. Storey*, at Los Angeles Harbor. He clambered down the engine room ladder.

"Where's Will Rogers, Jr.?" he asked the grimy men there.

"Here I am, sir," said a smiling lad in oilstained dungarees.

"Boy," said the official, "change your clothes and come ashore."

On the dock, the young about-to-be-seafarer was met by his cousin, Mary Ireland, who lives in Long Beach.

"Billy, your father's dead. He was killed in a crash with Wiley Post."

Stunned as though struck, young Will took the blow dry-eyed and rode silent to his ranch home with his cousin.

The vessel sailed late yesterday, with crew members silently sharing the grief of the boy who was a shipmate for an hour.

In Skowhegan, Maine, the news arrived in the forenoon. Betty Rogers, with Aunt Dick, was visiting with the occupant of a neighboring cottage. Betty saw a car coming up the road. It was driven by Grant Mills, the actor. He took Theda Blake aside and as Mrs. Rogers looked on with growing apprehension, he spoke agitatedly, though too low for Betty to understand him. Her "alarm turned to panic." Her first thought was that son Jimmy and his cousin Jimmy Blake had had a car accident. She was certain of it.

"Has something happened to Jimmy?" she asked.

Grant Mills did not answer; Aunt Dick then broke the news. "No, Betty, it's Will. Will has had an accident."

For the briefest of moments, Betty Rogers felt relief. Jimmy was all right and nothing could ever happen to Will. She thought that the news, most likely, concerned a forced landing, or some other minor mishap blown out of all proportion by a creative press. But the look on Aunt Dick's face dispelled any such notion. Betty could read the grim facts in her sister's eyes.

It was Grant Mills and Aunt Dick who had the task to tell Mary Rogers.

The family in Maine went into immediate seclusion and incoming telephone calls were screened. There were calls from eager reporters wanting statements; there were condolence calls; there were the curious and the morbid callers.

Governor W. Troy of Alaska sent messages of condolence to Betty Rogers and Mae Post. Colonel Charles Lindbergh, who was spending the summer with his family on North Haven Island, off the coast of Maine, spoke with Betty several times. He was an old friend of the family and offered his services. As a director of Pan American Airways, Lindbergh assured the family that Pacific Alaska Airways, a Pan-Am subsidiary company, would attend to all matters:

RXS488 38 = TDRO NORTHAVEN ME 16 829P

1935 AUG 16 PM 6:11

J K BLAKE =
WILL ROGERS OFFICE

PACIFIC ALASKA AIRWAYS IS SENDING PLANE TO BAR-ROW AND WILL ARRANGE ALL ALASKAN TRANSPOR-TATION STOP FOR YOUR CONFIDENTIAL INFORMA-TION THE PRESENT PLANS ARE FOR THE ALASKAN PLANE TO CONTINUE THROUGH DIRECTLY TO LOS ANGELES STOP WILL KEEP YOUR INFORMED =

CHARLES LINDBERGH

Later the colonel sent a telegram to New York City, to await Betty's arrival:

RXNAC173 70 = TDRO NORTHAVEN ME 16 850P

1935 AUG 16

PM 9: 32

MRS WILL ROGERS WALDORF HOTEL = =

TRANSCONTINENTAL AND WESTERN AIR IS OFFER-ING YOU TRANSPORTATION FROM NEWYORK TO

LOS ANGELES OVER THEIR LINE STOP LET ME KNOW
IF YOU WISH TO ACCEPT STOP PACIFIC ALASKA AIR-
WAYS IS SENDING PLANE TO BARROW AND WILL AR-
RANGE ALL TRANSPORTATION STOP PRESENT PLANS
ARE FOR ALASKAN PLANE TO CONTINUE DIRECTLY
TO LOS ANGELES STOP UNLESS WEATHER UNFAVOR-
ABLE PLANE SHOULD ARRIVE AT LOSANGELES IN
FROM THREE TO FIVE DAYS STOP WILL KEEP YOU
INFORMED =

LINDBERG. [sic]

Other old friends and associates also rallied to be of assistance. In California, Will's business manager James K. Blake and
Oscar Lawler, Will's lawyer and former neighbor, offered to make
arrangements on the West Coast. Lawler, who was in San Francisco on a business trip when he heard the news, immediately
telephoned, then wired:

RZ91 TWS PAID3 = WUX SANFRANCISCO CALIF
AUG 16 10 35 AM

MRS WILL ROGERS = SKOWHEGAN ME =

JUST PHONED MISS BLAKE WHO TELLS ME COL LIND-
BERGH IS TAKING SOME ACTION PLEASE TELL COL
LINDBERGH THAT HE IS FREE TO CALL UPON STAN-
DARD OIL COMPANY OF CALIFORNIA OR PACIFIC
TELEPHONE COMPANY FOR ANYTHING EITHER CAN
DO AND TO ADVISE ME HERE IF HE HAS ANY PARTIC-
ULAR DIRECTIONS COMMUNICATE WITH EITHER
COMPANY OR ME AT SANFRANCISCO =

OSCAR LAWLER 225 BUSH ST =

In the East, it was Jesse H. Jones, of Reconstruction Finance
Corporation fame and member of the National Emergency Council, who took control. His personal suite at the Waldorf Astoria
Hotel in New York City was immediately made available to the
family. The next day he left Washington for New York so he could

personally cater to the family members' needs and supervise arrangements for their transportation to California.

Mae Post was in Ponca City, Oklahoma, since Monday, August 12, visiting with old friends, the L. E. Grays. It was at their house that she learned the news. "I wish to God I had been with him when he crashed!" she cried out.

> She was prostrated by the tragic news and went to bed for several hours. When she rose, she left Ponca City by plane for Maysville, Okla., near which the parents of Post live. Mrs. Post had come to Ponca City from Oakland, Cal., by plane.

It was William Francis Post, Wiley's father, who first found inner composure. Sitting in a rocker on the porch of their modest home, he said, "This is the thing we have been dreading for years and years." The last time Wiley had been home was shortly before his fourth and final attempt at a substratospheric flight. Wiley's mother kept remembering their last parting. "Son, do be careful," she had pleaded, "but we hope you make good and that everything comes out right this time." And he had said: "I'll do my best."

Mrs. Cenie Post, Wiley's ninety-five-year-old grandmother, deaf and almost blind, sat in calm meditation for almost thirty minutes after being informed of her grandson's death. Then, as she slowly talked of Wiley, she wept. "I am sorry Mae didn't get to fall with him, instead of Mr. Rogers," she said. "She's always told us she wanted to die with him when he crashed. And I know she hates to be left like this."

Mae hurried to Maysville to confer with Wiley's parents about funeral arrangements. At first the elder Posts thought that funeral services for their son should be held in a small grove in front of their home so that local folks could gather to pay their last respects. "I think the best place would be right here at home. We could have the services out in the yard where it is shady." Later the gray-haired father changed his mind: "We may not be here always. We would like to know our son's grave never would go unattended." Mae had told them that she would agree with their decision.

Great consolation came to Mae Post when Betty Rogers called and the two women had a telephone conversation. "Mrs. Rogers was so brave, her conversation gave me courage," Mae told relatives.

In Maine, the next hours of Friday, August 16, were taken up with constant telephone callers, trying to make plans for everything from complicated travel arrangements to New York City to memorial services that evening over national radio networks. Betty and Mary were flooded with requests; Aunt Dick, fortunately, was able to shield them from much of it.

Messages arrived from most major capitals. In England, newspapers carried banner headlines on the tragedy in Alaska. *Associated Press* reported from London: "It was the greatest display of interest in British journals since Reichsführer Hitler announced the rearmament of Germany." French Air Minister Denain presented condolences to the United States Embassy on behalf of French aviation. Ireland's newspapers recalled for their readers Will Rogers' benefit performance of 1926, to assist the relatives of those who had perished in the Limerick County theater. Norway's newspapers honored Rogers' memory by publishing the words he had written into the Golden Book at Copenhagen, Denmark the previous summer, after a flying visit to Norway's high mountains: "Denmark is beautiful but I can't forgive the Danes who stole Greenland from my Norwegian friends." *O Globo*, Rio De Janeiro's great newspaper, wrote, "The disaster in Alaska deprives America of two of the highest expressions of her civilization."

Most revealing was Soviet reaction. In Moscow an official Russian spokesman expressed deep regret at the death of Wiley Post and Will Rogers: "Both victims were very popular in the Soviet Union. We were looking forward to their arrival in Russia with the greatest interest. The news of the disaster naturally came as a profound shock to us." Declaring that the Soviet Union expected "their arrival" indicates that the Russians knew the flight plans while the rest of the world only guessed.

Soviet Ambassador A. A. Troyanovsky transmitted his government's official condolences, and in a message to Secretary of State Cordell Hull, extended "sincere condolences to their families and to the nation for the loss of these famous and brave Americans."

From Hyde Park, New York, where President Franklin D. Roosevelt was weekending at the summer White House, he expressed his deep regret at the deaths of Will Rogers and Wiley Post. Informed of the tragedy when he returned from a motor trip through his estate, President Roosevelt authorized this statement:

> I was shocked to hear of the tragedy which has taken Will Rogers and Wiley Post from us. Will was an old friend of mine, a humorist and philosopher beloved by all. I had the pleasure of greeting Mr. Post on his return from his round-the-world flight. He leaves behind a splendid contribution to the science of aviation. Both were outstanding Americans and will be greatly missed.

From Honolulu, in the Territory of Hawaii, Shirley Temple was reported to have burst into tears when she learned of Will Rogers' death. The child star was a favorite of Rogers' and frequently the two "cut-up" together. Crying bitterly, Shirley was reported to have said: "I hate airplanes!"

Also in Honolulu was John Ford. Ford recalled how he had wanted Will to accompany him to Hawaii. Now he learned of his friend's death. He was too shocked for other than a grief-stricken exclamation. "God, that's terrible!" he cried.

Hal Roach, who had also asked Will to accompany him to Hawaii to play a series of polo matches there, had arrived in Honolulu when he learned of the crash.

Postmaster-General James A. Farley, too, was in Hawaii on a vacation when the news reached him: "I am inexpressibly shocked at word of Will's death. We were close personal friends," was all he could say.

In Washington, D.C., the governmental agency responsible for civil aviation issued a statement:

> Eugene L. Vidal, Director of Air Commerce in the Bureau of Air Commerce, Department of Commerce, upon being informed of the accident in which Will Rogers and Wiley Post were killed, made the following statement:

>Will Rogers has been regarded for years as the country's Number One air passenger. Wiley Post's exploits in round-the-world flying and in stratosphere tests are known wherever people know about airplanes.

>The news of their accident shocked and stunned all of us in the Bureau of Air Commerce. The loss of these able men cannot be measured.

>We have already set in motion the machinery for investigating the accident, to determine the cause, if possible.

>The Bureau of Air Commerce inspector in Alaska will proceed to the scene immediately and report to us when he has learned the facts.

>Wiley Post was flying a three-place Lockheed Orion Special which bore a Department of Commerce restricted license authorizing its operation on long cross country flights and special test work only.

>The plane was a special job, made up of an assembled Orion fuselage and Sirius wing. It was originally built in May 1933 and was licensed as a commercial plane, but was relicensed under a restricted license August 8, 1935 after being rebuilt. Its license number is NR 12283.

>Equipped with a controllable pitch metal propeller and 550 horsepower engine, it had a rated speed of approximately 180 miles.

The statement showed how little the responsible agency knew. The few reported facts contained basic errors, some of which would never be corrected; but Washington was a long way from Alaska and some news never reached back east.

Leaving Fairbanks at 11:15 in the forenoon, Alaska time, Crosson set his course for Barrow. The plane carried twelve five-gallon cans of gasoline. They just sat on the floor of the cabin and were not lashed down. Their own weight kept them in place. There was plenty of floor space as the crew had removed all but two of the seats. Bob Gleason would occupy one of them, directly behind the pilot's left shoulder. It was advantageous to have the radio operator that close to the pilot. With the roar of the engine making ordinary conversation difficult, Gleason could yell in Crosson's ear if he had to, or hand him a hastily scribbled note.

Bob sat with earphones clamped against his head, and a clip board with a hand key in his lap. The vacant floor space was a constant reminder of the purpose of that trip.

Asking for weather readings, Gleason heard from Wiseman and Barrow, and neither report was encouraging. The weather north of the Endicott Mountains was still the same as the day before: fog and cloud cover. Arrangements had been requested to have the Signal Corps observe a special broadcast schedule with Wiseman and Barrow so that updated weather summaries could be relayed to the plane in flight. This was done.

As Crosson and Gleason headed toward the Endicott Mountains and the solid weather beyond, they first had to negotiate the White Range and then cross the Yukon River. They had to attempt several passes, as some of them were closed in by fog and clouds. By the time they were through the mountains and were out over the flats—or tundra—they had flown close to five hours. Crosson set the plane down on the first lake that looked long enough to allow a comfortable landing and subsequent take off. Once the plane stopped its forward motion, the job of refuelling began. The two men emptied all twelve cans of gas. There was no way to save those cans. Gasoline fumes inside the cabin would have constituted a great danger. Bob simply dropped the emptied cans into the lake, where they filled with water and sank.

After gassing up, the engine was started with an inertial starter, which was a two-man operation. One person had to stand outside the plane and hand-crank the heavy flywheel rapidly; when a certain speed had been reached, the pilot inside the plane adjusted the throttle and engaged gears, which turn over the engine and start the motor.

Against his own advice, Crosson now set course directly for Barrow. Weather conditions were identical to those Wiley had encountered the day before. Dense fog and low clouds allowed very little visibility. But Crosson knew the North Slope. In Gleason's words, they had "hit Barrow just a little bit west of it—not much—we were very close to it and landed on Barrow's lagoon." The time was 5:15 in the afternoon. There was no ice on the lagoon, nor did there seem to be any ice on the Chukchi Sea. Ice floes, which only yesterday threatened a Coast Guard cutter, had completely disappeared in less than twenty-four hours. Heavy currents must have taken them further out to sea.

Securing the plane just a few feet from the lagoon's shore, the two men briefly discussed plans for their return trip. It was decided that they would wait until shortly after midnight, when it began to get light, before starting back. While there was no hurry to return to Fairbanks, it was Joe's axiom that it was "never wise to hang around Barrow too long, or the weather would shut you in." The time of departure set, Crosson made his way toward the village, to call on Dr. Greist and catch a few hours' rest.

Bob Gleason stayed with the airplane. Short wave communication in high latitudes is much more subject to ionospheric storms than in lower latitudes. Sometimes in the far North, short waves are useless. But on August 16, 1935, the PAA crew was fortunate that propagation via the ionosphere's reflecting layers was good and stable. Gleason used only 5692.5 KHz on the entire trip, which was PAA's regular daytime frequency.

Even bobbing on the water of Barrow's lagoon, Gleason was in contact with Chuck Huntley, the PAA key operator in Fairbanks. Through him he received news and weather updates from Fairbanks and Wiseman. Bob Gleason did not go into the village as he felt that he ought to stay at his post at the key. Stretching his legs, he took some photographs of the plane, then ate the hot meal brought from the village, but he did not sleep this night.

While Joe Crosson caught a few hours sleep, some other visitors to Barrow rested too. What had not been mentioned to either Crosson or Gleason was the fact that another plane had also arrived at Barrow that day. Its mission: to bring out the first photographs of the crash site and the wrecked plane.

For planes to arrive at Barrow may have been rare, but it was not unusual. The other plane was equipped with wheels, and it had landed away from the lagoon on the hard beach. It had reached Barrow along the upcoast from Nome, via Kotzebue and Wainwright on the west side of Alaska. In the next few hours there would develop a race between the two planes, but neither Crosson nor Gleason were as yet aware of it.

The Fairchild 71's gas tanks having been topped with fuel, twelve additional five-gallon cans of gasoline were taken aboard. Near eleven o'clock a silent crew of Eskimos carried the bodies of Wiley Post and Will Rogers with all possible care to the lagoon and placed them into the cabin of the waiting PAA plane. They were not lashed down. Close to midnight Crosson and Gleason started the engine. It would take some time to heat the engine oil to its prescribed minimum temperature of 40 degrees Centigrade (100 degrees Fahrenheit). The persistent roar of the motor, audible throughout the village, alerted the crew of the other plane, and the great photo race was on.

That is to say, this was the beginning for a race for the crew of the other plane, not for PAA. As far as Joe Crosson and Bob Gleason were concerned, they had simply flown north to bring away the bodies of Will Rogers and Wiley Post. The fact that at the same time they were taking along some rolls of film handed them at Barrow was of little importance to them. Crosson and Gleason had no information or instruction to race, nor was there any sense of urgency about their trip.

Once the Fairchild's engine had warmed up, the tether was released. Crosson maneuvered the plane into position for takeoff when one float ran aground. It was stuck on a barely submerged sandbank. Joe Crosson tried to gun the engine, to get the pontoon over the sandbar, but the plane would not budge. There was a pair of hip boots in the plane and Gleason had to put them on and step out into the water of the lagoon. He tied a fifty-foot rope, which was part of standard equipment, to the tail of the airplane. Walking now along the shore to one side as far as the rope would reach, Crosson gunned the airplane engine while Gleason pulled at the tail section. The plane could not be moved. Bob walked repeatedly from one side to the other, pulling first this way then the other, with Joe gunning at full throttle, until finally the plane slid off the bar. Crosson coasted, waiting for Gleason to detach the rope from the tail and get back aboard. The cabin door closed, Bob struggled out of the hip boots and took his seat; at last they were ready to go. Taxiing to one end of Barrow's lagoon, Crosson headed into the wind and took off. A small group of Eskimos stood watching and as the plane rose, waved a silent farewell. The time was 12:45 A.M., August 17. Stanley Morgan sat at his key for another hour, tapping out messages to the world before getting the first sleep in almost forty-eight hours.

While the world slowly learned of the tragedy, Crosson and Gleason faced the most dangerous part of their round-trip. "The ceiling was a hundred feet, visibility perhaps a half-mile, the weather was almost unflyable," Gleason remembered. There was no reason, or sense, to fly southwest to the crash site just for an aerial look. With the prevailing ceiling, there was little they could have learned; thus the thought of flying the few minutes out of their way, just to see the shattered plane, was not even discussed. There were other things far more important: The Endicott Range would have to be crossed, and this time from the shrouded side. It would be impossible to recognize, or even see, the passes from any distance.

Crosson's first task was to find the Colville River. The Colville River runs out of the Endicott Mountains then parallels the range, gathering tributaries rushing down the mountainside as it flows east then north toward the Beaufort Sea. Though one of Alaska's large rivers, it was not easy to locate when visibility was a mere half-mile. If Crosson took the plane up too high, he was enveloped in fog and clouds, and if he flew low he could not see far ahead.

Once he had located the river, Crosson followed it, staying close to the surface with the pontoons almost skimming over the low water. Now that night had returned to northern Alaska, the shorter daylight hours no longer supplied melted snow and ice as freely as they did during the earlier 24-hour summer days. The water in the streams was noticeably lower, as the supply from the mountains lessened. When a tributary from the south seemed wide enough, Joe would follow it upstream into the mountains, hoping that it would lead him to a pass. As Joe Crosson flew upstream, the rising terrain would soon force the small plane into solid overcast. The fog was almost impenetrable. There were no landmarks to be seen and Crosson had to fly still closer to the water's surface, as it was his sole guide. According to Gleason, the banks of these streams were:

> . . . about 20 feet high and we flew up the river and sometimes I couldn't see over the banks. I couldn't see the land, we were right down on the river. So we went on up there, of course there are a lot of tributaries into the Colville and Joe looked at two or three of those, but turned around and came back every time and finally we got through on one of them, I don't know which one it was. But all at once something wonderful happened. We broke out into clear weather. Sunshine! Sure did. Joe then

picked out a lake, which was Wild River Lake. And there
we started to gas up again; put the extra 60 gallons in.

While the two men were adding the fuel they heard a man,
apparently a miner, yelling at them. He was coming toward the
plane in a strange-looking boat which he had obviously made out
of a sluice box. It was about twelve inches wide and had little
outriggers on it. He was quite indignant. "Are you Frank Pollack?"
he demanded to know. When Joe assured him that neither he nor
Gleason was this Frank Pollack, the miner explained that he had
contracted with a Frank Pollack to fly in his winter supplies.
Pollack was a well-known, respected pilot, based in Fairbanks.
Joe Crosson assured the miner that Pollack was an honorable man
and would definitely be out later as agreed. Then Crosson surprised Gleason. He did something uncharacteristic. It was Joe's
habit never to discuss PAA business with anyone outside the
company. But this time he said, "we got the bodies of Will Rogers
and Wiley Post here, they were killed up at Point Barrow."
The old miner just looked at Crosson with a blank expression; neither name meant anything to him. Not being interested in
this news, the miner turned and began paddling back to his camp.
The Fairchild 71 took off but soon ran out of good weather.
Once Joe had crossed the Yukon River he ran into heavy rain. He
had yet to fly over one more range to get to the Tanana River and
then Fairbanks. The rain clouds were ever darker and menacing,
but this was an area where Joe had been many times and he knew
every stump.
It was just 7:35 A.M. when Crosson swooped low over the
center of Fairbanks. On instruction from PAA, Joe Crosson set the
plane down on the Chena Slough, just above the bridge at the foot
of Cushman Street. Ordinarily he would have landed at the
Spencer Homestead, where PAA had its base. Once the plane was
on the water, a small crowd gathered almost immediately. Several
volunteers, among them Lloyd Jarman, helped transfer the bodies,
which were then taken to the Hosea H. Ross Mortuary.
Crosson brought back from Barrow some of the personal
items belonging to Wiley and Will. Some had been dried by the
Greists; others were still soaking wet from drifting in the brackish
water of the lagoon. Joe took them home to Lillian, who dried
them out in her kitchen stove—the same oven on which only two

days earlier she had prepared Post's and Rogers' meal. The Crossons returned those items to the next of kin.

Joe Crosson and Robert Gleason now wanted to shower, shave, get a meal, and then a few hours of undisturbed sleep. They had fought the elements in the most inhospitable areas of Alaska; they had won and deserved some rest.

The two men did not know that another plane, too, was on its way to Fairbanks with the sole purpose of getting to Seattle first. The great photo race was on its initial lap and, while Pacific Alaska Airways still knew nothing about the contest, it had won the first round.

CHAPTER SEVEN

THE GREAT PHOTO RACE

[Lindbergh] said, "Come on, I will take you up
with me. . . ." The old plane looked like a weak
sister to me. It's almost sacrilegious to say that you
would be afraid with Lindbergh, for my only
chance of ever becoming immortal was to have
fallen with Lindbergh. But even at that I was too
big a coward to want to fall with him."
—Will Rogers, *Saturday Evening Post*,
June 9, 1928.

While the news of Will Rogers' and Wiley Post's deaths broke
too late in the morning for most American early newspapers,
there were still the midday, afternoon, and evening papers.
And then, of course, there were the "extras!" Those extras,
hawked by newsboys as they ran along the streets, were really
the same editions sold earlier, with the latest developments replacing some other story on the front page. Those new tidbits
could be major or minor, it mattered little. If a story was of some
momentary interest to the public, every single scrap of new
information was disseminated as an extra. Thus readers would
buy the same newspaper several times during the day, the only
difference being that the latest facts were simply added in red ink.
News services would compete fiercely for morsels of minutiae on
any major break, just to send those lucrative extra editions into
the streets.

   The deaths of Will Rogers and Wiley Post affected most
American homes. Post was the hero, admired, his exploits followed anxiously, his pictures on the front pages of every newspaper and magazine in the country. Rogers was the film star, the
humorist, the political analyst, the uncle everyone wanted. He
came into people's lives by way of the pages of 650 newspapers,
the radio, and the movies. And if one had remained untouched by

newspapers, radio, or movies, friends would forever quote what Will Rogers had written that same morning.

Few Americans did not personally feel the loss of either man. Thus the familiar cry of "Extry! Extry! Read all about it!" brought out eager buyers wanting to learn the latest developments in the unfolding story of the crash. Every detail of their lives was covered, from youth to their departure for Barrow. There were innumerable photographs of the two men in every imaginable pose: with or without their wives, leaving here, arriving there, their homes, Rogers' children (the Posts had none). There was just one major part of the story missing: there were no photographs of the final act—yet. But in Alaska, men were already challenging the elements to bring back the first pictures.

In Nome, on the western edge of Alaska, as in Barrow, the weather had been inclement for several days. As usual, by the middle of August every year, fog shrouded the coast, while rain was the expected norm, often turning to snow.

A local old-timer, Sam Anderson, had his own short-wave radio and early every morning he would listen to news broadcasts from the States. What he heard this particular morning was that Will Rogers and Wiley Post had crashed the evening before at Walakpa Lagoon, and both men had been killed. It gave him an idea; there was money to be made in getting the first picture of the crash site.

Anderson roused Chet Brown, an experienced bush pilot for the newly formed Wien Alaska Airways, Inc., one of the numerous small freight lines operating in Alaska. Chet immediately saw financial merit in Anderson's suggestion and went to see Alfred J. Lomen, of the Lomen Reindeer Corporation.

Lomen, a well-connected business man, was a man of action. He contacted the *Post-Intelligencer*, Seattle's foremost newspaper. He proposed to charter a plane with pilot and mechanic, hire a local photographer and bring to Seattle the first, exclusive pictures of the crash site and the wrecked plane. *The Post-Intelligencer* agreed at once. There was only one stipulation: Lomen would have to deliver the first photographs, or the deal was off. The Seattle newspaper would not pay if photos were already published elsewhere. Though he realized the risk, Lomen agreed. He was well aware of the fact that should Pacific Alaska Airways also carry films, it could easily beat him. The Wien

Alaska Airways planes available to Lomen were all slower than those used by PAA. Lomen would have to rely on his deal with the Seattle newspaper remaining a secret. He could only make money if PAA remained unaware that there was a competitor.

There were no pontoon planes available. Floats would have afforded a certain degree of safety in an emergency but wheels would have to do. The plane, a six-place, single-engine Bellanca, was on wheels. There was no reason to carry a radio operator, as the plane had no radio. It was a simple plane, with a basic turn and bank indicator, tachometer, compass, altimeter, and oil-pressure gauge as the only instruments. It did have a home-made type of heater, which was little more than a cover over the exhaust pipe, allowing almost as much deadly carbon monoxide as heat to enter the cockpit.

Hank Miller was to be Chet Brown's mechanic and co-pilot. Why supposedly rational people would entrust their lives to so ill-prepared a plane is astounding. It was a minimally equipped plane, with neither floats nor radio, flying into the same weather in which Post and Rogers had just crashed. To make things worse, the plane was going to carry four people. Alfred J. Lomen was not about to leave this mission to others; he was going along—to Barrow and then all the way to Seattle.

Now that he had a pilot and mechanic, he still needed a photographer. He chose Curtis Jacobs, a local photographer. There were others in town, but most were stringers for various news services. So far none of the other photographers had become aware of the crash near Barrow, and Lomen wanted to leave it that way. There was no sense in alerting the competition.

But Nome was covered by a blanket of fog and clouds and it was not until 11 A.M. that Friday morning, August 16, before weather conditions would allow a take-off. Even then, Chet Brown had to keep the landmarks in sight as he headed across the fog-shrouded Seward Peninsula toward Kotzebue, 175 air miles to the north.

Visibility was a great problem. Flying due north, Chet Brown would cross the Kigluaik and Bendeleben Mountains, with peaks as high as 4700 feet. There was no reason he could not fly at a higher altitude clearing all of them, but then he would lose visual contact with the ground. If Chet were to climb above the clouds, it would be most hazardous to descend through the cloud cover without knowing the altitude of the mountains below.

By one o'clock they had reached Kotzebue. No other plane had come up from Nome, and Alfred Lomen believed that so far he was ahead in the race to get photographs.

As soon as the fuel tanks were topped, the four men took off again. Their next stop: Barrow. Flying almost due north from Kotzebue, mountain ranges had to be crossed again. Parts of the Endicott Range, the Noatak Mountains, forced the tiny plane high above seven thousand feet. Exactly as Wiley Post had searched only a day earlier, Chet Brown now looked for a break in the thick cloud and fog carpet. Two hours had already elapsed and almost half their fuel was gone; the point-of-no-return had nearly been reached. Now what? Decisions had to be made. Should they turn around and backtrack to safety, or continue and take the risk of not finding a hole through which to descend? The consensus was to continue onward. Brown turned westward, hoping that he might be flying along the coast.

They found a break over Cape Lisburne. Now all they had to do was to fly low and follow the coastline right into Barrow. Just minutes out of Barrow, they spotted Walakpa Lagoon below. The pile of wreckage which was once a plane, now smashed, lay in a shallow pool of water, like a toy dropped by a giant.

This was what they had come to photograph. Now all Brown had to do was to find a place to land. His wheels were of little use on the lagoon. He circled several times, looking for an unbroken length of beach that looked like it would support their weight. Chet Brown, the veteran pilot, set the plane down gently as if he were on a concrete runway. Lomen and his photographer, Curtis Jacobs, walked back to the crash site. Several Eskimos in a skin boat were still there. Jacobs asked them to row him closer, for close-ups. It took but a few minutes to circle the debris and take several photographs.

Lomen began to question the Eskimos, trying not to sound anxious or arouse any suspicion; he wanted to know if any other plane had come to take photographs. The natives assured him that no plane had come all day. Lomen was still not quite satisfied that he held the only film of the wreck. He knew that the bodies of Rogers and Post had been recovered the night before. It occurred to him that perhaps some members of the rescue team had taken photographs. If that was the case then those films would be still in Barrow, unless—No! Who would have flown them south? Lomen was almost certain he held the film that was most likely to reach Seattle first.

It was almost 8 P.M., just twenty-four hours since the crash had occurred. Lomen was already thinking ahead about the return trip. First they had to get to Barrow, refuel, and rest. The Bellanca had difficulty getting out of the soft sand at the lagoon, but Chet managed to lift her off, landing minutes later on the beach at Barrow.

There was no way they could miss seeing the PAA float plane bobbing in the lagoon. Inquiring about it, they learned that it had come to pick up the bodies of Post and Rogers, and that it would take some undeveloped rolls of film back to Fairbanks. Naturally none of the four men would discuss their own mission, and no one asked them.

By this time, at least one other Nome-based team was trying to get to Walakpa Lagoon. Frank H. Whaley had been hired by Universal News to fly a cameraman from Nome to the crash site. But the same heavy fog that had troubled Wiley Post a day earlier, and Chet Brown and Joe Crosson this day, had now become impenetrable. Despite the fact that Whaley was an excellent pilot—or perhaps because of it—he turned back after getting to within a hundred miles of Walakpa Lagoon.

Brown needed gasoline for his trip to Fairbanks. The major supplier would have been Pacific Alaska Airways, which, however, was not in the business of selling aviation gasoline to competitors, no matter how small. Brown was able to buy twenty-five gallons of automobile gasoline from Brower's store, but it was not enough to reach Fairbanks. They would have to fly via Kotzebue and buy aviation fuel there.

They ate dinner with their host Charles Brower and then decided to turn in. On the move since 6 A.M. that morning, they had had a full day with enough excitement and worry to last a full week; and there was still more to come.

Lomen wanted to keep an eye on his precious film, so he and photographer Jacobs were to sleep at Brower's, while Brown and Hank Miller were to bed down on the other side of the village with Frank Daugherty, the school teacher.

The time was close to midnight, and Lomen had not yet fallen asleep, when he heard Crosson's plane being warmed up. Tired as he was, he could not afford to allow Crosson and Gleason to get too far ahead, especially since his crew had to fly out of their way, via Kotzebue. Hearing Crosson's engine start, the four men met at their plane without any prearrangement. They all had the same thought. Using the last aviation gasoline remaining in one fuel tank for take-off, Brown switched to the automobile gas once the plane had reached altitude. Thus they flew into the new day, August 17; only some thirty hours had elapsed since the crash.

Arriving in Kotzebue at 4:30 A.M., Brown filled his tanks with aviation gasoline. There was a message for Lomen from the office of Wien Alaska Airways, saying that on his arrival in Fairbanks, another plane would be standing by, ready for an all-night flight to Seattle. The tanks topped, the engine checked, it was back into the air by 6:20 A.M. Lomen constantly urged greater speed, since there was no time to lose; he had a long way to go and there was a lot of money at stake. Three hours later, Brown had to make a refueling stop at Ruby, on the Yukon River. The Bellanca landed at Weeks Field in Fairbanks almost twenty-four hours after leaving Nome.

From here a new crew was to take over. Brown and Miller had completed their jobs perfectly; Jacobs, too, was no longer needed. The new pilot was Noel Wien; his mechanic, Victor Ross. Noel had the reputation of being one of the most steady, most reliable pilots in the Territory. He would not take unnecessary chances and every one of his exploits showed careful planning and thorough attention to detail.

Wien could have taken Chet Brown's wheel-equipped plane and flown it to Whitehorse, then on to Juneau and finally into Seattle, though that was usually the route taken by float planes. But somehow Noel did not trust Brown's plane without a thorough overhaul. He chose, instead, to fly a Bellanca with a Wasp Jr. engine. This plane, too, was equipped with wheels. Obviously, flying mostly over water, wheels would be almost useless in an emergency. Noel also pored over maps and decided on a different course into Seattle, namely via Whitehorse in Canada's Yukon Territory, Prince George, British Columbia, and then non-stop into Seattle. It was an eighteen-hundred-mile trip, six hundred miles to Whitehorse, then some seven hundred miles to Prince George, and finally almost five hundred miles into Seattle. It was longer than the coastal route, but it would be entirely over land

and presented a small margin of safety, even though it led over the inhospitable granite spikes of the Canadian Rockies.

Meanwhile, Lomen tried to learn whether Crosson and his plane were still in Fairbanks. When he heard that Crosson and Gleason were at their homes, asleep, he must have heaved a sigh of relief. So far his secret seemed safe, and he was to be off immediately for Seattle.

But Wien's Bellanca was not quite ready. To make the long night flight to Seattle, additional fuel tanks and gas cans would have to be carried for on-board fuelling. On a night flight, it would not be possible to land the plane and empty the cans directly into its tanks. The way commonly used to make such a transfer while in flight was a simple wobble pump, a horizontal siphon-pump which was worked by pushing and pulling a lever back and forth. The installation took time and almost three hours were lost in Fairbanks. An impatient Lomen must have been seething. Though the work was going on in secrecy inside a closed hangar and any competitor would be unaware of their preparations, Lomen was only too keenly aware that every minute on the ground increased the danger of being scooped. Some other photographer could also fly to Barrow and bring back pictures. Crosson, himself, could wake refreshed and fly those rolls of film to Seattle; and PAA's Fairchild 71s and Lockheed Electra 105s were faster planes. There were any number of other scenarios of what could go wrong if too much time was lost.

Lomen was risking a lot of money—his own—and there was no pay-off if he was late. There is no record whether Alfred Lomen had had any sleep since getting up in Nome some thirty hours earlier. Chances are that he caught some short naps while in flight. But the man who was not going to get any chances of sleep for many hours to come, was Noel Wien. He had just come back on a night flight from Dawson, and was not too anxious to go out again. But Alfred Lomen was impatiently prodding everybody, urging everyone on.

It was 1:15 in the afternoon before the single-engine Bellanca was finally ready to leave. It was carrying a capacity 112 gallons in its tanks and twelve five-gallon drums of aviation gasoline in the cabin. Six hours and forty-five minutes later, Wien's Bellanca landed at Whitehorse, Yukon Territory. They cleared customs and Noel consulted the latest weather information and refueled the empty wing tanks. He also replenished his cache of gasoline cans. They would have to cross the mountains during the coming hours, and the last thing Wien needed was added worries over running out of fuel. As a matter of record, Noel's careful nurturing of his fuel supply and respect for his equipment made him cruise at 1650 rpm, which would only use fourteen gallons an hour.

Alfred Lomen, always the driving spirit, was for taking off immediately on the next leg. Noel just sat down, stretched out his legs, leaned back and relaxed. Lomen, who was paying the bill, became irritated. What did Wien think resting at a time like this, he demanded? Did he not realize that every minute counted? They might just as well return to Fairbanks as sit here doing nothing!

Wien was undisturbed and composed. Patiently he explained that if they left Whitehorse now, they would arrive over Prince George in total darkness; since the airfield there was not equipped with lights, there would be no way to land. What they had to do, Noel tolerantly clarified, was to leave Whitehorse so they would arrive at Prince George with the coming of light. Having given one of the longest speeches of his life, Noel Wien continued to rest; he was a thoughtful pilot. His ambition was to die in bed of old age, not crushed like Wiley Post.

In Fairbanks, a PAA twin-engine Lockheed Electra 10, a cabin monoplane, was being checked by mechanics. Warren Tilman, Rogers' new friend from Juneau and Fairbanks, and Ron and Vaughn Taylor removed the seats and welded a platform with fasteners in their place. This plane would bear the bodies of Will Rogers and Wiley Post to Seattle. Its crew was to be Joe Crosson, pilot, William Knox, co-pilot, and Bob Gleason as radio communicator. It was to fly to Whitehorse, then non-stop to Seattle.

The much smaller Fairchild 71, which had brought the bodies and rolls of film from Barrow, was also checked and refuelled. It had been chartered by Associated Press. When Joe Crosson had flown to Barrow, Pacific Alaska Airways operation in Fairbanks had found itself one plane short. That missing Fairchild 71 was needed for pilot Al Monson to deliver the U.S. mail down along the Yukon River. To cover the temporary shortage, pilot Alex Holden and mechanic Lloyd Jarman, stationed in Juneau, had been ordered to bring a replacement Fairchild 71 to Fairbanks. By an odd coincidence, Lloyd Jarman remembered that the plane transferred from Juneau was the same one having the damaged pontoons which eventually ended up on Wiley's plane.

Now that Crosson had returned from Barrow, Holden and Jarman were to take that extra plane back to its home base. Their cargo: the rolls of film containing photos of the crash site, the same received by Crosson from David Brower and Frank Daugherty. Both United Press and Associated Press were clamoring for those photographs. PAA was fully aware of the importance of these films and its obligation to deliver them as fast as possible. But no one outside the Lomen group had any knowledge that another plane was racing photos to Seattle for the rival International News Service.

Holden and Jarman, in their fast Fairchild 71, left Fairbanks about 2 P.M., a half-hour ahead of Noel Wien. The destination for refueling was Burwash Landing on Kluane Lake, Yukon Territory. Their plan then called for a night flight to Juneau, where a fresh pilot would take another plane to Seattle.

As Lloyd Jarman reported, it was not a pleasant flight. He complained that the plane handled like a "truck." It balked and reared and would not fly a straight line. He felt certain that Crosson's brush with the sand bank in Barrow lagoon somehow changed the alignment of the pontoons, causing air turbulence.

It seems odd that Holden would take Crosson's plane back to Juneau, instead of the one he and Jarman had brought to Fairbanks. Besides, if it was indeed the plane Crosson had flown to Barrow and back to Fairbanks, he had not encountered any such quirks. Surely, being the careful executive he was, Crosson would never have allowed anyone else to fly a plane he did not think airworthy.

Holden and Jarman reached Burwash Landing, where their plane was immediately refueled. They took off into the semidarkness, heading for Juneau. Jarman had to strike matches to read compass headings for Holden. Not long out of Burwash Landing, they ran headlong into a howling storm and, rather than risk facing into it all night while having to fly through Chilkoot Pass, they decided to return to Kluane Lake and wait it out. There they managed to land safely and secure the plane. After some deliberation, they concluded that the smartest thing to do was to catch some sleep and set the alarm clock for 3 A.M. As employees of PAA, they reported their new plan to the resident radio operator. The tiny PAA radio facility at Burwash Landing, being in the Yukon Territory, was manned by Royal Canadian Air Force personnel. These men worked for PAA, but were also members of the Canadian military. It was a strange but necessary arrangement, as Canadian authorities would not allow Americans to operate radios on their territory. As standard procedure, the radio operator at Burwash Landing reported the new flight plan to other PAA radio facilities up and down the line. As no plane was now due to move until after 3 A.M., the various stations shut down until then.

Lomen, Wien, and Vic Ross were at the Whitehorse Inn, in Whitehorse, waiting until it was time to take off. The arrival of strangers in a small town always brought out residents eager to hear the latest first-hand news from the outside world. Quite a number of men had assembled around the visitors when Ronny Greenslide, one of PAA's radio operators in Whitehorse, walked into the inn. Having just come off-duty, he had some late news. Not aware that his company, Pacific Alaskan Airways, was involved in a big race, he innocently announced to one and all within earshot that "Alex Holden and Lloyd Jarman are staying in Burwash until morning. We're going back to work at 3 A.M." Lomen must have shot quick, knowing glances at Wien and Ross when he heard that their only rivals were bedded down for the night. This was good news. They had dreaded that Holden and Jarman were ahead of them, and now they learned that not only was the other plane a hundred miles northwest behind them, but that its crew would sleep until at least 3 A.M.

Still another PAA employee unwittingly helped his company's competitors. The station manager at Whitehorse made it possible for Wien to take off in darkness, offering to light the runway with the headlights of his old Ford automobile, parked at the far end of the landing field. At 11 P.M., aiming his plane at the two lighted spots at the far end of the field, Noel raced over ground he could not see. Finally the heavily laden plane lifted off. He set the compass course for Prince George and flew through the moonless night over some of the most craggy, hostile mountains in the world. The night was absolutely clear, and the faint starlight silhouetted the mountain ridges all around the plane. The slightest miscalculation, the sudden malfunction of the engine, the wrong compass setting, an inaccurate reading of the maps—any one of them could mean death. In an emergency, lakes or rivers, even had they been visible, would have been useless to a plane equipped with wheels. There were no landing fields amid the cliffs of the steep mountains; and if by chance some level ground appeared, and Noel Wien could have seen enough to set the plane down, search teams would have never found them in the Alaskan vastness. Without a radio aboard, they could neither learn of the weather ahead, nor could they ascertain or confirm their position. They were blind, deaf, and invisible to the world.

Promptly at 3 A.M. Holden and Jarman arose at Burwash Landing. The storm had cleared, but the wind was still brisk. As Jarman walked to the lake to warm up the engine, he could hear the hungry wolves howl nearby. By 4 A.M. Holden and Jarman were ready to take off. The waves were running pretty high on Kluane Lake and Alex could not get the plane on the float step for take-off. He raced along the surface for over a mile and still the plane would not rise. He turned back to the landing and tied up.

Jarman had to loosen the propeller blades and alter the pitch by three degrees, since the plane's propeller blades had been set for sea-level pitch, and Kluane Lake was at an altitude of over six thousand feet. In the darkness he tried to adjust them evenly, checking his settings with matches that blew out as fast as he lit them.

On their next attempt, Holden was at last able to lift the plane off the water and the two men headed for Juneau. It was now 4:30 A.M. Sunday, August 18. Three hours and forty-five minutes later, Alex Holden landed at Juneau. Bob Ellis, a seasoned pilot, and Paul Brewer, his mechanic, had been waiting for them. Their plane, Alaska's fastest single-engine plane, a Lockheed Vega on floats, was warmed up. Extra cans of gasoline had been put aboard to make it possible to fly the more than nine hundred miles non-stop to Seattle. They, too, would have to use a wobble pump. Ellis and Brewer took off five minutes after Holden's Fairchild 71 touched the water of Gastineau Channel. It was now up to them to take the film into Seattle, south along the coastline. By this time, PAA had become fully aware that Noel Wien was also carrying film, and the race was on to Seattle. PAA had communicated to Juneau that there was no report of Noel Wien's flight. None of the regular airfields in Alaska had reported seeing him. PAA assumed that the storm, which had forced Holden and Jarman

back to Kluane Lake, had also forced Wien to set down. PAA
simply believed that Wien, known as a cautious flyer, was still
sitting in some safe spot. The thought that Wien had left Alaska
and was at the moment flying across Canadian territory apparently never occurred to anyone at PAA. Bob Ellis, therefore, left
Juneau at 8:20 A.M., with Pacific Alaska Airlines convinced that
their plane was ahead of Wien in his slower Bellanca. With that
information, Bob Ellis had little doubt in his mind as to who
would win, especially as he was now in the much speedier Vega.
Even though his plane was slowed by floats, he knew that it could
out-cruise Wien's Bellanca by thirty miles an hour. Only now, at
this late point, the simple task of flying film to Seattle had developed into a real race.

At the time Bob Ellis and Paul Brewer left Juneau, Joe
Crosson, Bill Knox and Bob Gleason had already left Fairbanks.
Hosea Ross, the local undertaker, had driven to Weeks Field,
bringing the bodies of Will Rogers and Wiley Post. Ross had a
startling opinion: "Post died instantly," he told Tilman, "but
Rogers, you can tell by the blood in the face, he probably didn't
know it, but he probably lived a little bit. . . ."

Warren Tilman and Ron and Vaughn Taylor helped carry the
bodies into the plane and lashed them down. When both bodies
were securely fastened, Tilman satisfied a strange urge. He had
long wanted to know just how short Wiley Post was and how tall
Will Rogers had been. He used his own bizarre way to find out:

> Post was a short guy, but Rogers was a pretty big guy.
> Boy, 'cause I laid down on the side of each one of 'em,
> you know, wrapped, and Ron said: "God, he says, don't
> do that, you make me sick."

Warren Tilman tried to calm his co-worker: "They're just
bodies now." But Ron Taylor did not quite see it that way.

The salvaged belongings, some still soaked from Walakpa
Lagoon, were also placed into the plane. Some of the men seri-
ously considered taking souvenirs. One man offered Tilman
Rogers' knife and watch, or at least the soggy copy of *Arctic
Village*, but Warren wanted none of it. He finally took a water-
logged sheet of paper. It was the bill from Seattle's Northwest Air
Service, for the plane's structural conversion to pontoons, which

Rogers had paid. Tilman kept it for years, then one day it was gone; taken by another souvenir hunter.

The trio of Lomen, Wien, and Ross knew nothing of this. After a flight of seven hours and fifteen minutes, they had landed at Prince George, British Columbia, at six o'clock in the morning. They were now sixteen and three-quarter hours out of Fairbanks and had covered 1,300 miles; it was almost two days since Noel Wien had slept. Everything had gone according to his plan. The question was just how much longer his good fortune could last.

Time-wasting trouble developed almost at once. Having landed in British Columbia, the trio was informed by officious airport management that they would have to go through customs. The fact that they had gone through customs at Whitehorse, in the Yukon—which, after all, was Canadian territory too—and had not left the country since then, was not accepted. They would have to do it again. Since the trio carried only rolls of film, there should have been no problem, but there was: no Canadian customs inspector was on duty.

An hour went by before an inspector was located, but he refused to come to the airport until his tour of duty was to start. In fact, the inspector was irritable, having been disturbed at his home and at a time when he was off-duty.

It was promptly at eight o'clock, two hours after they had landed, that the Canadian customs officer appeared. After hearing the facts of the case, he saw immediately that there was no need for the fliers to pass customs, as they were leaving the country, not entering it.

While there is no official, or even unofficial, record of what Alfred Lomen said at that moment when he found that two priceless hours had been wasted, it is known that Lomen had the vocabulary and the temperament to be quite articulate.

Noel Wien had another five hundred miles to go. He was tired and the trio was dispirited. There was little doubt at that moment that they had lost the race. But they would just go through the motions, anyway. Now that it was daylight, the rest of the flight was easy. Noel followed the Fraser River west, then cut south below Vancouver. The usual morning fog along this coast was burned off. Seattle sparkled in the early afternoon sun as Noel put the Bellanca down at Boeing Field at 1:45 P.M., local time. Before Wien could even cut the Wasp engine, the cabin door was jerked open, identifications were hurriedly exchanged and the film was snatched from Lomen's hands.

Bob Ellis, coming south from Juneau, claimed that he and Brewer had an easy nine-hundred-mile flight: "The weather was beautiful. The weather bureau reported 'not a cloud in the sky from Fairbanks to San Diego.' I read magazines all the way to Seattle. Another airplane in the sky was a rare sight in those days. Really, a hum-drum trip." At 3:35 P.M. he landed at Seattle's Boeing Field. He shut off the engine, grabbed the precious films, and walked into the administration building. The first thing he saw was someone reading a copy of the Seattle *Post-Intelligencer*, with pictures of the wrecked plane splashed across the front page. Noel Wien had beaten PAA by almost two hours.

But all was not lost for Associated Press. Having come in second in the race to Seattle merely meant the loss of a single market; it still left the rest of the country, indeed the whole world. AP split the number of negatives right in Seattle, some being retained for immediate service from that point, the remaining photos were dispatched to San Francisco.

Edison Mouton, an outstanding pilot, had flown a special plane north to make the final relay. He took off at 4:30 P.M., stopped at Eugene, Oregon, from 6:05 to 6:15 P.M., and then completed the 716-mile hop to San Francisco's airport at 9 P.M. The picture packages were rushed to the Associated Press office by motorcycle, and first prints were soon made and distributed by wire photo throughout the country.

Wien Alaska Airways, Inc., received $3,500 for the flight, based on a fee of fifty dollars per flying hour of a round-trip, the usual rate. Noel, being in Seattle, immediately used the money for a down-payment on a Ford Tri-motor, previously owned by North-West Airline.

Delayed in Seattle, Noel Wien acquired several paying passengers for the return trip, among them Alfred Lomen. Both men arrived back in Fairbanks more then two weeks after they had left that Saturday, August 17.

CHAPTER EIGHT

LAST RITES

Can you imagine when I die and St. Peter asks me
what I did on earth to qualify for heaven and I
answer: "I spun a rope and kidded myself so's
other people wouldn't kid me first."
—Will Rogers, *News-Week*, August 24, 1935.

Betty Rogers, her sister Theda Blake (Aunt Dick), and daughter
Mary left Skowhegan, Maine, Friday night, August 16, by train.
Their first destination was New York City. Will Jr., leaving Los
Angeles, was aboard an eastbound United Airlines plane to join his
family. Questioned by a reporter at the airport whether he now
feared flying, Will Jr. said, "The accident was just unfortunate. It
will not keep me from flying." Younger son Jimmy was in New
York City, and would await the arrival of the family members there.

Betty received a telegram from Amon Carter, publisher of
the *Fort Worth Star-Telegram*, a powerful political force in Texas
and a long-time friend of Will Rogers. He wanted Betty's permission to fly to Seattle and sit in the plane which was to bring his old
friend's body back to California. Betty wired her consent.

While Betty, Theda, and Mary were aboard the crack train
speeding south, the deaths of Rogers and Post had different reper-
cussions in countless parts of the United States. In Washington,
D.C., the Department of Commerce, through its Bureau of Air
Commerce, announced that it had dispatched Inspector Murray
Hall from Anchorage, Alaska, to the scene of the Rogers-Post
accident to gather all possible data. "No inspector will be sent
from here, the bureau said." Congress, too, announced an investigation, albeit little ever came of it. Preparations were made for

the funerals of Will Rogers and Wiley Post in Los Angeles and Oklahoma City, respectively, each city assuming the role of a hometown, though neither was.

Nome, Alaska, sorrowfully canceled arrangements for a grand reception. (Will Rogers had been quoted in an Associated Press story that he wanted to rope a reindeer, and Nome citizens had had the deer all picked out for him to lasso.)

In Bartlesville, Oklahoma, heavy folds of black crepe hung around the *Winnie Mae*, Wiley's plane that brought him world fame. Colonel Art C. Goebel, eminent pilot and Wiley's friend, supervised the draping of the plane. By a strange twist in the path of events, this was the same Art Goebel who had years earlier refused to accept delivery of that Lockheed Explorer that Roy Ammel subsequently wrecked in the Canal Zone. Wiley later bought that Explorer's wing from Charley Babb and joined it to the Orion fuselage which carried him to his death.

From St. Louis, Missouri, United Press carried the announcement that the *Spirit of St. Louis* medal for outstanding contribution to aviation would be awarded posthumously to Will Rogers. The award was originated in 1929 by the aeronautics division of the American Society of Mechanical Engineering. Will Rogers, the third person so honored, had been selected for the award weeks earlier and the announcement was originally to have been withheld until the Society's October meeting. Rogers, so the dispatch stated, had been selected for the honor because of his consistently constructive publicizing of aeronautics.

The *Seattle Daily Times* of August 17 reported an episode from the Los Angeles Legion Stadium, about the usual sight of Hollywood characters packing the house for the weekly fights. Rogers rarely attended the bouts, but other motion-picture people did. One regular was the famous and beloved wide-mouthed comedian, Joe E. Brown. Every Friday night he would climb into the ring, clown, turn handsprings, and challenge the fighters. The crowd always howled. But this night Brown had a different tone. He paid a touching tribute to Will Rogers. Case-hardened gallery spectators listened in silence. "Movie stars, sharp-faced blondes, bankers, merchants—in other words the fans—stood with bared heads as Brown recalled the name of Will Rogers.

"Mae West at the ringside seemed to have trouble with her eyes. Maybe it was a tear, and perhaps she was thinking of the time of the gala premiere of one of her first motion pictures. She wasn't very well known and some of the long established stars may have resented her drive toward popularity. Anyhow, few of the big stars turned out for the premiere. But Will Rogers, who seldom goes to gala affairs of this sort, did.''

In Ventura, California (so Associated Press reported), the *Ventura Free Press* in an editorial urged President Roosevelt to declare a national day of mourning in tribute to Will Rogers and Wiley Post.

In Wilmington, North Carolina, the local newspaper, the *Wilmington Star-News*, called on newspapers across the nation to join an effort to erect a memorial in Will Rogers' hometown, Claremore, Oklahoma.

In Sidney, Iowa, the rodeo contests were halted, pausing in memory of Will Rogers.

Arkansas, Betty Rogers' home state, observed a day of mourning, as decreed by the governor.

A special pine tree on the western shore of Lake Tahoe, on the border between California and Nevada, was draped in black as a tribute of love and respect for Will Rogers. The tree, which was near Tahoe Tavern, had been dedicated to Rogers July 23, 1933, when he had come there with a group of state governors on their way to a conference at Sacramento. Larger trees in the grove, known as *Governors' Grove*, were dedicated at the same time with suitable ceremonies to governors from each state of the union.

At that time, Rogers was led to a very small tree bearing a plaque reading, ''Dedicated to ''Governor'' Will Rogers, Beverly Hills.'' Governors and other spectators, anticipating a wise crack, waited in silence as Rogers measured with his eyes the height of ''his'' tree against the size of the governors' trees. ''Well,'' he finally drawled, ''I guess it'll grow to be a big tree some day.'' Will knew the area well. He had spent some time there during the filming of his motion picture *Lightnin'*.

From Chicago came the suggestion to have four hundred carillons in the United States and Canada chime in tribute to Will Rogers at the hour of his private funeral. J. C. Deagan, secretary of a company that made carillons, announced he had airmailed letters to owners of the chimes requesting a five-minute toll followed by the playing of Chopin's ''Funeral March'' and ''Abide With Me.''

The National Broadcasting Company and the Columbia Broadcasting System canceled two thirty-minute national programs to allow for special coast-to-coast broadcasts. Political leaders, fliers and motion-picture celebrities, speaking from Washington, New York, Chicago, and Los Angeles, told of their admiration and affection for the two men.

Captain Edward V. Rickenbacker opened the NBC program. Others participating included Speaker of the House of Representatives Joseph W. Byrns; Senator Joseph T. Robinson, Democratic leader in the Senate; Senator Thomas P. Gore of Oklahoma; former Secretary of War Patrick J. Hurley; and Will H. Hays, president of the Motion Pictures Producers and Distributors of America.

In Chicago, in the studios of CBS, former President Herbert Hoover, en route to his California home, joined General Charles G. Dawes, former Vice-President; round-the-world flier Jimmy Mattern; and Jack Knight, veteran airline pilot, in a radio tribute.

Mayor F. H. LaGuardia, speaking from New York's own municipal broadcasting station WNYC, told of the personal sadness he felt at the death of two men who were his friends: "How often," he said, "Will Rogers has given each of us something to smile about or something to reflect upon. His wise and humorous philosophy developed into a distinct school of thought. Every day, 'Will Rogers Says' started conversation at the breakfast tables of millions of American families. Wiley Post is another martyr to the progress of aviation development. He was another pioneer, a great and courageous flyer. Both men typified to the world, although each in a different way, all that is finest and best in the fiber and soul of American manhood."

A memorial program presented in New York City was directed by Bide Dudley, newspaper man and drama critic. Others taking part in the program were Jimmy Durante, Victor Moore, Dorothy Stone, and Frank M. Hawks.

Another program broadcast in New York included eulogies by Senators Warren B. Austin of Vermont; Jesse H. Metcalf of Rhode Island; W. Warren Barbour of New Jersey; James F. Byrnes of South Carolina; William E. Borah of Idaho; Daniel O. Hastings of Delaware; Henry F. Ashurst of Arizona; and Tom Connally of Texas.

At the conclusion of the eastern program, the NBC studios in Los Angeles continued the tribute. Darryl F. Zanuck, vice-president of Twentieth Century-Fox (Rogers' home studio), paid tribute, as did Colonel Roscoe Turner, an aviator who had flown Will many times, and Fred Stone, Will's closest friend. Ruth Etting concluded the program by singing *"Just a 'Wearyin' For You."*

In Seattle, Washington, Dr. James Whitcomb Brougher, Sr., pastor of the Hinson Memorial Baptist Church, prepared to leave Portland for Glendale, California. Betty Rogers had specifically requested that Dr. Brougher, an old friend of the Rogers family, be asked to officiate at the funeral service.

The nation's flags hung at half-mast in honor of Will Rogers and Wiley Post. *The Los Angeles Times* of August 17, 1935 printed a photograph of a large cross surrounded by flowers and a praying, shawled woman on her knees. The headline was: OLVERA STREET MOURNS. (Olvera Street is deep in the Spanish-speaking section of the city.) The caption under the photograph read:

> When news of the death of Will Rogers was received in Olvera Street, voices were hushed and heads bowed in sorrow. Quickly dahlias, gladioluses and other blooms taken from vases were placed at the foot of the cross at the street's entrance. They were soon woven into a gorgeous wreath which was placed on the cross. Beneath the wreath an artist printed on a placard the words: *"Will Rogers, Los Mexicanos de La Calle Olvera Lemantan Tu Muerte"* (The Mexicans of Olvera Street lament thy death). Then a large candle was lighted at the foot of the cross.

News of the crash shocked the U. S. capital. As soon as a quorum was assembled, Senator Joseph T. Robinson of Arkansas, Majority Floor Leader, arose from his seat and announced the deaths of Will Rogers and Wiley Post.

In the House of Representatives, Jed Johnson from Oklahoma, and a friend of both men, was selected by Speaker Byrns to announce the deaths to the House.

A number of crusades started at once, the most immediate of which was filmdom's ban on actors and actresses flying. New contracts contained a strict clause against the use of airplanes, while established stars with longtime contracts were persuaded to take the train.

Francis Lederer, Czechoslovakian–born stage star, announced his plan to build a memorial for Rogers and Post as "Leaders for Peace." Lederer himself was a prime leader in the world peace movement.

Postmaster-General James A. Farley was requested by the *Denver Rocky Mountain News* to authorize a special air-mail stamp in tribute to Will Rogers and Wiley Post. A Will Rogers stamp was issued in 1938, a second one in 1979.

Newspapers all over the country had banner headlines and featured the story daily. Some consulted public and self-appointed experts for their analyses of the crash near Barrow. Magazines devoted pages upon pages to recreate the accident. All aspects of the lives of the two men were told and retold. Interviews with friends, acquaintances, co-workers, competitors, and anyone who ever had come within a mile of either man were cited as if they were the most important news.

Without a shred of first-hand information, writers would point to the cause for the crash. The most common reason offered was the most simplistic: carburetor icing. They argued their finding on grounds that temperature and moisture conditions were right for the formation of tiny ice crystals which temporarily blocked the free flow of fuel in the carburetor. The engine stalled, they claimed, and the plane fell. It was an easy conclusion and placed the blame on the weather, which was convenient and to many even persuasive. The country was handed a culprit for the tragedy. But at a time of a world-wide Depression, another tragedy was not exactly what was needed. Will Rogers' death was an enormous loss to America. President Roosevelt evaluated the nation's grief correctly: "He loved and was loved by the American people. His memory will ever be in benediction with the hosts of his countrymen who felt the spell of his kindly humor which, while seeing facts, could always laugh at fantasy."

In the east, the ladies of the Rogers family were aboard the express train, the *Down-Easter*, speeding toward New York City. Before leaving Maine, Betty Rogers had telephoned Dorothy Stone in New York City. Dorothy, Fred Stones's famous daughter, was married to actor-dancer Charles Collins. With Betty, the three developed a plan.

Expecting a crowd of reporters and curious onlookers at New York's Grand Central Terminal it was decided that the family would leave the train at Stamford, Connecticut, and motor the remaining forty miles to the Waldorf Astoria. As Dorothy remembers it was left to her and Charles to make the necessary arrangements and drive to Stamford to pick up the family:

> The next morning Charley and I got up at 5 o'clock to drive to Connecticut to meet the train. The station master, naturally knowing of the unscheduled stop, informed the police, so that Mrs. Rogers could have a police escort—something she didn't want. And that was how the newspaper people found out where Mrs. Rogers would leave the train. When we got to the station, everybody was taking pictures, and this poor, darling woman and Mary stumbled off the train; she was just ready to fall when Charley caught her. That's how Charley ended up on the front page of some tabloid, and since no one knew who he was, the caption read "Jimmy Rogers meets his mother." We finally got back to the car and had to drive all over the countryside, through woods and everything, until we finally lost the pursuing newspaper cars. Then we met another car, I think it was a cousin's, and they whisked her away. When we returned home—we lived in Forest Hills at the time—our front lawn was covered with reporters, demanding to know where Mrs. Rogers was. And we could truthfully say we didn't know. One reporter even came into the house, pretending that he was a Western Union boy, trying to deliver a telegram.

At the Waldorf Astoria Hotel Betty was reunited with her son Jim, who, with his cousin Jim Blake, had awaited her here, rather than continue his drive to Maine.

Ever-faithful Oscar Lawler telegraphed Betty at the Waldorf Astoria:

NE100 60 DL = SANFRANCISCO CALIF 16 12 57
                                                    1935 AUG 16 ON 4 37

MRS WILL ROGERS = WALDORF ASTORIA HOTEL =
COLONEL LINDBERGH PHONES ARRANGEMENTS GO-
ING FORWARD AS REPORTED TO YOU STOP TRANS-

PORTATION WILL BE BY AIR TO JUNEAU AND TO LOSANGELES BY STEAMER STOP STANDARD EM- PLOYEES IN ALASKA DIRECTED TO COOPERATE FULLY STOP I WILL PROBABLY RETURN LOSANGELES TONIGHT STOP DO NOT HESITATE TO COMMAND STOP HILDA ADVISED OF PARTICULARS AND SHE IS IN TOUCH WITH YOUR HOME STOP =

OSCAR LAWLER

Lawler, on a business trip in San Francisco, must not have been aware of developing arrangements. He was referring to newspapers reporting a plan which called for the bodies to be brought back from Barrow aboard the Coast Guard cutter *Northland*. At the time Lawler sent the telegram, Crosson and Gleason were still on their way to Barrow. It had been Joe Crosson's own plan; it was something Crosson felt he had to do and was not ordered by either Lindbergh or any officer of PAA. In fact, Lindbergh had not yet formulated any definitive strategy and Crosson's own plan merely called for bringing the bodies to Fairbanks.

Some time in the next few hours the final program evolved:

5RXS488 38 = TDRO NORTHAVEN ME 16 829P
(STAMPED 1935 AUG 16 PM 6/1

J K BLAKE =
　　WILL ROGERS OFFICE

PACIFIC ALASKA AIRWAYS IS SENDING PLANE TO BARROW AND WILL ARRANGE ALL ALASKAN TRANS- PORTATION STOP FOR YOUR CONFIDENTIAL INFOR- MATION THE PRESENT PLANS ARE FOR THE ALASKAN PLANE TO CONTINUE THROUGH DIRECTLY TO LOS ANGELES STOP WILL KEEP YOU INFORMED =

CHARLES LINDBERGH

By 7 A.M., local time, James K. "Sandy" Blake in Los An- geles knew all about the current preparations:

NF65 37 DL BEVERLYHILLS CALIF 17 718A

1935 AUG 17 AM 11 11
MRS WILL ROGERS = WALDORF HOTEL =

COL LINDBERGH TELEPHONED THIS MORNING
PLANE SHOULD BE IN FAIRBANKS THIS MORNING
AND SHOULD ARRIVE LOS ANGELES WITH BOTH
BODIES MONDAY IF WEATHER PERMITS WILL TAKE
MR POST ON TO OKLAHOMA BETTER GET IN TOUCH
WITH HIM LOVE

                                                    SANDY

Some hours later, Oscar Lawler, still in San Francisco, wired
Betty:

NG268 104 DL = BEVERLYHILLS CALIF 17 135P
                        HAND STAMPED 1935 AUG 17 5 54
MRS WILL ROGERS =
WALDORF ASTORIA HOTEL =

AS IS NOT UNNATURAL THERE IS MUCH LOCAL SOLIC-
ITUDE FOR YOU INCLUDING INQUIRY AS TO FINAL
ARRANGEMENTS AND DESIRE FOR DEMONSTRA-
TIONS OF RESPECT STOP WE HAVE ANSWERED ALL
INQUIRIES THAT ARRANGEMENTS ENTIRELY UP TO
YOU AND WE WERE WITHOUT INSTRUCTIONS STOP
SO FAR AS WE KNOW PARTICULARS AS TO TRANSPOR-
TATION NOT KNOWN TO ANY OUTSIDER HERE AND
WE WILL SAY NOTHING UNTIL AFTER HEARING FROM
YOU DIRECT STOP COLONEL YOUNG PAN AMERICAN
ARIWAYS [sic] SANFRANCISCO ARRIVES SEATTLE SUN-
DAY EVENING AND BY DIRECTION COLONEL LIND-
BERGH WILL ATTEND ALL DETAILS THERE AND WILL
ADVISE US HERE AND REPORT ALSO TO LINDBERGH
STOP DO NOT HESITATE TO COMMAND =

                                    OSCAR LAWLER.

Charles Lindbergh consulted with Betty and kept her informed of all developments, but when decisions about transportation had to be conveyed, it was Lindbergh who issued the

commands. He proved a loyal, dependable friend who had come forward on his own when he was needed. The friendship between Rogers and Lindbergh began in 1927 in Mexico, when U. S. Ambassador Dwight Morrow had invited Will Rogers and Charles Lindbergh to help close a rift with that country. Morrow's plan not only had worked well, but the ambassador ended up gaining a son-in-law. Anne Spencer Morrow, the ambassador's daughter, and Charles Augustus Lindbergh were married in May 1929.

Following the 1932 kidnapping and death of the Lindbergh's infant, Charles, Jr., the distraught parents were hounded by the press. The crime, perhaps the most sensational of the Thirties, and the trial that was to follow, were constant news. Trying to escape pursuing reporters on a visit to Los Angeles in 1934, Anne and Charles Lindbergh had found solitude and privacy at the Rogers ranch in Pacific Palisades, California.

Over the years, the common interest in aviation further deepened the friendship between the two families. It was in keeping with Lindbergh's character that he would contact Betty and offer his services immediately upon hearing of the crash, even though the family was in the midst of celebrating son Jon's birthday.

Another old friend, chairman of the Reconstruction Finance Corporation, Jesse Jones, came to New York City from Washington to act as spokesman for the family and help them complete funeral arrangements. As he had put his personal suite at the Waldorf Astoria at the disposition of the Rogers family, he had to look for accommodations first.

Definite plans for the family's westward trip were not made until after the arrival of Will Rogers, Jr., from California. Transcontinental and Western Airway had offered the family transportation to California but plans to make the trip by air were canceled at the last moment. As Jesse Jones explained, "Mrs. Rogers asked me to say that the manner of her husband's death had no bearing on her decision to make the trip by train. It was found that there was no necessity for hurry, and as there was a large party and much luggage, it was decided that it would be more convenient to go by train. But she has no feeling against air travel. And she was deeply appreciative of Colonel Lindbergh's offer of assistance."

Perhaps it was also felt that the time spent on the train would allow the family to recover enough composure to face the ordeal ahead in Los Angeles.

Later, when the family emerged from the Waldorf Astoria, Betty Rogers looked drawn, but composed. The strain of the tragedy was plainly visible on the family's faces. Mary, her golden curls mostly hidden under a small dark blue hat, was close to tears as she stood beside her mother while flashlights exploded. She wore no makeup and leaned heavily on her brother's arm. Betty greeted reporters and photographers who crowded around. When she spoke there was a tremor in her voice. "Don't forget to tell the boys that Mr. Rogers was always your friend and he always will be your friend. He was one of you and I know he would want me to give you this message."

It was a large party that drove to Pennsylvania Station on August 18. Betty Rogers was accompanied by her daughter Mary; her two sons, Will Jr. and Jim; her sister, Theda Blake; her nephew, Jim Blake; and Dorothy Stone. Will's long-time friend, Frank Phillips, the oil millionaire from Bartlesville, Oklahoma and sponsor of the last four stratosphere flights by Wiley Post, would also share the private coach.

That same Sunday, August 18, Pacific Alaska Airways' twin-engine Lockheed Electra 10 cabin monoplane, bearing the bodies of Will Rogers and Wiley Post, had left Fairbanks at 6:05 A.M., local time. Joe Crosson was at the controls, Bill Knox co-pilot and Bob Gleason radio operator. The weather was good in Fairbanks; it was a beautiful morning. The flight plan called for a refuelling stop at Whitehorse, Yukon, a hop of close to five hundred miles; then it would be on to Prince George, British Columbia, and from there to Seattle, Washington. Ordinarily crossing the Canadian border was a routine procedure easily resolved at the time of landing. This time protocol was strictly observed. Whether it was the fact that corpses were taken across an international boundary, or whether it was the world fame of the bodies, is not known; in any case, the United States Department of State sought authorization from the Government of Canada for the plane to fly over its territory. The State Department acted at the request of Mrs. Will Rogers and Mrs. Wiley Post and also on representations of Pan-American Airways, Pacific Alaska Airways' parent company. Ottawa immediately granted permission.

At Whitehorse, the plane was checked and refuelled. Considering the ease of the flight so far, and the trouble-free weather, the three men realized that with the fuel reserve aboard, they could reach Seattle without any further stop, provided the weather remained good.

Crosson's planned route lay over more than a thousand miles of rugged, towering peaks and mountainous plateaus. This day it was an easy, almost monotonous flight. Trying to avoid crowds at points where refuelling stops were usually made, Bob Gleason made the flight practically without radio contacts except for several required position checks and mandated reports.

Leaving New York early that same Sunday afternoon, Betty Rogers and her party traveled in a special car attached to the *Pennsylvania Limited*. It was the private coach of General W. W. Atterbury, former president of the Pennsylvania Railroad. The party was scheduled to arrive in Chicago at 7:35 A.M. Monday morning. There they would have to change terminals. Their journey would continue aboard the Santa Fe railroad's crack train, *The Chief*, scheduled to reach Los Angeles Wednesday afternoon, August 21. Will's sister, Sallie, of Chelsea, Oklahoma, was to meet the train at the Kansas City Station. She was some sixteen years Will's senior, and had raised her ten-year-old brother after their mother's death. Now she would accompany Betty to California to be present at her brother's funeral service. Will had loved Sallie, perhaps more like the mother he had lost and could hardly remember. The two had been very close and Will never missed a chance to visit her at "Maplewood," her house at Chelsea. Of the eight children their parents had had, only Sallie was left.

While changing trains in Chicago, Will Jr. acted as the family's spokesman. He told the press that the funeral would be held in Los Angeles on Thursday, August 22, with a private funeral in the afternoon. The body, he said, would be placed in a vault in Los Angeles and would later be interred in the family's plot at Claremore.

Even while Betty was in transist, Charles Lindbergh kept her informed of developments. When the Rogers party reached Chicago, two telegrams were waiting. The first,

RXB2349 15 = TDRO NORTHHAVEN ME 18 725P

1935 AUG 18 PM 7 01

MRS WILL ROGERS, CARE CONDUCTOR = ON SANTA-

FE CHIEF WHICH LEAVES CHICAGO FOR LA 11 15
MONDAY CHGO =

ALASKAN PLANE MAY ARRIVE LOSANGELES MONDAY
NIGHT IF WEATHER FAVORABLE STOP OTHERWISE
SHOULD ARRIVE TUESDAY =

CHARLES LINDBERGH

had been followed by another one sent some two hours later:

RXBB 417 12 = TDRO NORTHHAVEN ME 18 101 OP
1935 AUG 18 PM 9 40

MRS WILL ROGERS, CONDUCTOR ON SANTAFE
CHIEF = LEAVES CHICAGO FOR LA ABOUT 11 AM
MONDAY CHGO =

ALASKAN PLANE LANDED VANCOUVER SUNDAY
NIGHT IS DUE LOSANGELES MONDAY NIGHT =

LINDBERGH

This second message might have puzzled the Rogers family.
Why would the plane have landed in Canada? Why not in Seattle,
as planned? Was this a garbled message? Was something wrong?

The Lockheed Electra 10 had indeed landed in Vancouver
just after 4 P.M., Fairbanks time. A few minutes earlier, while over
Squamish, thirty miles to the north, Robert J. Gleason had tapped
out the message: "PLEASE NOTIFY VANCOUVER AUTHORI-
TIES WE ARE ARRIVING. THANKS." Crosson's flight from Fairbanks to Vancouver, completed in ten hours and six minutes, was
the equivalent of a transatlantic flight from Newfoundland to
Ireland. But he need not have hurried, for now the plane would
spend the night in Vancouver, instead of Seattle. There was a
simple explanation for the delay. According to Gleason, the plan
had been to make the transfer of the bodies in Seattle quickly and
without ostentation, but

> . . . all at once we got our message: "Land at Vancouver's
> Sea Island Airport."

> We actually queried that message to be sure that
> that was what they wanted us to do . . . the problem was
> that the Pan-American airplane which was coming up
> from Texas to meet us at Seattle wasn't there yet. . . . So
> we stayed overnight and they told us to arrange to arrive in
> Seattle at—I don't know whether it was 9 a.m. or 10 a.m.

The airport at Vancouver was almost deserted, since its Sunday activity was minimal. Crosson was directed toward an empty hangar and he taxied into it. Once Crosson, Knox, and Gleason had assured themselves that their equipment was in proper hands, they walked into the administration building. The three refused to be drawn into interviews: instead, Crosson made several long-distance telephone calls to New York City and San Francisco, reporting his whereabouts to Pan-American Airways officials and receiving new instructions.

The next morning, Monday, August 19, after Canadian officials had placed a wreath aboard the ship as Vancouver's tribute to the dead men, Crosson took off from Sea Island Municipal Airport at 8:22 A.M. and reached Seattle forty-seven minutes later. Crosson was met by an army plane and escorted to the airport. Three navy planes, which had met him midway between Seattle and Vancouver, followed him to Boeing Field in the southern part of the city and circled over the airport, but did not land.

The funeral ship, with the curtains of the passenger cabin closely drawn, was met at the field by a large group of civic representatives.

A crowd of some fifteen thousand, some of which had been at the airport all night, was held back from the hangar apron by the police. There had been more than twenty thousand at the airport the day before, waiting for a plane that did not come.

Now it had arrived. Without stopping the motors Crosson taxied the plane into a United Air Lines hangar at the side of the field and the doors were locked.

The hangar was then completely surrounded by an honor guard of twenty Marine Corps reserves and by the state patrol.

Waiting inside the hangar was thin, dark-haired Colonel Clarence M. Young, Former Assistant Secretary of Commerce for Aeronautics, now Pacific Coast manager of Pan American Airways. With him was Amon Carter, who had flown north from

Fort Worth, Texas. Also awaiting the plane from Fairbanks was a Douglas DC-2 transport plane piloted by William A. Winston, with a crew of five men.

Once the huge doors of the hangar had closed and security was assured, the bodies were transferred into the after-cabin of the waiting transport. The transfer took place under the care of three undertakers who had arrived earlier.

Again the bodies of the two famous men were strapped down, still wrapped in plain white sheeting. Between them were a dozen floral pieces, placed aboard at Seattle. Blue curtains, drawn over the windows, darkened the interior. Somewhere in the emptiness of the cargo plane, Amon Carter found a place to sit down and spend the next hours in private mourning.

At 11:53 A.M., the large DC-2 air transport plane rolled out of the hangar and took off for Los Angeles, California. Pilot Winston charted his course southward, mostly along the Pacific coastline. The plane made a single stop, a brief pause at Alameda, where the plane was checked and refueled.

Because of the fantastic popular interest in Will Rogers and Wiley Post an effort at secrecy had been made. It was feared that if large crowds gathered, injuries would result. Therefore no departure times or arrival times were announced. All that was known was that funeral services for both Rogers and Post would take place at the same time, Thursday, August 22. Will's rites would be held in the Wee Kirk o' the Heather, at Forest Lawn Cemetery in Glendale, California. Wiley's service would take place in Oklahoma City, Oklahoma.

Nor could the press find out the plans for transporting Wiley Post's body to Oklahoma City. It was assumed that efforts would be made to fly clear of large cities and well-known airports to prevent the gathering of large crowds.

What readers of the nation's newspaper did learn was that Senator William Gibbs McAdoo had introduced Senate Resolution S.3436: "A BILL TO AUTHORIZE THE INTERMENT IN THE ARLINGTON NATIONAL CEMETERY OF THE REMAINS OF THE LATE WILL ROGERS AND WILEY POST." Though the Senate passed it, the House of Representatives blocked the resolution. The objection was that "the soil of Arlington is hallowed ground reserved exclusively for those who have served in the nation's armed forces."

Monday evening, August 19, at 10:20 P.M., the gray funeral plane bearing the bodies of Will Rogers and Wiley Post landed at Union Air Terminal, Burbank, California.

Hours before the funeral plane was expected, crowds had begun to gather at the Terminal. In an effort to reduce the throng to a manageable crowd, the rumor was started that the funeral plane would land at the Grand Central Air Terminal, in Glendale. This only drew several hundred to the other field, and even those returned quickly to Burbank. Somehow the crowd knew where the bodies would arrive.

Once on the ground, the plane was wheeled into a hangar where funeral cars waited to take Will's body to Forest Lawn Cemetery. A scuffle broke out when police discovered a photographer hidden in the rafters of the hangar, high above the plane. The intruding photographer was dragged down by police; his camera was smashed and he was placed under arrest. Outside the hangar, police engaged in hand-to-hand skirmishes with photographers and curious spectators who pressed in a body against the doors. Removal of Will Rogers' body was delayed for almost half an hour. Then, preceded by twenty motorcycle policemen, a hearse and two limousines sped out of the hangar and headed for the cemetery.

The Rogers family wanted personally to express their gratitude to Joe Crosson for his effort to recover the bodies. Again it was Charles Lindbergh who informed the family:

S75 49 3 EXTRA = TDRO NORTHHAVEN ME VIA FA
LOSANGELES CALIF   AUG 21, 1935

BILL ROGERS, CARE SANTAFE CHIEF CAR 319 DUE 1
10 PM

CROSSON PROCEEDED WITH ALASKAN PLANE FROM LOSANGELES TO OKLAHOMACITY STOP PLANE WILL GO FROM OKLAHOMA CITY TO TEXAS STOP CROSSON WILL RETURN FROM OKLAHOMACITY TO JUNEAU ALASKA STOP ADVISE YOU CONTACT HIM IMMEDIATELY CARE MRS POST OKLAHOMACITY AND ARRANGE FOR MEETING AT MUTUALLY CONVENIENT TIME AND PLACE =

LINDBERGH

THE CHICAGO DAILY NEWS

FRIDAY, AUGUST 16, 1935—THIRTY-FOUR PAGES.   THREE CENTS

WILL ROGERS AND POST DIE IN ALASKAN AIR CRASH

FINAL EDITION

FILM HUMORIST AND NOTED FLIER DIE IN AIR CRASH

Land in Fog, Then Wreck in Takeoff at Eskimo Camp

Humor Made Rogers Famous; Set Records

'PLATONIC FRIEND' OF MORRISON'S TELLS HER STORY

Clockwise, from top left: August 16, 1935, front page. (Photo: *Chicago Daily News.*) Joe Davidson statue in center of the Will Rogers Memorial at Claremore, Oklahoma. A duplicate stands in Statuary Hall in the U.S. Capitol in Washington, D.C. (Photo: NBC Project XX.) Original monument erected by private citizens on the embankment overlooking crash site. Covered with ice and snow, this photograph was taken during the months-long winter night. (Photo: Will Rogers Memorial.) In 1982, this new monument to Will Rogers and Wiley Post was dedicated near the airport in Barrow, Alaska. (Photo: Tom "Butch" Girvin.) The forenoon of August 22, 1935. More than one-hundred thousand mourner file past Will Rogers' closed coffin at Forest Lawn Cemetery in Glendale, California. (Photo: L.A. Library System.) Salvaged original Lockheed trademark and official restricted license number from the tail section of Wiley Post's plane; now on display in Mattie's Cafe in Barrow. (Photo: B. B. and F. N. Sterling.)

Even before the Rogers family arrived back in Los Angeles funeral arrangements for Thursday, August 22, were made public:

> 7 A.M. to 12 noon - Body lies in state at Forest Lawn Memorial Park.
> 2 P.M. - Private funeral rites at Forest Lawn Memorial Park, restricted to the family and friends with cards.
> 2 P.M. - Memorial services in Hollywood Bowl, open to the public.
> 2 P.M. - Memorial service, Beverly Hills Community Church.
> 2 P.M. - Services at motion picture studios.

In Oklahoma City, Oklahoma's Governor Ernest W. Marland proclaimed Thursday, August 22, a day of public mourning. The schedule there was shorter.

> 12 noon - Memorial service on the south steps of the capitol, following a period when the body would lie in state in the marble rotunda, and coinciding with the hour of Rogers' funeral in Los Angeles.
> 2 P.M. - Funeral service in First Baptist church, followed by burial in Memorial Park.

Governor Marland was scheduled to direct public memorial services. Frank Phillips, who had backed the Post stratosphere flights, became chairman of a delegation of 150 honorary pall-bearers, including Harold Gatty, co-pilot of Post's first globe-circling flight; Jimmy Mattern, famous pilot who was lost for some time in Siberia in an attempt to break Post's around-the-world record; and Art Goebel, winner of the Dole-Hawaii race. Joe Crosson, Wiley's closest friend, was to be one of the active pall-bearers.

Governor Marland had telegraphed Mrs. Will Rogers, offering the use of Oklahoma's State Capitol for the body of her husband to lie in state: "If you are going to bury Will in Oklahoma, the people of Oklahoma would appreciate the privilege of showing their respect, and I tender the use of the State Capitol at whatever day and hour you choose for the body to lie in state," the wire read. "The flag on the State Capitol is now flying at half-mast, with deepest sympathy."

The offer was seriously considered but the decision to hold services in Los Angeles instead of Olkahoma was reached when Mrs. Rogers expressed the feeling that she was unequal to another long trip from the coast back to Oklahoma after the transcontinental journey from Maine.

In Los Angeles, several proposals were made to erect a monument to the memory of Will Rogers. One movement was started by Joseph Mesmer, a pioneer civic leader and president of the Los Angeles Historical Society. He suggested that the public be invited to participate and that he would contribute $100 to start the fund.

In a separate effort, a Committee of eight was formed to plan a memorial to filmdom's number-one male box-office attraction. Chairman Stanley Anderson, Mary Pickford, Mrs. Oscar Lawler, Mayor Edward Spence, Chief of Police Charles Blair of Beverly Hills, Woodworth Clum, Norman Pabst, and Municipal Judge Arthur Erb suggested that a part of the Rogers estate abutting Beverly Boulevard might afford a possible site. Later a site on Sunset Boulevard would be recommended.

Eventually a new, most prestigious commission was established to consider and decide on the type and character of a memorial to Will Rogers. The commission's stated purpose was: "To crystalize the nation-wide sentiment which calls for some tangible expression of the regard in which Will Rogers was held by people in all walks of life."

This commission, headed by Vice President Nance Garner, had 230 members. Its treasurer was Will's friend, Jesse Jones. Vice-chairmen were: E. W. Marland, governor of Oklahoma; Fred Stone; Amon G. Carter; and Rex Beach. The list of commission members was almost an abstract of *Who's Who in America* and included many of Will's personal friends: Herbert Hoover, Alfred E. Smith, Walter P. Chrysler, Marion Davies, T.E. Braniff, Thomas Gore, George Ade, Mrs. August Belmont, Arthur Brisbane, Billie Burke, Clarence Darrow, James A. Farley, Edsel Ford, Bernard Gimble, Evangeline C. Booth, Patrick J. Hurley, Mountain K. Landis, Louis B. Mayer, Mrs. Dwight Morrow, William S. Paley, Mary Pickford, Hal Roach, Sr., Elliott Roosevelt, Joseph M. Schenck, Igor Sikorsky, Alfred P. Sloan, Juan Trippe, Henry Ford, Amelia Earhart, Eddie Cantor, Mrs. Woodrow Wilson, Owen D. Young, Vincent Astor, Irvin S. Cobb, Frank Phillips, Waite Phillips,

Bernard M. Baruch, William E. Boeing, W. E. Borah, Gene Buck, Richard E. Byrd, James Doolittle, Marshall Field, Dr. A. H. Gianini, Harry F. Guggenheim, Joseph P. Kennedy, Alice Roosevelt Long-worth, Joseph Pershing, Mrs. Adolph S. Ochs, A. W. and W. L. Mellon, Eddie Rickenbacker, Grover Whalen, Harry Sinclair, Nelson Rockefeller, Arthur Hays Sulzberger, Cornelius V. Whitney, and Charles M. Schwab.

This commission raised a huge sum of money, but it never built a memorial. The money collected went to establish a 'Will Rogers Memorial Scholarship Fund' in three states. UCLA, the University of California at Los Angeles, received a check for $125,000. It was presented by Jesse Jones, with Betty Rogers, motion-picture czar Will Hays, Fred Stone, Amon G. Carter, and Oscar Lawler in attendance. Another scholarship fund in the amount of $125,000 was established at the University of Okla-homa, and a $60,000 fund at the University of Texas. The first scholarships were to be awarded from proceeds in February 1940.

The State of Oklahoma would raise its own memorial to Will Rogers in 1938, though none to Wiley Post.

As so often is the case, a fraudulent element saw a splendid opportunity to benefit from a nation in grief. Nonexistent com-mittees which pretended to collect for memorials, for statues, for plaques, for shrines—unfortunately preyed upon the trusting public. Some were arrested and tried, most were not. For some time afterwards, Betty Rogers was called upon to testify in court that specific sham organizations had not been empowered to collect funds for a Will Rogers memorial.

Acting on Betty Rogers' telegraphed instructions from the east coast, Sallie and Tom McSpadden selected the casket in which Will would be buried. It was an inexpensive bronze coffin of plain design. Mrs. Rogers stressed specifically that no undue expense or display should mar the funeral or burial. Her husband, she was quoted, must go to his final resting place in a manner conforming to the simplicity of his life and with proper regard to the dislike he held for any form of ostentation.

It was announced that Rogers' body would be removed to the gold room of the Forest Lawn chapel. Will Rogers would lie in a blue serge suit—the one he called his "dress-up" suit—a plain garment of the commonest cut and design. He would wear a soft-collared shirt and his familiar black bow tie.

But to the disappointed thousands who hoped to look one more time on the features of Will Rogers as he lay in state, it was announced that the casket would remain closed. The explanation given by a spokesman for the family was that it had been Will's own wish; that more than once in his life he had said he hoped his casket would not be open at his own funeral.

Five times during 1935, Wiley Post had taken off from Union Air Terminal in Burbank. Four of those flights were attempts to set transcontinental speed records flying in the stratosphere. He always took off at dawn and few were around to see it; usually only a small number of newspapermen were present. Once Will Rogers had been an interested spectator; he had driven over from his ranch home in Santa Monica Canyon, "just to blather," he said. On that flight it had been Will's hand that was the last to shake Wiley's and Will's voice that was the last to wish him success.

The fifth time Post had left Union Air Terminal this year was the start of the Alaskan trip on which Will Rogers joined him in San Francisco. Now, for the last time, Wiley would leave from Union Air Terminal to return to Oklahoma. No longer was he the pilot; this time Wiley lay in a darkened cabin with silken shades drawn tightly to bar the morbidly curious. The same crew that had brought Will Rogers and Wiley Post to Los Angeles only hours earlier again manned the east-bound airliner. Bill Winston was at the controls; J. L. Fleming, junior pilot; T. W. Dowling at the radio; Tom Ward, mechanic; Colonel Clarence M. Young, Pacific Coast manager of Pan American Airways; and Joe Crosson, who wanted to accompany the body of his friend to its final resting place. As the family's friend, Crosson wished to stand by them, to help them in case he was needed.

Wednesday afternoon, August 21, Santa Fe's super train, *The Chief*, stopped at Victorville, California, less than a hundred miles from Los Angeles. Here, far from the crowd waiting in downtown Los Angeles, Betty Rogers and her daughter, Mary, left the train to continue the journey home by automobile. At Azusa, some twenty-five miles from Los Angeles, most of the rest of the relatives and friends of the family detrained and transferred into waiting automobiles. Associated Press reported that "They were met by Fred Stone, the actor, who embraced his daughter, Dorothy, and the Rogers boys with tears in his eyes." Eventually the family gathered again in the rambling ranch house in Santa Monica canyon. It was the eve of the funeral, and though they were a rather large group, each of them was alone with thoughts of the morrow.

There may have been a world beyond, but America paid little heed. Most people spoke only about the funerals. Many cities lowered their flags to half-staff. Letters and telegrams offering condolences to the Rogers family flooded the post office and telegraph office in Beverly Hills. Will's last gift to Betty also arrived by mail and was delivered to his Beverly Hills office. The package bearing a Juneau postmark, was addressed in the humorist's own hand, and contained the red fox fur he had bought as a present.

Hollywood's film colony announced that it would participate in the greatest funeral demonstration ever given one of its number. Fox Studios, where Rogers worked, would close at 1 P.M.

The nation's newspapers wrote banner headlines on the eve of the two funerals. "HOMAGE WILL BE GREATEST EVER ACCORDED TO PRIVATE CITIZENS," shouted a Los Angeles daily. "FAMILY OF ROGERS RETURNS HOME ON EVE OF MEMORIAL," blared the *Tulsa World*. Talking about preparations in Oklahoma City, *Associated Press* sent out a report that "WILEY POST'S HOME TOWN PAYS LAST TRIBUTE TO NOTED FLYER." Referring to the scheduled radio broadcast, another screamed "NATION WILL HEAR SERVICES IN HOLLYWOOD BOWL." Radio indeed planned its tribute to the man whose own broadcasts had been of such great unifying importance throughout the nation. He had rallied his countrymen in the depth of the Depression and he had, as President Roosevelt said, "brought hope where there had been despair." Now radio, which had brought Will's voice into the remotest villages, was to broadcast across a transcontinental network of stations the services held for him at the Hollywood Bowl. Los Angeles station KNX was to carry it. The Yankee and Mutual networks would carry the broadcast to the East and Midwest through their local stations. For the first time ever, other radio stations were to observe thirty minutes of silence, starting at 2 o'clock, the time of the funeral services.

Not only would radio stations observe silence, but motion-picture houses across the country would interrupt performances; screens would darken with a two-minute break.

California's Governor Merriam issued a proclamation asking that all flags within the state be lowered to half-mast: "We cannot let death take Will Rogers and Wiley Post from us, without giving expression to our sense of personal loss." The governor further proclaimed that a moment of reverent silence be observed at precisely 2 P.M. in every town and hamlet of the state.

In his proclamation, Mayor Edward Spence of Beverly Hills urged that all business activity in that city be suspended from 2 until 4 P.M. out of respect for Will Rogers. And in the records of Los Angeles' Municipal Court the following order was transcribed: "In memory of the late Will Rogers and Wiley Post, it is hereby requested that everyone rise and stand for one minute in silent tribute to these two great men who have passed on." At the Hall of Justice a bugler would sound taps and at 2 P.M. there would be a minute of silence to honor Will Rogers and Wiley Post.

The Post family home in Maysville, Oklahoma, in the Washita Valley, was a tiny frame bungalow. It had no telephone and no electricity. Without any of their neighbors' knowledge, William Francis and Mae Quinlan Post had gone to Oklahoma City to be present when the body of their son arrived from Los Angeles. As the gleaming transport plane rolled to a stop, Mae broke into tears: "It was just what Wiley would have wished—coming back in an airplane."

The plane also brought Wiley's battered cowhide suitcase, his companion on all his flights. In it were a dozen maps, still damp from the brackish waters of Walakpa Lagoon. The bag also contained Wiley's damp, gray double-breasted suit. It was immediately sent out to the cleaners, as the family had decided that Wiley should be buried in it. A hearse took Wiley's body to the Watts & McAtee Funeral Home.

The small farming community of Maysville had never experienced such bustle. For two hot, sweltering days, its citizens had prepared their mourning community for services for their world-famous townsman. Streets in the modest business section had been made pristine by sweeping and washing. Flags were liberally displayed, most of them at half-mast along the main thoroughfare. Unpaved streets within a radius of one or two blocks of the line of procession were periodically sprinkled to settle the dust that thousands of feet would quickly stir into clouds again. Everything was ready before the bronze casket's scheduled arrival time of 1 P.M.

A company of the 120th Oklahoma Engineers took charge of the town early in the day, directing traffic and furnishing the guard of honor, which would form a lane through which Post's casket would be carried to the church. Little groups gathered around the bank and the hardware, dry goods and drug stores, with solemn residents sharing their own memories of the small town's most famous citizen. "He sat right here," said Fred Berry, pointing to a corner of his auto-dealer's office, "and he told me all the details of his last world flight. I said: 'Wiley, don't you have any doubts or fears?' He said: 'Not a bit.' He knew he would make it."

Berry, who would be one of the pall-bearers, then showed— to all who wanted to see and touch it—an obsolete propeller that Wiley had given him a long time ago.

"Wiley never was talkative," another in the crowd remembered. "He'd just stand around the streets or up against a tree, grinning, and talk like one of the boys. He never forgot his people. That's why we saw him after he got famous, being famous didn't change him."

The Landmark Missionary Baptist Church, a little white frame building that Wiley's father had helped build, had been beautifully decorated solely with flowers grown by people in the community. The ceremony in Maysville was simple and most dignified. Not only were Wiley's former neighbors and fellow townsfolk lining the street, but admirers, acquaintances and the curious, came from as far as 250 miles away.

A steady line, two abreast, of plain men and women, neighbors, friends, and admirers walked between guardsmen at arms and through the church to get a fleeting glimpse at the famous flier's face. It took more than two hours for all to walk beneath the maples and sycamores, enter the one-room church, past the open coffin and exit by the back door. The number who viewed the remains here was conservatively estimated at near seven thousand.

About four o'clock, after the crowd had begun to thin, Mr. and Mrs. Frank Post, Wiley's parents, arrived. With them was the widow, Mae Post. Then the doors were closed to give the family privacy. Later, after the relatives had left for their nearby farm, Post's body was taken back to Oklahoma City.

On Thursday, August 22, 1935, in Oklahoma City, Wiley Post's body was on view in the rotunda of the State Capitol for two hours. The beautiful, open bronze casket, guarded by a National Guard detail, was seen by fifteen thousand people, many of them Post's friends. Hundreds of floral displays had arrived and were placed around the coffin. Even A. A. Troyanovsky, ambassador of the Union of Soviet Socialist Republics, had sent a wreath. It was made of five hundred pink carnations and decorated with lily-of-the-valley and roses. His note expressed deepest sympathy for the family.

The display sent by Joe and Lillian Crosson was a large propeller made of flowers, on which were the lavender letters "Q.B."—signifying *Quiet Birdmen*, aviation's most exclusive organization.

Mrs. Post, touched by the outpouring shown by the thousands of flowers, asked that they be distributed to Oklahoma City hospitals.

At noon, while thousands of mourners still awaited an opportunity for a last look at the flyer's face, the state's official observance began. President Roosevelt had ordered that he be represented at the funerals of Post and Rogers through the War and Navy Departments by men with the rank of general or admiral. These officers were to lay wreaths on behalf of the president and the government. Brigadier General H. W. Butner of Fort Sill, representing President Roosevelt, accompanied by Governor Marland, walked to the second floor where the body lay, through a lane forced open by guardsmen. Overhead airplanes dipped their wings in salute. Governor Marland, in a short address, said: "Wiley Post flew around the earth. Wiley Post ascended above the earth to heights unattained by man. Today Wiley Post precedes us, his friends, on that greater journey we all must take some day. . . . Happy landing Wiley Post in that heaven of all brave souls. The body of Oklahoma's son begins the sleep eternal beneath the sod he loves. Nothing we poor mortals can do or say will add to the lasting glory or prestige of these two Oklahoma sons. Fare thee well, Will Rogers, fare thee well, Wiley Post. Happy landing."

There followed a brief invocation by the Rev. William Slack, a former naval airman and now minister of the Methodist Church at Lawton, Oklahoma; then, the casket was moved toward the south steps of the capitol and to a hearse. Because of the crowds progress toward the church was difficult.

Final rites at Oklahoma City's First Baptist Church began at 2 P.M. Services were conducted by the Rev. W. R. White, pastor of the church, and the Rev. J. H. Gardner of Sentinel, Oklahoma. The church was filled to overflowing; hundreds gathered outside, including a large number who had been unable to get into the Oklahoma capitol earlier for the state's tribute.

When the news made the rounds that the famous Joe Crosson, the heroic flier who had brought the bodies back from the top of the world, was with the funeral party, everyone wanted to have him pointed out. People pressed in on him, to touch him or to get his autograph.

The service was simple, as simple as Wiley, the man, had been. There was a prayer; a quartet sang "Lead Kindly Light," and the Rev. W. R. White delivered a brief sermon. He read from Isaiah: "Who are these that fly as a cloud, and as the doves to their windows?"

As soon as services were finished, the church was cleared of everyone except immediate relatives. For a few moments more the members of the family were allowed to be alone with their dead. Then, on a signal, the national guardsmen and police cleared a path to the waiting hearse. Borne aloft by Wiley's friends, the coffin was placed in the hearse and taken along crowded streets to the mausoleum.

Thousands rushed forward toward the hearse as it started on its way to Fairlawn Cemetery. Planes swooped low to scatter roses over Wiley's coffin and in its path. The thin police line was easily broken and several women fainted in the crush to catch some of the flowers strewn from the sky, but the crowd remained orderly. Slowly the procession made its way to Fairlawn's mausoleum, where Wiley Post's body was to rest that night with members of the State Militia standing guard.

Wiley's body was interred in Edmond, Oklahoma, his grave marked by a small, flat stone that may easily escape the searcher.

At the very hour of the funeral procession in Oklahoma City, New York City fliers paid their own tribute to Will Rogers and Wiley Post in a massed flight over the city. The plans for this display were made by the executive committee of the Gascraft Club, which was composed of representatives of the aviation, motorboat, and automobile industries. Wiley Post had been one of its founders.

Led by five navy planes, a squadron of twenty-four planes followed a carefully mapped course from Floyd Bennett Field on Long Island, up New York Bay to the Hudson River, and then north over Manhattan and finally back to the field over Brooklyn. It was a display watched by more than a million.

The flotilla, trailing black streamers from rudders, was led by Captain William C. Allison and included Clyde Pangborn, famous 'round-the-world flyer. One woman pilot, Miss Viola Gentry, was among the fourteen civilian pilots.

Philadelphia, too, bade goodbye to Will Rogers and Wiley Post. Numerous state, city, and naval officials, as well as civic leaders, delivered eulogies. Airplanes flew over the assembled crowd, dipping their wings in tribute to the great proponents of aviation. Hundreds attended the memorial services at Mustin Field in the Philadelphia Navy Yard. City Hall flags were lowered to half-mast.

The Santa Monica Chamber of Commerce received and endorsed a proposal that Route 66, the major highway that originated in Chicago, passed through Claremore, Oklahoma, and terminated at Santa Monica, California, be renamed the Will Rogers Highway. Indeed, the highway became known by that name though no official action was ever taken by the federal government.

In San Diego, California, sorrow stopped the California Pacific International Exposition in Balboa Park. A crowd of ten thousand, asked by a loud-speaker announcement, stood with bared heads as the American flag at the Plaza del Pacifico fluttered slowly down the pole to half-mast and a bugler from the Thirtieth U. S. Infantry rifle company sounded taps in farewell to Will Rogers and Wiley Post. A contingent of soldiers conducted modified military funeral services. They marched down the Avenue of Palaces to the measured strains of Chopin's funeral march. The solemn procession came to rest as the band took its stance in front of the Palace of Science. The soldiers stood at parade rest. Dr. Roy Campbell, Congregational minister, delivered a short and simple eulogy: "In order for this ceremony to express the wholehearted sentiment of this great audience," he said, "I need say no more than this: Will Rogers, we loved him. He is gone. Let us recite the Shepherd's Prayer."

Even concession barkers and musicians were silent, and the Fair was hushed for the tribute.

The Los Angeles Examiner of August 20 announced that "next Sunday afternoon at Taborian Hall, Negroes who had worked with Will in several of his pictures, are arranging for a mass meeting of Los Angeles' colored population to pay tribute to the actor. The meeting will be under the auspices of the Friends of Ethiopia, a society numbering 5000 members here, according to the Rev. L. B. Brown.''

In the far away North Country of Alaska, twenty-two WAM-CATS stations of the U.S. Signal Corps remained silent for five minutes, from noon to 12:05, out of respect for Will Rogers and Wiley Post.

At Claremore, Oklahoma, the county seat of Rogers County and Will's proclaimed hometown, conducted its own service. Here, too, a sweltering crowd broiled under the searing August sun; the thermometer had topped 100 degrees early in the day. Gathered at 2 P.M. at the single brownstone hangar of modest Will Rogers Airport, men and women, little girls and boys fidgeted in the almost unbearable heat through the speeches and songs. Within the uncomfortable, sweaty crowd were some of Will's relatives by blood and marriage; there were neighbors and boyhood friends, and there were his fellow Shriners from the Akdar Temple in Tulsa, who had come in twenty motor cars led by six motorcycle policemen.

Will's friends had come from nearby Chelsea and Muskogee and Tahlequah and Pryor. It was not the most spectacular ceremony held that day, but it was the most heartfelt. A small hometown had turned out for its beloved, favorite son. The mourners were there because of their kinship with Willie, the boy grown man. Will, who had been one of them—who had left them to go out into the world and who had made good—had made the world aware of their little town, Claremore, along Route 66 on the way to Tulsa. And now Uncle Clem Rogers' boy, Willie, was gone, and each of them had lost part of themselves. There would never be another one like him. That much they all knew.

The ceremony ended with the Spartan Dawn Patrol, three privately owned small planes, flying over the dusty field. Perhaps it was fitting that one of those planes was a Lockheed Orion. Then an American Air Express plane, en route from Los Angeles to New York, circled the airport once and dipped its wing out of respect. (It was understood that American Air Express had given orders for all their planes flying over Claremore during the next ten days to pay similar tribute.)

Then it was over. The extended family had met and prayed and remembered—and they would remember to the end of their days.

Minutes before midnight announcing the day of the funeral, Betty Rogers arrived at Forest Lawn's mortuary and looked on the body of her husband. She had not seem him since that night at the airport, when they had kissed goodbye and he was off on a trip to Alaska. Their daughter, Mary, and their two sons, Will Jr. and Jim, were at their mother's side as she stepped from the car that had brought them for this last private visit. A nurse was also in attendance.

In another car, Sally McSpadden with three of her daughters and J. K. Blake, Betty's brother-in-law, joined them. The police guard at the door directed them to the entrance of the room where the casket rested.

Now, in the dim lights of the mortuary, Betty studied once more the features she knew so well. He looked so natural— asleep, she thought. There was none of what she had dreaded to see; no disfiguring marks, no scars, no pain in his face—just serenity and peace.

There was a heavy silence in the little room as the party stood about the still form. Scarcely a word was spoken. After a few moments, with bowed head and supported by her sons, Betty Rogers turned and left. She sobbed softly, but showed no sign of collapse. It was her last private moment with her husband. From now on she would share her sorrow with millions.

The early hours of Thursday, August 22, 1935, saw a multitude gather outside Forest Lawn Memorial Park in Glendale, California. Gates were to open at 7 A.M. but by 1 A.M. men and women began to arrive to stand in line. Automobiles of mourners began to clog highways for miles and San Fernando Road, the main artery leading directly to the cemetery from surrounding communities in the Los Angeles area, was jammed with automobiles. Traffic slowed to a snail's pace as early as 5 A.M. Side streets were choked with cars looking for parking spaces. Snack joints for miles around did a brisk business, as almost any food would sell.

Glendale and Los Angeles police, deputy sheriffs, and other law enforcement officers had held several meetings to arrange rules for preserving decorum, to keep people in line and moving, and to avoid the usual confusion on such occasions. Final plans called for every road and highway leading to Forest Lawn to be posted; four hundred members of the traffic squad of the Los Angeles police department would be assigned to special duty at the cemetery. To further enlarge the number of available enforcement officers, soldiers and marines were detailed to assist the regular agencies. The strategies worked perfectly, and at the end of the service, the police would report that they had never directed a more orderly throng.

The honor guard was in place by 7 A.M. It consisted of forty noncommissioned officers, four commissioned officers and four flying cadets from March Field, under Lieutenant Jesse Auton, First Wing U.S. Army. Major General H. H. (Hap) Arnold of March Field was in command of the detail. The family decided that the active pall-bearers would be chosen from the honor guard of March Field pilots. There would be no honorary pall-bearers as "Rogers had so many friends that we wouldn't know where to start or leave off if we began selecting pall-bearers," Oscar Lawler was quoted.

For five hours they would stand guard over Will Rogers' casket. Eight at a time, they would stand beside his floral draped bier. At half-hour intervals there was a brisk changing of the guard, commanded by Lieutenant Auton, who had known Will Rogers personally. Then the new eight noncommissioned fliers stationed themselves at attention, and, according to the *Los Angeles Times*, "their eyes never wavering from their straight gaze toward the heights of the Hollywood Hills."

When the gates of Forest Lawn swung open precisely at 7 A.M., the line of mourners extended for more than a mile and the crowd increased at the rate of a block every fifteen minutes. The approach of the crowd to the main gate was in three roped lanes. Spectators began filing past the flower-banked casket on a catafalque, at the rate of 90 a minute; then that number had to be increased dramatically. Police, sheriff's officers and state troopers kept the line moving. There was scarcely a break as the mourners passed the coffin. In the first hour, ten thousand men, women, and children walked past the catafalque. The roped lane led close to the casket, around it and back out through the gate.

In back of the casket, in the middle of the semi-circle along which the public passed, a number of newsreel cameramen recorded the flow of mourners. It was a hushed, sober procession. Many were deeply affected, a large number openly crying. Nobody spoke, nobody stepped out of line.

The crowd's patience and devotion were especially surprising, as mourners could do no more than glance quickly at the mountain of flowers and the simple closed coffin, which had a floral cover arranged into a huge American flag. They had known beforehand that they would not be able to look one more time at Will's face, but still they had come.

Hundreds of those filing by brought flowers. Some came with a single flower, others brought expensive bouquets or wreaths. As no one was allowed to touch the casket, the flowers were placed at the base of the bier. A small coil of rope decorated with a single sprig of fern and one rose—the token of a small boy—was placed near the coffin. The card read, "Just my lariat."

Some were somberly dressed in mourning, while others wore their everyday clothing. The crowd consisted mostly of women, generally middle-aged or elderly. The men approached the bier usually with bare heads, their hats held over their hearts.

The hours went by and still they came, thousands upon thousands. Police reports of the total number varied, depending on the source and newspaper account. The actual figure was somewhere in between the two extremes cited: one-hundred to one-hundred-and-fifty thousand. As the closing hour of noon approached, officers in charge realized that the thousands still lining up would never get to see the coffin. To avoid disappointment, police officers first doubled, then quadrupled the lines and mourners were "rushed through past the casket in droves, though good order was still maintained," as the wire services reported. Police could claim that all those who had come to say their farewell to Will Rogers had been able to do so. Promptly at noon, the entrance was barred and the last mourner allowed to leave.

Only four hundred relatives and friends of the family were invited to attend the strictly private ceremony in the Wee Kirk o' the Heather in Forest Lawn Memorial Park. Even so, the small chapel could only seat 125 persons, and chairs had to be placed immediately outside the stone building.

Among those invited were generals and ranch hands, movie stars and unknowns, relatives and hired help. The only criterion was that they be either family or close friend. For the curious mourners standing patiently outside the guarded gates, there was enough glamor among the arriving mourners to satisfy any fan. As each car arrived and slowed down for identification at the gate, those closest would try to identify the occupants; then, by word of mouth, the names made their way through the crowd. Many arrivals were unknown, but among those identified were Jack Blystone, John Boles, M/M Ed Borein, M/M Frank Borzage, M/M Joe E. Brown, Billie Burke, David Butler, M/M Eddie Cantor, M/M Harry Carey, Leo Carillo, Harry Carr, Amon G. Carter, Charles Chaplin, M/M Irvin S. Cobb, Walt Disney, Amelia Earhart Putnam, M/M James A. Farley, Charles Farrell, Stepin Fetchit, Pauline Frederick, Clark Gable, James Gleason, M/M Samuel Goldwyn, Sid Grauman, William S. Hart, M/M Will Hays, William R. Hearst, Jack Holt, Howard Hughes, M/M Henry King, Carl Laemmle, M/M Oscar Lawler, Rabbi Magnin, Paul Mantz, George Marshall, M/M Louis B. Mayer, Mary Pickford, M/M Chic Sale, Gertrude Sandmeier, Joseph Schenck, Harry F. Sinclair, M/M Fred Stone and daughters Dorothy, Carol and Paula, Irving Thalberg, Spencer Tracy, Col./M Roscoe Turner, Cornelius Vanderbilt Jr., M/M Rob Wagner, Walter Wanger, Jack Warner, Guinn Williams, M/M Sol Wurtzel, Darryl F. Zanuck, and Patricia Ziegfeld.

At Will Rogers' funeral, Rear Admiral W. T. Tarrant, U.S.N. of San Diego, commandant of the Eleventh Naval District, was designated to represent his Commander in Chief, President Franklin D. Roosevelt. Brigadier General H. H. "Hap" Arnold, represented the army. Gene Vidal, chief of the aeronautics division of the United States Department of Commerce, was to represent that branch of the Government.

Escorted by a detachment of motorcycle policemen from the Beverly Hills police department, Betty Rogers, members of the family, and some friends left the Pacific Palisades ranch at 1:20 P.M. to drive to Glendale. In the first car were Betty and her three children, Mary, Will Jr., and James. The motorcade of some seventeen cars left the home by a back road without being noticed by the press, which had laid siege to the Rogers retreat.

While the family and some friends were en route to the cemetery, the coffin was transferred from the catafalque to the Wee Kirk o' the Heather, which stood on a rise overlooking the gentle slope. A squad of ten noncommissioned officers and cadets marched at parade step to the casket and stood at attention.

At an order from the officer, the men lifted the casket and bore it at a slow march some 250 feet to the waiting hearse, flanked by thirty-six soldiers at salute. The hearse then moved slowly up the incline to the chapel. Arriving there at a slow pace, a squad of thirty deputy sheriffs in full regalia formed a guard of honor. It was a disappointment to Will's friends when they learned that there would be no honorary pall-bearers. Many had hoped to take an active part in this, the last function.

At the chancel, the coffin was covered by a mass of flowers. There were wreaths, arrangements, figures, bouquets, and funeral pieces not only from individuals but representing a city or a state; some were sent by organizations, groups of aviators, the Baseball Writers Association of America, the grand British veterans, the government of the Soviet Union, the Chuck Wagon Trailers, and "the boys from the stables." The entire slope outside the Wee Kirk, stretching down the whole side of the hill, was blanketed by flowers. (Later, on Betty Rogers' instructions, the flowers were carefully collected and distributed among hospital wards in Los Angeles and Glendale.)

Through the open doors of the chapel the plaintive strains of *"Old Faithful"* could be heard. It was one of Will's favorite hymns. As the organ played within, the body was borne into the chapel. Softly the pipe organ played the familiar *"Old Rugged Cross,"* then other familiar airs Will must have heard often as a boy—*"In the Cross of Christ I Glory," "Beautiful Isle of Somewhere," "Saved by Grace,"* and *"I Love to Tell the Story."*

The service began promptly after the family arrived. Betty and the closest relatives were seated in an alcove from where they could view the casket but were themselves partially out of view of the congregation.

The Reverend Dr. James Whitcomb Brougher, Sr., delivered the eulogy. For the better part of an hour he mixed poetry and simple words, painting a picture of Will as the world knew him. Often close to tears himself, he moved his listeners. Clark Gable sobbed almost continually. Billie Burke, one of the few wearing black, was supported by two men and almost had to be carried from the chapel at the conclusion of the service.

Dr. Brougher had known Will Rogers for a long time. Once, in the early Twenties, they had staged a mock debate; "Resolved, that the movies have been more beneficial to humanity than preachers.'' ''It's the most uneven question I suppose ever debated,'' wrote Will. ''I have the movie side, and he is such a nice fellow that I really feel ashamed to see him try and bring preaching up to the level of one of the arts.''

Dr. Brougher delivered his tribute, carefully building the mosaic that was the life of Will Rogers. He said what men and women in the nation would have said if they had had the pulpit and the words:

> . . . There are many streams, but only here and there a great Mississippi;
>
> There are many echoes, but only now and then an original voice;
>
> There are many musicians, but only now and then a Mendelssohn or a Mozart;
>
> There are many people, but only now and then an outstanding individual;
>
> When a great personality suddenly appears, the world stops in its busy rush to look and listen. The monotony of life is broken for a moment. A man who is ''different'' has attracted the attention of all. He soon becomes a hero, for men and women bow before a strong and magnetic personality. Such has been the unique and commanding position of Will Rogers during the last quarter of a century. He has been the one figure in the life of our nation who had drawn to himself the admiration and the love of all classes of people. It is no exaggeration to say that no man has been so universally appreciated and loved as Will Rogers. . . .
>
> He was a man of sympathetic kindness. He understood human nature. He knew its weaknesses and the struggles. He could forgive our sins while he made us laugh at our mistakes. . . . He had the sympathy of a mother for her child and the kindness of a friend for a friend. He understood human nature so well that he did not misjudge men and women. He was so thoughtful and considerate of others that he would not permit himself to be unjust or unkind or unfriendly. . . .
>
> He did not have a shadow of intolerance or prejudice in his make-up. He was a brother to all mankind.

Like his Master, he "went about doing good" to all classes and races of men. . . .

The last two times I had the great pleasure and privilege of appearing with him on the platform, I was introducing him to do his share for the McKinley Orphan Boys' Home. And after that, for the raising of money for the colored people in one of our large Baptist churches in Southern California. When drought or flood or earthquake or storm brought suffering and starvation to his fellowmen, he gave his service without thought of himself to minister through the Red Cross and other agencies. His place in the hearts of the people of our nation is secure, because of his sacrificing spirit and helpful ministry to the various needs of mankind. . . .

Will Rogers was pre-eminently the apostle of good humor. He was a humorist who made fun that was good-natured without the sting of acid or the barb of spite. . . . Will Rogers was the master magician who with a simple phrase could turn laughter into tears and tears into laughter. . . . he had a genius for love. He loved people. . . .

Betty Rogers left the small chapel leaning heavily on the arms of her sons, Will Jr. and James, and seemed close to collapse. She and her family returned directly to the Pacific Palisades ranch home. Their cars were again escorted by police guard. A short time later, several more cars bearing friends and relatives were admitted to the private, serpentine road leading to the home. Guards at the gates would be maintained throughout the day and night.

While rites were being held at Forest Lawn, the life of America virtually stopped. Business paused; public offices were closed; millions huddled around the radio to hear the Hollywood Bowl service; more than a dozen Hollywood film studios were silent. "Never," so Associated Press claimed, "in the history of this country has a private citizen been handed over to eternity amid such a demonstration of public love and admiration as the homage paid to Will Rogers." New York's *Herald Tribune* was even more impassioned: "Will Rogers hadn't a living peer in the affection of America's millions. Wiley Post ranked next to Lindbergh as their hero of the air."

At the same time, 2 P.M., nearly twenty thousand men and women came together for a special service at the Hollywood Bowl. Nestled in the Hollywood Hills, the large amphitheater accommodated those who had not been able to participate in the services at Forest Lawn.

Friends, associates, or just plain fans, all came to be part of this gigantic tribute to Will Rogers. Some arrived in elegant limousines driven by uniformed chauffeurs, but most had to walk the long, steep road to the Bowl. But rich or poor, they all had to endure a broiling sun. Many, arriving without hats, hastily fabricated sunshades out of folded newspapers.

The Hollywood American Legion singing group opened the service with *"Nearer My God to Thee."* The invocation was offered by Dr. Frank C. McKean, president of the Hollywood Ministerial Association. Dr. Roy L. Smith, pastor of the First Methodist Church, read from the Bible. After reciting the Nineteenth and Ninety-First Psalms, he quoted passages from the Fourteenth Chapter of the Gospel of St. John: "Let not your heart be troubled, neither let it be afraid."

Author Rupert Hughes began his eulogy: "If anybody had told Will Rogers that when he was dead he would be made the object of these great ceremonies, he would have rubbed his nose, shuffled his feet, shifted his gum and grinned, wondering why. . . . Never in history had a man gained and held so large an audience."

Movie star Conrad Nagel, fighting to keep back tears, quoted from "Thanatopsis" by William Cullen Bryant:

> So live, that when thy summons comes to join
> The innumerable caravan which moves
> To that mysterious realm where each shall take
> His slumber in the silent halls of death
> Thou go not like the quarry-slave at night
> Scourged to his dungeon, but sustained and soothed
> By an unfaltering trust, approach thy grave
> Like one that wraps the drapery of his couch
> About him, and lies down to pleasant dreams.

Famous opera and screen star Lawrence Tibbett sang John Masefield's *"By A Bier Side."* The Hollywood Legion band then played Beethoven's funeral dirge, after which Dr. Cleveland Kleihauer, president of the Federated Protestant Churches of Los Angeles, pronounced the invocation.

The service was simple, as simple as the man himself. Yet it left thousands in the audience with tears streaming down their faces. Millions at home, by their radios, must have been similarly affected. It was a way to share the loss, but the pain remained. As every speaker pointed out that day, there was no one to take Will Rogers' place.

Coinciding with the Hollywood Bowl observance, services were being held by the Community Presbyterian Church on Santa Monica Boulevard, Beverly Hills. Will and Betty had been some of the organizers of the church and had consistently contributed to its upkeep. The minister, Rev. Dr. R. M. Donaldson, had instructed the Rogers children in the principles of religion and morality. Will, who was raised a Methodist, became nonsectarian and claimed no membership in any particular faith. He was, as his life amply demonstrated, a man of deep religious fervor. His religion was a constant, vigorous influence. His conduct relied solely on his early teachings of "love thy neighbor as thyself" and observation of The Golden Rule.

Led by Beverly Hills Mayor Edward E. Spence, some 650 people crammed into the beautiful small church. Rev. Donaldson, though retired, still came to give the eulogy. He was assisted by ministers from the Episcopal, the Presbyterian and Community churches in the area.

At almost every movie studio, stars and extras, secretaries and directors, cameramen and grips assembled to honor and remember Hollywood's number-one male star. Not a handsome leading man, not a dashing hero adept at swordplay, but a most homey, comfortable friend.

At these private services, John Boles, film actor, sang the cowboy-philosopher's favorite, *"Old Faithful,"* at one studio; James Melton, radio star, sang *"Home on the Range"* at another; Joe Morrison, actor-singer, sang *"The Last Round-up,"* at still another; and Nino Martini, celebrated opera singer, intoned *"Agnus Dei."*

The Soviet Union's film industry paid homage to the memory of Rogers in a cablegram received at Twentieth Century-Fox studio, Rogers' home studio:

THE GREAT LOSS OF WILL ROGERS SADDENS OUR
HEARTS. THE SOVIET CINEMA IS CONFIDENT THAT
THE BRIEF BUT SPLENDID LIFE OF THIS MASTER
ARTIST WILL INSPIRE HUNDREDS OF CINEMA WORK-
ERS TO A SIMILAR DEVOTED AND SINCERE SERVICE
TO THE GREAT CINEMA ART.

The cable was signed by Soviet actors and officials.

More than three thousand attended memorial services at
Warner Bros., Burbank Studios, honoring Will Rogers. Officials
of the newly formed Twentieth Century-Fox Corporation would
dedicate a just completed, modern sound stage in his honor. With
hundreds of old friends in attendance, a plaque was unveiled. It
showed a likeness of Will with these words embossed beneath:

THIS STAGE WE DEDICATE TO YOUR MEMORY, WILL
ROGERS, YOU WHO MADE THE WHOLE WORLD
LAUGH AND MADE THE WHOLE WORLD LOVE YOU.

But all was not well at Twentieth Century-Fox. Since March
1929, Will had been under contract to Fox Film Corporation,
which had just merged with Twentieth Century Pictures. During
negotiations for this consolidation, Rogers' films, which had been
grossing $7,000,000 annually, were important considerations.
Fox had brought along into this union as its major assets Hollywood's two greatest money-makers, Will Rogers and Shirley
Temple. Now Will's death, besides being a grievous personal
shock, was a multimillion-dollar blow.

There was another important point to consider. Will Rogers
was obligated under a new contract for six productions following
his latest release, *Doubting Thomas*. Two of those sure-fire films,
expected to earn $1,500,000 profit each, had already been pro-
duced and were ready for release to the public. They were *In Old
Kentucky*, directed by George Marshall, and *Steamboat Round
the Bend*, directed by John Ford. The question was simply what to
do with them. How would the public react to seeing and hearing
their beloved Will Rogers on the screen, knowing that he had just
died? Perhaps it would be wiser, some suggested, to wait; allow
the public its time of grief; then it might be more receptive to
seeing his films later.

Perhaps, other executives suggested, the two films representing an investment of approximately $750,000 should be scrapped. True, this would mean a loss of three or four million dollars to the studio, but it might be worth it to avoid having the public condemn the newly merged studio as being ghoulish, trying to cash in on a tragedy. It was a dilemma, which was solved by the unemotional heads of commerce.

Running advertisements in the form of news releases, Twentieth Century-Fox prepared the public of its intentions. FOX TO PAY TRIBUTE TO ROGERS IN PRESENTATION OF NEW FILM, read the headline over one article, which explained that it was "with the deepest and most sincere respect that Fox has released his finest picture. . . . Mrs. Rogers, knowing her husband's wishes, requested that the two pictures completed before his departure on this last trip, be released so that once again he might bring pleasure and inspiration to his millions of friends. *Steamboat Round the Bend* is the greatest story ever played by this great star. . . . Some of Will Rogers' best friends are in the cast. . . . "

Management carefully screened the two films and decided that *Steamboat Round the Bend*, which was made after *In Old Kentucky*, was the superior of the two films. The decision to release it first was simply based on the conviction to go with the best, hoping that it would overcome a possible public objection against seeing the film of a dead actor. If that worked, then it would be easier to release *In Old Kentucky*, the lesser of the two films.

Only one scene in *Steamboat Round the Bend* was cut, the newspapers reported. The original closing scene showed Will Rogers on the rear deck of his steamboat sailing off and waving farewell. Had the scene been allowed to remain, so it was thought, every spectator would have felt that he saw Will waving farewell to the world. Twentieth Century-Fox executives made the final decision that "it wouldn't do to send audiences away from the theater crying."

On Friday, August 24, 1935, nine days after Will's death, *Steamboat Round the Bend* opened in Los Angeles at Grauman's Chinese Theatre and Loew's State, as well as key theaters in the Midwest. Pleased with the initial response by audiences, the film was released in the entire country.

By mid-November, *Steamboat Round the Bend* had set new earning records for any Rogers film. Twentieth Century-Fox

Films reported that it had out-drawn any of his other pictures by more than forty percent. With this encouragement, Rogers' other film, *In Old Kentucky*, was released the following week.

A large number of memorials to Will Rogers, and to a smaller degree to Wiley Post, were built in the years that followed. Streets, parks, schools, churches, motion picture theaters, office buildings, airports, an airport observation platform, navigational lights and even an atomic submarine bore either the name of Rogers or Post or both.

In 1938, the Will Rogers Memorial at Claremore, Oklahoma opened its doors. It was financed by Will's native state and stands on twenty acres Will had purchased in 1911 as a site for his eventual retirement home. Its rising ground overlooks the small city Will claimed as his hometown. Betty had been approached to donate the land as an ideal site for the Memorial and she agreed.

For nine years the body of Will Rogers rested in a vault at Forest Lawn's mausoleum. Then, in 1944, after a brief, private ceremony in Glendale, the casket was taken to Oklahoma. In the rose garden of Claremore's Will Rogers Memorial it was placed into a massive stone crypt, together with the body of Will's twenty-three-month-old son, Fred, who had died in 1920. "He rests now amid familiar scenes," said Reverend John R. Abernathy of Oklahoma City, "The long journey is ended. He is at home."

Accompanying the body on its journey east had been Jim and Astrea Rogers, Will's son and daughter-in-law; Ewing Halsell, of Vinita, Oklahoma, a cattleman and childhood playmate of Rogers; and Lew Wentz, a Ponca City oil-man. Will's widow was unable to make the trip because of her failing health.

A month later, Betty Rogers died and was buried alongside her husband and infant son.

CHAPTER NINE

THE INVESTIGATION

When I die, my epitaph or whatever you call those signs on gravestones is going to read: "I joked about every prominent man of my time, but I never met a man I didn't like." I am so proud of that, I can hardly wait to die so it can be carved. And when you come to my grave you will find me sitting there proudly reading it.
—Will Rogers, *Boston Globe,* June 16, 1930.

The government's investigation into the crash that killed Will Rogers and Wiley Post was a travesty. It began with an obligation to candor, but it ended with the much older obligation to protect the status quo.

The Air Commerce Act of 1926 charged the Secretary of Commerce with regulating air commerce, certificating aircraft for airworthiness, and investigating the causes of accidents in civil air navigation. This was an entirely new area of responsibility for the established government department. In the Thirties aviation was in a state of rapid evolution, growing from infancy to maturity without going through adolescence, from precarious novelty to respectable necessity. But in the Thirties, faced with America's Great Depression, President Franklin D. Roosevelt's need for economy created a special hardship for aviation. Congress wielded a well-honed axe, cutting the department's appropriation by 10 percent to $7.7 million, a severe blow that the president aggravated by impounding an additional third. By 1934, the Air Commerce section was cut to about half the budget it had when Roosevelt took office.

Naturally, such a drastic slash was felt all along the line. The work force was reduced by exactly one-third; specifically, all associate and junior airway engineers, all junior civil engineers, and all but six assistant airways engineers were fired. The travel allowance for aeronautical and airplane inspectors was cut by fifty percent, and the Aeronautics Research Division in the Bureau of Standards was abolished.

While morale was low and further cut-backs were feared, the Bureau of Air Commerce retained its enviable position. Not only did the Bureau make the laws that regulated air traffic and safety, but it enforced them and—in case of accidents—acted as judge, jury, and hangman. It was an ideal vantage point from which to whitewash the Bureau's own complicity or culpability, whenever or wherever found.

In 1935, the Secretary of Commerce was Daniel Calhoun Roper. He was well qualified for the position, having served his apprenticeship in various elected and appointed positions connected with Commerce, Trade, and Tariff. He had started in the House of Representatives of his native South Carolina at age twenty-seven and reached the position of first assistant postmaster general before becoming U. S. Commissioner of Internal Revenue in 1917. In 1921, with the Democrats no longer in control of the White House, Roper headed the law firm of Roper, Hagerman, Hurrey, Parks & Dudley until 1933, when Franklin D. Roosevelt called him into his cabinet.

Air Commerce was under the umbrella of the Commerce Department but had its own chief executives. The men principally involved were Eugene Vidal, Director of Air Commerce, and his assistant, Colonel J. Carroll Cone, Assistant Director; and Denis Mulligan, Chief of the Enforcement Section, Air Regulations Division. Each was a highly competent, honorable man who was forced to work within the governmental bureaucracy. Each knew what to do, but each also knew enough about bureaucracy to bow to whatever government dictated. It must again be remembered that aviation was not yet thirty-two years old and that the public's confidence in governmental supervision of the field had to be retained. Furthermore, Wiley Post was not an ordinary pilot, but a hero who had conquered the air and ridden high-altitude winds. If one was not safe flying with Post, could one ever fly safely?

There was enough irresponsibility and guilt to go around and destroy a number of reputations and careers. They all had to be protected from the public, if not entirely from internal scrutiny. Thanks to a commendable spark of departmental honesty,

documents have survived—though scattered in various reposi-
tories—that show the Department's massive contributory negligence, guilt, and responsibility for the accident. Two lives were
lost, for which there were a half-dozen reasons. As in almost all
such investigations, someone's head would have to roll—as long
as it did not belong to anyone of importance. Thus the search for a
scapegoat began.

Investigations had been announced. On August 18, the *Los
Angeles Times* wrote in large type, "SENATE GROUP OPENS
PROBE OF DISASTER." The article explained that Senator Cope-
land, Democrat from New York, had convened a special committee to investigate fatal air accidents. The committee had been
appointed just three months earlier, following the crash that had
killed—among others—Senator Bronson Cutting of New Mexico.
In the evening of May 6, 1935, a scheduled TWA DC-2 crashed in
bad weather near Kansas City, its radio inoperative on night
frequency. Learning that earlier weather reports had substantially
changed, the pilot tried to reach an alternate, unfamiliar airport
under adverse atmospheric conditions. The pilot and four passengers were killed, eight injured.

Here, as in Wiley Post's case, the weather played a part in
the crash. It is interesting to note the different procedures em-
ployed to investigate the earlier accident by the Department of
Commerce. Immediately after the accident, five Department of
Commerce airline inspectors from different parts of the Midwest
were dispatched to the crash scene. Vidal sent two Bureau of Air
Commerce officials, Denis Mulligan, Chief of the Enforcement
Section, Air Regulations Divisions, and R. W. "Shorty" Schroe-
der, Chief of the Air Line Inspections Service, Air Regulations
Division, to Kansas City. Completing the Bureau of Air Commerce
Accident Board were Dr. R. E. Whitehead, Richard C. Gazley, and
Jesse L. Lankford.

Six days of hearings followed, while fifty-nine witnesses
were questioned and more than nine hundred pages of testimony
recorded. Despite all this apparent thoroughness, the findings are
all the more bewildering. On June 14, almost six weeks after the
accident, the determinations were made public. In what must be
the most ridiculous of board findings on record, the Bureau of
Air Commerce announced, "The probable direct cause of this
accident was an unintentional collision with the ground while the

airplane was being maneuvered at a very low altitude in fog and darkness.''

Stripped of its excessive language the investigation revealed that the ''probable'' reason for Senator Cutting's death was the plane hitting the ground. It was a glorious revelation of the obvious.

Little was ever determined by the senatorial investigating committee. It was hardly competent to inquire into a plane crash; certainly not as qualified as the Bureau of Air Commerce, and it certainly was grossly ineffective, as the Cutting air wreck investigation had demonstrated.

In contrast, the investigation of the Post–Rogers crash was carried on via long distance—by second– and third–hand reports, by hearsay and rumor, by mail, or telegrams.

For example, on August 27, three days prior to the issuance of the first and most important governmental report on the crash, Eugene Vidal, the Director of Air Commerce, was still seeking tangential answers:

JUAN TRIPPE, PRESIDENT, PAN AMERICAN AIRWAYS INC, CHRYSLER BUILDING, NEW YORK

IN CHECKING FACTORS LEADING UP TO POST ROGERS CRASH WOULD LIKE TO KNOW WHETHER OR NOT PAN AMERICAN WAS IN ANY WAY INVOLVED WITH POSTS FLIGHT OR PROPOSED FLIGHTS

VIDAL

It is unclear how any connection with PAN AM would in any way shed light on the crash. But there were other telegrams:

DAYLETTER, ALFRED LOWMAN [sic], COLMAN BUILD-ING, SEATTLE WASHINGTON:

DISCUSSED POST ROGERS ACCIDENT WITH YOUR BROTHER TODAY AND WOULD APPRECIATE YOUR WIRING US WHAT CONCLUSIONS YOU MIGHT HAVE REACHED OR SPECULATIONS AS TO CAUSE OF ACCIDENT AFTER VISITING WRECK STOP ALSO IT WOULD

ASSIST US IF YOU MAILED SKETCH OF LAGOON AND
PATH OF PLANE

VIDAL, DIRECTOR OF AIR COMMERCE

Alfred J. Lomen had been to the crash site, but he was neither a
pilot nor a mechanic. His "speculations" could not be of value.
And he certainly would have no idea of the "path of plane." Vidal
sent another telegram:

DAYLETTER, EDO FLOAT COMPANY, COLLEGE POINT,
LONG ISLAND, N Y

WOULD APPRECIATE YOUR MAILING IMMEDIATELY
ALL INFORMATION AND DRAWINGS FOR ARRANGE-
MENT OF FLOATS ON WILEY POST PLANE

EUGENE L. VIDAL DIRECTOR OF AIR COMMERCE

The EDO Float Company in Queens, New York, could not possibly have any valid information about Wiley Post's plane. Such a
query should have been directed to Northwest Air Service in
Seattle.

Director Eugene Vidal did fly to Los Angeles and talk
to the Department's Inspector James E. Reed. Reed had crossed
Wiley's path many times and was important to this investigation.
It was he who had licensed Post to operate an aircraft radio.
And it was Reed who had observed the daily progress of the work
done on Wiley's plane at Pacific Airmotive Corporation in Burbank. It was Reed who had approved the issuance of the restricted
license. But neither as pilot not passenger had he ever flown
the plane.

It does seem difficult to accept that an experienced employee of the Bureau of Air Commerce with the rank of an
inspector would not question the airworthiness of such a hap-
hazardly assembled plane, or suspect that it was nose-heavy.

It is established that Inspector Reed had not tested Wiley's
plane; he admitted it. But then there had been further alterations
at Seattle; was the plane supposed to have been inspected again
for airworthiness?

Director Eugene Vidal's foremost thought seemed to have been to protect the Bureau of Air Commerce and prove absence of any contributory responsibility. Vidal should have insisted on an on-site investigation, on the interviews with the eyewitnesses, on an examination of the wreck, on questioning the various mechanics who had worked on the plane. Instead he ordered an internal search to determine the limits of his Department's obligations. Did an inspector really have to test for "airworthiness?" What about a restricted license? Did a plane given a restricted license also have to be tested?

On August 27, 1935, Eugene L. Vidal sent an inter-office memo to Denis Mulligan, Chief of the Enforcement Section, Air Regulations Division:

> Following discussions with Colonel Johnson, [Assistant Secretary of Commerce] it was decided to check into the authority of the Department regarding the "R" license in the case of the Wiley Post plane. We are anxious to find out whether or not an inspector should have checked over the plane in Seattle after Post had changed from wheels to floats, which change, by the way, resulted in a very nose-heavy characteristic.

Denis Mulligan's detailed report was devastating. Every possible excuse, every rear escape hatch by which the Bureau of Air Commerce might have tried to dodge responsibility, was slammed shut. Eight days after receiving the order, on September 4, 1935, Denis Mulligan filed his response. The date is significant, as it is precisely the same date on which the U.S. Department of Commerce, Bureau of Air Commerce, presented its first official findings on the causes of the crash. Actually that report had been prepared several days earlier, but bore the restriction: "For Release Morning papers Wednesday, September 4, 1935." It is obvious that an official conclusion was reached and published while the investigation had barely begun.

In his report to Director Vidal, Mr. Mulligan was extremely thorough. "This information has been obtained," he pointed out, "through consultation with members of the Registration, Engineering, and General Inspection Sections."

Mulligan quoted pertinent points from every applicable law and reference work; these are among the most incriminating:

"Inspector's Handbook of Instructions,
CHAPTER IV.—AIRCRAFT INSPECTION FOR LICENSE
Section A.—Field Inspection of Airplanes

#3. Inspection Procedure.

Since you are responsible for the airworthy condition of every airplane which you approve for license, an investigation into the operation and thorough inspection of each airplane should be made to satisfy yourself that it is eligible for license and airworthy.

#4. When Airplane is Approved for License

(a) In case of restricted license . . .write on card "No passenger other than bona fide members of the crew may be carried".

#8. Restricted Airplane Licenses

Primarily restricted licenses are intended for airworthy airplanes which are being used for some special class of operation . . . Crop dusting, Sky writing, Photography . . .

Restricted Licenses will not be issued to aircraft used for pleasure flying or for commercial operation for which a commercially licensed airplane could normally be used. Airplanes bearing restricted licenses may not carry passengers and are permitted to carry only the pilot and such crew as is necessary for the type of restricted operation for which it is licensed.

#10. Alterations.

In general, airplanes which have been altered from the approved design as shown in the licensing specifications are not eligible for license and should, therefore, not be approved by inspectors in the field without written or telegraphic authority from the Washington office. Certain minor alterations are permissible. In order to enable inspectors to have a clear understanding regarding the matter of alterations, the following classification of alterations is set up with instructions as to the necessary action on the part of the inspector in each case:

Class A.—

The following changes are examples of alterations from the approved design which will necessitate submission of technical data and possible flight test. Planes so altered may not be licensed until approval of the changes has been issued by the Washington office

X Increase in fuel and oil capacity;
   Increase in seating capacity;
X Structural changes of any part or component;
X Changes in control surfaces or systems;
X Changes in seating arrangement where load distribution is altered in such a manner that it may affect the stability;
X Installation of pontoons;
   Installation of skis;
   Installation of wheel pants.''

[Those identified with "X" apply to Wiley Post's plane. Ed.]

Sec. 11. It shall be unlawful . . .

(3) To navigate any aircraft registered as an aircraft of the United States . . . in violation of the terms of any such certificate.

Denis Mulligan's search clearly exposed several significant violations of departmental rules by both inspectors and Wiley Post. The Restricted Aircraft License No: NR 12283, issued August 8, 1935, specifically stated under the item "Passengers (less crew): "NONE." In order to qualify as a bona fide member of the crew, and be possibly considered an "observer," that observer would have to be technically qualified to "observe" something, say, the performance of the plane, or some equipment aboard. Surely an observer looking out the window at the landscape below would not qualify as an "observing" crew member. It could be argued—however feebly—that Rogers was aboard as a special crew member; his functions being to tie up, or release, the float-equipped plane upon landings and departures, so Post could remain at the controls. No similar argument could ever be advanced for Rogers' and Mae Post's presence on the flight to Arizona, New Mexico, Utah, Nevada, and back to Los Angeles when the plane was on wheels.

Post again breached the conditions of his restricted license when he flew Mae to Seattle.

Inspector Mulligan supplied Director Vidal with still further abstracts of rules and regulations:

> Aeronautical Bulletin No. 7, The Air Commerce Regulations:
>
> Sec. 25. Grounds for Revocation or Suspension
>
> (F) Remodeling the airplane structure and flying the airplane without having it first re-rated as airworthy by the Secretary of Commerce.

This stipulation clearly applied. The landing gear with wheels was removed and a new support system for pontoons was substituted.

Denis Mulligan's conclusion to Director Vidal was clear:

> The answer to the question asked in your memo . . . is that when Post changed his plane from wheels to floats at Seattle, he should have requested an inspection, and an inspection would have been in order by one of our inspectors.

Perhaps, just perhaps, after such a comprehensive recitation of violations, Denis Mulligan wanted to soften the blow:

In conference with Messrs. Shumate, Kerber, and Gazley, it was learned that in granting "R" licenses to aircraft as much leeway as possible is given for development, exploration, and for other special purposes. Regulation, therefore, is of secondary consideration. The inspection given prior to the issuance of an "R" license goes to workmanship, condition of material, where such condition is obvious, and to the general design of the craft, assuming it be of a standard type. Airworthiness as such is not required. Prior to the issuance of an "R" license the airplane is not flown by an inspector.

Maybe that was the lax, indulgent practice in the field. No regulation is cited that allows that a plane could be declared "airworthy" without that plane having been in the air. It was not incumbent on any inspector to simply ignore so basic a requirement as a plane's ability to fly safely. Especially in this case, when no "scientific project" was even envisioned. This was simply Wiley's "bastard" in which he wanted to do a little hunting and fishing, and fly a paying passenger leisurely in search of an airline route.

Not even the most indulgent inspector could, after considering "the general design of the craft," come away "assuming it be of a standard type," as Denis Mulligan, Chief of the Enforcement Section, Air Regulations Division, had mentioned. This plane was neither "general" nor "standard"—it was unique.

Washington realized at once that there had been a serious omission on Inspector Reed's part. One could say that he was awed by Wiley Post's accomplishments; and that if Post thought the plane was "airworthy," who was Reed to question it?

Having established Reed's failure to follow the dictates of the *Inspector's Handbook of Instructions*, it was time to review the actions of the inspector in Seattle. The Bureau, having found one possible culprit, now went after another who could be made to share the blame.

WESTERN UNION TELEGRAM DAY LETTER, PAID.
WASHINGTON D.C. AUGUST 30, 1935.

W. S. MOORE, SCHOOL INSPECTOR, BOEING FIELD, SEATTLE WASHINGTON. ADVISE WIRE WHETHER

YOU INSPECTED INSTALLATION PONTOONS WILEY
POST LOCKHEED NR ONE TWO TWO EIGHT THREE
ALSO GIVE NUMBER LOCATION CAPACITY GAS TANKS
STOP FORWARD AIRMAIL ALL INFORMATION COVER-
ING ALTERATIONS MADE SUBJECT AIRCRAFT AT SEAT-
TLE AND REPORT COVERING INSPECTION IF MADE.

But Inspector Moore was not to be reached. Western Union
Telegraph Company notified Washington that the telegram sent
to W. D. [sic] Moore "is undelivered for the following reason:
Addressee left city will return Sept. 3, Signed: Shumate."

At Oakland, a Bureau of Air Commerce officer named Bedinger showed initiative. He contacted Northwest Air Service in
Renton, Washington, and found all the correct answers. He then
notified his superiors in Washington, D.C., via telegram - collect,
dayletter.

Somehow the vacationing Inspector Moore was suddenly
found, and the Washington Bureau was informed on August 31
that the telegram addressed to W. S. Moore had been telephoned
to him. There is no indication where or how he had been contacted. But he obviously received the message, for that day, as
instructed, he filed his written report. He repeated all the details
Bedinger had already supplied and he freely admitted that he had
not inspected Wiley's plane:

. . . There was no inspection made of the airplane after
the installation of pontoons at Seattle.

The installation and other work on the airplane
was completed the evening of August 5, and Mr. Post
departed Renton airport at 9:20 AM August 6 . . .

This letter was stamped as having been received in Washington, DC, on September 4, 1935, 2:01 P.M. Questioned whether
he had performed an inspection, Inspector Moore had his excuse
ready. He replied that the floats attachment had been completed
in the evening of August 5, and that Post left at "9:20 AM August
6." His implication is that Post and Rogers left town before he,
Moore, had an opportunity to make the necessary inspection. The
intimation to Washington was clearly that had the plane stayed

longer he, Moore, would surely have performed his duty. This seemed to satisfy the U.S. Department of Commerce.

The facts are that Northwest Air Service indeed finished work on Post's plane late in the afternoon of August 5. But the plane with Post and Rogers aboard did not leave Seattle until 9:15 A.M. on August 7, a full twenty-four hours later than misstated by Inspector Moore. Wiley had taken the plane up that August 6 for a test flight and had invited Gordon Williams and Bob McLarren to join him.

It was also on August 6 that Will Rogers played polo at the Olympic Riding and Driving Club's new polo field. Newspaper articles and photographs exist to substantiate that date.

Northwest Air Service is not involved in any of this controversy. As far as its workmanship was concerned, no inspection was needed. It was a government-licensed, accredited station and any work performed by the company was considered officially accepted. The company had no authority to question the plane's airworthiness, or demand that Post request an inspection.

As for the U. S. Department of Commerce, nagging questions remained: was the plane, now equipped with floats, safe to be flown? Was it less safe to be flown than it was before the floats were attached? As the investigation progressed, it became quite obvious to all that neither Inspector Reed in Burbank, nor Inspector Moore in Seattle, nor Director Vidal, nor his Bureau of Air Commerce had gone by the book. Nor indeed, did any of them seem to know the regulations in that book.

The Department now had two government inspectors culpable for failing to inspect the plane, and a third inspector was about to join their ranks. Though the least culpable, he would end up the most castigated; it was his head that would roll. But it would not roll because of anything he had done, or failed to do, but because of something he was yet to do.

Inspector Murray Hall was stationed in Anchorage, but mid-August 1935, found him in Fairbanks, which lay within his jurisdiction. Colonel J. Carroll Cone of the Bureau of Air Commerce, reached Hall by telegraph:

REPORT RECEIVED POST AND ROGERS KILLED THIS
MORNING ENROUTE NORTH FROM ANCHORAGE OR
FAIRBANKS STOP RADIO AVAILABLE INFORMATION

IMMEDIATELY STOP USE ARMY RADIO IN CODE IF
THIS DOES NOT CAUSE DELAY OTHERWISE REGU-
LAR CHANNELS

Dutifully, Inspector Hall wired back at once:

REWIRE POST AND ROGERS . . . PREPARATION BEING
MADE TO MAKE TRIP TO BARROW NS9 DEPARTURE
TOMORROW MORNING STOP HAVE MADE ARRANGE-
MENTS WITH CROSSON TO OBTAIN ALL DETAILS
AVAILABLE STOP TRIP CONSIDERED HAZARDOUS
ADVISE IF ABSOLUTELY NECESSARY FOR BEST IN-
TEREST OF BUREAU STOP

The NS9 referred to was Murray Hall's wheel-equipped,
Stinson Reliant SR-SE, a short-range plane. It was hardly the right
type of craft to be taken by a lone pilot on a hazardous, long-
distance flight to Barrow.

Still on that same day, August 16, Colonel Cone in Washington sent Hall a surprising reply:

RETEL COAST GUARD CUTTER NORTHLAND DE-
PARTED FROM BARROW YESTERDAY AND IS RETURN-
ING TO BARROW TO PICK UP BODIES STOP YOUR
TRIP TO BARROW NOT NECESSARY STOP GET ALL
DETAILS FROM CROSSON AND RADIO ME STOP FOL-
LOW WITH LETTER AND COMPLETE INFORMATION.

By the time Hall received this telegram, he had already
spoken to Joe Crosson and Robert Gleason, who had returned
from Barrow. Crosson had brought back new information and
Form AB-87, the official Aircraft Accident Report, which Hall had
given him for Sergeant Stanley Morgan to complete. Yet all Hall
learned was what the two fliers had been told. Nobody had
actually examined the plane or the engine. In fact, neither Crosson
nor Gleason had even seen the wreckage from the air.

On August 17, as ordered, Hall sent a full report, both by
telegraph and hand-written, telling all that he had learned from
Joe Crosson. The basic details were old news by now, but there
were some new, pertinent facts, and a revealing addendum:

. . . Joe Crosson reported to me that the ship must have
been very nose heavy, for he had heard Wiley say so, and
that he had heard Wiley direct Mr. Rogers to sit to the
rear of Cabin [sic] and keep the heavy baggage to the rear
especially when taking off and landing . . . The ship
would climb very fast and at a steep angle after leaving
the water. A take-off of this nature was made upon leaving the slough at Fairbanks for Harding Lake preliminary
to departing for Barrow . . .

Murray Hall enclosed a meteorological report, without
identifying it further. While two reports by meteorologists have
now been found, only the one signed by R. L. Frost, assistant
meteorologist, was dated early enough to be attached to Inspector Hall's hand-written letter.

Mr. Frost's report gave weather statistics before and after
the accident and restated information that was known from other
sources; but it also presented several new facts:

. . . During the time Post was in Fairbanks he never came
in contact with the Weather Bureau Officials or telephoned for weather information . . .

. . . Shortly after noon on the 14th the Pacific Alaska
Airways requested information regarding the landing
conditions at Point Barrow and also requested an Airway
Weather report for the following morning on the regular
10:00 am radio schedule. It was not stated that this
information was desired for Post and it was not known at
the time that Post and Rogers intended to fly to Point
Barrow . . .

. . . People who witnessed the take off from the river
stated that Post made a very steep and unnecessary climb
after leaving the water and it is the general impression
that this was his usual method of taking off . . .

. . . At Walakpi the plane landed in shallow water . . . It
is said that after leaving the water the plane rose in a very
steep climb. The motor stopped and the plane came

down and landed upside-down. It is also said that after
leaving the water the plane banked sharply to the right at
an elevation of fifty or sixty feet. The motor stalled and
as the plane came down the right wing and pontoons
struck the water. The country in the vicinity is reported
to be very low and flat. It is difficult to understand why
the pilot found it necessary to rise in an unusually steep
climb or to make a sharp bank to the right. There were no
obstructions to be avoided . . .

. . . It would seem that Post took unnecessary chances in
attempting this flight, particularly so when considering
the fact that he was not familiar with the country. Pilots
with years of flying experience in Alaska would not
think of making a flight from Fairbanks to Point Barrow
with no weather reports and Post was advised against it
by the best pilot in the Territory.

> Respectfully
> (signed) R. L. Frost
> Asst. Meteorologist.

From this report, which far exceeded the limits of a meteorological summary, it will be seen that the Bureau of Air Commerce had facts and data in its possession which were never used
in its official statements.

On August 19, the Bureau of Air Commerce was quoted in
the newspapers as having received no further word from Inspector Hall. "Transportation is pretty slow up there," a Commerce
Department official explained to reporters. "Hall has to travel by
dog sled sometimes, or any other way he can. He has one land
plane, but I doubt if he is using it now." Whoever that spokesman
was, he revealed complete ignorance of conditions the Department's inspectors faced.

There had been no further telegraphed details because
Inspector Murray Hall had nothing further to report. He had by
then wired and written all he had heard and he had been given no
further instructions.

Suddenly Washington became self-conscious. It had publicly announced to the press and the nation that it would send an
inspector to the wreck scene to investigate the crash. And then, it

had told the only inspector in Alaska that it was "NOT NECES-SARY" to go to the crash site. True, Air Commerce had heard several reports about *what* had happened, but it had absolutely no idea *why* it had happened. This was not the public image the Bureau wanted to present; action was indicated. Developing an acute case of impeccable hindsight, a prodded Colonel Cone sent Hall another wire that Monday, August 19:

> SOME DEPARTMENT PERSONNEL PUZZLED WHY YOU DID NOT ACCOMPANY CROSSON TO BARROW STOP . . . . RADIO REPLY REGARDING FAILURE TO MAKE TRIP WITH CROSSON

If, according to Cone, the Department personnel was puzzled, one can imagine what poor Murray Hall must have thought. He had asked his superiors whether he should fly to Barrow, and they had informed him that it was not necessary. There was no sense denying it; Hall had not been anxious to go to Barrow. It was a dangerous trip, especially on a day when even the birds on the North Slope walked. But now, three days later, Washington suddenly wanted to know why he had not gone. Being the ever compliant civil servant, Murray Hall did not simply stand up and wire back: I didn't go because you told me it wasn't necessary! Instead of talking back to his superior, Hall assumed the blame for not going to Barrow. He set out to pretend that he had really wanted to go with Crosson and Gleason, but that logic and consideration for their safety would not permit him to do so. Thus Hall began to fabricate details into his narrative. It was a foolish decision, which would haunt him in the days to come:

> RE WIRES OF NINETEENTH STOP JOE CROSSON AND RADIO OPERATOR GLEASON LEFT FAIRBANKS CHENA SLOUGH AT ELEVEN FIFTEEN AM THE SIXTEENTH FOR POINT BARROW STOP THE AIRPLANE USED WAS FAIRCHILD SEVENTY ONE . . . THE PAY LOAD OF THIS AIRPLANE ON FLOATS IS APPROXIMATELY FOUR HUNDRED SIXTY POUNDS STOP . . . IT WAS DESIRABLE TO LOAD THE AIRPLANE CABIN WITH FIVE GALLON CANS OF GASOLINE TO *THE LIMIT* OF THE *SHIPS PERFORMANCE* STOP . . . ABOUT TEN CASES OR ONE

HUNDRED GALLONS OF FUEL WAS IN THE SHIPS
CABIN STOP WITH THIS LOAD THE SHIP WAS *UNABLE
TO TAKE OFF* THE WATER STOP TAKE OFF WAS MADE
ON THE THIRD ATTEMPT AFTER *THIRTY GALLONS*
OF GASOLINE HAD BEEN *REMOVED* FROM THE CABIN
STOP I WAS PRESENT DURING THESE ATTEMPTS AND
INDICATED TO JOE THE DESIRE TO ACCOMPANY HIM
STOP HE SAID TO ME THAT HE WOULD BE GLAD TO
TAKE ME BUT DID NOT KNOW WHETHER HE COULD
GET OFF WITH THE LOAD ALREADY ON BOARD STOP
IN VIEW OF THE NECESSITY OF CARRYING EXTRA
FUEL FOR HIS OWN SAFETY AND THE FACT THAT THE
RETURN TRIP WOULD HAVE TO BE MADE WITH *THE
ADDITIONAL WEIGHT OF THE BODIES AND EFFECTS
OF THE UNFORTUNATE MEN* IT DID NOT APPEAR
THAT GOOD JUDGMENT WOULD PERMIT ME TO AC-
COMPANY HIM STOP . . . I DO NOT BELIEVE *ANY
ADDITIONAL KNOWLEDGE* COULD HAVE BEEN OB-
TAINED AS ONLY ONE PERSON A NATIVE ACTUALLY
SAW THE ACCIDENT . . . AND IT IS ALWAYS DESIRABLE
AT THAT POINT TO DEPART AS SOON AS POSSIBLE TO
AVOID THE CHANCE OF HAVING THE WEATHER SHUT
DOWN STOP . . . THE ONLY CLUE THAT I HAVE TO
SUGGEST AS A CAUSE FOR THE ACCIDENT IS THAT IF
THAT THE [sic] LAGOON NEAR POINTBARROW WILEY
CLIMBED HIS PLANE TOO STEEPLY AND *STALLED* OR
APPROACHED A STALL AS THE MOTOR MISSED HE
MAY *NOT HAVE BEEN ABLE TO HOLD* IT OUT OF THE
ENSUING DIVE STOP IF STILL DESIRABLE I WILL PRO-
CEED TO POINTBARROW AND MAKE THE BEST POSSI-
BLE EXAMINATION OF THE WRECKAGE STOP IF THIS
DESIRABLE PLEASE ADVISE AUTHORITY CHARTER RA-
DIO EQUIPPED AIRPLANE FOR TRIP OR OK USE NS
NINE GROUNDED AT PRESENT ACCOUNT PROPELLER
BLADES

The fiction and inaccuracies are immediately glaring. A
Fairchild 71 was an airplane designed to accommodate the pilot
and six adult passengers. Official specifications state that as a land
plane, the Fairchild 71 was allowed a maximum payload of 1500

pounds. Equipped with pontoons, as this plane was, the payload was cut back to 1160 pounds. It is unreported what made Inspector Hall claim that "THE PAY LOAD OF THIS AIRPLANE ON FLOATS IS APPROXIMATELY FOUR HUNDRED SIXTY POUNDS?" It is plain that seven people would weigh more than a total of 460 pounds.

Errors in mathematics are instantly evident in Murray Hall's claim that Crosson had the cabin filled "WITH FIVE GALLON CANS OF GASOLINE . . . ABOUT TEN CASES OR ONE HUNDRED GALLONS OF FUEL WAS IN THE SHIPS CABIN." Ten cases of five gallons each would be a total of only fifty gallons. Since each U. S. gallon of gasoline weighs six pounds the payload was only three-hundred pounds. But the plane carried neither one-hundred gallons, nor fifty gallons.

Robert J. Gleason, who was aboard this flight, remembers no difficulties with the take-off: "As I recall, we had twelve five-gallon cans of Red Crown gasoline, sixty gallons." There would be no reason for Crosson to experience difficulties taking off from Chena Slough. The weather was perfect, the weight of the gasoline was only the weight of two male passengers. This was a seven passenger plane and it was 800 pounds short of capacity load. Why should there be any problem in taking off?

There was enough weight allowance and space available to accommodate Murray Hall, had he seriously wished to fly to Barrow. And on that point, after earlier volunteering to fly his NS9 to Barrow, Hall now claimed that it was grounded because of "propeller blades."

Murray Hall's version of his conversation with Joe Crosson pertaining to a trip to Barrow, and his claimed "good judgment," was immediately questioned in Washington. It was discussed at a meeting in Assistant Secretary Johnson's office (same day, Monday, August 19) with several staff members present. The official report of that meeting, included in Colonel Cone's Memorandum, is an unwitting self-indictment by their second-highest ranking official in the Bureau of Air Commerce. Wrote Colonel J. Carroll Cone:[1]

> It was felt that since the Secretary had released information to the Press to the effect that the Bureau had sent someone to investigate the accident, it would be advis-

able to make some gesture to make clear the Bureau's
interest in the accident.

". . . it would be advisable to make some gesture?" Is that
what the men who ran the Bureau of Air Commerce thought? Just
"a gesture to make clear the Bureau's interest?" Was that all the
Bureau wanted? A gesture. Two men had died, and the Bureau of
Air Commerce thought it "advisable to make some gesture" to
find out why they lay dead?

Well, what was their "gesture?" It was first proposed to
send Mr. Mulligan to Los Angeles to interview Mr. Crosson. Cone
pointed out that this would engender undesirable publicity, as his
specialized duties as Chief of the Enforcement Section would
"raise the question as to whether or not violations were involved
and indicate that some punitive action was warranted."

It was next suggested that Colonel Cone be sent, but he
pointed out that as head of the Regulations Division his participation could be considered in much the same light as Mr. Mulligan's.
Cone finally suggested that Eugene Vidal, the director, would be
the logical choice. After all, his activities embraced all functions
of the Bureau and no adverse inference could be drawn. The
obvious impression made by this conversation and subsequent
action is that the so-called "investigation" now had deteriorated
into a case of appearance over substance: "How does it look,"
and "What will they say about us?"

Mr. Vidal left for Los Angeles on Tuesday, August 20, when
it was announced that he would represent the Bureau at Will
Rogers' funeral. Unfortunately Joe Crosson, the man he wanted to
see, was in Oklahoma City for the funeral of his friend Wiley Post.
Vidal, however, did meet Crosson later in Los Angeles, when Joe
was on his way back to Alaska.

On Vidal's return to Washington, he brought with him
some news. Crosson had told him that he had indeed invited Hall
to accompany him to Barrow, but had told him that Hall would
have to arrange for other means of transportation for returning to
Fairbanks.

The Bureau then concluded, as stated by Colonel Cone: "It
appeared from this that Hall had sent inaccurate and erroneous
reports." It was then decided that the Bureau of Air Commerce
wanted Hall's scalp.

It seems strange that the Bureau's main target now was an inspector, when it should have concentrated on information. The crashed plane was still lying in two feet of brackish water at the top of the world and no one had gone to examine it; there were dozens of people to interview who could have added helpful information. There seemed to be a lack of interest in following any leads. Had the Bureau already made up its mind what to tell the public? Was the Bureau's main objective now to make Inspector Hall confess that he had lied?

Vidal contacted Hall on Tuesday, August 27, to secure written data "for file purposes," and in order to remove any doubt of a possible misunderstanding:

> PLEASE RADIO WHETHER OR NOT CROSSON IN-
> FORMED YOU HE COULD TAKE YOU TO BARROW BUT
> NOT ON RETURN TRIP ALSO WHETHER OR NOT YOU
> CONSIDERED BARROW FLIGHT HAZARDOUS.

Colonel Cone also contacted Hall that same day, although by letter.[2] Addressing him informally as "Dear Murray," he came quickly to the meat of the matter: "There have been several slightly conflicting statements made to various officials as to what actually happened in connection with Crosson's flight to Point Barrow and the reasons why you did not accompany him, and in order that the matter may be completely cleared up once and for all, I think it would be beneficial to all parties concerned to have a first-hand statement from Crosson, which statement I am sure will eliminate any vestige of doubt as to the proper functioning of the Regulation Division, particularly your own activities. I understand, among other things, that Crosson has stated that he invited you to go with him to Point Barrow but at the same time advised you that you would have to arrange for some other transportation on your return trip . . . Kindest personal regards."

This letter, dated August 27, shows that the Bureau of Air Commerce had indeed formed an opinion at long distance, and was no longer interested in obtaining facts. Cone says so:

> We in the Regulation Division are fully satisfied that we
> know the reasons for the accident and that a trip on your
> part to the scene of the accident would not have devel-

oped any new information. We feel that the accident was caused primarily by motor failure while the ship was in a steep climb, which resulted in the stalling condition of the aircraft. We have rather complete information as to the flying characteristics of the aircraft.

Having spun the web for Inspector Murray Hall to fully entangle himself in his own "slightly conflicting statements," the Bureau of Air Commerce in Washington now had to prove its own impeccability. It had to lay the groundwork by spelling out the sequence of events in an orderly, easy to understand fashion. It was necessary to touch all the bases, reminding all those involved and those who would read the report just as to who said what, and when, and how it all was to tumble into place. It was never intended to become public reading matter; it was merely the foundation for not divulging all that was known. The delicate task of writing this document fell again to J. Carroll Cone, the assistant director of Air Commerce.

Hall could still have claimed that he had asked the Bureau whether he really had to go to Barrow, and the Bureau's reply had been that it was not necessary. He had also been told that even had he gone, no new information would have developed. What then was this pre-occupation with what either he or Crosson had said? But Hall did not use those arguments. Instead he replied at once:

REWIRE TWENTY SEVENTH STOP JOE CROSSON MADE NO DEFINITE OFFER TO TAKE ME TO POINT BARROW NOR DID HE SAY THAT HE COULD NOT TAKE ME STOP THE ADVISABILITY OF MY ACCOMPANYING HIM WAS DISCUSSED AND IT WAS I THAT DEFINITELY DECIDED NOT TO INSIST OR PRESS HIM FOR PASSAGE IN VIEW OF HIS DESIRE TO CARRY ALL POSSIBLE EXTRA FUEL STOP . . .

Of course, this was in direct contradiction to Joe Crosson's statement to Director Vidal. Crosson had no ulterior motives to make false statements; he would most certainly have taken an official along. It would have been an act of courtesy, and good public relations for Pacific Alaska Airways, which was under the jurisdiction of this same Murray Hall.

Just to have Joe Crosson's reply on record for his files, Colonel Cone wired some questions to Crosson on August 27. If this had been a court room, Cone would have been challenged for leading the witness:

> WOULD APPRECIATE YOUR ASSISTANCE IN CLEARING SLIGHTLY MISLEADING INFORMATION RELATIVE HALLS [sic] FAILURE TO ACCOMPANY YOU TO BARROW STOP HALL STATED HE WANTED TO GO BUT THAT DUE TO NECESSARY GASOLINE LOAD IT WAS INADVISABLE AND IMPOSSIBLE STOP OTHER STATEMENTS TO EFFECT YOU INVITED HALL TO ACCOMPANY YOU BUT THAT HE WOULD HAVE TO FIND OTHER MEANS FOR RETURNING STOP WOULD APPRECIATE COMPLETE STATEMENT BY WIRE COLLECT AS TO ANY MISUNDERSTANDING THAT MAY EXIST STOP YOUR STATEMENTS FOR OFFICIAL USE ONLY AND NOT FOR PUBLICITY STOP DEPARTMENT APPRECIATES COOPERATION YOU HAVE ALWAYS GIVEN IT STOP REGARDS.

On Thursday, August 29, Cone had his reply from Crosson. Instead of clearing matters up, it muddied the waters. In what must appear to be an act of generous friendship, Joe Crosson now contradicted his own report to Eugene Vidal and backed up Murray Hall's excuses. In his earliest telegram Hall had pointed out that a trip to Barrow was hazardous; and he had queried the Bureau whether it really wanted him to fly to Barrow. Now friend Crosson stated: "NO QUESTION CAN BE RAISED REGARDING HALLS DESIRE ACCOMPANY ME PT BARROW STOP HALL REQUESTED MAKE TRIP . . ." Crosson went even further to help Hall. He declared that his first impression had been that Hall could accompany him to Barrow, but that it would be necessary for him to make other arrangements about his return to Fairbanks; that after checking the amount of gas necessary to make the trip safely, he found it inadvisable and impossible for Hall to come along. Crosson protected Hall even further; "UNDER EXISTING CONDITIONS FAIRBANKS THAT DAY CONSIDERABLE DIFFICULTY WAS EXPERIENCED GETTING PLANE OFF WATER AND GAS LOAD WAS REDUCED BELOW DESIRED AMOUNT BEFORE POSSIBLE TO TAKE OFF STOP."

There was never a logical reason for Joe Crosson to decline taking Inspector Hall to Barrow. Robert Gleason and Joe Crosson had maintained that there was no problem taking off in Fairbanks.

As for the claim that Crosson was willing to take Hall to Barrow, but could not return him, that would have been correct. On the return trip there would have been the additional weight of the two bodies, which would take up more room. But Hall could not have come back as soon as Crosson did in any case. He would have needed time to interview several eyewitnesses. Then Hall would have had to travel to Walakpa Lagoon and thoroughly inspect the wreck. He would have had to salvage the engine and possibly take it apart. All that would have taken far more time than the few hours Crosson and Gleason spent at Barrow.

Hall's protestations, and Crosson's willingness to help a friend, were of no help. Thursday and Friday, August 29 and 30, Cone spent with Director Vidal and members of his staff, discussing the question of Hall's transfer for "failure to go to the scene of the accident." Vidal felt that although Hall should be transferred as punishmnent, no action should be taken until he had discussed the matter with Secretary of Commerce Daniel Calhoun Roper.

The conclusion was the expressed belief that there was cause for a punitive transfer, but if Hall were transferred now, there would be created a suspicion of inefficiency on the part of the Department and the question would be raised as to the propriety of the action.

The only thought remaining is just to which assignment Inspector Hall could have possibly been transferred as a form of punishment? Surely after spending several harsh winters in Alaska, almost any other assignment would have seemed a promotion.

It is obvious that the investigation was neither thorough nor complete; and it was equally obvious that it would never go much further. Yet the Department of Commerce issued an account of its findings two weeks after the crash. With just partial information on hand, with both public and internal investigations barely begun, the Department of Commerce somehow felt qualified to draw conclusions.

The report was dated August 30, 1935, with instructions "For Release Morning Papers Wednesday, September 4, 1935."[3] In almost 1,300 words, Eugene L. Vidal, director of the Bureau of Air Commerce, displayed its lack of basic information about the accident that had killed Wiley Post and Will Rogers near Barrow, Alaska, on August 15, 1935.

To the public it was an eagerly awaited disclosure. At least millions of fans thought they were learning the truth about the deaths of their idols. What they learned sounded reasonable and there was no cause to distrust it. Only a few knew that Washington was guessing, while protecting its own.

What was excluded from this Bureau of Air Commerce statement was as massive as the mistakes it contained. Two weeks after the beginning of the investigation, Eugene L. Vidal, the director of the Air Service Bureau, the top man in the Bureau, still thought that Wiley had substituted a "Sirius" wing, when it was the wing of an "Explorer" model.

Vidal quoted a statement Post supposedly had made to Inspector Reed. Wiley—so Reed had claimed when asked—was satisfied with "the plane's flying characteristics, particularly its stability, balance, and ease of maneuverability." However, once the plane had received its license from Reed, Wiley had no hesitation to say openly how difficult a plane it was to fly. But Vidal never heard of that.

Someone must have told Vidal that the plane had no radio equipment aboard, and that the plane had to be started by hand. Both particulars are incorrect. Every inspection report in the Bureau's own files, including the very last one signed by Inspector Reed, indicates that the plane carried 135 pounds of radio equipment—adding to the nose-heaviness.

Vidal's report claimed that there was "neither snow nor ice on either land or water." There are numerous statements that on August 15, 1935, there was so much ice on the water that the U. S. Coast Guard cutter *Northland* had moved fifty miles southward out of Barrow, lest it become icebound. Clair Okpeaha, on his dash to Barrow, abandoned his oomiak as the sea covered with ice floes was too hazardous. David Brower, coming with his party from Barrow, reported treacherous and slow progress due to ice on the ocean. It was an easy fact to check before disclaiming it in a statement that more than a hundred million Americans and foreigners would read and believe.

Vidal's report claimed that: "their last accurate navigation check was over two hundred miles from that point . . ." There was no way Vidal could have knowledge that Post had made any accurate navigation check. Since Post died in the crash he could not have made a report about any of his activities while in flight; since there was no radio contact between Post and anyone on the ground, no one else could have known about this supposed "navigation check."

Vidal's contention "that the airplane had become nose-heavy on take-offs and landings following the installation of the floats" is a misstatement. The Department had in its possession documentation that the plane was quite nose-heavy even before the installation of floats and any inspector should have been aware of it. In the Bureau's files was a report that indicated that only on the day Vidal dictated this "report" did he bother to send an inquiry about the plane's weight distribution to one of his own assistants, L. V. Kerber, chief, Manufacturing Inspection Service. Kerber acted promptly and had sent his reply the next day, August 31. By that time, however, Vidal's report was finished and in the hands of the press. Therefore Kerber's information never became part of the Bureau's published findings.

What Kerber submitted was information that Inspector Reed should have requested weeks earlier; failing that, anyone investigating the crash should have asked for it on the first day of the inquiry. Kerber determined within 24 hours that ". . . the center of gravity of Post's Special Lockheed as a land plane was approximately 4", or 5% . . . further forward than the same airplane as approved before alterations."

Chief Kerber's report continued, stating that the weight of the pontoons moved the center of gravity still further forward. The much higher wind resistance of pontoons "acting below the center of gravity induces a considerable diving moment which is the equivalent of a still further forward movement of the center of gravity."

Kerber's conclusion was a death sentence:

> . . . the balance of the seaplane was such that, in the event of loss of propeller blast over the tail due to engine failure, an uncontrolled dive would ensue, from which recovery could not be expected under an altitude of 300 to 400 feet.

This meant that once the plane's single engine had stalled—for whatever reason—the plane would immediately nose-dive; a pilot would need between 300 and 400 feet of altitude before he could recover control of the plane. Wiley's estimated altitude at the time of the stall over Walakpa Lagoon was, at best, 200 feet.

When no facts were available for Vidal's report, supposition took over. He claimed that at Walakpa Lagoon "Post probably looked over his plane from the pontoons before the motor was started by hand." Every pilot will inspect his engine before starting it, but there was no need to start the plane by hand. The electric starter was working, or one of the Eskimos would have reported so obvious an effort as little Wiley Post starting an engine with a three-bladed propeller by hand.

Vidal kept his opinion about the cause of the crash to the end of his summary:

> It appears reasonable to believe that Post was banking the plane to the right while still in a slight climb, since with the low ceiling he would turn in the direction of Point Barrow along the coast line immediately after gaining sufficient altitude for maneuvering. . . . The combination of the plane in a banking turn, with still low flying speed immediately following the take-off and climb, the motor failure and the airplane's nose heaviness, could result in such a stall. . . . We are inclined to believe that with the moisture in the air as it existed that day, and the temperature as it was reported, ice could have developed in the carburetor. Either that, or the spray from the water in taking off could have entered the scoops and in that way caused icing.

This summary is interesting for its diplomacy, if not for its persuasion. Mr. Vidal carefully walked the narrow path among a number of possibly guilty parties, only to find no one to indict. Although Post maneuvered "the plane in a banking turn, with still low flying speed immediately following the take-off and climb."—an unspeakable crime according to any pilot's Bible—there is no word of reproach. Carburetor icing is mentioned as a possible culprit, and it might be—though not in the mind of many Alaskan pilots or mechanics. And spray from the surface of the lagoon entering the scoops, is Mr. Vidal's third, and least likely, candidate for the crash.

Reading Director Vidal's statement about the events of the crash while sitting in his home in Fairbanks, Jim Hutchison shook his head. Working for PAA, Jim was an experienced airplane mechanic and wise to the ways of Alaskan aviation. He had had a good chance to study Wiley's plane. "I didn't think much of it. I don't think anyone else did, either. Wooden airplane, low wing, had Fairchild 71 floats on it,—I don't know—the thing was built up from different models, big prop—big three-bladed propeller— but the engine is the thing that worried me on account of the size of the thing, great big cowling and he couldn't see too good over it . . . I looked at the airplane sitting out there and I could tell that it looked funnier than the Dickens . . . I don't think I would have flown in that plane, I didn't like the looks of it . . . We do know what happened—I do in my own mind. When he took off from this lagoon, he had flown all the way from here, I bet you he was short of gas—not too short, but when he took off he made this steep climb and bank and he tips his wing up, there was no gas in this tank on the upper side of the wing, or anyway near dry . . . when he banked like that—even though the lower tanks may have a lot of gas, if that wasn't enough to get into the outlet and fill the pump, you know, the pump sucked air, it only took one instant and the engine quit."

Jim Hutchison paused, he usually didn't talk this much, but he had given this matter a lot of thought over the years. "If he would have listened to old Crosson, he would be alive today, too . . . . Crosson would have taken him up there with his own— one of the Pan American airplanes . . . in a Fairchild 71 on floats. . . . Sure Crosson wanted to, he tried every which way to talk him out of taking that thing up there. . . ." Jim Hutchison's voice trailed off.

Jim had mentioned a critical point, although he had not realized it. He had probably come up with the only correct reason for the crash. For the major part of his flying career, Wiley Post had piloted Lockheed Vegas, high-wing planes which supplied fuel to the carburetor by gravity feed. The tanks were in the wing above the engine and the fuel flowed downward into the carbure-tor. On his hybrid "bastard," which was a low-wing plane, fuel had to be pumped by suction from the tanks in the wings below the fuselage, up to the carburetor. Most pilots flying a low-wing plane would try to keep one tank only for take-offs. Once in flight, they would switch to another one. The reasoning was, that when taking off with the plane in a steeply inclined position, the fuel intake line would always come from a full tank, rather than from one that might be near empty. The tank used for take-offs usually contained a higher octane rated fuel than the gasoline used in cruising. Wiley was not used to low-wing planes and their idiosyncrasies. The take-off at Walakpa Lagoon was the first one Post made with this plane when all the tanks were not full. Leaving from Chena Slough to fly to Harding Lake, there was plenty of gasoline in the tank he was using, though the rest had not been filled. But when Post took off from the lagoon, he was most likely on the same tank he had used when landing, and no one will ever know how much—or rather how little—fuel there was left in that tank. Not even Wiley would have known accurately, for he had no fuel gauges on five of his six tanks. There was no warning system to alert the pilot that fuel in the tank was too low for a steep ascent. With Wiley's habit of draining the last drop of fuel from a tank before switching to a fresh one, it is natural to assume that he followed that same pattern on this flight. Climbing abruptly, as was reported by eyewitnesses, and banking to the right, all six tanks would be in a tipped position. The residue of fuel in a tank would thus seek the lowest point. If there is insufficient fuel left, the fuel pump would suck air into the carburetor, forcing the engine into a mechanical stall. The conclusion reached by the Bureau of Air Commerce never considered human error. It should have.

Warren Tilman, too, had worked on Wiley's plane and had inspected it closely. Wondering how Wiley Post rated the strange-looking aircraft, Tilman asked him. The 'round-the-world traveler admitted: "Screwiest damn plane I ever flew." Tilman would never forget Post's words, and no amount of money could have induced him to fly in that plane.

Both Hutchison and Tilman had worked on the plane and they had examined it carefully, but nobody from Washington ever came to question Jim or Warren; not even the government's inspector, Murray Hall, who was right there with them in Fairbanks, and who had been ordered to investigate the crash.

Roscoe Turner, one of America's foremost fliers, shared Jim Hutchison's key to the cause of the crash. Roscoe Turner was convinced that the accident was due to using a fuel-feed from an almost empty tank. This, he said, would easily account for the engine stopping just after take-off.

In a copyrighted story from Seattle, Universal Service quoted the dean of Alaskan fliers, Noel Wien. As so many men who were thoroughly familiar with the north country, he did not even consider carburetor icing, but blamed "impossible weather and fuel supply failure" as the causes of the crash. The press service reported:

> Noel Wien declared that it was his belief that Post emptied one of the gasoline tanks of his monoplane, and then failed to switch to the other. He said Post probably had no warning of the fuel shortage until he attempted to bank sharply when only a few feet above the lagoon in which he and Rogers had landed to ask the way to Point Barrow. . . .
>
> A climbing turn, such as Post tried to make, according to the descriptions of native witnesses to the tragedy, would have put the entire strain of carrying the plane on the motor, then, if the motor failed, it would be too bad—as it was.

The United States Senate sat in safe, sweltering Washington, D.C., and no senator was about to go on a dangerous investigating junket to Barrow, Alaska. Of course, the Senate investigating committee did not know that Inspector Hall had already filed a hearsay report. He, like the senators, had not been too anxious to take the perilous trip. Vidal had relied on Joe Crosson's first-hand knowledge of what took place in Juneau and Fairbanks, and what Post had told him. As to the crash itself, everybody relied on someone else's hearsay and beliefs, for no one had reliable, first-hand information.

And then, there had been Inspector Phil C. Salzman's letter. It was typed on official Department of Commerce stationery, Office headquarters Sixth Inspection District, Kansas City Airport, K.C. Missouri, and was dated August 23, 1935. It told of the writer sharing a plane ride with Joe Crosson, who was on his way back to California, having attended Wiley Post's funeral in Oklahoma. The letter contained bits of new information:

>Mr. Crosson said . . . that he believed had Post been
>flying a Vega and not an Orion seaplane, with which he
>was not too familiar, he would have gotten away with it
>and would have made a safe landing.
>
>Mr. Post had requested Crosson to fly the air-
>plane, as he did not like the characteristics, and Crosson
>said he wished he had done so as he probably would
>know more about what happened.

Wiley and Joe talked as close friends and fellow pilots. They would freely exchange the straightforward facts. Wiley had no reason either to cover up the shortcomings of his plane, nor did he have to exaggerate. Therefore, when Wiley Post admitted that he "did not like the [plane's] characteristics," we have confirmation of Wiley's statement to Warren Tilman "Screwiest damn plane I ever flew." Crosson's opinion that Wiley would "have gotten away with it" if he had been flying a Vega and not an Orion seaplane, "with which he was not too familiar," is the conclusion of an expert that Wiley was not too adept at handling this type of plane. It corroborated a belief widely held in the flying community.

It is also significant to note that Joe Crosson declined the offer to fly Wiley's plane. Instead he had offered to fly Wiley to Barrow, but not in Wiley's plane!

The Department of Air Commerce, having issued a prelimi- nary report, was now in an awkward position. Sooner or later it would have to render a final decision on an accident about which it knew relatively little. It could not declare once again that the cause for the crash was the fact that the plane hit the water; it would have to satisfy one hundred thirty million Americans, and half the world. It would have to sound knowledgeable, sincere, logical, while hurting no one's ego or damaging anyone's reputa- tion. It seemed an almost impossible task. It was perhaps easiest for all concerned to point accusingly in the direction of carbure- tor icing. It had a certain ring of logic that could not be entirely refuted, nor disproved. A little hint that the engine had stalled— for whatever cause, did not hurt; that is, it did not hurt the Department. But it could do enormous damage to Pratt & Whitney, the manufacturers of that engine.

It is always convenient to claim malfunction of an engine. After all, did not the engine stop in mid-air? But it could have

stalled for a number of reasons. There could have been an aerodynamic stall, caused by too steep an angle of climb on Post's part;
then there could have been a stall due to Post's sharp right turn
and the intake pipe sucking air instead of fuel into the carburetor.
Then, of course, the stall could have been due to tiny ice particles
blocking finely adjusted needle valves. None of these could be
even remotely considered a malfunction of the engine. But because of this initial blame on a carburetor blockage—which in
most minds translated into a fault of the Pratt & Whitney engine—
the company kept in the background. It was, after all, possible
that there could have been something drastically wrong with
some engine part.

An internal memorandum, dated August 28, 1935 and
signed by H. M. Horner, Pratt & Whitney's assistant corporate
secretary, later chairman of the board, suggested that "this engine
be written off immediately. It is now in the consignment account
at $3500." The following day, a response to this memo signed
D. L. Brown, Pratt & Whitney's president, agreed and suggested:
"Personally, I feel that we should drop the matter and write the
engine off in our year-end adjustment." Even though Pratt &
Whitney felt quite certain that its engine was not responsible for
the crash, the company believed that it was cheaper to write the
engine off as a total loss, than invite additional adverse publicity.
Efforts to recover the engine were sure to make new headlines.
Only immeasurable harm could result from a close association
with an engine connected with the number one tragedy in the
country.

But matters became known that began to shed a different
light on the crash. In New York, Wiley's "flying acquaintances"
offered a new image. Pilots who knew the globe-girdling flier
intimately could not recall that he ever had flown a marine type
plane. Veteran seaplane pilots said that the unaccustomed bulk of
these floats might be disastrous even to a pilot of Post's ability, if
he found himself in a sudden jam. These reports caused quite a
flurry as for the first time some guilt was cast on America's hero,
Wiley Post. But Wiley himself might have contributed to that
opinion. "I don't know much about Alaska," Post had been
quoted in the *Seattle Post–Intelligencer*, "I haven't had much
experience flying planes with pontoons. I wonder how it's going
to work out."

This onset of open doubt in Wiley Post's hitherto unquestioned mastery of the air caused a change of heart at Pratt & Whitney. No longer did the company want to be disassociated from any involvement in the crash; it now considered reclaiming the engine. Actually, this decision may have been triggered by another developing news item. Newspapers reported that Sergeant Stanley R. Morgan, in Barrow, Alaska, had answered an inquiry about the salvage of Wiley Post's plane. He stated that he believed salvage operation with a crew of 15 or 20 men could load the fuselage and the engine on small boats and bring them to Barrow. He estimated the cost to be approximately $500, including men and boats. He doubted that pontoons and other small parts were worth salvage unless for a particular purpose other than repair.

Before action was taken by any Washington agency, Charles Brower, as the Commissioner in charge, took it upon himself to send "twenty-five men with a couple of lighters and a launch to try and save what was left of the wrecked plane." Winter was coming fast, and with it he expected serious damage to any part of the plane immersed in water. It turned out to be a two-day job. Lashed to two whale boats, pontoon-like, and towed by the motor boat, the men brought back what was left of the fuselage, the engine and propeller. Brower stashed the fuselage out in the open where the early snow soon spread a blanket over it. He took the engine and the propeller into his warehouse. Then on September 9, 1935, he wired Pratt & Whitney:

> ON ACCOUNT OF WEATHER CONDITIONS WITH-
> OUT AUTHORITY HAVE SALVAGED ENGINE AND
> BROUGHT SAME TO BARROW STOP . . .

Brower suggested that if Pratt & Whitney were interested, he would clean and inspect the engine for a small additional charge. Pratt & Whitney ordered him to go ahead.

Three weeks later, September 30th, 1935, Charles D. Brower wrote:

> At your request I have taken to pieces and cleaned
> your engine. Reassembled the same and crated it for
> shipment the coming summer . . .

I found that the main part of the engine was all-most [sic] perfect in its working parts. The engine had evidently stoped [sic] dead before the crash as the principal parts were in perfect working order after cleaning. allthough [sic] every place in the inside was full of sand even the cylinders and timing gear were full. but [sic] after cleansing and oiling they worked perfectly.

Of Course [sic] all the outside parts were smashed beyoud [sic] repair. [sic] and the Alloy parts that had been under water so long were all eaten away and turned to a grey clay which rapidly dissolved in gasolene [sic] . . .[4]

In late December newspapers across America carried a little item, stating Brower's surprising deduction:

Charles D. Brower, veteran of half a century as an Arctic trader, whaler and trapper, said today the motor of the Wiley Post–Will Rogers plane stored in his warehouse here, is in perfect condition despite the crash which cost the lives of the two flyers last August.

Brower's knowledge of gas engines is extensive.

The engine may have been found to be in fine working order, but by that time the governmental investigations had long ended and the official conclusion had been published. Case closed!

A lengthy telegraphic exchange ensued between Charles Brower and Pratt & Whitney about the return of the engine. Though a whole year would pass before the engine finally reached East Hartford, Connecticut, the company's home, Pratt & Whitney was glad to have its engine back. Charley Brower charged $400 for salvage; it was only $40 more than his actual cost.

At the factory, the engine was thoroughly checked and was found to be in perfect working condition, just as Charley Brower had stated. There was no reason not to use the engine in other aircraft. It was rebuilt and sent out. Yet somehow a certain aura of failure followed this engine. It was never installed in a contract-winning model.

On February 9, 1937, the engine went to Northrop in Inglewood, California, for use in the Gamma 2J, a plane that was entered into use as a demonstrator in competition for the U.S. Army contract for basic and advanced trainers. Some ignition problems developed, along with installation mount complications in this particular aircraft, and the engine was returned to the plant sometime later that year.

On April 6, 1937, the engine went back out on consignment to Seversky Aircraft, Farmingdale, New York, for their XBC, Experimental Basic Combat trainer. Again the engine was used for demonstration purposes in competition for the U.S. Army trainer contract that North American eventually won.

After the engine came back from Seversky, it was finally sold on December 21, 1938, to Compania de Aviacion Faucett, in Lima, Peru, for domestic flight use. As far as it is known, the engine that carried Will Rogers and Wiley Post to their deaths may still be in use today.

The fuselage belonged to Mrs. Post, and Charles Brower notified her that he had it and asked for her instructions. Mae Post replied that she was most anxious to have the instrument panel returned. She needed those instruments to consummate the sale of the *Winnie Mae* to the Smithsonian Institution. The requirement for the transaction had been that the plane be restored to the exact condition at the time of the solo 'round-the-world flight, in 1933. Without the completed instrument panel, the deal would have fallen through.[5]

By the time Mae Post's request was received, winter had come and there was no further physical contact with the outside world. The instruments did not leave Barrow until April, 1936.

As far as the rest of the plane was concerned, Mae Post wanted it destroyed so that it would never be used by souvenir hunters or sellers. As it turned out she was too late. Many of the Eskimos, including Clair Okpeaha, had already used some of the metal parts to make rings. Some of these were worn by the Eskimos themselves, while many more were sold.

In the Arctic spring Tom Brower, in accordance with Mae Post's wishes, towed the rest of the plane out to sea and sank it—that is, all but one item: it was one of the pontoons that looked so much like a kayak. "Looking at it," he said in an interview, "it wasn't damaged—I used it—I took it out to the ranch and I was going to use if for a little skiff, you know, towed behind the boat in case I had to come ashore, but we got in a storm and I lost it.

One of the big lakes, it went right down, never came out—I just cut the rope—it got swamped . . ."

Commissioner Brower kept two items from the plane for himself. One was the Lockheed trademark, the other the official license number, both cut from the tail section of the plane. These two items still hang in Mattie's Cafe in Browerville, a section of Barrow, Alaska. The cafe, once called Brower's Cafe, is now owned by Tom Brower's daughter and carries her name. Like all buildings on the North Slope, it stands on stilts driven into the permafrost, between the Brower home and Brower's Trading Post, just a few feet from the edge of the Beaufort Sea.

If Rogers and Post had reached Barrow safely, they would have been guests of Charley Brower, probably staying at his home. They would have walked these same gravel surfaces, perhaps buying some staples at the Trading Post, or drinking the strong, hot coffee while munching crispy, thin Eskimo doughnuts at the Cafe.

The Bureau of Air Commerce received a number of inquiries from insurance companies and lawyers. Their concerns were almost identical. To settle insurance claims on the life of Will Rogers they all requested to know whether Wiley Post was a licensed pilot, and whether they could have abstracts of his and the plane's licenses. Among those asking for documentation were: Duncan & Mount, 27 William Street, NYC; United States Aviation Underwriters, 80 John St., NYC; Swett & Crawford, 621 So. Hope Street, Los Angeles;[6] Lawler & Degnan, 800-810 Standard Oil Bldg., Los Angeles; and Republic Investment Corporation, 6331 Hollywood Blvd., Hollywood, California.

The following cable added an air of mystery to the Commerce Department's doings:

GRAY
London

Secretary of State
Washington
470, September 25, 3 p.m.　　　　dated Sept. 25, 1935.
　　　　　　　　　　　　　　　　Recd 11:20 a.m.
FROM COMMERCIAL ATTACHE FOR COMMERCE.

STRICTLY CONFIDENTIAL. 21. CABLE IMMEDIATELY TYPE OF LICENSE FOR WILEY POST PLANE INVOLVED

IN FATAL ACCIDENT AND WHETHER CERTIFICATE
OF AIRWORTHINESS PERMITTED CARRIAGE OF NON-
FAREPAYING PASSENGER AND WHETHER CERTIFI-
CATE WAS INVALIDATED BECAUSE OF NOSE-HEAVI-
NESS OR SUBSTITUTION OF FLOATS FOR WHEELS.
INFORMATION URGENTLY NEEDED IN ORDER TO RE-
COVER PORTION OF ROGER'S INSURANCE.

BINGHAM

This is what the State Department answered:

SEPTEMBER 26, 1935
27e
BUREAU OF FOREIGN AND
DOMESTIC COMMERCE.

COMMERCIAL ATTACHE   LONDON, ENGLAND

YOUR TWENTYONE AIR COMMERCE ADVISES LI-
CENSE RESTRICTED ISSUE UNDER SECTION FIFTEEN
AIR COMMERCE REGULATIONS STOP NONFARE PAY-
ING PASSENGER PERMITTED AS MEMBER CREW
SUCH AS OBSERVER NAVIGATOR ETCETERA STOP
LICENSE NOT INVALIDATED CHANGE OF EQUIP-
MENT PERMITTED UNDER RESTRICTED LICENSE
WHEN IN FURTHERANCE PARTICULAR PURPOSE
FOR WHICH LICENSE ISSUED.

MURCHESON

It can be assumed that the inquiry was prompted by the
insurance policy taken out with Lloyd's of London just hours
before the fatal crash. But it is interesting to see how government
likes to stay on both sides of an argument at all times. Knowing
that Will Rogers was a "fare paying passenger" in all but the
issuance of a ticket, it still did not wish to offer insurance companies a legal argument on which to refuse payment of claims. To
do so would have meant shouldering liability; and accepting

responsibility—as Will Rogers would have been the first to point out—is never governmental policy.

The final official word about the accident came exactly two months after the crash.[7] It appeared in the *AIR COMMERCE BULLETIN*, Vol.7, No.4, October 15, 1935, p.94. It was the report of the "Accident Board," and was signed Jesse Lankford, secretary. It repeated all that had been said before, and concluded:

> The exact cause of the engine failure cannot be determined. The temperature at the time was about 40 and the failure could have been due to the engine having become cool while standing on the lagoon or to ice or water condensate forming in the carburetor. It is the opinion of the accident board that the probable cause of this accident was loss of control of the aircraft at a low altitude after sudden engine failure, due to the extreme nose-heaviness of the aircraft.

The findings were naive. Though shut off for ten minutes, the engine could not have cooled in so short a time; nor would any ice have formed in the carburetor. As for claiming that the "probable" *cause* for the accident was "loss of control at a low altitude after sudden engine failure, due to the extreme nose-heaviness of the aircraft" is incorrect; it was not the "cause," it was the *result*. The "cause" was not the plane's nose-heaviness, which would have taken several hundred feet of altitude to allow a skilled pilot to bring the plane into a gliding attitude and land; the cause for the accident was that this plane was ever licensed to fly.

From the moment Wiley Post told Inspector Reed that he liked "the plane's flying characteristics, particularly its stability, balance, and ease of maneuverability," just to get a license for his "Bastard," this plane had a rendezvous with tragedy. It is perhaps a credit to Wiley Post's flying ability that it had not happened earlier, for it had to happen eventually. But the Bureau of Air Commerce would not admit it.

All was as had been expected. What the Bureau disclosed was a dream—a mirage in which there were no guilty parties, no contributory negligence, no disregard of rules, no violation of laws, no omissions, no lies. No one was to blame, no one had erred, no one had either by commission or by omission contributed to the accident. It was all conveniently blamed on carburetor icing, some tiny ice crystals that would immediately melt in the sun, leaving no trace. Two men had died, and the experts in their infinite wisdom had determined that it was no one's fault.

It was exactly as Will Rogers had written about another investigation in April, 1934:

> . . . investigations start out so sensationally and peter out so quietly. Investigations are held just for photographers.

CHAPTER TEN

POSTSCRIPT

This thing of being a hero, about the main thing to
it is to know when to die. Prolonged life has
ruined more men then it ever made.
—Will Rogers, *Daily column*, July 17, 1928

A large number of letters flooded into the Bureau of Air Commerce, suggesting possible causes for the crash. Almost all of
them were written by well-meaning people. One such letter, still
available, suggested the cause to be Wiley Post's cigarette smoking.
Of course, Wiley hardly ever smoked. The writer's assumption
was based on Post's endorsements of Camel cigarettes. Will
Rogers also did not smoke, though he, too, at one time had
endorsed a cigarette tobacco, Bull Durham. But he had made it
clear at the time that while he endorsed this tobacco, he, himself,
did not use it.

In another letter dated September 9, 1935, and addressed
to Eugene Vidal, a Captain C.J. Hutchinson from Seattle, Washington, suggested another cause for the crash. Apparently in 1906,
Captain Hutchinson was a member of the U.S. Geological Survey

> . . . doing North Arctic exploration and [I] traveled in an
> open boat along the coast line to Point Barrow. We
> would experience great difficulty with the air currants
> [sic]—sometimes the native boats of the Eskimo would
> be lifted out of the water and our own large dory boat
> tossed like a chip. They were known as "woolies". The
> perpinduclar [sic] ocean beach line rising abruptly and

sometimes very high from the waters [sic] edge seemed
to start a "twister". Could it not have been this that
caused the Rogers-Post plane disaster?

In his reply, dated September 24, 1935, Eugene Vidal
thanked the writer but pointed out that weather and wind conditions "were in all probability not the deciding factors, except for
the fact that there was a low ceiling and also freezing temperature
at the time of the crash."

But Captain Hutchinson was adamant and wrote again. It is
Director Vidal's second response, dated October 8, 1935, which
carries a partial admission never included in any official statement. Wrote Eugene Vidal:

> In the case of the Post-Rogers accident, however, we do
> not feel that strong or peculiar air currents played any
> material part. To the contrary, the few witnesses to the
> accident were in good agreement as to the flight path
> from the take-off from the lagoon to the point of impact.
> This path was just what might be expected under the
> circumstances and showed no indication of influence
> from unusual air currents.
>   These witnesses also agree on engine failure. Just
> what caused the engine to fail will never be known as the
> engine was buried in several feet of mud and water. The
> causes suggested in our public statement are *very theo-
> retical*, but are possibilities. [Emphasis added.]

This candor is surprising and hidden in a letter, but even here it
does not go far enough. While the causes suggested by the
Department of Air Commerce were indeed "possibilities," they
were not all the possibilities, merely the convenient ones. It is
understandable that the authorities neither wanted to accept responsibility, nor did they wish to point an accusing finger in any
direction.

     This assertion is obvious. The Department of Air Com-
merce spent more time and effort on establishing the limits of its
obligations than it did on trying to check the plane, the engine,
mechanics, or even interviewing eyewitnesses.

A letter dated October 3, 1953, addressed to Duncan & Mount, 27 William Street, NYC, NY, and signed for J. M. Johnson, assistant secretary of Commerce, reads:

> Said aircraft license . . . permitted three persons to be aboard said airplane while in flight *provided that none of them were passengers carried for hire.* Restricted aircraft licenses "R" or "NR" are issued to aircraft not eligible for commercial passenger carrying licenses, *but on inspection and approval by a Department of Commerce inspector are found to be airworthy for specially designated purposes.* [Emphasis added.]

Either everybody trusted everybody to do the right thing, or nobody really cared. Certainly nobody went by the book. No inspector tested Wiley's plane for airworthiness. Wiley evidently never told an inspector that the plane was nose-heavy. The Department never once alluded to the most obvious cause for the engine to stall, that air was sucked into the carburetor. Nowhere is it mentioned that Post was unfamiliar with low-wing planes and sea planes in particular. Stating such facts would have meant identifying those officials whose actions, or inactions, contributed to two deaths. And when there is active, or even inactive, participation in the death of others, a culpable act has been committed.

Will Rogers trusted Wiley Post; he thought him one of the great pilots of the age. Wiley tried to publicly rationalize Will's presence by claiming he was an observer. Rogers paid for repairs, for fuel and for all other expenses, hardly the action of an "observer." The reality is that Rogers paid for the privilege of having Wiley act as his private pilot. Mae Post stated in an interview that Rogers was paying for the trip and therefore had her stay behind when the two men flew to Alaska. This surely indicates that Will Rogers was a paying passenger, an infraction of the terms of the restricted license. If further proof for this breach is necessary, it is provided by the "manifest" issued by Canadian authorities when Will and Wiley crossed into the Northwest Territory. Will is simply described as "1 Passenger"—mind you, not "1 Observer" or "1 Crew Member."

It could be argued that Wiley probably needed Will's generosity to make the search for the air route possible. Will was surely very happy with the arrangement he had with Post. But those are merely rationalizations, simple excuses, and none of them sufficient to warrant the loss of two lives.

The facts are that two men died and the question remains whether it was an accident, unavoidable, an act of God, or merely the result of the heedlessness of men. Could Will Rogers' and Wiley Post's deaths have been averted? Surely the plane should have been denied a license as not being "airworthy." Post should never have allowed Rogers aboard that plane, nor indeed his own wife, or both of them, as he did on their flight to New Mexico, Arizona, Utah, and Nevada earlier in July.

And why did two rational men take off from a secure haven at Fairbanks and rush toward a perilous Barrow harbor where the latest information available had told them plainly that they would be unable to land? Why would two men fly against the advice of seasoned local pilots and weathermen? Because these were not two ordinary men. Knowing the dangers would never deter them—either one of them. They had absolute faith in themselves and they were totally convinced of their indestructibility.

Could their violent deaths have been avoided? Certainly! At least that day in August, 1935. But if given a choice, each man would have gladly elected this type of exit.

WILL ROGERS

His kindness and the innocuous way in which he delivered his most pointed observations disarmed the world. It was not that his comments fell short of their mark. There was usually stinging criticism in what he said, but his most acid statements were invariably couched in such delicious phraseology that it moved one victim to remark that Mr. Rogers was like a dentist who pulled your tooth first and gave you laughing gas afterwards.
—*NY Herald Tribune*, August 17, 1935.

P.P.S.

Mrs. Wiley Post received $25,000 from the sale of the *Winnie Mae* to the Smithsonian Institution. She used the money to purchase a 500-acre cotton farm in the Texas Panhandle. She operated the farm and lived there quietly. She rarely gave interviews. Mrs. Post never remarried; she died in 1984, and was buried beside her husband in Edmond, Oklahoma.

The rotating warning signal on the eastern support of the George Washington Bridge, spanning the Hudson River between New Jersey and New York, was named the Will Rogers–Wiley Post Beacon. A plaque was unveiled at the Newark, New Jersey, airport observation deck, dedicating it to Wiley Post and Will Rogers. The Wiley Post Airport in Oklahoma City, Oklahoma, is one of several honors due his achievements. Two air-mail stamps have been issued in Wiley Post's memory, but only a single major biography was ever written. A statue detailing his achievements was erected in Oklahoma City's Civic Center in 1963. It is regrettable that Wiley Post's great accomplishments and his important contributions to aviation have been allowed to be forgotten and ignored.

Mrs. Will Rogers continued to live quietly on the couple's ranch in Pacific Palisades, California. She wrote *Will Rogers, His*

Wife's Story, which was serialized in the Saturday Evening Post and made into a motion picture, starring Will Rogers, Jr., and Jane Wyman. Mrs. Will Rogers never remarried; she died in 1944 and was buried beside her husband and infant son, Fred, in the crypt at the Memorial in Claremore, Oklahoma.

Will Rogers' popularity has been maintained through various shrines: The Will Rogers Memorial and Museum in Claremore, Oklahoma; Will Rogers' birthplace, Oologah, Oklahoma; The Will Rogers State Park (his home), in Pacific Palisades, California; the Will Rogers Beach (once his property), in Pacific Palisades; the Will Rogers Shrine of the Sun, Colorado Springs, Colorado; Will Rogers World Airport, Oklahoma City, Oklahoma; and numerous parks, buildings, and highways. The United States issued two postage stamps. A set of five stamps was issued by Nicaragua to express gratitude for his help after the earthquake of 1931. The Will Rogers Institute was renamed in his honor, dedicated to research and to help those in show-business who need medical assistance. His statue stands in Statuary Hall in the U.S. Capitol, in Washington, D.C., representing the state of Oklahoma. When the Cowboy Hall of Fame was created, Will Rogers was the first inductee. Busts stand in a number of places, paintings are in Oklahoma's state capitol and elsewhere. He has been the subject of many books and several stage presentations, including ''Will Rogers' U.S.A.'' and ''The Will Rogers Follies.''

EPILOGUE

He loved and was loved by the American people. His memory will ever be in benediction with the hosts of his countrymen who felt the spell of that kindly humor which, while seeing facts, could always laugh at fantasy. That was why his message went straight to the hearts of his fellow men. . . .

. . . we pay grateful homage to the memory of a man who helped the nation to smile. And, after all, I doubt if there is among us a more useful citizen than the one who holds the secret of banishing gloom, of making tears give way to laughter, of supplanting desolation and despair with hope and courage. For hope and courage always go with a light heart.

There was something infectious about his humor. His appeal went straight to the heart of the nation. Above all things, in a time grown too solemn and sober he brought his countrymen back to a sense of proportion.

With it all his humor and his comments were always kind. His was no biting sarcasm that hurt the highest or the lowest of his fellow citizens. When he wanted people to laugh out loud he used the methods of pure fun. And when he wanted to make a point for the good of mankind, he used the kind of gentle irony that left no scars behind it.

Franklin Delano Roosevelt

NOTES

Chapter One

1. Joseph (Joe) Crosson was to become chief pilot for Pacific Alaska Airways and one of the foremost Alaskan bush pilots. He came to national prominence for his mercy flights, bringing serum to Nome during a diphtheria epidemic.

2. Mrs. Hall died late in 1930.

3. *Revolution in the Sky*, Richard Sanders Allen, page 82.

4. The actual flying time for the 15,474 miles was 107 hours and 2 minutes, which meant that the *Winnie Mae* averaged 144.57 miles per hour. Consuming 3,455 gallons of fuel, the Wasp engine averaged 4.479 miles per gallon, or 32.28 gallons for the average hour in flight.

5. Bennie Turner was the aviation editor of the *Daily Oklahoman* and one of Wiley's friends.

6. *Oklahoma City Times*, July 31, 1933.

7. "It was only a two passenger plane; let's face it. No, she was never going." From interview with Fay Gillis Wells, November 12, 1985.

8. Ibid.

9. Interview and correspondence with Lyman Brewster, General Reindeer Superintendent, Department of the Interior (1932–1936), headquarters at Nome, Alaska:

   As related to me by Lyman Peck . . . Lyman felt sorry for him [Post], off-handedly mentioned that Rogers had mentioned going to Alaska. Peck never forgave himself for that ill-considered remark . . . Peck would nearly cry when he later related his involvement. Lyman [Peck] said he made it to get Post out of his hair.

Chapter Two

1. Interview with Joe Keaton, *Seattle Daily Times*, August 22, 1935.

2. *London Times*, Thursday, May 24, 1906, p. 12, col. 5.

3. *New York Times*, November 3, 1935, Section VII, p. 4.

4. Will Rogers, *Weekly Article*, December 25, 1925.

5. *Seattle Sunday Times*, August 18, 1935.

6. Interview with Anne Shoemaker, June 21, 1977.

7. Will Rogers, *Daily Column*, August 1, 1934.

Chapter Four

1. *Will Rogers*, Betty Rogers, page 305.

2. Section based on Rex Beach's account.

3. Interview with Warren Tilman, July 21, 1986.

4. Interview with Mrs. Lillian Crosson Frizell.

5. Ex: official statement by Department of Commerce, Washington D.C., released September 4, 1935.

Chapter Six

1. Ex: letter written December 27, 1935 by Charles D. Brower to Bert Bernet, St. Louis, MO.

2. *Nursing under the North Star*, Mollie Greist, page 143.

3. Ibid.

Chapter Nine

1. MEMORANDUM   August 30, 1935
   To: Assistant Secretary Johnson
   Through: Director of Air Commerce
   From: Assistant Director of Air Commerce (Regulations)

   1. For your information and files, and for the possible future information of the Secretary, there follows a summary of incidents securing, and action taken by me subsequent to the Post–Rogers accident in Alaska. I shall be pleased to amplify this document with further details at your request at any time. It is my firm belief that you can easily conclude from this summary that each action was logical and justifiable, and that no additional or different steps could, or should have been taken.
   2. As soon as I heard on Friday, August 16, the report that Post and Rogers had been killed in Alaska, I radioed our Inspector in Alaska to make an immediate investigation and supply at the earliest possible moment all available details. I also contacted your office and you instructed me to keep you informed regarding developments and you were given the information that I had contacted the Signal Corps of the Army, and the Coast Guard for assistance and any information and that the Coast Guard suggested that upon request from you it might be possible for them to turn the Coast Guard cutter *Northland* around, which had left the day before from Point Barrow and send it back to Barrow to return the bodies. I quote herewith the first radiogram sent to Inspector Hall and his reply which was received the same day.
   "REPORT RECEIVED POST AND ROGERS KILLED THIS MORNING ENROUTE NORTH FROM ANCHORAGE OR FAIRBANKS STOP RADIO AVAILABLE INFORMATION IMMEDIATELY STOP USE ARMY RADIO IN CODE IF THIS DOES NOT CAUSE DELAY OTHERWISE

REGULAR CHANNELS"

"REWIRE POST AND ROGERS DEPARTED FAIRBANKS FOR POINT BARROW ONE THIRTY PM FIFTEENTH STOP RADIO REPORT FROM BARROW INDICATES ACCIDENT OCCURRED ABOUT EIGHT PM SAME DAY STOP POST HAD STOPPED AT LAKE FIFTEEN MILES FROM BARROW AND ASKED DIRECTION TO BARROW FROM NATIVES LIVING ON LAKE STOP TAKING OFF FROM LAKE REPORT INDICATED SHIP CRASHED INTO SHALLOW WATER AFTER OBTAINING ALTITUDE OF FIFTY FEET KILLING BOTH INSTANTLY STOP NATIVE RAN TO BARROW WITH NEWS AND IT IS REPORTED THAT PARTY LEFT BARROW IN SKIN BOATS TO RESCUE BODIES STOP WEATHER AT BARROW HAZARDOUS POOR VISIBILITY FOG AND FREEZING TEMPERATURE STOP JOE CROSSON AND RADIO OPERATOR GLEASON LEFT FAIRBANKS FOR BARROW ELEVEN FIFTEEN AM TODAY AND WILL PROBABLY RETURN BODIES TO FAIRBANKS STOP NO OTHER DEPENDABLE INFORMATION NOW AVAILABLE STOP PREPARATION BEING MADE TO MAKE TRIP TO BARROW NS9 DEPARTURE TOMORROW MORNING STOP HAVE MADE ARRANGEMENTS WITH CROSSON TO OBTAIN ALL DETAILS AVAILABLE STOP TRIP CONSIDERED HAZARDOUS ADVISE IF ABSOLUTELY NECESSARY FOR BEST INTEREST OF BUREAU"

4. Before answering this wire, I received from the Registration Section, through the Manufacturing Inspection Service, information to the effect that the airplane was a Lockheed Orion 9E originally built in May, 1933, approved, and licensed as a landplane with 160 gallons of fuel and a 450 horsepower engine. It was changed to an Ohion 9E Special in November, 1933, because the engine was changed to a Wasp S1D1, 550 horsepower engine, approved, and licensed.

It was purchased by Post in February, 1935, whereupon he had it rebuilt and considerably altered. He retained the same fuselage, but installed the 'Sirius' model wing, the Wasp S3H1-G 550 horsepower engine which is 145 pounds heavier, 250 gallon fuel tank, and a Hamilton Standard 3 bladed controllable pitch propeller which was approximately 50 pounds heavier. Both the engine and the propeller changes must necessarily have increased the nose-heaviness of the airplane. In Seattle Post installed Edo J-5300 pontoons. The effect of changing from land gear to pontoons generally moves the center of gravity forward, that is, increases nose-heaviness, and, in addition, the much greater drag of pontoons below the center of gravity always induces a greater diving moment which is the equivalent of greater nose-heaviness. Since it was known that the airplane fell off on one wing at 50 feet and dove into the ground, it was clear that the engine failed and that he was unable to overcome the nose-heaviness, without the benefit of the propeller blast over the tail. Because of weather conditions it is quite likely that icing conditions in the carburetor caused the engine to miss after idling for some time.

It was obvious that Hall could learn nothing by visiting the scene of the accident that Crosson could not learn and report to Hall. However I also knew that the trip would be hazardous for Hall to attempt for several reasons. Flying conditions in the Arctic Circle are generally worse than elsewhere, the weather conditions were bad, Hall is not a blind flyer and was not familiar with the terrain to be traversed, and his airplane NS9 was totally unsuited for the trip along the shore line from Kotzebue to Point Barrow because of its limited range and the fact that no intermediate refueling stations exist.

5. I therefore prepared the following radiogram to Hall:

"RETEL COAST GUARD CUTTER NORTHLAND DEPARTED FROM BARROW YESTERDAY AND IS RETURNING TO BARROW TO PICK UP BODIES STOP YOUR TRIP TO BARROW NOT NECESSARY STOP GET ALL DETAILS FROM CROSSON AND RADIO ME STOP FOLLOW WITH LETTER AND COMPLETE INFORMATION. [emphasis in original]

Before sending the above on August 16, I called you and read to you Hall's message and my proposed reply. You remarked, "All right, keep me advised," and the message was sent at 8:30 P.M.

On Saturday, August 17, Hall mailed a written report, appended hereto, incorporating everything learned of the accident from Crosson and other.

7. At about 11 A.M. Monday, August 19, the Director asked me if I had sent Hall to the scene of the accident and then why I had not. I explained to him that I was unable to locate him on Friday, that I had communicated with you, and then enumerated to him all the detailed reasons above mentioned. The Director had the wwiredof [sic] Saturday, August 17, to me, which, up to this time, I had not seen.

8. The above mentioned message from Hall follows:

"JOE CROSSON ARRIVED FAIRBANKS WITH BODIES ABOUT EIGHT THIRTY AM TODAY STOP PLANE NOW IS TO CONTINUE TO SEATTLE SOUTHERN CALIFORNIA AND OKLAHOMA USING LOCKHEED ELECTRA AND LEAVING FAIRBANKS TOMORROW MORNING STOP MOTOR FAILURE IMMEDIATELY AFTER TAKEOFF PRIMARY CAUSE OF ACCIDENT STOP THERE WAS ONLY ONE EYE WITNESS A NATIVE STOP THE WEATHER NOT RESPONSIBLE STOP AB 87 AND LETTER FOLLOWS". [sic]

9. Rather than wait for Hall's written report to reach here by mail, and after discussion with you, I radioed Hall (Monday, August 19) as follows:

"THE SECRETARY WISHES YOU TO SEND A COMPLETE RADIO REPORT IN DETAIL OF ALL INFORMATION RELATIVE TO POST ROGERS ACCIDENT STOP THIS SHOULD INCLUDE EVERYTHING IN WRITTEN REPORT ALREADY MAILED AND ANY ADDITIONAL INFORMATION OBTAINABLE STOP EXPENSE NO CONSIDERATION BUT TIME IS AN IMPORTANT ELEMENT".

10. Later the same day, Monday, August 19, I was called into your office, with Messrs. Vidal, Martin, Kerlin and St. Clair present. You asked my why I had told you that Hall had been sent to the scene of the accident [underline in original]. I thereupon reminded you of my having read to you Hall's message and my proposed reply (paragraph 5 above). You recalled this incident at that time and also remembered that Mr. Martin told you that he would send a man to the scene of the accident.

The question was then raised as to why Hall had not accompanied Crosson on his flight to pick up and return the bodies. The reason which I advanced as probable will be seen later to have been substantially correct from the subject matter of a subsequent paragraph wherein Hall gives the real reasons.

11. I then wired Hall (same day, Monday August, 19) as follows:

"SOME DEPARTMENT PERSONNEL PUZZLED WHY YOU DID NOT ACCOMPANY CROSSON TO BARROW STOP WOULD SUCH A TRIP HAVE GAINED ADDITIONAL KNOWLEDGE REGARDING ACCIDENT AND WOULD IT HAVE BEEN ADVISABLE IN VIEW OF WEATHER AND RETURN LOAD STOP CONTINUE INVESTIGATION AND SEND COMPLETE DETAILS AT EARLIEST MOMENT BY MAIL STOP RADIO REPLY REGARDING FAILURE TO MAKE TRIP WITH CROSSON". [sic]

12. Hall's self-explanatory reply to this message and to the one quoted in paragraph 9 quoted herewith:

"RE WIRES OF NINETEENTH STOP JOE CROSSON AND RADIO OPERATOR GLEASON LEFT FAIRBANKS CHENA SLOUGH AT ELEVEN FIFTEEN AM THE SIXTEENTH FOR POINT BARROW STOP THE AIRPLANE USED WAS FAIRCHILDSEVENTY ONE WITH FUEL TANK CAPACITY OF ONE HUNDRED FORTY EIGHT GALLONS STOP THE PAY LOAD OF THIS AIRPLANE ON FLOATS IS APPROXIMATELY FOUR HUNDRED SIXTY POUNDS STOP BECAUSE OF WEATHER UNCERTAINTIES IT WAS DESIRABLE TO LOAD THE AIRPLANE CABIN WITH FIVE GALLON CANS OF GASOLINE TO THE LIMIT OF THE SHIPS PERFORMANCE STOP THIS ALSO DESIRABLE BECAUSE NO INTERMEDIATE FUELING POINTS EXIST STOP

ABOUT TEN CASES OR ONE HUNDRED GALLONS OF FUEL WAS IN
THE SHIPS CABIN STOP WITH THIS LOAD THE SHIP WAS UNABLE
TO TAKE OFF THE WATER STOP TAKE OFF WAS MADE ON THE
THIRD ATTEMPT AFTER THIRTY GALLONS OF GASOLINE HAD
BEEN REMOVED FROM THE CABIN STOP I WAS PRESENT DURING
THESE ATTEMPTS AND INDICATED TO JOE THE DESIRE TO AC-
COMPANY HIM STOP HE SAID TO ME THAT HE WOULD BE GLAD
TO TAKE ME BUT DID NOT KNOW WHETHER HE COULD GET
OFF WITH THE LOAD ALREADY ON BOARD STOP IN VIEW OF
THE NECESSITY OF CARRYING EXTRA FUEL FOR HIS OWN
SAFETY AND THE FACT THAT THE RETURN TRIP WOULD HAVE
TO BE MADE WITH THE ADDITIONAL WEIGHT OF THE BODIES
AND EFFECTS OF THE UNFORTUNATE MEN IT DID NOT APPEAR
THAT GOOD JUDGMENT WOULD PERMIT ME TO ACCOMPANY
HIM STOP IT WAS THEN THAT I HAD PREPARED NS NINE FOR
THE FLIGHT WHICH I PLANNED TO MAKE BY WAY OF KOTZBUE
[sic] AND WAINWRIGHT STOP ALSO ARRANGED WITH JOE
CROSSON TO OBTAIN ALL POSSIBLE INFORMATION FOR ME AND
SUPPLIED HIM WITH AB EIGHTY SEVEN WHICH REPORT HE RE-
TURNED TO ME AND HAS BEEN MAILED YOUR OFFICE STOP BY
GOING TO BARROW WITH JOE I DO NOT BELIEVE ANY ADDI-
TIONAL KNOWLEDGE COULD HAVE BEEN OBTAINED AS ONLY
ONE PERSON A NATIVE ACTUALLY SAW THE ACCIDENT AND JOE
DID NOT TAKE TIME TO GO TO THE SCENE TO THE ACCIDENT
SINCE THE BODIES WERE REMOVED TO POINTBARROW [sic]
AND IT IS ALWAYS DESIRABLE AT THAT POINT TO DEPART AS
SOON AS POSSIBLE TO AVOID THE CHANCE OF HAVING THE
WEATHER SHUT DOWN STOP JOE ARRIVED AT POINTBARROW
ABOUT FIVE PM AND DEPARTED FOR FAIRBANKS SHORTLY AF-
TER MIDNIGHT ARRIVING FAIRBANKS AT SEVEN THIRTY AM MY
REPORT INCLUDING COPIES OF FAIRBANKS NEWS MINER AND
AB EIGHTY SEVEN RETURNED FROM BARROW BY CROSSON
SHOULD ARRIVE YOUR OFFICE SOMETIME TUESDAY THE DATE
YOU RECEIVE THIS TELEGRAM AS IT WAS CARRIED TO SEATTLE
BY CROSSON IN ELECTRA AND CARRIED AIR MAIL POSTAGE FOR
THE TRIP TO WASHINGTON STOP INFORMATION ALREADY SUB-
MITTED NO DOUBT SEEMS MEAGER AND I HAVE NOT HEARD
ANYTHING DEFINITELY TO ADD TO MY WRITTEN REPORT AND
ONLY LITTLE TO MY PREVIOUS TELEGRAM REPORT STOP POSTS
AIRPLANE WAS SERVICED AT FAIRBANKS BY PAA AND EVERY-
THING WAS IN GOOD ORDER EXCEPT GENERATOR WHICH
COULD NOT BE DUPLICATED LOCALLY AND POST DECLINED A
SUBSTITUTE AT THAT TIME I BELIEVE BECAUSE THEY MAY HAVE
EXPECTED TO RETURN TO FAIRBANKS AFTER A SHORT VISIT AT

POINTBARROW STOP THE MORNING OF THE FIFTEENTH THE
PLANE WAS FUELED TO ONLY PART CAPACITY AT PAA DOCK IN
CHENA SLOUGH AT FAIRBANKS AND FLOWN BY POST TO LAKE
HARDING WHERE THE SHIP WAS COMPLETELY FUELED STOP
THIS DONE BECAUSE CHENA SLOUGH IS NOT STRAIGHT
ENOUGH TO GET OFF EASILY WITH HEAVY LADEN AIRCRAFT
STOP A SPECIAL WEATHER REPORT WHICH HAD BEEN RE-
QUESTED THE DAY BEFORE HAD NOT ARRIVE FORM
POINTBARROW STOP THE FAILURE OF THE REPORT TO ARRIVE
WAS DISCUSSED BY THE FLIERS AND JOE CROSSON WHO WAS
WITH THEM UNTIL THEY DEPARTED FOR HARDING LAKE AND
IT WAS DECIDED THAT THEY MIGHT JUST AS WELL GO ALONG
ANY WAY AND IF THE WEATHER BAD THEY WOULD LAND ON
SOME LAKE OR RIVER AND WAIT TILL IT WAS BETTER STOP
POST AND ROGERS WERE ALSO ADVISED THAT THEY COULD
PHONE IN FROM HARDING LAKE AND ASK IF REPORT YET RE-
CEIVED BUT THIS WAS NOT DONE STOP THE REPORT ARRIVED
AT FAIRBANKS AT ONE THIRTY PM AND READ NIL NIL STOP THE
FLIERS DEPARTED FROM HARDING LAKE ABOUT TWO PM THE
EXACT HOUR OF THE ACCIDENT HAS NOT BEEN LEARNED STOP
JOE CROSSON INFORMED ME THAT THE MEN LANDED ON A LA-
GOON APPARENTLY TO ASK THE DIRECTION TO
POINTBARROW THEY STOPPED THE PLANE ON THE BEACH OF
THE LAGOON IN FRONT OF NATIVE HUTS AND ASKED THE ONE
NATIVE PRESENT FOR DIRECTION STOP THEY REMAINED THERE
FOR POSSIBLY TEN MINUTES AND TOOK OFF AND AFTER RISING
ONLY FIFTY FEET OR SO TURNED RIGHT AND PLUNGED INTO
SHALLOW WATER STOP THE NATIVE RAN TO BARROW WITH
WORD THAT AN AIRPLANE HAD BLOWN UP STOP PARTY FROM
BARROW WAS ORGANIZED AND WENT BACK TO RECOVER OR
AID STOP WILEYS WATCH STOPPED AT EIGHT SEVENTEEN AND
ROGERS WATCH WAS RUNNING STOP ONLY KNOWLEDGE OF
PLANES BEHAVIOR OR CHARACTERISTICS WAS THAT POST HAD
TOLD JOE CROSSON IT WAS VERY NOSE HEAVY AND THAT HE
HAD TO KEEP TELLING WILL SIT TO THE REAR AND KEEP THE
LUGGAGE REAR WHEN LANDING AND TAKING OFF STOP WHEN
LEAVING CHENA SLOUGH FOR HARDING LAKE POST CLIMBED
HIS PLANE AT TAKE OFF VERY STEEPLY ACCORDING TO SEV-
ERAL WITNESSES INCLUDING JOE CROSSON STOP THE ONLY
CLUE THAT I HAVE TO SUGGEST AS A CAUSE FOR THE ACCIDENT
IS THAT IF THAT THE [sic] LAGOON NEAR POINTBARROW WILEY
CLIMBED HIS PLANE TOO STEEPLY AND STALLED OR AP-
PROACHED A STALL AS THE MOTOR MISSED HE MAY NOT HAVE
BEEN ABLE TO HOLD IT OUT OF THE ENSUING DIVE STOP IF

STILL DESIRABLE I WILL PROCEED TO POINTBARROW AND MAKE THE BEST POSSIBLE EXAMINATION OF THE WRECKAGE STOP IF THIS DESIRABLE PLEASE ADVISE AUTHORITY CHARTER RADIO EQUIPPED AIRPLANE FOR TRIP OR OK USE NS NINE GROUNDED AT PRESENT ACCOUNT PROPELLER BLADES." [Emphasis in original.]

13. This reply of Hall's was discussed at a meeting in your office (same day, Monday August 19) with Messrs. Kerlin and St. Clair present. It was felt that since the Secretary had released information to the Press to the effect that the Bureau had sent someone to investigate the accident, it would be advisable to make some gesture to make clear the Bureau's interest in the accident. It was first proposed by Mr. St. Clair to send Mr. Mulligan to Los Angeles to interview Mr. Crosson. I pointed out that this would engender undesirable publicity in view of the fact that Mr. Mulligan's participation, because of his specialized duties as Chief of the Enforcement Section, would raise the question as to whether or not violations were involved and indicate that some punitive action was warranted. It was next suggested by Mr. Kerlin that I be sent, but I pointed out that as head of the Regulations Division my participation could be considered in much the same light an Mr. Mulligan's. I suggested that the Director, whose activities embrace all functions of the Bureau, would be the logical choice. This was concurred in by all present, and Mr. Vidal left for Los Angeles on Tuesday, August 20.

14. On Mr. Vidal's return, he advised me that Crosson had told him that he (Crosson) had invited Hall to accompany him to Point Barrow, but that Hall would have to arrange for other means of transportation for returning.

15. It appeared from this that Hall had sent in inaccurate and erroneous reports. I thereupon wrote to both Crosson and Hall on Tuesday August 27 as per appended copies of my letters, both in order to secure written data for file purposes, and in order to remove any doubt of possible misunderstanding along the lines of events.

16. The Director radioed Hall on the same day (Tuesday, August 27th) as follows for undoubtedly the same reason:

"PLEASE RADIO WHETHER OR NOT CROSSON INFORMED YOU HE COULD TAKE YOU TO BARROW BUT NOT ON RETURN TRIP ALSO WHETHER OR NOT YOU CONSIDERED BARROW FLIGHT HAZARDOUS."

17. Hall's reply of August 27th to the above message is quoted herewith:

"REWIRE TWENTY SEVENTH STOP JOE CROSSON MADE NO DEFINITE OFFER TO TAKE ME TO POINT BARROW NOR DID HE SAY THAT HE COULD NOT TAKE ME STOP THE ADVISABILITY OF

MY ACCOMPANYING HIM WAS DISCUSSED AND IT WAS I THAT
DEFINITELY DECIDED NOT TO INSIST OR PRESS HIM FOR PAS-
SAGE IN VIEW OF HIS DESIRE TO CARRY ALL POSSIBLE EXTRA
FUEL STOP CROSSON ARRIVED IN FAIRBANKS FROM BARROW
WITH LESS THAN ONE HALF HOURS [sic] FUEL REMAINING STOP
IDID [sic] AND STILL DO CONSIDER A TRIP TO POINTBARROW
HAZARDOUS STOP SINCE RECEIVING YOUR WIRE I HAVE ASKED
TWO FAIRBANKS PILOTS WHETHER THEY FELT THAT A BAR-
ROW TRIP WAS HAZARDOUS STOP BOTH SAID THAT THEY DID
STOP IT WOULD NOT BE AS HAZARDOUS TO MAKE TRIP IN SHIP
EQUIPPED TO REPORT ITS POSITION BY RADIO FOR THEN IN
EVENT OF FORCED LANDING FOR ANY REASON SEARCHERS
WOULD HAVE GOOD CLUE AS TO WHERE TO SEARCH STOP NS
NINE ASSIGNED ME HAS RADIUS OF ACTION OF TWO HUNDRED
FORTY MILES STOP DISTANCE FAIRBANKS TO BARROW OVER
FIVE HUNDRED MILES STOP ENDICOTT MOUNTAIN RANGE LIES
BETWEEN BARROW AND FAIRBANKS AND CROSSING IS USU-
ALLY GAINED THROUGH ONE OR TWO LOWER PASSES STOP I
HAD PLANNED TO MAKE TRIP BY WAY OF NOME KOTZEBUE
AND COAST LINE TO BARROW STOP SUGGEST THAT YOU CON-
TACT CAPT HEZ MCCLELLAN AIR CORPS WASHINGTON FOR
FIRST HAND INFORMATION AS HE RECENTLY MADE TRIP TO
POINT BARROW FROM NOME AND RETURNED DIRECT TO FAIR-
BANKS STOP FOR YOUR FURTHER INFORMATION I HAVE BEEN
COORDINATING AND PARTICIPATING IN SEARCH FOR PILOT
ART HINES AND THREE PASSENGERS LOST ON AUGUST NINE-
TEENTH AFTER DEPARTING FROM DAWSON YT FOR FAIRBANKS
STOP THE AREA SEARCHED IS TWO HUNDRED AND SIXTY MILES
LONG BY ONE HUNDRED FIFTY WIDE STOP ONLY ONE CLUE AS
TO POSSIBLE LOCATION IN WHICH A PLANE WAS HEARD THAT
DAY HAS BEEN RECEIVED STOP THIS AREA HAS BEEN COMBED
RELENTLESSLY STOP APPROXIMATELY THIRTY FIVE THOUSAND
MILES HAVE BEEN FLOWN IN AREA BY SEARCHING PLANES TO
DATE WITH NO SIGN OF TRACE OF PLANE OR OCCUPANTS BE-
ING FOUND STOP THE FOREGOING IS AN INDICATION OF THE
DIFFICULTY OF FINDING A LOST PLANE IN AN AREA MORE OR
LESS DEFINITELY BOUNDED STOP WOULD LIKE TO RECEIVE
YOUR OPINION AS TO HOW LONG SUCH A SEARCH SHOULD BE
CONTINUED AND IF ANY MONEY IS AVAILABLE TO DEFRAY ALL
OR PART OF THE EXPENSES OF THE SEARCHERS STOP THE TER-
RITORY HAD ALREADY MADE AVAILABLE MAXIMUM OF FORTY
SEVEN HUNDRED DOLLARS WHICH IS NOT YET EXHAUSTED
STOP TO DATE SEARCHERS HAVE BEEN PROMISED ONLY GAS OIL
AND SUBSISTENCE [sic] STOP IN FURTHER REFERENCE TO YOUR

WIRE JOE CROSSON IS STILL IN STATES AND NO DOUBT COULD
BE LOCATED THRU PANAMERICAN AIRWAYS NEW YORK AND
CONTACTED OVER TELEPHONE PERSONALLY FOR INFORMA-
TION RELATIVE TO BARROW TRIP STOP RESPECTFULLY.''

18. On Wednesday, August 28, in order to make our records
clear for your information and to procure for our files a document
on which to clarify in the minds of interested persons the action of
the Bureau of Air Commerce and since reply to my letter to Crosson
of the 27th could not be expected at an early date, I wired Crosson
as follows:

''WOULD APPRECIATE YOUR ASSISTANCE IN CLEARING
SLIGHTLY MISLEADING INFORMATION RELATIVE HALLS FAILURE
TO ACCOMPANY YOU TO BARROW STOP HALL STATED HE
WANTED TO GO BUT THAT DUE TO NECESSARY GASOLINE
LOAD IT WAS INADVISABLE AND IMPOSSIBLE STOP OTHER
STATEMENTS TO EFFECT YOU INVITED HALL TO ACCOMPANY
YOU BUT THAT HE WOULD HAVE TO FIND OTHER MEANS FOR
RETURNING STOP WOULD APPRECIATE COMPLETE STATEMENT
BY WIRE COLLECT AS TO JUST WHAT ACTUAL CONDITIONS
WERE IN ORDER OR CLEAR UP ANY MISUNDERSTANDING THAT
MAY EXIST STOP YOUR STATEMENTS FOR OFFICIAL USE ONLY
AND NOT FOR PUBLICITY STOP DEPARTMENT APPRECIATES CO-
OPERATION YOU HAVE ALWAYS GIVEN IT STOP REGARDS.''

19. On Thursday, August 29, I received the following reply
from Crosson which threw additional light on the question as to the
danger of a trip by Hall alone and the possibility of Hall accompanying Crosson:

''NO QUESTION CAN BE RAISED REGARDING HALLS DESIRE
ACCOMPANY ME PT BARROW STOP HALL REQUESTED MAKE
TRIP MY FIRST IMPRESSION WAS THAT HALL COULD ACCOM-
PANY ME TO BARROW BUT WOULD BE NECESSARY MAKE
OTHER ARRANGEMENTS RETURN FAIRBANKS STOP AFTER
CHECKING ABOUT GAS NECESSARY MAKE TRIP SAFELY <u>WE
FOUND IT INADVISABLE AND IMPOSSIBLE FOR HALL ACCOM-
PANY ME</u> STOP UNDER EXISTING CONDITIONS FAIRBANKS
THAT DAY CONSIDERABLE DIFFICULTY WAS EXPERIENCED GET-
TING PLANE OFF WATER AND GAS LOAD WAS REDUCED BELOW
DESIRED AMOUNT BEFORE POSSIBLE TO TAKE OFF STOP
WEATHER CONDITIONS WERE VERY UNFAVORABLE DURING
TRIP TO AND FROM BARRROW AND <u>I WOULD CONSIDER THIS
TRIP EXTREMELY HAZARDOUS TO ONE NOT FAMILIAR WITH
ARCTIC CONDITIONS</u> REGARDS.'' [Emphasis in the original.]

20. On Thursday or Friday, while in your office with the Director, the question of transferring Hall for failure to go to the scene of

the accident was discussed and you stated that although felt that he should be transferred, that no action be taken until you had discussed the matter with the Secretary.

21. It is my hope that a review of all the happenings concerning this case will obviate in the minds of all interested, any necessity for transferring Hall. He was very carefully selected for this detail and his services have been highly efficient and satisfactory to all parties concerned. In this connection your attention is called to the fact that preceding Hall's permanent location in Alaska, it had been the policy of the Bureau to send an Inspector to Alaska about every six months for a three-month period and that although we sent experienced Inspector on each occasion, none of them has done as satisfactory work as Hall.

22. Your attention is also called to the fact that up until about a year ago the morale of the Inspection force, due to certain changes, transfers, etc., and rumors from the Washington area, was at a very low ebb but since that time that morale had been built up to the point that the industry as a whole state that the Inspection force as constituted is working more efficiently than ever before.

Hall's transfer now, I am afraid, will not only be displeasing to the Alaskan authorities, they being highly complimentary of the service rendered by Hall, but would have a bad effect on the morale of the whole field force.

So far as I can learn from all available sources outside of the Department of Commerce, there is no criticism of the Department's actions in the Post–Rogers crash investigation, but I believe that if Hall is transferred there will be created a suspicion of inefficiency on the part of the Department and the question will be raised as to the propriety of our action, [sic]

I am writing this lengthy memorandum only in an effort to clarify the whole situation and to prevent the possibility of prompting editorial and other criticism. Heretofore, the Air Regulation Division of the Bureau of Air Commerce has not brought any criticism upon the Secretary or the Department and has been very diligent in its efforts to reflect credit on the Department.

J. Carroll Cone,
Assistant Director of Air Commerce
(Air Regulations)

2. Mr. Murray Hall   August 27, 1935
   Supervising Aeronautical Inspector
   Bureau of Air Commerce
   Anchorage, Alaska

Dear Murray:

I am enclosing copy of a letter I have written to Crosson, which is self-explanatory to a certain extent.

There have been several slightly conflicting statements made to various officials as to what actually happened in connection with Crosson's flight to Point Barrow and the reasons why you did not accompany him, and in order that the matter may be completely cleared up once and for all, I think it would be beneficial to all parties concerned to have a first-hand statement from Crosson, which statement I am sure will eliminate any vestige of doubt as to the proper functioning of the Regulation Division, particularly your own activities.

I understand, among other things, that Crosson has stated that he invited you to go with him to Point Barrow but at the same time advised you that you would have to arrange for some other transportation on your return trip.

We in the Regulation Division are fully satisfied that we know the reasons for the accident and that a trip on your part to the scene of the accident would not have developed any new information. We feel that the accident was caused primarily by motor failure while the ship was in a steep climb, which resulted in the stalling condition of the aircraft. We have rather complete information as to the flying characteristics of the aircraft.

Of course the reason for the unusual interest on the part of the officials of the Department of Commerce in this accident is occasioned by the prominence of the pilot and passenger.

Kindest personal regards.

Sincerely yours,
J. Carroll Cone,
Assistant Director of Air Commerce

3.   From: DEPARTMENT OF COMMERCE, WASHINGTON D.C.
(For Release Morning Papers Wednesday, September 4, 1935)

The Department of Commerce today made public the following memorandum of Eugene L. Vidal, Director of the Bureau of Air Commerce, to Secretary Roper on the airplane accident in which Wiley Post and Will Rogers were killed near Point Barrow, Alaska, August 15, 1935:

August 30, 1935

Memorandum to the Secretary of Commerce:

Subject: Wiley Post–Will Rogers Fatal Airplane Accident near Point Barrow, Alaska.

To date, certain information regarding the accident in which Wiley Post and Will Rogers lost their lives has been secured. The details preceding the crash were obtained, directly or indirectly, from an Eskimo who saw the plane fall, Sergeant Morgan of the United States Army, located at Point Barrow, a radio report from Inspector Hall of the Bureau of Air Commerce, located in Alaska. Also, I visited personally Mr. Crosson who flew to Point Barrow from Fairbanks in order to return the bodies to this country, Inspector Reed of the Department of Commerce, who licensed the airplane at Glendale, Calif., and others who had contact with Post and Rogers either at Los Angeles or enroute. As you know, I traveled to Los Angeles in order to discuss with Mr. Crosson the probable cause and any other details which might have aided us in determining such causes of this crash.

Inspector Reed, one of our representatives in Los Angeles, informed me that he had inspected at Glendale almost daily the alterations of the original Orion 9E airplane which Post had purchased in February, 1935. Inspector Reed, as a result of his regular and frequent inspections was satisfied with every detail from a construction standpoint. He told me that as to workmanship, it was *a splendid job* [emphasis added]. Mr. Reed did not fly the airplane, but watched Post's test flights and discussed with him its flight characteristics, which, by the way, were pleasing to Post. The Department could not issue an ''NC'' license for the plane because of the fact that a wing from another type of plane, a ''Sirius,'' had been substituted for the regular Orion wing and a larger motor and gas tanks had been installed. The plane was granted an ''R'' or restricted license. Mr. Post at various times expressed satisfaction over the plane's flying characteristics, particularly its stability, balance, and ease of maneuverability.

Mr. Post substituted for his wheel landing gear a pair of pontoons at Seattle and after being joined by Will Rogers, proceeded to Alaska from that point. At Fairbanks, Alaska, Post informed Crosson of Pan American Airways that the airplane had become nose-heavy on take-offs and landings following the installation of the floats, that on take-offs, he had instructed Rogers to sit as far to the rear as possible, and also to keep the equipment and the luggage well aft.

At Fairbanks, both Post and Rogers discussed with Crosson and others their proposed flights, and it was apparent that they had no actual schedule, no set plans, and no particular reason for departures and arrivals at any place on any certain date. Post remarked that in their flying about Alaska, under no circumstances would he fly with Rogers in or above any cloud or fog bank. His plan was to travel as safely as possible by so-called ''contact flying,'' turning back and landing in lake or river at any time when the weather made it dangerous to proceed. It was because of this attitude or policy that their reported indifference to weather reports could not be considered careless.

Pan American Airways base personnel at Fairbanks checked the plane and the motor and declared "everything in good order," with exception that a generator failure eliminated self-starting the motor, thus making it necessary to start the motor by hand. The plane had no radio equipment and Post was navigating by compass and map.

Prior to their departure from Fairbanks a weather report from Point Barrow was requested. This report hadn't been received when they were preparing to depart. Post decided that they would start out and if the weather proved unfavorable, would land on some lake, of which there were many, or river, and wait until conditions had improved. The weather report arrived at Fairbanks at 1:30 P.M., and read "zero-zero." It was reported later that weather conditions improved and at the time of the arrival of Post and Rogers at the lagoon near Point Barrow that evening, our information is that the ceiling was about 200 feet, and visibility satisfactory. The temperature was reported from 40 to 45 degrees, with neither snow nor ice on either land or water. The next day when Crosson made the flight, practically the same weather conditions prevailed, according to his report.

The fliers departed Harding Lake at about 2:00 P.M., and landed at a lagoon near Point Barrow shortly after 8:00 P.M.

The lagoon in which Post landed lies almost perpendicular to the coast line and separated from it by a flat sand bar. Since their last accurate navigation check was over 200 miles from that point, naturally, Post could not be sure on reaching the ocean whether Point Barrow was at his right or left. On seeing the huts and the native alongside the lagoon, it was very much in order for Post to land and make sure whether or not Point Barrow was to his right or left. Point Barrow does not show up at a very great distance from the air even with good visibility, so with the low ceiling, the landing and inquiry was quite logical. There could be very little accuracy in the report that Post was having trouble with either the plane or the motor, because he would not have attempted to take off from the lagoon with Rogers as a passenger if both the plane and the motor were not functioning properly. Post probably looked over his plane from the pontoons before the motor was started by hand.

The fliers landed at the lagoon, asked the native the location of Point Barrow, remaining possibly 10 minutes. The Eskimo's first story, before being pressed and possibly confused later by a number of people, was that the plane took off toward the coast line, turned to the right in the direction of Point Barrow, and then plunged into the shallow water immediately after the noise from the motor had ceased. While the Eskimo reported that the plane had risen about 50 feet, it seems quite apparent that Post had climbed to a higher altitude, probably almost 200 feet, which was the lower level of the fog bank. The near perpendicular nosing-in of the plane and its turning on its back would indicate that an altitude higher than 50 feet had been gained prior to its stalling.

It appears reasonable to believe that Post was banking the plane to the right while still in a slight climb, since with the low ceiling he would turn in the direction of Point Barrow along the coast line immediately after gaining sufficient altitude for maneuvering. He naturally would not enter the fog bank in his last few minutes search for Point Barrow. The combination of the plane in a banking turn, with still low flying speed immediately following the take-off and climb, the motor failure and the airplane's nose heaviness, could result in such a stall. There can be only speculation as to the cause of the motor failure, the motor being buried in the mud underneath some two feet of water. We are inclined to believe that with the moisture in the air as it existed that day, and the temperature as it was reported, ice could have developed in the carburetor. Either that, or the spray from the water in taking off could have entered the scoops and in that way caused icing.

Eugene L. Vidal
Director of Air Commerce

4. From United Technologies archives.

5. The *Winnie Mae* hangs today in the Air and Space Museum of the Smithsonian Institution.

6. During the week of August 29, 1935, Swett & Crawford settled one of Will's aviation insurance policies for $262,500.

7.   LOCKHEED ORION
POST–ROGERS CRASH 1935   Seaplane Conv.
"Statement of probable cause concerning an aircraft accident which occurred to a privately owned plane on August 15th, 1935, at Walakpi [sic], Alaska.

On August 15, 1935, at about 6 P.M. at Walakpi, Alaska, about 15 miles south of Point Barrow, Alaska, an airplane, owned and piloted by Wiley Post and carrying Will Rogers, fell out of control while taking off, with resultant death to both men and the complete destruction of the aircraft.

The airplane, at the time of purchase by Mr. Post, was a Lockheed Orion, model 9E, and bore Dept. of Commerce license. Prior to the flight, however, the airplane was completely rebuilt and several major changes incorporated which changed it from the original model. The engine, propeller, wings and fuel tanks were changed entirely. This remodeling was inspected and approved for workmanship by the Dept. of Commerce restricted license number NR-12283, which limited its use to long-distance and special test flights. The pilot, Wiley Post, held a Dept. of Commerce transport pilot's license.

At Seattle, Washington, pontoons were substituted for the wheel landing gear. No inspection of the airplane was requested after this change. Mr. Rogers joined the flight at this point. At Fairbanks, Alaska, the airplane was partially refueled and flown to Lake Harding, about 40 miles away, to be completely refueled for the Point Barrow flight.

The take-off for Point Barrow was accomplished at some time between 1:30 and 2:30 P.M. When next heard of, the airplane had landed on a small lagoon about 15 miles south of Point Barrow where Mr. Post inquired the direction of Point Barrow. Having obtained this information, he proceeded to take off from the lagoon and, when an altitude of about 50 feet had been reached, the engine was heard to stop and the airplane fell to the water out of control. Both occupants were killed instantly.

A study of the effect of the various changes made on the airplane indicated that it was decidedly nose-heavy and must have been extremely difficult, if not impossible, to properly control without the aid of the engine. A statement made by the pilot after the change to pontoons confirms this conclusion.

The exact cause of the engine failure cannot be determined. The temperature at the time was about 40 and the failure could have been due to the engine having become cool while standing on the lagoon or to ice or water condensate forming in the carburetor. It is the opinion of the accident board that the probable cause of this accident was loss of control of the aircraft at a low altitude after sudden engine failure, due to the extreme nose-heaviness of the aircraft.''

Signed for the Accident Board:

Jesse W. Lankford
Secretary

ACKNOWLEDGMENTS

We thank the following for their memories and information but above all, their courteous willingness to share them with us:

Authors and Writers

Jim Bedford, Fairbanks, AK;
Jerry Belcher, *Los Angeles Times*, Los Angeles, CA;
Ben Lucian Berman (*Steamboat Round the Bend*, 1935);
Sharon Cooper Calhoun, *Oklahoma Heritage*;
Homer Croy (*They Had to See Paris*, 1929; *Down to Earth*, 1932; *Our Will Rogers*, 1953);
Jean Devlin, Editor, *Oklahoma Today*, Oklahoma City, OK;
Mollie Greist (*Nursing Under the North Star*, 1968);
John Grierson (*Challenge to the Poles*);
Kay Kennedy, Fairbanks, AK;
Paula McSpadden Love, Curator, Will Rogers Memorial, Claremore, OK;
Charles V. McAdam, McNaught Syndicate, Bal Harbour, FL;
Tricia Olsen, features editor, *News-Miner*, Fairbanks, AK;
C.R. Roseberry, *The Challenging Skies*;
Archie Satterfield, *Alaska Bush Pilot in the Float Country*;
Andrew Sinclair, *John Ford*;
Dr. Richard K. Smith, Washington, DC;
Patricia Ziegfeld Stephenson, Los Angeles, CA;

Kent Sturgis, editor, *News-Miner*, Fairbanks, AK;
Walt Woodward, radio and newspaper reporter, Juneau, AK.

Aviation

Mr. and Mrs. Randy Accord, Air Museum, Fairbanks, AK;
Richard Sanders Allen, Lockheed authority, Albany, NY;
Robert E. Ames, mechanic, Fairbanks, AK;
Mrs. Charles H. Babb, Los Angeles, CA;
Emerson Bassett, Shelton, WA.;
Alan L. Blum, Northwest Air Service, Seattle, WA;
Ashley 'Ash' Bridgham, Northwest Air Service, Renton, WA;
Sid Brustin, pilot, Los Angeles, CA;
Harvey Christen, Pasadena, CA.;
Max Christman, mechanic, Mercer Island, WA;
Lionel B. Clark, veteran mechanic, E. Hartford, CT;
Randall S. Crosby, Dir., Operations, Search & Rescue, Barrow, AK;
Gen. James 'Jimmy' Doolittle, Carmel, CA;
John W. Dudley, wireless authority, Seattle, WA;
Robert Ellis, pilot, author, Ketchikan, AK;
Lillian (Mrs. Joe) Crosson Frizell, Seattle, WA;
Lt. Col. Robert J. Gleason, Communications Superintendent with Pacific
     Alaska Airways, Fairbanks, AK;
Wes Gordeuk, United Technologies, E. Hartford, CT;
Capt. John E. Grimmett, Tucson, AZ.;
Jesse Hendershot, United Technologies, E. Hartford, CT;
Jim Hutchison, mechanic, Fairbanks, AK;
Lloyd Jarman, mechanic, author, Bellevue, WA;
Dr. Nickolas Komons, FAA historian, author, Washington, DC;
Harvey H. Lippincott, Corp. Archivist, United Technologies (Pratt &
     Whitney), East Hartford, CT;
Sol London, Lockheed Corporation, CA;
Everett Long, Air museum, Fairbanks, AK;
Dr. Anne Millbrooke, Corp. Archivist, United Technologies, East Hart-
     ford, CT;
Dr. Stanley R. Mohler, Dayton, OH;
Denis J. Mulligan, Chief of Enforcement Section, Air Regulation Divi-
     sion, Bureau of Air Commerce, Upper Montclair. NJ;
Anne C. Rutledge, Archivist, Museum of Flight, Seattle, WA;
Duncan Shand, pilot, Tacoma, WA;
Ted M. Spencer, Director, Alaska Hist. Aircr. Soc., Anchorage, AK;
Capt. Robert W. Stevens, pilot, author, Seattle, WA;
Warren Tilman, mechanic, Fairbanks, AK;

Orville Tosch, Tosch Aircraft Industries, Tacoma, WA;
Donald P. Turley, Sr., Pacific Airmotive, Burbank, CA;
Fay Gillis Wells, veteran pilot, writer, reporter, Alexandria, VA;
Frank Whaley, pilot, Valley Center, CA;
N. Merrill Wien, pilot, Kent, WA;
Gordon S. and Marcie Williams, aviation authorities, Bellevue, WA;
Anne Whyte, Pan Am Airways, New York, NY.

Private and Public Contributors

Jesse Anderson, Fairbanks, AK;
Forbes Baker, Redmond, WA;
Renee Blahuta, University of Alaska, Fairbanks, AK;
Eileen Bowser, Museum of Modern Art, New York City, NY;
Lyman Brewster, Reindeer Superintendent, Nome, AK;
Jeffrey Briley, Curator, State Museum of History, Oklahoma City, OK;
Jane Brower, Barrow, AK;
Thomas Brower, Barrow, AK;
Joseph H. Carter, Director, Will Rogers Memorial and Museum, Clare-
    more, OK;
Michelle Lefebvre Carter, Public Relations, Claremore, OK;
Chester Cowen, Photographic Archivist, Oklahoma Historical Society,
    Oklahoma City, OK;
Alma Despot, Medina, WA;
William Dugovich, public relations, Seattle, WA;
Robert H. Fowler, National Archives, Washington, DC;
John M. Gerard, Seattle, WA;
Thomas 'Butch' Girvin, Barrow, AK;
Dr. and Mrs. Elwood Greist, Livermore, CA;
Molly Greist, Barrow, AK.;
R. Ann Ogle, Oklahoma Historical Society, Oklahoma City, OK;
Rose Okpeaha Leavitt, Barrow, AK;
Robert W. Love, Manager, Will Rogers Memorial, Claremore, OK;
Patricia Lowe, Librarian, Will Rogers Memorial and Museum, Claremore
    OK;
Gregory Malak, Curator, Will Rogers Memorial & Museum, Claremore,
    OK;
Barrow and Donna Morgan, Nome, AK;
Prof. Claus Naske, University of Alaska, Fairbanks, AK;
Earlene Paddock, Seattle, WA;
Fred Okpeaha, Barrow, AK;
Patrick Okpeaha, Barrow, AK;
Robert Okpeaha, Barrow, AK;

Don and Donna Raymond, Pacific Palisades, CA;
James B. Rogers, CA;
Mary Rogers, CA;
Will Rogers, Jr., AZ;
Gene Rogge, Fairbanks, AK.;
Emil and Trudy Sandmeier, Pacific Palisades, CA;
Max and Dorothy Sherrod, Palmer, AK.;
Charles Silver, Museum of Modern Art, New York City, NY;
Inez Snell, Fairbanks, AK;
Dace Taube, Regional Historical Archives, University of Southern California, Los Angeles, CA.

Publications, News Media

Akron Times-Press, Akron, OH;
Alaska History, Anchorage, AK;
Alaskan Empire, Anchorage, AK;
Anchorage Times, Anchorage, AK;
Associated Press; New York, NY;
Daily Oklahoman, Oklahoma City, OK;
Fort Worth Star-Telegram, Fort Worth, TX;
Houston Chronicle, Houston, TX;
Juneau Daily Empire, Juneau, AK;
Kansas City Star, Kansas City, KS;
London Daily Mail, London, England;
London Times, London, England;
Los Angeles Chronicle, Los Angeles, CA;
Los Angeles Examiner, Los Angeles, CA;
Los Angeles Herald-Express, Los Angeles, CA;
Los Angeles News, Los Angeles, CA;
Los Angeles Post-Record, Los Angeles, CA;
Los Angeles Times, Los Angeles, CA;
Maysville News, Maysville, OK;
Muskogee Times-Democrat, Muskogee, OK;
News Miner, Fairbanks, AK;
News-Week, New York, NY;
New York American, New York, NY;
New York Evening Post, New York, NY;
New York Herald Tribune, New York, NY;
New York Journal, New York, NY;
New York Mirror, New York, NY
New York News, New York, NY;
New York Post, New York, NY;

New York Sun, New York, NY;
New York Times, New York, NY;
New York World Telegram, New York, NY;
Oklahoma Today, Oklahoma City, OK;
The Pilot;
Ponca City News, Ponca City, OK;
Rocky Mountain News, Denver, CO;
Seattle Post-Intelligencer, Seattle, WA;
Seattle Times, Seattle, WA;
TIME, New York, NY;
Tulsa World, Tulsa, OK;
United Press, New York, NY;
Ventura Free Press, Ventura, CA;
Washington Evening Star, Washington, DC;
Washington Herald, Washington, DC;
Washington Post, Washington, DC;
Wilmington Star-News, Wilmington, NC.

Research Centers

Alaska Historical Aircraft Society, Anchorage, AK;
California State University, Northridge, Northridge, CA;
Federal Aviation Administration, Oklahoma City, OK;
Federal Aviation Administration, Washington, DC;
George Eastman House, Rochester, NY;
Library of Congress, Washington, DC;
Los Angeles Public Libraries, Los Angeles, CA;
Museum of Flight, Seattle, WA;
Museum of History and Industry, Seattle, WA;
Museum of Modern Art, New York, NY;
National Air & Space Museum Library, Washington, DC;
National Archives, Washington, DC;
National Cowboy Hall of Fame and Western Heritage Center,
     Oklahoma City, OK;
National Museum of American History, Washington, DC;
National Press Club, Washington, DC;
New York City Public Library, New York, NY;
New York State Public Records, New York, NY;
Oklahoma Historical Society, Oklahoma City, OK;
Oklahoma State University, Stillwater, OK;
Public Library, London, England;
Seattle Public Library, Seattle, WA;
Smithsonian Institution Library, Washington, DC;

Toronto Public Libraries, Toronto, Canada;
Twentieth Century Fox Library, Los Angeles, CA;
University of Alaska, Fairbanks, AK;
University of California, Berkeley, CA;
University of California, Los Angeles, CA;
University of Michigan, Ann Arbor, MI;
University of Oklahoma, Norman, OK;
University of Southern California, Los Angeles, CA;
Westminster Research Library, London, England;
Will Rogers Memorial and Museum, Claremore, OK;
Will Rogers Ranch, Pacific Palisades, CA.

Show Business

Academy of Motion Picture Arts and Sciences, Los Angeles, CA;
American Film Institute, Los Angeles, CA;
American Film Institute, Washington, DC;
Lew Ayres, actor (*State Fair*, 1933);
Hermione Baddeley, actress (Charles Cochran Revue, 1926);
Clarence Badger, director (*Almost A Husband*. 1919; *Jubilo*, 1919; *Water, Water Everywhere*, 1919; *The Strange Boarder*, 1920; *Jes' Call Me Jim*, 1920; *Cupid, The Cowpuncher*, 1920; *Honest Hutch*, 1920; *Guile Of Women*, 1920; *Boys Will Be Boys*, 1921; *An Unwilling Hero*, 1921; *Doubling For Romeo*, 1921; *A Poor Relation*, 1921; *The Ropin' Fool*, 1921; *Fruits Of Faith*, 1922; *One Day In 365*, 1922);
British Film Institute, London, England;
Tom Brown, actor (*Judge Priest*, 1934);
David Butler, director (*A Connecticut Yankee*, 1931; *Business And Pleasure*, 1931; *Down To Earth*, 1932; *Handy Andy*, 1934; *Doubting Thomas*, 1935);
Harry (Dobe) Carey, Jr., actor;
Olive Carey, actress;
Charles Collins, actor/dancer;
Dorothy Stone Collins, musical comedy star (*Three Cheers*, 1928–29);
Fifi D'Orsay, actress (*They Had To See Paris*, 1929; *Young As You Feel*, 1931);
John Ford, director (*Doctor Bull*, 1933; *Judge Priest*, 1934; Steamboat Round the Bend, 1935);
Janet Gaynor, actress (*State Fair*, 1933);
Ira Gershwin, lyricist;
Jetta Goudall, actress (*Business And Pleasure*, 1931);
Sterling Holloway, actor (*Life Begins At Forty*, 1935; *Doubting Thomas*, 1935);

Rochelle, Hudson, actress (*Dr. Bull*, 1933; *Mr. Skitch*, 1933; *Judge Priest*, 1934; *Life Begins At Forty*, 1935);

Maria Jeritza, diva;

Henry King, director (*Lightnin'* 1930; *State Fair*, 1933);

Myrna Loy, actress (*A Connecticut Yankee*, 1931);

Joel McCrea, actor (*Lightnin'*, 1930; *Business and Pleasure*, 1931);

George Marshall, director (*Life Begins At Forty*, 1935; *In Old Kentucky*, 1935);

Evelyn Venable Mohr, actress (*David Harum*, 1933; *The County Chairman*, 1935);

Hal Mohr, director of photography (*David Harum*, 1933; *State Fair*, 1933; *The County Chairman*, 1935);

Irene Rich, actress (*Water, Water Everywhere*, 1919; *The Strange Boarder*, 1920; *Jes' Call Me Jim*, 1920; *Boys Will Be Boys*, 1921; *The Ropin' Fool*, 1922; *Fruits Of Faith*, 1922; *They Had To See Paris*, 1929; *So This Is London*, 1930; *Down To Earth*, 1932);

Hal E. Roach, Sr., producer/author (*Hustling Hank*, 1923; *Two Wagons, Both Covered*, 1923; *Jus' Passin' Through*, 1923; *Uncensored Movies*, 1923; *The Cake Eater*, 1924; *The Cowboy Sheik*, 1924; *Big Moments From Little Pictures*, 1924; *High Brow Stuff*, 1924; *Going To Congress*, 1924; *Don't Park There*, 1924; *Jubilo, Jr.*, 1924; *Our Congressman*, 1924; *A Truthful Liar*, 1924; *Gee Whiz, Genevieve*, 1924);

Anne Shoemaker, actress (*Ah, Wilderness!*, 1934);

George R. Spota, producer, (*Will Rogers' U.S.A.*);

Peggy Wood, actress, singer, author (*Almost A Husband*, 1919; *Handy Andy*, 1934);

Keenan Wynn, actor.

INDEX